THE EUROPEAN CONVENTION ON HUMAN RIGHTS AND ITS IMPACT ON NATIONAL PRIVATE LAW

THE EUROPEAN CONVENTION ON HUMAN RIGHTS AND ITS IMPACT ON NATIONAL PRIVATE LAW

A Comparative Perspective

Edited by
Matteo Fornasier
Maria Gabriella Stanzione

Cambridge – Antwerp – Chicago

Intersentia Ltd
8 Wellington Mews
Wellington Street | Cambridge
CB1 1HW | United Kingdom
Tel: +44 1223 736 170
Email: contact@larcier-intersentia.com
www.larcier-intersentia.com

Distribution for the UK and
Rest of the World (incl. Eastern Europe)
NBN International
1 Deltic Avenue, Rooksley
Milton Keynes MK13 8LD
United Kingdom
Tel: +44 1752 202 301 | Fax: +44 1752 202 331
Email: orders@nbninternational.com

Distribution for Europe
Lefebvre Sarrut Belgium NV
Hoogstraat 139/6
1000 Brussels
Belgium
Tel: +32 (0)2 548 07 13
Email: contact@larcier-intersentia.com

Distribution for the USA and Canada
Independent Publishers Group
Order Department
814 North Franklin Street
Chicago, IL 60610
USA
Tel: +1 800 888 4741 (toll free) | Fax: +1 312 337 5985
Email: orders@ipgbook.com

The European Convention on Human Rights and its Impact on National Private Law. A Comparative Perspective
© The editors and contributors severally 2023

The editors and contributors have asserted the right under the Copyright, Designs and Patents Act 1988, to be identified as authors of this work.

No part of this book may be reproduced, stored in a retrieval system, or transmitted, in any form, or by any means, without prior written permission from Intersentia, or as expressly permitted by law or under the terms agreed with the appropriate reprographic rights organisation. Enquiries concerning reproduction which may not be covered by the above should be addressed to Intersentia at the address above.

Artwork on cover: © Gravure Francaise / Alamy Stock Photo

ISBN 978-1-83970-342-3
D/2023/7849/52
NUR 822

British Library Cataloguing in Publication Data. A catalogue record for this book is available from the British Library.

PREFACE

This book is the fruit of an international symposium that we organised at the German-Italian Centre for the European Dialogue, Villa Vigoni, in the summer of 2021. The aim of the conference was to gather experts from many different fields of private law to obtain a broader view of the interaction between the European Convention on Human Rights and national private law. The volume contains the papers presented at the symposium, which have been updated to cover more recent legal developments and reflect the insights from our discussions at Villa Vigoni.

Originally, the conference was scheduled for May 2020. However, in the spring of that year, COVID-19 started to spread across Europe. The Italian region of Lombardy, where Villa Vigoni is located, was particularly affected by the pandemic. Suddenly, German universities would not permit their staff to take business trips abroad, many countries, including Italy, closed their borders, and the Centre for the European Dialogue was temporarily shut down and fell silent. For us, who had been used to travelling freely from country to country as modern day *clerici vagantes*, those events went beyond our imagination. They were a powerful reminder that open national frontiers are nothing we can take for granted, not even in Europe, and need to be defended, not just against viruses and other diseases, but likewise against all kinds of political threats.

Eventually, the conference was postponed to the end of August 2021. For most participants, the symposium at Villa Vigoni was the first in-person event after almost one and a half years of online meetings. This, together with the magnificent location of the Villa overlooking Lake Como, undoubtedly contributed to the pleasant and inspiring atmosphere of our gathering.

We are grateful to many institutions and persons who have supported our research project and made the publication of this book possible: the Deutsche Forschungsgemeinschaft for providing the funding for the conference; the German-Italian Centre for the European Dialogue, Villa Vigoni, and its staff for hosting the event, with special thanks to Julian Steffenelli, Luca Giovannelli, Vivien Kiliani, Anna-Katharina Klus, Linda Rossmann, Caroline Schmitt-Mücke, Benedict Walter, Ben Wennrich and

Madlen Wolter for various kinds of assistance during different stages of the project. Moreover, we would like to thank Rebecca Moffat, Ahmed Hegazi and the whole team of Intersentia Publishing for their extraordinary diligence in reviewing and editing 16 manuscripts by 16 different authors and turning them into a book. Last but not least, we would like to express our gratitude to all participants of the conference for providing invaluable input to the research project and to the contributors of the volume for their commitment and patience.

The editors
Bochum/Salerno, March 2023

CONTENTS

Preface v
List of Cases xiii
List of Contributors xxix

The European Convention on Human Rights and its Impact on National Private Law: An Introduction
    Matteo FORNASIER and Maria Gabriella STANZIONE 1

1. The Application of the Convention in Horizontal Relationships 1
2. The Court's Role in Private Law Disputes 2
3. The Impact of the ECHR on Private Law During the Last Two Decades: Some Examples 4
4. Aim and Outline of the Book 6

PART I. SETTING THE STAGE: THE EUROPEAN CONVENTION ON HUMAN RIGHTS AND NATIONAL LAW

The European Convention on Human Rights in the German Legal System: A Qualitative and Quantitative Introduction
    Andreas ENGEL 11

1. The Formal Rank of the ECHR in the German Legal System 12
2. The Relevance of the ECHR for the Interpretation of German Law: Qualitative Remarks 17
3. Quantitative Remarks 27

The Role of the Italian Courts in the Effective Implementation of the European Convention on Human Rights: Introductory Remarks
    Laura VAGNI 43

1. Premise 43
2. The Interpretation in Conformity with the European Convention: The Italian Doctrine of Consolidated Case Law 46

3. The Lack of Ratification of Protocol 16 to the Convention by Italy 50
4. Lights and Shadows in the Effective Implementation of the European Convention 59

PART II. FAMILY LAW

Parental Autonomy and Child Protection Measures: Procedural and Substantive Standards
Konrad DUDEN 65

1. Introduction 65
2. The ECtHR Case Law: *Wetjen* and *Tlapak* 67
3. Procedural Standards 70
4. Substantive Standards 76
5. Influence of National Constitutional Law 82
6. Conclusion 84

The Status of Biological Fathers: An Example for the Impact of the European Convention on Human Rights on National Family Law
Anatol DUTTA 87

1. Introduction 87
2. Biological Fathers and Legal Fatherhood 89
3. Easier Access to Legal Fatherhood for Biological Fathers Required? 92
4. At Least Some Parental Rights for the Biological Father? 95
5. The Impact on National Family Law 96
6. Conclusion 97

Shaping New Families: Same-Sex Couples' Rights in the Dialogue between the Courts
Maria Gabriella STANZIONE 99

1. The Role of the ECtHR in the Recognition of Same-Sex Couples' Right to Family Life 99
2. Legal Recognition of Same-Sex Couples in Europe: The Comparatist's Laboratory 105
3. Some Conclusions 113

PART III. RIGHT TO PRIVACY AND DATA PROTECTION

Shaping the Right to Privacy: The Interplay between Karlsruhe, Strasbourg, and Luxembourg
Katharina DE LA DURANTAYE 119

1. Introduction 119
2. The Baseline: The *von Hannover* Cases 120
3. The 'Right to be Forgotten': Shaping the Future, Shaping the Past 125
4. Connecting the Dots 135

Data Protection in Private Relations and the European Convention on Human Rights
Christian HEINZE and Dominik EBEL 137

1. Europeanisation of Data Protection Law...................... 138
2. Different Concepts of Data Protection 141
3. Consequences of the Privacy-Based Concept of the ECHR for Private Relations.. 145
4. Conclusion.. 153

Copyright as a Fundamental Right and the Influence of the Case Law of the European Court of Human Rights and of the European Court of Justice
Giovanni Maria RICCIO 157

1. The Confusing Age of Copyright 157
2. Is Copyright a Fundamental Right? 162
3. Copyright as a Fundamental Right in Other International Conventions... 164
4. The Case Law of the ECJ 166
5. The Case Law of the ECtHR 169
6. The 'Propertisation' of Copyright and the Need for a Different Approach 172

PART IV. PROCEDURAL LAW

The Relationship between Article 6 of the European Convention on Human Rights and International Commercial Arbitration
Francesca BENATTI.. 177

1. Introduction 177

2. Access to Justice 180
3. Independence, Impartiality and Neutrality..................... 183
4. Conclusion.. 194

The European Convention on Human Rights and the Protection of Foreign Direct Investment: The Role of 'Legitimate Expectations'
Giacomo Rojas Elgueta 197

1. Introduction 198
2. The Notion of Investment under IIL and the ECHR.............. 201
3. The Use of 'Legitimate Expectations' in IIL and the ECHR System.. 206
4. Conclusions.. 222

The EU Principle of Mutual Recognition before the European Court of Human Rights
Denise Wiedemann... 225

1. Introduction 226
2. The Impact of Fundamental Rights on the Implementation of Judgments 227
3. Recognition and Enforcement of Judgments within the EU 234
4. The Impact of the ECHR on the EU Mechanisms of Recognition and Enforcement... 237
5. Summary and Outlook.. 249

PART V. LABOUR LAW

Freedom of Association for the Armed Forces: A Fruitful Dialogue between the European Court of Human Rights and the Italian Constitutional Court
Edoardo Ales 253

1. The Collective Dimension in the Armed Forces and the Decisions of the Italian Constitutional Court.................... 254
2. Freedom of Association and the State as Employer in the ECHR, as Interpreted by the ECtHR.................................... 260
3. The Case Law of the Italian Constitutional Court on the Impact of ECHR Provisions on National Legislation 264
4. The Case Law of the ECHR on the Armed Forces................. 266

5. The Case Law of the Italian Constitutional Court in Light of
   Article 117, Para. 1 of the Constitution......................... 268
6. Conclusion... 271

The Impact of the European Convention on Human Rights on German Labour Law: A Special Focus on Collective Labour Law
Gabriele BUCHHOLTZ....................................... 273

1. Introduction 273
2. Case Law History 275
3. Binding Effect of the ECHR 278
4. Assessing the Impact of the ECHR on the German Right
   to Strike 279
5. Conclusion and Outlook 281

PART VI. CONCLUSIONS

Comparative Law at the European Court of Human Rights: Does Context Still Matter?
Filippo VIGLIONE 285

1. Introduction 285
2. The Use of Comparative Remarks 287
3. European Consensus and its Contradictions 292
4. Comparative Law in the Advisory Opinions of the ECtHR:
   Conclusions.. 297

Harmonisation through the Back Door? The Impact of the European Convention on Human Rights on National Private Law
Matteo FORNASIER 305

1. Introduction 306
2. The Channels of Harmonisation.............................. 308
3. Direct Harmonising Effects................................... 314
4. Indirect Harmonising Effects 327
5. Conclusion... 332

Bibliography... 339
Index... 357

LIST OF CASES

SUPRANATIONAL

COURT OF JUSTICE OF THE EUROPEAN UNION

Case C-6/64, *Flaminio Costa v. E.N.E.L*, 15 July 1964,
ECLI:EU:C:1964:66 327
Case C-11/70, *Internationale Handelsgesellschaft mbH v. Einfuhr- und Vorratsstelle für Getreide und Futtermittel*, 17 December 1970,
ECLI:EU:C:1970:114 327
Case C-106/77, *Amministrazione delle Finanze dello Stato v. Simmenthal SpA*, 9 March 1978, ECLI:EU:C:1978:49 327
Case C-7/98, *Dieter Krombach v. André Bamberski*, 23 September 1999,
ECLI:EU:C:2000:164 .... 242, 248
Case C-369/98, *The Queen v. Minister of Agriculture, Fisheries and Food, ex parte Trevor Robert Fisher and Penny Fisher*, 14 September 2000,
ECLI:EU:C:2000:443 140
Case C-465/00, *Rechnungshof v. Österreichischer Rundfunk and Others and Christa Neukomm and Joseph Lauermann v. Österreichischer Rundfunk*, 20 May 2003, ECLI:EU:C: 2003:294 140
Case C-116/02, *Erich Gasser GmbH v. MISAT Srl.*, 9 December 2003,
ECLI:EU:C:2003:657 246
Case C-479/04, *Laserdisken ApS v. Kulturministeriet*, 12 September 2006,
ECLI:EU:C:2006:549 168
Case C-275/06, *Productores de Música de España (Promusicae) v. Telefónica de España SAU*, 29 January 2008, ECLI:EU:C:2008:54 168
Case C-211/10 PPU, *Doris Povse v. Mauro Alpago*, 1 July 2010,
ECLI:EU:C: 2010:400 239
Case C-70/10, *Scarlet Extended NV v. Belgische Vereniging van Auteurs, Componisten en Uitgevers CVBA (SABAM)*, 24 November 2011,
ECLI:EU:C:2011:771 168
Case C-360/10, *Belgische Vereniging van Auteurs, Componisten en Uitgevers CVBA (SABAM) v. Netlog NV ('Netlog')*, 16 February 2012,
ECLI:EU:C:2012:85 168
Case C-156/12, *GREP GmbH v. Freistaat Bayern*, 13 June 2012,
ECLI:EU:C:2012:342 243
Case C-131/12, *Google Spain SL and Google Inc. v. Agencia Española de Protección de Datos (AEPD) and Mario Costeja González*,
13 May 2014, ECLI:EU:C:2014:317 .... 126–127, 310

Opinion 2/13, 18 December 2014, ECLI:EU:C:2014:2454 . . . . 226, 237, 244, 246
Joined Cases C-404/15, C-659/15 PPU, *Aranyosi* and *Căldăraru*,
  5 April 2016, ECLI:EU:C:2016:198 246
Case C-70/15, *Emmanuel Lebek v. Janusz Domino*, 7 July 2016,
  ECLI:EU:C:2016:524 239
Case C-160/15, *GS Media BV v. Sanoma Media Netherlands BV and Others*,
  8 September 2016, ECLI:EU:C:2016:644 169
Case C-610/15, *Stichting Brein v. Ziggo BV, XS4ALL Internet BV*,
  14 June 2017, ECLI:EU:C:2017:456. 171
Case C-414/16, *Vera Egenberger v. Evangelisches Werk für Diakonie und
  Entwicklung E.V.*, 17 April 2018, ECLI:EU:C:2018:257 331
Case-673/16, *Relu Adrian Coman and Others v. Inspectoratul General
  pentru Imigrări and Ministerul Afacerilor Interne*, 5 June 2018,
  ECLI:EU:C:2018:385 115
Case C-68/17, *IR v. JQ*, 11 September 2018, ECLI:EU:C:2018:696. 331
Case C-684/16, *Max-Planck-Gesellschaft zur Förderung der Wissenschaften
  eV v. Tetsuji Shimizu*, 6 November 2018, ECLI:EU:C:2018:874 310
Joined Cases C-798/18 and C-799/18, *Federazione nazionale delle imprese
  elettrotecniche ed elettroniche (Anie) and others and Athesia Energy S.r.l.
  and others v. Ministero dello Sviluppo Economico and Gestore dei servizi
  energetici (GSE) S.p.A.*, 15 April 2021, ECLI:EU:C:2021:280. 216
Case C-129/21, *Proximus*, 27 October 2022, ECLI:EU:C:2022:833 136

EUROPEAN COMMISSION OF HUMAN RIGHTS

De Becker v. Belgium, no. 214/56, ECommHR 9 June 1958 309
Council of Civil Service Unions et al v. the United Kingdom, no. 11603/85,
  ECommHR 20 January 1987 . . . . 261, 263
M. & Co. v. Germany, no. 13258/87, ECommHR 9 February 1990. 238
Smith Kline and French Laboratories Ltd. v. The Netherlands, no. 12633/87,
  ECommHR 4 October 1990. 170

EUROPEAN COURT OF HUMAN RIGHTS

Case '*Relating to certain aspects of the laws on the use of languages in education
  in Belgium*' *v. Belgium*, nos. 1474/62, 1677/62, 1691/62, 1769/63, 1994/63
  and 2126/64, ECtHR 23 July 1968 44
Golder v. the United Kingdom, no. 4451/70, ECtHR 21 February 1975 227
National Union of Belgian Police v. Belgium, no. 4464/70, ECtHR
  27 October 1975. . . . . 267, 275
Schmidt and Dahlström v. Sweden, no. 5589/72, ECtHR 6 February 1976. 275
Swedish Engine Drivers' Union v. Sweden, no. 5614/72, ECtHR
  6 February 1976 . . . . 20, 260

List of Cases

Kjeldsen, Busk Madsen and Pedersen v. Denmark, nos. 5095/71, 5920/72
and 5926/72, ECtHR 7 December 1976 65
Tyrer v. the United Kingdom, no. 5856/72, ECtHR 25 April 1978 .... 290, 320
Sunday Times v. the United Kingdom, no. 6538/74, ECtHR 26 April
1979 292
Marckx v. Belgium, no. 6833/74, ECtHR 13 June 1979 .... 2–3, 100, 309, 319
Deweer v. Belgium, no. 6903/75, ECtHR 27 February 1980 178
Dudgeon v. the United Kingdom, no. 7525/76, ECtHR 22 October 1981 295
X. v. the United Kingdom, no. 9702/82, ECtHR 6 October 1982 139
Öztürk v. Federal Republic of Germany, no. 8544/79, ECtHR
21 February 1984 288
Sporrong and Lönnroth v. Sweden, no. 7151/75, ECtHR 18 December 1984 169
X and Y v. Netherlands, no. 8978/80, ECtHR 26 March 1985 .... 314, 316
James et al. v. the United Kingdom, no. 8793/79, ECtHR 21 February 1986........20
Lithgow v. the United Kingdom, nos. 9006/80, 9262/81, 9263/81, 9265/81,
9266/81, 9313/81 and 9405/81, ECtHR 8 July 1986 178
Leander v. Sweden, no. 9248/81, ECtHR 26 March 1987 .... 139, 144
Axelsson v. Sweden, no. 11960/86, ECtHR 13 July 1990 180
Philis v. Greece, nos. 12750/87, 13780/88 and 14003/88, ECtHR
27 August 1991.. 227
Observer and Guardian v. UK, no. 13585/88, ECtHR 26 November 1991 20
Drozd and Janousek v. France and Spain, no. 12747/87, ECtHR 26 June 1992 231
Sigurður A. Sigurjónsson v. Iceland, no. 16130/90, ECtHR 30 June 1993 321
Keegan v. Ireland, no. 16969/90, ECtHR 26 May 1994 319
Kroon and Others v. The Netherlands, no. 18535/91, ECtHR
27 October 1994...319–320
Scollo v. Italy, no. 19133/91, ECtHR 28 September 1995 228
Z v. Finland, no. 22009/93, ECtHR 25 February 1997.................... 146, 149
Hornsby v. Greece, no. 18357/91, ECtHR 19 March 1997..................... 227
Eriksen v. Norway, no. 17391/90, ECtHR 27 May 1997 291
Matthews v. the United Kingdom, no. 24833/94, ECtHR 18 February 1999...... 240
Waite and Kennedy v. Germany, no. 26083/94, ECtHR (GC) 18 February 1999.....227
Suovaniemi v. Finland, no. 31737/96, ECtHR 23 February 1999........... 178–179
Salgueiro da Silva Mouta v. Portugal, no. 33290/96, ECtHR
21 December 1999.. 295
Beyeler v. Italy, no. 33202/96, ECtHR (GC) 5 January 2000................... 205
Ignaccolo-Zenide v. Romania, no. 31679/96, ECtHR 25 January 2000 .... 73, 233
Mazurek v. France, no. 34406/97, ECtHR 1 February 2000 294
Rotaru v. Romania, no. 28341/95, ECtHR (GC) 4 May 2000.......... 144, 148, 155
Elsholz v. Germany, no. 25735/94, ECtHR 13 July 2000 .... 66, 77–80
Gnahoré v. France, no. 40031/98, ECtHR 19 September 2000...................77
Kudła v. Poland, no. 30210/96, ECtHR 26 October 2000......................44
Krombach v. France, no. 29731, ECtHR 13 February 2001................... 248
Mata Estevez v. Spain, no. 56501/00, ECtHR 10 May 2001 .... 103, 289
K. and T. v. Finland, no. 25702/94, ECtHR 12 July 2001.............. 66, 73, 77–79
Pellegrini v. Italy, no. 30882/96, ECtHR 20 July 2001 230–232

P.G. and J.H. v. the United Kingdom, no. 44787/98, ECtHR
  25 September 2001 146
Unison v. the United Kingdom, no. 53574/99, ECtHR 10 January 2002 275
Fretté v. France, no. 36515/97, ECtHR 26 February 2002 289
Kutzner v. Germany, no. 46544/99, ECtHR 26 February 2002 .... 73, 77, 79
Burdov v. Russia, no. 59498/00, ECtHR 7 May 2002 227
Goodwin v. the United Kingdom, no. 28957/95, ECtHR 11 July 2002 101
Taylor-Sabori v. the United Kingdom, no. 47114/99, ECtHR
  22 October 2002 148
Peck v. the United Kingdom, no. 44647/98, ECtHR 28 January 2003 146
Sahin v. Germany, no. 30943/96, ECtHR (GC) 8 July 2003 315
Craxi v. Italy (no. 2), no. 25337/94, ECtHR 17 July 2003 150
Perry v. the United Kingdom, no. 44647/98, ECtHR 17 July 2003 146
Sylvester v. Austria, no. 54640/00, ECtHR 9 October 2003 229–230
Cooper v. the United Kingdom, no. 48843/99, ECtHR 16 December 2003 291
Von Hannover v. Germany (no.1), no. 59320/00, ECtHR
  24 June 2004 .... 5, 121, 324
Pla and Puncernau v. Andorra, no. 69498/01, ECtHR 13 July 2004 4
Kopecký v. Slovakia, no. 44912/98, ECtHR 28 September 2004 215
Odd F. Lindberg v. Sweden, no. 48198/99, ECtHR 15 December 2004 232–233
Fociac v. Romania, no. 2577/02, ECtHR 3 February 2005 227
Plotnikovy v. Russia, no. 43883/02, ECtHR 24 February 2005 227
Bosphorus Hava Yolları Turizm ve Ticaret Anonim Şirketi v. Ireland,
  no. 45036/98, ECtHR 30 June 2005 .... 238, 240, 243–244, 247
Jahn and Others v. Germany, nos. 46720/99, 72203/01 and 72552/01,
  ECtHR (GC) 30 June 2005 222
Broniowski v. Poland, no. 31443/96, ECtHR (GC) 28 September 2005 222
Süss v. Germany, no. 40324/98, ECtHR 10 November 2005 73
Eskinazi and Chelouche v. Turkey, no. 14600/05, ECtHR 6 December 2005 231
Sørensen and Rasmussen v. Denmark, nos. 52562/99 and 52620/99,
  ECtHR (GC) 11 January 2006 321
Tüm Haber Sen et Çınar v. Turkey, no. 28602/95, ECtHR 21 February 2006 262
Sukhovetskyy v. Ukraine, no. 13716/02, ECtHR 28 March 2006 292
Cocchierella v. Italy, no. 64886/01, ECtHR (GC) 29 March 2006 44
Sürmeli v. Germany, no. 75529/01, ECtHR 8 June 2006 74
Anheuser-Busch Inc. v. Portugal, no. 73049/01, ECtHR (GC) 11 January 2007 ... 170
Sisojeva and Others v. Latvia, no. 60654/00, ECtHR 15 January 2007 249
Evans v. the United Kingdom, no. 6449/05, ECtHR (GC)
  10 April 2007 .... 289, 314, 316
Wagner and JMWL v. Luxembourg, no. 76240/01, ECtHR 28 June 2007 233
Maumousseau and Washington v. France, no. 39388/05, ECtHR
  6 December 2007 238
EB v. France, no. 43546/02, ECtHR 22 January 2008 295
Guja v. Moldova, no. 14277/04, ECtHR (GC) 12 February 2008 312
Hülsmann v. Germany, no. 33375/03, ECtHR 18 March 2008 94–95
McDonald v. France, no. 18648/04, ECtHR 29 April 2008 230
Bevacqua and S. v. Bulgaria, no. 71127/01, ECtHR 12 June 2008 66

Liberty and Others v. the United Kingdom, no. 58243/00, ECtHR
  1 July 2008. 147
I. v. Finland, no. 20511/03, ECtHR 17 July 2008 150
Leschiutta and Fraccaro v. Belgium, nos. 58081/00 and 58411/00, ECtHR
  17 July 2008. 233
Boivin v. France, Belgium and 32 other Contracting Parties, no. 73250/01,
  ECtHR 9 September 2008. 238
Demir and Baykara v. Turkey, no. 34503/97, ECtHR (GC) 12 November
  2008 . . . . 5, 19, 263–264,
    267, 274, 276
K.U. v. Finland, no. 2872/02, ECtHR 2 December 2008 150
S. and Marper v. the United Kingdom, nos. 30562/04 and 30566/04,
  ECtHR (GC) 4 December 2008 145
Saccoccia v. Austria, no. 69917/01, ECtHR 18 December 2008 229–230
Burdov v. Russia (no. 2), no. 33509/04, ECtHR 15 January 2009 227
Sud Fondi srl and Others v. Italy, no. 75909/01, ECtHR 20 January 2009. 47
Enerji Yapı-Yol Sen v. Turkey, no. 68959/01, ECtHR 21 April 2009. . . . . 5, 19, 274,
    276, 322
K.H. and Others v. Slovakia, no. 32881/04, ECtHR 28 April 2009. 150
Codarcea v. Romania, no. 31675/04, ECtHR 2 June 2009. 316
Opuz v. Turkey, no. 33401/02, ECtHR 9 June 2009 303
Vrbica v. Croatia, no. 32540/05, ECtHR 1 April 2010 . . . . 227, 229
Macready v. Czech Republic, nos. 4824/06 and 15512/08, ECtHR
  22 April 2010 75
Schalck and Kopf v. Austria, no. 30141/04, ECtHR 24 June 2010 . . . . 103, 289,
    295, 319
Neulinger and Shuruk v. Switzerland, no. 41615/07, ECtHR
  6 July 2010. . . . . 77–78, 80, 238
Rumpf v. Germany, no. 46344/06, ECtHR 2 September 2010 74
Uzun v. Germany, no. 35623/05, ECtHR 2 September 2010 146
Obst v. Germany, no. 425/03, ECtHR 23 September 2010 328
Schüth v. Germany, no. 1620/03, ECtHR 23 September 2010 . . . . 6, 29, 317, 328
Korolev v. Russia, no. 38112/04, ECtHR 21 October 2010 229
A, B and C v. Ireland, no. 25579/05, ECtHR 16 December 2010 . . . . 289, 297, 308
Anayo v. Germany, no. 20578/07, ECtHR 21 December 2010. 95
Chavdarov v. Bulgaria, no. 3465/03, ECtHR 21 December 2010. 319
Siebenhaar v. Germany, no. 18136/02, ECtHR 3 February 2011 328
Kuppinger v. Germany, no. 41599/09, ECtHR 21 April 2011 73–74
Negrepontis-Giannisis v. Greece, no. 56759/08, ECtHR 3 May 2011 . . . . 230, 233
Mosley v. the United Kingdom, no. 48009/08, ECtHR 10 May 2011 150
Fabris v. France, no. 16574/08, ECtHR 21 July 2011 294
Heinisch v. Germany, no. 28274, ECtHR 21 July 2011. . . . . 5, 312, 326
Schneider v. Germany, no. 17080/07, ECtHR 15 September 2011. 95
Khelili v. Switzerland, no. 16188/07, ECtHR 18 October 2011. 149
Bergmann v. Czech Republic, no. 8857/08, ECtHR 27 October 2011 75
S.H. and Others v. Austria, no. 57813/00, ECtHR (GC)
  3 November 2011. 313

Othman (Abu Qatada) v. the United Kingdom, no. 8139/09, ECtHR
   17 January 2012 231
Axel Springer v. Deutschland, no. 39954/08, ECtHR (GC) 7 February 2012 129
Von Hannover v. Germany (no.2), nos. 40660/08 and 60641/08,
   ECtHR (GC) 7 February 2012 ....3, 124, 315, 325, 335
Ahrens v. Germany, no. 45071/09, ECtHR 22 March 2012................ 5, 93–94
Kautzor v. Germany, no. 23338/09, ECtHR 22 March 2012................. 93–94
Konstantin Markin v. Russia, no. 30078/06, ECtHR 22 March 2012............ 303
Alkaya v. Turkey, no. 42811/06, ECtHR 9 October 2012 150
Catan and Others v. Moldova and Russia, nos. 43370/04, 8252/05 and
   18454/06, ECtHR 19 October 2012..65
Michaud v. France, no. 12323/11, ECtHR 6 December 2012 .... 243, 247, 241
Koppikar v. Germany, no. 11858/10, ECtHR 11 December 2012 93–95
De Souza Ribeiro v. France, no. 22689/07, ECtHR 13 December 2012............44
Ashby Donald and Others v. France, no. 36769/08, ECtHR
   10 January 2013 170
Eweida and Others v. the United Kingdom, nos. 48420/10, 36516/10,
   51671/10 and 36516/10, ECtHR 15 January 2013......................... 315
Fabris v. France, no. 16574/08, ECtHR (GC) 7 February 2013 ....2, 4
Vojnity v. Hungary, no. 29617/07, ECtHR 12 February 2013....................81
Bernh Larsen Holding AS and Others v. Norway, no. 24117/08,
   ECtHR 14 March 2013 147
Animal Defenders International v. the United Kingdom, no. 48876/08,
   ECtHR 22 April 2013... 290
Boeckel and Gessner-Boeckel v. Germany, no. 8017/11, ECtHR
   7 May 2013 313
Shindler v. the United Kingdom, no. 19840/09, ECtHR 7 May 2013 290
Avilkina and Others v. Russia, no. 1585/09, ECtHR 6 June 2013............... 148
Sofia Povse and Doris Povse v. Austria, no. 3890/11, ECtHR
   18 June 2013 ....232, 238–242
Sindicatul 'Păstorul Cel Bun' v. Romania, no. 2330/09, ECtHR (GC)
   9 July 2013... 5, 314, 318
Von Hannover v. Germany (no.3), no. 8772/10, ECtHR
   19 September 2013.. 124
Varvara v. Italy, no. 17475/2009, ECtHR 29 October 2013 47
Vallianatos and Others v. Greece, nos. 29381/09 and 32684/09,
   ECtHR (GC) 7 November 2013............................. 5, 105, 295, 319
Söderman v. Sweden, no. 5786/08, ECtHR (GC) 12 November 2013 150
X v. Latvia, no. 27853/09, ECtHR 26 November 2013 238
*National Union of Rail, Maritime and Transport Workers (RMT) v. the
   United Kingdom*, no. 31045/10, ECtHR 8 April 2014 .... 5, 321–322
Radu v. Republic of Moldova, no. 50073/07, ECtHR 15 April 2014......... 146, 148
Fernández Martínez v. Spain, no. 56030/07, ECtHR (GC)
   12 June 2014..6, 328–329
Labassee v. France, no. 65941/11, ECtHR 26 June 2014 .... 5, 52, 233
Mennesson v. France, no. 65192/11, ECtHR 26 June 2014 .... 5, 52, 233, 311
S.A.S. v. France, no. 43835/11, ECtHR 1 July 2014 290

Hämäläinen v. Finland, no. 37359/09, ECtHR 16 July 2014 296
Cakicisoy and Others v. Cyprus, no. 6523/12, ECtHR 23 September 2014 147
Adefromil v. France, no. 32191/09, ECtHR 2 October 2014 266–268
Hrvatski liječnički sindikat v. Croatia, no. 36701/09, ECtHR
 27 November 2014 5
Adebowale v. Germany, no. 546/10, ECtHR 2 December 2014 93–95
Matelly v. France, no. 10609/10, ECtHR 2 January 2015 266–268
Kuppinger v. Germany, nos. 62198/11, ECtHR 15 January 2015 73–75
M.A. v. Austria, no. 4097, ECtHR 15 January 2015 233
Markgraf v. Germany, no. 42719/14, ECtHR 10 March 2015 93
Oliari and Others v. Italy, nos. 18766/11 and 36030/11, ECtHR
 21 July 2015 . . . . .3, 5, 105, 111, 113, 319–320
Parrillo v. Italy, no. 46470/11, ECtHR 27 August 2015 290
M. and M. v. Croatia, no. 10161/13, ECtHR 3 September 2015. 66
Mandet v. France, no. 30955/12, ECtHR 14 January 2016 94
Avotiņš v. Latvia, no. 17502/07, ECtHR 23 May 2016 . . . . 230, 239–240,
 242–246, 250
Geotech Kancev GmbH v. Germany, no. 23646/09, ECtHR
 2 June 2016 5
Chapin and Charpentier v. France, no. 40183/07, ECtHR 9 June 2016 296
Vukota-Bojić v. Switzerland, no. 61838/10, ECtHR 18 October 2016 148
L.D. and P.K. v. Bulgaria, nos. 7949/11 and 45522/13, ECtHR
 8 December 2016 . . . . 5, 93–94
Béláné Nagy v. Hungary, no. 53080/13, ECtHR 13 December 2016 . . . . 210, 214
Satakunnan Markkinapörssi Oy and Satamedia Oy v. Finland, no. 931/13,
 ECtHR (GC) 27 June 2017 146
Bărbulescu v. Romania, no. 61496/08, ECtHR (GC) 5 September 2017 . . . . 6, 146,
 150–151, 155,
 316, 326
Antović and Mirković v. Montenegro, no. 70838/13, ECtHR
 28 November 2017 152
Ben Faiza v. France, no. 31446/12, ECtHR 8 February 2018 148
Mockutė v. Lithuania, no. 66490/09, ECtHR 27 February 2018 . . . . 146, 148
Royer v. Hungary, no. 9114/16, ECtHR 6 March 2018 246–250
Tlapak and Others v. Germany, nos. 11308/16 and 11344/16,
 ECtHR 22 March 2018 . . . . 67–73, 75–82
Wetjen and Others v. Germany, nos. 68125/14 and 72204/14,
 ECtHR 22 March 2018 . . . . .67–73, 75, 77,
 79–82, 315
Pirozzi v. Belgium, no. 21055/11, ECtHR, 17 April 2018 245
Benedik v. Slovenia, no. 62357/14, ECtHR 24 April 2018 148
G.I.E.M. s.r.l. and Others v. Italy, nos. 1828/06, 34163/07 and
 19029/11, ECtHR (GC) 28 June 2018 48–49
M.L. and W.W. v. Germany, nos. 60798/10 and 65599/10, ECtHR
 28 June 2018 . . . . 127, 131
Denisov v. Ukraine, no. 76639/11, ECtHR (GC) 25 September 2018 216
Petrov and X v. Russia, no. 23608/16, ECtHR 23 October 2018 316

Vicent Del Campo v. Spain, no. 25527/13, ECtHR 6 November 2018 149
Mehmedovic v. Switzerland, no. 17331/11, ECtHR 11 December 2018 147
Deaconu v. Romania, no. 66299/12, ECtHR 29 January 2019 4
Advisory Opinion, no. P16-2018-001, ECtHR (GC)
  10 April 2019 . . . . 52, 298, 312
Ilgar Mammadov v. Azerbaijan, no. 15171/13, ECtHR (GC)
  29 May 2019 61
Nicolae Virgiliu Tănase v. Romania, no. 41720/13, ECtHR (GC)
  25 June 2019 317
Romeo Castano v. Belgium, no. 8351/17, ECtHR 9 July 2019 245–246
López Ribalda and Others v. Spain, nos. 1874/13 and 8567/13,
  ECtHR (GC) 17 October 2019 . . . . .6, 150, 152, 155,
                                                                                  315–316, 326
Buturugă v. Romania, no. 56867/15, ECtHR 10 February 2020 150
Advisory Opinion, no. P16-2019-001, ECtHR (GC) 29 May 2020 52
D v. France, no. 11288/18, ECtHR 16 July 2020 . . . . 55, 312
Koychev v. Bulgaria, no. 32495/15, ECtHR 13 October 2020 . . . . 5, 93–94
Honner v. France, no. 19511/16, ECtHR 12 November 2020 97
Advisory Opinion, no. P16-2020-001, ECtHR (GC)
  14 December 2020 52
Bivolaru and Moldovan v. France, nos. 40324/16 and 12623/17,
  ECtHR 25 March 2021 246
Liebscher v. Austria, no. 5434/17, ECtHR 6 April 2021 . . . . 150, 153
Valdís Fjölnisdóttir and Others v. Iceland, no. 71552/17, ECtHR
  18 May 2021 . . . . 88, 312, 317
BEG S.P.A. v. Italy, no. 5312/11, ECtHR 20 May 2021 194
*Trade Unions (LO) and Norwegian Transport Workers' Union (NTF) v.
  Norway*, no. 45487/17, ECtHR 10 June 2021 . . . . 5, 323
Hurbain v. Belgium, no. 57292/16, ECtHR 22 June 2021 131–132
Fedotova and Others v. Russia, no. 40792/10, ECtHR 13 July 2021 102
Spinelli v. Russia, no. 57777/17, ECtHR 19 October 2021 238
Kupás v. Hungary, no. 24720/17, ECtHR 28 October 2021 238
Sousa v. Portugal, no. 28/17, ECtHR 7 December 2021 245
Abdi Ibrahim v. Norway, no. 15379/16, ECtHR 10 December 2021 88
Advisory Opinion, no. P16-2021-001, ECtHR (GC), 26 April 2022 52
*Association of Civil Servants and Union for Collective Bargaining
  and Others v. Germany*, nos. 815/18, 3278/18, 12380/18, 12693/18
  and 14883/18, ECtHR 5 July 2022 . . . . 5, 323
Advisory Opinion, no. P16-2021-002, ECtHR (GC), 13 July 2022 52
Dolenc v. Slovenia, no. 20256/20, ECtHR 20 October 2022 231–232
Veres v. Spain, no. 57906/18, ECtHR 8 November 2022 233
D.B. and Others v. Switzerland, nos. 58817/15 and 58252/15, ECtHR
  22 November 2022 55
K.K. and Others v. Denmark, no. 25212/21, ECtHR
  2 December 2022 55

List of Cases

INTER-AMERICAN COURT OF HUMAN RIGHTS

Atala Riffo and Daughters v. Chile, Inter-Am. CtHR 24 February 2012,
 case no. 12.502 297

INTERNATIONAL CENTRE FOR SETTLEMENT OF INVESTMENT DISPUTES

Salini Costruttori S.p.A. and Italstrade S.p.A. v. Kingdom of Morocco
 (ICSID Case No. ARB/00/4), Decision on Jurisdiction
 (23 July 2001) 204
MTD Equity Sdn. Bhd and MTD Chile S.A. v. Republic of Chile (ICSID
 Case No. ARB/01/7), Award (25 May 2004) 208
Continental Casualty Company v. The Argentine Republic (ICSID
 Case No. ARB/03/9), Award (5 September 2008) 219
*Suez, Sociedad General de Aguas de Barcelona, S.A. and Vivendi Universal,
 S.A. v. Argentine Republic* (ICSID Case No. ARB/03/19), Decision on
 Liability (20 July 2010) 209
Total S.A. v. Argentine Republic (ICSID Case No. ARB/04/1), Decision
 on Liability (27 December 2010) 208, 210
El Paso Energy International Company v. The Argentine Republic (ICSID
 Case No. ARB/03/15), Award (31 October 2011) 216
Electrabel S.A. v. Republic of Hungary (ICSID Case No. ARB/07/19),
 Award (25 November 2015) 217
*Philip Morris Brands Sàrl, Philip Morris Products S.A. and Abal Hermanos
 S.A. v. Oriental Republic of Uruguay* (ICSID Case No. ARB/10/7),
 Award (8 July 2016) 211
Blusun S.A., Jean-Pierre Lecorcier and Michael Stein v. Italian Republic
 (ICSID Case No. ARB/14/3), Final Award (27 December 2016) 211, 217
Stadtwerke München GmbH and others v. Kingdom of Spain (ICSID
 Case No. ARB/15/1), Award (2 December 2019) 218
ESPF Beteiligungs GmbH and others v. Italian Republic (ICSID
 Case No. ARB/16/5), Award (14 September 2020) 214
Silver Ridge Power BV v. Italian Republic (ICSID Case No. ARB/15/37),
 Award of the Tribunal (26 February 2021) 211, 214

PERMANENT COURT OF ARBITRATION

Jürgen Wirtgen and others v. The Czech Republic (PCA Case No. 2014-03),
 Dissenting Opinion of Arbitrator Gary Born (11 October 2017) 212
Antaris GMBH and Dr. Michael Göde v. The Czech Republic (PCA
 Case No. 2014-01), Award (2 May 2018) 211, 218

PERMANENT COURT OF INTERNATIONAL JUSTICE

S.S. Lotus (France v. Turkey), no. 9, 7 September 1927, PCIJ (Series A) No. 10 228

STOCKHOLM CHAMBER OF COMMERCE

Greentech Energy Systems A/S, et al. v. Italian Republic (SCC
    Case No. 2015/095), Dissenting Opinion of Arbitrator Giorgio Sacerdoti
    (5 December 2018) 220
CEF Energia B.V. v. Italian Republic (SCC Case No. 2015/158), Award
    (16 January 2019). 213, 219
Sunreserve Luxco Holdings S.À.R.L. and others v. Italian Republic (SCC
    Case No. 2016/32), Final Award (25 March 2020) 213

NATIONAL

AUSTRIA

Constitutional Court

VfGH 30 June 2022 – G 230/2021-20 313

Supreme Court of Justice

OGH 1 October 2019 – 18 OCg 5/19p 192
OGH 23 July 2020 – 18 ONc 3/20s 180

FRANCE

Constitutional Court

Conseil Constitutionnel, 17 May 2013, no. 2013-669 107

Court of Cassation

Cass. Civ., 1ère, 28 March 2013, no. 11-27.770 181
Cass. Civ., 1ère, 5 July 2017, no. 15-28-597; no. 16-16-901; no. 16-16-455
    and no.16-20-052. 52
Cass., Ass. plén., 4 October 2019, no. 10-19053. . . . . 54, 298
Cass. Civ., 1ère, 18 December 2019, no. 19-11815 and no. 18-12327. 54

GERMANY

Federal Constitutional Court

BVerfG 10 May 1957 – 1 BvR 550/52, *BVerfGE* 6, 389 18
BVerfG 16 December 1958 – 1 BvR 449/55, *BVerfGE* 9, 36 .... 18, 30
BVerfG 5 August 1966 – 1 BvR 586/62, 1 BvR 610/63 and 1 BvR 512/64,
    BVerfGE 20, 162 18
BVerfG 3 October 1969 – 1 BvR 46/65, *BVerfGE* 27, 71 18
BVerfG 4 May 1971 – 1 BvR 636/1968, *BVerfGE* 31, 58 18
BVerfG 5 June 1973 – 1 BvR 536/72, *BVerfGE* 35, 202 18
BVerfG 29 May 1974 – 2 BvL 52/71, *BVerfGE* 37, 271 (*Solange I*) 244
BVerfG 15 December 1983 – 1 BvR 209/83, 1 BvR 484/83, 1 BvR 440/83,
    1 BvR 420/83, 1 BvR 362/83 and 1 BvR 269/83, *BVerfGE* 65, 1 .... 139, 142
BVerfG 4 June 1985 – 2 BvR 1703/83, 2 BvR 1718/83, 2 BvR 1718/83
    and 2 BvR 856/84, *BVerfGE* 70, 138. 329
BVerfG 22 October 1986 – 2 BvR 197/83, *BVerfGE* 73, 339 (*Solange II*) 244
BVerfG 13 January 1987 – 2 BvR 209/84, *BVerfGE* 74, 102 26
BVerfG 26 March 1987 – 2 BvR 589/79, 2 BvR 750/81 and 2 BvR 284/85,
    BVerfGE 74, 358 .... 14, 18
BVerfG 29 May 1990 – 2 BvR 254/88 and 2 BvR 1343/88, *BVerfGE* 82, 106 ..... 18, 26
BVerfG 14 November 1990 – 2 BvR 1462/87, *BVerfGE* 83, 119 18
BVerfG 12 July 1994 – 2 BvE 3/92, 2 BvE 5/93, 2 BvE 7/93 and 2 BvE 8/93,
    BVerfGE 90, 286 15
BVerfG 24 Ocotber 1996 – 2 BvR 1851/94, 2 BvR 1852/94, 2 BvR 1875/94
    and 2 BvR 1853/94, *BVerfGE* 95, 96. 16
BVerfG 6 May 1997 – 1 BvR 409/90, *BVerfGE* 96, 56 84
BVerfG 15 December 1999 – 1 BvR 653/96, *BVerfGE* 101, 361 (*Caroline
    von Monaco*) 120
BVerfG 11 December 2000 – BvR 661/00, *NJW* 2001, 961. 84
BVerfG 9 April 2003 – 1 BvR 1493/96 and 1724/01, *FamRZ* 2003, 816 91
BVerfG 14 October 2004 – 2 BvR 1481/04, *BVerfGE* 111, 307
    (*Görgülü*) 12, 18, 20–21,
                                                              25, 27, 123, 278
BVerfG 26 February 2008 – 1 BvR 1602/07, 1 BvR 1606/07 and
    1 BvR 1626/07, *BVerfGE* 120, 180 (*Caroline von Hannover*) 18, 21, 27,
                                                              41, 124
BVerfG 10 November 2009 – 1 BvR 1265/08, *BVerfGK* 14, 38. 83–84
BVerfG 24 November 2009 – 1 BvR 2678/08, *NJW* 2012, 1643. 124
BVerfG 4 May 2011 – 2 BvR 2365/09, 2 BvR 740/10, 2 BvR 2333/08,
    2 BvR 1152/10 and 2 BvR 571/10, *BVerfGE* 128, 326 .... 13, 17–18, 21, 27
BVerfG 20 June 2011 – 1 BvR 303/11, *FamRZ* 2012, 433 83
BVerfG 28 February 2012 – 1 BvR 3116/11, *BVerfGK* 19, 295 84
BVerfG 7 April 2014 – 1 BvR 3121/13, *FamRZ* 2014, 907 83–84
BVerfG 22 May 2014 – 1 BvR 2882/13, *FamRZ* 2014, 1266 83
BVerfG 22 October 2014 – 2 BvR 661/12, *BVerfGE* 137, 273. 330
BVerfG 25 April 2015 – 1 BvR 3326/14, *FamRZ* 2015, 1093 84

BVerfG 13 July 2017 – 1 BvR 1202/17, *FamRZ* 2017, 1577 83–84
BVerfG 12 June 2018 – 2 BvR 1738/12, 2 BvR 646/15, 2 BvR 1068/14
    and 2 BvR 1395/13, *BVerfGE* 148, 296 .... 15–16, 18–23, 27, 277,
                                                                 279–280, 311, 334
BVerfG 26 March 2019 – 1 BvR 673/17, *BVerfGE* 151, 101 26
BVerfG 6 November 2019 – 1 BvR 16/13, *BVerfGE* 152, 152
    (*Recht auf Vergessen I*) 129–130, 143, 309, 311
BVerfG 6 November 2019 – 1 BvR 276/17, *BVerfGE* 152, 216
    (*Recht auf Vergessen II*) 24, 241
BVerfG 1 December 2020 – 2 BvR 1845/18 and 2 BvR 2100/18,
    BVerfGE 156, 182 24
BVerfG 8 August 2021 – 2 BvR 171/20, *BeckRS* 2021, 24992 32
BVerfG 14 November 2021 – 1 BvR 1525/20, *NZFam* 2021, 953 83

Federal Court of Justice

BGH 19 December 1995 – VI ZR 15/95, *BGHZ* 131, 332 (*Caroline
    von Monaco*) 120
BGH 6 March 2007 – VI ZR 13/06, *NJW* 2007, 1981 (*Abgestuftes
    Schutzkonzept*) 124
BGH 6 March 2007 – VI ZR 51/06, *BGHZ* 171, 275 (*Winterurlaub*) 5, 124
BGH 6 March 2007 – VI ZR 52/06, *ZUM* 2007, 470 124
BGH 1 July 2008 – VI ZR 67/08, *NJW* 2008, 3141 (*Urlaubsfoto von
    Caroline*) 124
BGH 15 December 2009 – VI ZR 227/08 and VI ZR 228/08, *BGHZ*
    183, 353 (*Online-Archiv*) 126
BGH 9 February 2010 – VI ZR 243/08 and 244/08, *NJW* 2010, 2432
    (*Spiegel-Dossier*) 126
BGH 20 April 2010 – VI ZR 245/08 and VI ZR 246/08, *NJW* 2010,
    2728 126
BGH 13 November 2012 – VI ZR 330/11, *MDR* 2013, 151
    (*Apollonia-Prozess*) 129
BGH 10 December 2014 – XII ZB 463/13, *BGHZ* 203, 350 311
BGH 5 October 2016 – XII ZB 280/15, *FamRZ* 2016, 2082 97
BGH 16 June 2021 – XII ZB 58/20, *FamRZ* 2021, 1375 97

Federal Administrative Court

BVerwG 29 June 1957 – II C 105.56, *BVerwGE* 5, 153 18

Federal Labour Court

BAG 7 February 1990 – 5 AZR 84/89, *NJW* 1990, 2082 318
BAG 8 September 2011 – 2 AZR 543/10, *NZA* 2012, 443 330
BAG 28 July 2016 – 2 AZR 746/14 (A), *NZA* 2017, 388 330
BAG 20 February 2019 – 2 AZR 746/14, *NZA* 2019, 901 332

Higher Regional Courts

OLG Hamburg 29 July 2008 – 7 U 30/08, *BeckRS* 2010, 1974 126
OLG Nürnberg 11 June 2015 – 9 UF 1430/14, *FamRZ* 2015,
    1908 .... 68–69, 73, 77, 80, 82

Regional Court

LG Hamburg 29 February 2008 – 324 O 459/07, *BeckRS* 2010, 3447 126

ITALY

Constitutional Court

Corte Cost., 14 February 1973, no. 16 254
Corte Cost., 18 December 1973, no. 183 264
Corte Cost., 22 December 1980, no. 188 265
Corte Cost., 5 June 1984, no. 170 .... 264, 270
Corte Cost., 29 April 1985, no. 126 257
Corte Cost., 23 July 1987, no. 278 270
Corte Cost., 11 January 1989, no. 24 256
Corte Cost., 13 November 1997, no. 350 57
Corte Cost., 13 December 1999, no. 449 .... 258, 270
Corte Cost., 24 October 2007, no. 348 and no. 349 .... 46, 264
Corte Cost., 14 January 2010, no. 4 107
Corte Cost., 14 April 2010, no. 138 107
Corte Cost., 7 July 2010, no. 276 107
Corte Cost., 4 April 2011, n. 113 61
Corte Cost., 14 January 2015, no. 49 .... 47–48, 334
Corte Cost., 22 January 2015, no. 3 57
Corte Cost., 13 June 2018, no. 120 269
Corte Cost., 9 March 2021, no. 33 302
Corte Cost., 23 February 2022, no. 79 56

Court of Cassation

Cass. Civ., Sez. I, 15 March 2012, no. 4184 .... 109, 114
Cass. Civ., Sez. I, 9 February 2015, no. 2400 109
Cass. Civ., Sez. I, 21 June 2016, no. 19599 57
Cass. Civ. Sez. Un., 8 May 2019, no. 12193 .... 56, 301
Cass. Pen., Sez. Un., 24 October 2019, no. 8544 49
Cass. Civ., Sez. I, 29 April 2020, no. 8325 .... 55, 57–58, 301
Cass. Civ., Sez. I, 21 January 2022, no. 1842 59
Cass. Civ., Sez. Un., 30 December 2022, no. 38162 59

Court of Appeal

Court of Appeal of Venice, Ord., sez. III, 16 July 2018 56

PORTUGAL

Constitutional Court

Tribunal Constitucional de Portugal, 4 November 2009, Acórdão
n.º 359/2009 106

SPAIN

Constitutional Court

Tribunal Constitucional de España, 11 January 2012, Sentencia 198/2011 106

SWITZERLAND

Federal Supreme Court

TF, 10 June 2010, 4A_458/2009 *(Adrian Mutu)*.............................. 188
TF, 9 October 2012, 4A_110/2012 194

UNITED KINGDOM

Supreme Court

Halliburton Company v. Chubb Bermuda Insurance Ltd (formerly known as Ace Bermuda Insurance Ltd) [2020] UKSC 48 190

Court of Appeal

Locabail (UK) Ltd v. Bayfield Properties Ltd [2000] QB 451................... 187
Taylor v. Lawrence [2003] QB 528 191

High Court

Guidant LLC v. Swiss Re International SE [2016] EWHC (Comm) 1201 186
W Ltd. v. M SDN BHD [2016] EWHC 422 (Comm). 189, 193

UNITED STATES OF AMERICA

Supreme Court

Mazer v. Stein, 347 U.S. 201 (1954) 155
Commonwealth Coatings Corp v. Continental Casualty Co, 393 U.S.
  145 (1968) 186
Obergefell v. Hodges, Director, Ohio Department of Health et al., 135 S.
  Ct. 2584 (2015). 112

Courts of Appeals

*Merit Insurance Company v. Leatherby Insurance Company a/k/a Western
  Employers Insurance Company*, 714 F.2d 673 (7th Cir. 1983) 186
*Morelite Constr. Corp. v. New York City District Counsel Carpenters Benefit
  Fund*, 48 F.2d 79 (2d Cir. 1984) 190
Applied Indus. Materials Corp. v. Ovalar Makine Ticaret Ve Sanayi, A.S.,
  492 F.3d 132 (2d Cir. 2007).. 194

LIST OF CONTRIBUTORS

Edoardo Ales
Full Professor of Labour Law and Industrial Relations, University of Naples 'Parthenope', Italy

Francesca Benatti
Associate Professor of Comparative Law, Catholic University of Sacred Heart, Milan, Italy

Gabriele Buchholtz
Junior Professor (Tenure Track) of Social Security Law, with a focus on digitalisation and migration, University of Hamburg, Germany

Katharina de la Durantaye
Full Professor of Civil Law, Commercial Law, Competition Law and Intellectual Property, Free University Berlin, Germany

Konrad Duden
Full Professor of Private Law and Private International Law, Leipzig University, Germany

Anatol Dutta
Full Professor of Private Law, Private International Law and Comparative Law, Ludwig Maximilian University of Munich, Germany

Dominik Ebel
Research Fellow and Ph.D. candidate, Heidelberg University, Germany

Andreas Engel
Senior Research Fellow (Akademischer Rat a.Z.), Heidelberg University, Germany

Matteo Fornasier
Full Professor of Civil Law, Labour Law, Private International Law and Comparative Law, Ruhr University Bochum, Germany

Christian Heinze
Full Professor of Civil Law, Commercial Law, European Law and Comparative Law, Heidelberg University, Germany

List of Contributors

Giovanni Maria Riccio
Full Professor of Comparative Law, University of Salerno, Italy

Giacomo Rojas Elgueta
Associate Professor of Private Law, Roma Tre University School of Law, Italy

Maria Gabriella Stanzione
Associate Professor of Comparative Law, University of Salerno, Italy

Laura Vagni
Full Professor of Private Comparative Law, University of Macerata, Italy

Filippo Viglione
Full Professor of Comparative Law, University of Padova, Italy

Denise Wiedemann
Senior Research Fellow, Max Planck Institute for Comparative and International Private Law, Hamburg, Germany

THE EUROPEAN CONVENTION ON HUMAN RIGHTS AND ITS IMPACT ON NATIONAL PRIVATE LAW

An Introduction

Matteo Fornasier and Maria Gabriella Stanzione

1. The Application of the Convention in Horizontal Relationships...... 1
2. The Court's Role in Private Law Disputes 2
3. The Impact of the ECHR on Private Law During the Last Two Decades: Some Examples.. 4
4. Aim and Outline of the Book 6

1. THE APPLICATION OF THE CONVENTION IN HORIZONTAL RELATIONSHIPS

As Norberto Bobbio writes, human rights are historical rights; that is to say they are born in definite circumstances, marked by the efforts to protect new freedoms against old privileges.[1] Civil liberties are the fruit of the struggles of parliaments against absolute rulers, religious freedom is the result of the wars of religion, political and social freedom emerged with the rise of the labour movement, and so on. Precise claims arise, in fact, only when specific needs arise, in correspondence with the changes in society.

In this perspective, early human rights proclamations such as the Virginia Declaration of Rights of 1776, the French Déclaration des droits de l'homme et du citoyen of 1789, or the United States Bill of Rights, adopted in the same year, had the aim of limiting the power of the

---

[1] N. Bobbio, *L'età dei diritti*, Einaudi, Torino 1990.

sovereign over its citizens. Similarly, the fundamental rights enshrined in the constitutions of many modern states are primarily concerned with the vertical relationship between individuals and public institutions, and seek to safeguard the former against arbitrary coercion and interference by the latter. However, over the last few decades, it has become widely accepted that human and fundamental rights also matter in the horizontal relations between private parties, since the interests protected by those rights may be threatened not just by public authorities, but likewise by private actors.

These observations also apply to the European Convention on Human Rights (ECHR or Convention). When the Convention was drafted in 1949/50, it was meant to be a response to the atrocities committed by totalitarian states during the first half of the 20th century. Almost 30 years later, the European Court of Human Rights (ECtHR) developed, in *Marckx v. Belgium* – a historic case concerning family as well as succession law – the notion of 'positive obligations', which paved the way for the application of the ECHR in private law disputes. According to the Court, the Contracting States are not only under a negative duty to abstain from direct interference with the rights and freedoms guaranteed under the Convention: they may be equally obliged, depending on the circumstances, to adopt active measures to secure the relevant rights and to prevent other individuals from interfering with those rights.[2]

2. THE COURT'S ROLE IN PRIVATE LAW DISPUTES

The doctrine of positive obligations, aimed at protecting human rights also in horizontal relationships between individuals, shifts the focus to private law. As the ECtHR rightly points out, '[it] is not in principle required to settle disputes of a purely private nature'.[3] Rather, the Strasbourg Court assumes the role of a 'quasi-constitutional court',[4] exercising supervision of the Contracting States' private law legislation. Thus, in the *Marckx* case mentioned above, the Court scrutinised the Belgian provisions on the legal status of children born out of wedlock and found those provisions to be in breach of the Convention, in particular

---

[2] *Marckx v. Belgium*, no. 6833/74, § 31, ECtHR 13 June 1979.
[3] *Fabris v. France*, no. 16574/08, § 60, ECtHR (GC) 7 February 2013.
[4] E. BATES, *The Evolution of the European Convention on Human Rights*, OUP, Oxford 2010, pp. 155 *et seq*.

Article 8 on the right to respect for family life, and Article 14 prohibiting discrimination on grounds of birth, as they put 'illegitimate' children in a less favourable position compared to 'legitimate' children with regard to the procedure of establishing maternal affiliation, as well as in relation to maintenance and inheritance rights.[5] Moreover, the Court may not only find violations of Convention rights in the ways that national legislatures actively regulate private law relationships; breaches of the Convention may also result from the absence of legislation conferring rights and duties to individuals in their mutual relations. An example is the case of *Oliari and Others v. Italy*, regarding the right of same-sex couples to respect for private and family life under Article 8 of the Convention. Here, the Strasbourg Court held that the Italian legislature had violated the Convention by refraining from enacting a legal framework granting legal recognition and protection to persons of the same sex living in a relationship.[6]

Besides scrutinising the Contracting States' domestic legislation, the ECtHR also performs a supervisory role over the decisions of national civil courts, ensuring that, when they adjudicate disputes between private parties, the relevant rules of private law are applied in a manner consistent with the guarantees of the Convention. This is particularly important where the resolution of the dispute requires striking a balance between the competing rights and interests of the parties, all of which are, in principle, protected by the Convention. Here, the task of the ECtHR is, in its own words, 'to review, in the light of the case as a whole, whether the decisions [the national courts] have taken pursuant to their power of appreciation are compatible with the provisions of the Convention relied on.'[7] In *Pla and Puncernau v. Andorra* the Court went one step further still. It held that domestic courts have to interpret not just the Contracting States' laws and regulations, but also legal acts by private individuals, such as testamentary dispositions and contractual agreements, in conformity with the Convention. In the case under consideration, the courts in Andorra had interpreted a clause in a will, which dated back to 1939, to the effect that only biological descendants were entitled to inherit the testatrix's estate, excluding the adoptive grandchildren from succession. The ECtHR, in its majority opinion, took the view that such a reading of the will was

---

[5] *Marckx v. Belgium*, no. 6833/74, §§ 35 *et seq.*, ECtHR 13 June 1979.
[6] *Oliari and Others v. Italy*, nos. 18766/11 and 36030/11, §§ 165 *et seq.*, ECtHR 21 July 2015.
[7] *Von Hannover v. Germany (No. 2)*, nos. 40660/08 and 60641/08, § 105, ECtHR (GC) 7 February 2012.

discriminatory, and thus violated Article 14 of the Convention.[8] The Court stated that,

> in exercising the European supervision incumbent on it, it cannot remain passive where a national court's interpretation of a legal act, be it a testamentary disposition, a private contract, a public document, a statutory provision or an administrative practice appears unreasonable, arbitrary or ... blatantly inconsistent with the prohibition of discrimination established by Article 14 and more broadly with the principles underlying the Convention.[9]

3. THE IMPACT OF THE ECHR ON PRIVATE LAW DURING THE LAST TWO DECADES: SOME EXAMPLES

In the last two decades, the ECtHR has come to play a major role in a broad range of private law issues. At the turn of the century, the Convention was still believed to have only a very limited impact on private law.[10] In 2004, however, the Strasbourg Court delivered its decision in the case of *Von Hannover v. Germany*: a decision which the former Judge and Vice President of the ECtHR, Angelika Nussberger, described as a 'wake-up call for private law scholarship' in Germany.[11] In this case, the ECtHR held that the established case law of the German Federal Court of Justice, on the protection of the right to privacy of public figures against the publication of photographs about their private lives in the press, violated the right to respect for private and family life under Article 8 of the Convention, to

---

[8] *Pla and Puncernau v. Andorra*, no. 69498/01, §§ 51 *et seq.*, ECtHR 13 July 2004. Judges Bratza and Garlicki dissented, arguing that private individuals are, in principle, not bound by the Convention. Therefore, the testatrix in the case at hand was not precluded from differentiating between biological and adoptive children in her decision on to whom to leave her property. Consequently, the two judges maintained that the national courts were allowed to give effect to such a testamentary disposition even though it was discriminatory.

[9] *Pla and Puncernau v. Andorra*, no. 69498/01, § 59, ECtHR 13 July 2004. See, to the same effect, *Fabris v. France*, no. 16574/08, § 60, ECtHR (GC) 7 February 2013; *Deaconu v. Romania*, no. 66299/12, § 24, ECtHR 29 January 2019.

[10] See J. Basedow, 'Europäische Menschenrechtskonvention und Europäisches Privatrecht', *RabelsZ* 63 (1999), 409, 411, who argues that the ECHR is unlikely to produce any effects on German private law that are substantially different from those emanating from domestic constitutional law.

[11] A. Nussberger, 'Die Europäische Menschenrechtskonvention und das Privatrecht', *RabelsZ* 80 (2016), 817, 825.

the extent that it permitted the dissemination of pictures which did not contribute to any debate of public interest.[12] As a result, the Federal Court of Justice had to develop a new approach to the resolution of conflicts between the right to privacy of public figures, on the one hand, and the right to freedom of the press, on the other.[13]

The Court's case law also led to far-reaching changes in other fields of private law. In the sphere of family law, the ECtHR strengthened the legal protection afforded to individuals living in de facto family relationships, where such relationships are not officially recognised under the applicable national law. This may be the case, depending on the jurisdiction, for same-sex couples,[14] for biological fathers vis-à-vis their children,[15] or for the relationship between children born through surrogacy and their intended parents.[16] In the ambit of labour relations, the Court acknowledged that specific trade union rights, such as the right to bargain collectively with the employer and the right to strike, are essential elements of the freedom of association guaranteed by Article 11 of the Convention,[17] thus causing a significant increase in the number of cases involving collective labour law brought before the Court.[18] Likewise, the Strasbourg Court is keen to secure the rights of individual employees, for example by restricting the freedom of employers to dismiss employees for 'whistle-blowing',[19] or by scrutinising, in the context of church employment, the duties imposed on employees also to comply with certain moral or religious precepts of

---

[12] *Von Hannover v. Germany*, no. 59320/00, §§ 61 *et seq.*, ECtHR 24 June 2004.
[13] BGHZ 171, 275= *NJW* 2007, 1977.
[14] *Vallianatos and Others v. Greece*, nos. 29381/09 and 32684/09, ECtHR (GC), 7 November 2013; *Oliari and Others v. Italy*, nos. 18766/11 and 36030/11, ECtHR 21 July 2015.
[15] *Ahrens v. Germany*, no. 45071/09, § 58, ECtHR 22 March 2012; *L.D. and P.K. v. Bulgaria*, nos. 7949/11 and 45522/13, § 54, ECtHR 8 December 2016; *Koychev v. Bulgaria*, no. 32495/15, § 44, ECtHR 13 October 2020.
[16] *Mennesson v. France*, no. 65192/11, ECtHR 26 June 2014; *Labassee v. France*, no. 65941/11, ECtHR 26 June 2014.
[17] *Demir and Baykara v. Turkey*, no. 34503/97, § 154, ECtHR (GC) 12 November 2008; *Enerji Yapı-Yol Sen v. Turkey*, no. 68959/01, § 24, ECtHR 21 April 2009.
[18] See, e.g. *Sindicatul "Păstorul Cel Bun" v. Romania*, no. 2330/09, ECtHR (GC) 9 July 2013; *National Union of Rail, Maritime and Transport Workers (RMT) v. United Kingdom*, no. 31045/10, ECtHR 8 April 2014; *Hrvatski liječnički sindikat v. Croatia*, no. 36701/09, ECtHR 27 November 2014; *Geotech Kancev GmbH v. Germany*, no. 23646/09, ECtHR 2 June 2016; *Trade Unions (LO) and Norwegian Transport Workers' Union (NTF) v. Norway*, no. 45487/17, ECtHR 10 June 2021; *Association of Civil Servants and Union for Collective Bargaining and Others v. Germany*, nos. 815/18, 3278/18, 12380/18, 12693/18, 14883/18, ECtHR 5 July 2022.
[19] *Heinisch v. Germany*, no. 28274, ECtHR 21 July 2011.

the employer in their private lives.[20] Moreover, the Court has limited the right of employers to monitor employees in the workplace through CCTV cameras and other surveillance technologies.[21] Many more examples, from other fields of private law, could also be added to this list.

What is striking is that the impact of the case law of the ECtHR appears to be particularly strong in areas of private law where the European Union (EU) lacks the power to legislate, such as in family law, or in relation to trade union rights.[22] The same is true for matters on which the Member States take quite different – and often unreconcilable – approaches, making it difficult to reach a political consensus on legislative instruments at EU level. This is the case, for example, in respect of the conflict between freedom of the press and the right to privacy.[23] Here, the normative vacuum at the level of supranational law, resulting from the absence of EU law, is filled by the ECHR and the case law of the Strasbourg Court.

4. AIM AND OUTLINE OF THE BOOK

This book is the fruit of an international symposium we organised at the German-Italian Centre for the European Dialogue, Villa Vigoni, in the summer of 2021. Its aim is to obtain a broader view on the impact of the ECHR on national private law. To that end, the first two chapters shed some light on the interaction between the Convention and the States Parties' domestic law, focusing on two jurisdictions: Germany and Italy. As the two examples show, Contracting States adopt quite

---

[20] *Schüth v. Germany*, no. 1620/03, ECtHR 23 September 2010; *Fernández Martínez v. Spain*, no. 56030/07, ECtHR (GC) 12 June 2014.

[21] *Bărbulescu v. Romania*, no. 61496/08, ECtHR (GC) 5 September 2017; *López Ribalda and Others v. Spain*, nos. 1874/13, 8567/13, ECtHR (GC) 17 October 2019.

[22] According to Article 153(5) TFEU, the EU lacks legislative competence on 'pay, the right of association, the right to strike or the right to impose lock-outs'.

[23] The reluctance of the EU to adopt legislation on this matter is reflected, e.g. by Article 85(2) of the EU General Data Protection Regulation (GDPR), which provides that, for the processing of personal data carried out for journalistic purposes, Member States are free to derogate from the rules of the GDPR. Similarly, Article 1(2)(g) of the Rome II Regulation refers, for the determination of the law applicable to non-contractual obligations arising from violations of privacy and rights relating to personality, to the Member States' domestic choice-of-law rules. The reason is that especially British media outlets lobbied against the creation of a common European conflict rule out of fear that, under such a provision, they could more easily incur liability for defamation under foreign law, which in their view might impose stricter limitations on the freedom of the press than the law of their home jurisdiction.

different approaches as to how the guarantees of the Convention and the case law of the ECtHR are to be implemented into national law. The following 11 chapters, which form the main part of the book, examine the influence of the ECHR on a number of fields of private law, covering family law, data protection law, media law, copyright law and labour law, as well as private international law and procedural law. The survey of cases reveals many common features, but likewise some inconsistencies, in the decisions of the ECtHR involving issues of private law. At times, the Court confines itself to setting procedural standards for the protection of human rights in private law relations: it merely requires national authorities to adequately take into account and balance the competing rights and interests of the private individuals involved in the dispute, without prescribing which rights or interests are to take precedence in the case under consideration. In other judgments, the Court has assumed a less deferential role and defined in detail the substantive content and scope of the human rights at stake, giving instructions to national authorities as to which rights should prevail in the balancing test. Also, the Court sometimes infers the standard of human rights protection from current trends in international law, as well as from the laws and practices of the Contracting States, whereas in other cases, the Court has come up with its own standards and criteria. The last two chapters of the book build on these general observations and address some overarching issues: the role of comparative law in the reasoning of the ECtHR, and the contribution of the Convention to European harmonisation of private law, respectively.

The comparative analysis carried out throughout this work allows the authors to address more general questions: does the 'horizontal' application of the ECHR in private law relationships rest on an 'excessive' interpretation of the Convention, or is it, on the contrary, a sound approach to render the protection of human rights more effective? Is the procedural framework provided for under the ECHR suited to the settlement of disputes between private parties? These questions are closely connected with the more fundamental issue of whether the constitutionalisation of private law, i.e. the increasing influence of human and fundamental rights on private law, is a welcome and positive development.

What becomes apparent from the various chapters of the book is that the European Convention on Human Rights, as an essential component of a European koinè of principles and rights, together with the common constitutional traditions and the European Charter, is developing into an important element of a common European private law grounded – more than in dialogue – in a real common action.

PART I
SETTING THE STAGE
The European Convention on Human Rights and National Law

THE EUROPEAN CONVENTION ON HUMAN RIGHTS IN THE GERMAN LEGAL SYSTEM

A Qualitative and Quantitative Introduction

Andreas ENGEL*

1. The Formal Rank of the ECHR in the German Legal System 12
   1.1. Rank of a Federal Statute (Art. 59 Para. 2 GG) 12
   1.2. Why not Accord a Higher Formal Rank to the ECHR?
        Roads not Taken 14
        1.2.1. The ECHR and its Institutions as an International
               Organisation in the Sense of Art. 24 GG? 15
        1.2.2. ECHR Rules as General Rules of International Law
               According to Art. 25 GG 15
        1.2.3. The ECHR as Part of the Constitution (Art. 1 Para. 2 GG
               or the Rule of Law According to Art. 20 Para. 3 GG) 16
2. The Relevance of the ECHR for the Interpretation of German Law:
   Qualitative Remarks 17
   2.1. Current Approach 18
   2.2. Foundations for the Current Approach in the Basic Law 19
   2.3. Adaptation: Focus on Outcomes, not on Underlying
        Concepts 20
   2.4. Relevance of ECtHR Judgments 20
   2.5. Limitations 22
   2.6. Application of EU Fundamental Rights and the ECHR 24

---

* I am grateful to Matteo Fornasier and Maria Gabriella Stanzione, and the participants of the workshop 'The European Convention on Human Rights and its impact on private law', and to Andreas M. Fleckner, Stefan Korch, Timo Rademacher and Dominik Rennert for their valuable hints and comments. Many thanks also to Marietta Ostendorf for her helpful assistance with the collection and handling of the data for the final part of this chapter.

2.7. Bringing an ECHR Violation before the Courts 24
  2.8. Observations on the ECHR in Action 26
3. Quantitative Remarks 27
  3.1. Data and Methodology 28
  3.2. Caveats 30
  3.3. Quantitative Observations 32
  3.4. Discussion 40

This chapter serves as a general introduction to the role of the European Convention on Human Rights (ECHR) in the German legal system, with an eye on qualitative as well as quantitative aspects. It first qualitatively discusses the formal rank of the ECHR: in the German legal system, the ECHR is accorded the (sub-constitutional) rank of a federal statute (section 1). Still, the ECHR has an eminent de facto importance for the interpretation of German law, which will be explored qualitatively in the second part (section 2). The final part aims to supplement and deepen this introduction with a quantitative analysis: it describes and explores how often decisions by German courts refer to the ECHR (section 3).

1. THE FORMAL RANK OF THE ECHR IN THE GERMAN LEGAL SYSTEM

The ECHR is accorded the rank of a federal statute in the German legal system (section 1.1). While several suggestions have been made as to how the ECHR could be construed as higher-ranking, none of these have ultimately been accepted (section 1.2).

1.1. RANK OF A FEDERAL STATUTE (ART. 59 PARA. 2 GG)

Formally, the ECHR has the rank of a federal statute within the German legal system. Germany follows an approach of moderate dualism towards international law.[1] In accordance with this approach,[2] the ECHR,

---

[1] BVerfGE 111, 307 para. 34; F. HOFFMEISTER, 'Germany: Status of European Convention on Human Rights in domestic law' (2006) 4 *International Journal of Constitutional Law* 723, 726–27.

[2] See R. GEIGER, *Staatsrecht III*, 7th ed., C.H. Beck, München 2018, §7.II, and also the in-depth analysis by F.C. MAYER, 'Einleitung' in U. KARPENSTEIN and F.C. MAYER, *Konvention zum Schutz der Menschenrechte und Grundfreiheiten*, 3rd ed., C.H. Beck, München 2022, paras. 72–76.

as an international treaty, was approved by parliamentary statute on 9 December 1952,[3] and ratified on 5 December 1952; the Convention entered into force for Germany on 3 September 1953, after it had been ratified by 10 states.[4] Thus, in accordance with Art. 59 para. 2 Grundgesetz (Basic Law – GG), the ECHR was accorded the rank of a federal statute.[5]

From an international law perspective, Germany is obligated to respect the ECHR.[6] The way in which it implements the convention is left to Germany, as long as the Convention is implemented effectively.[7] Unlike European Union (EU) law, the ECHR does not claim primacy of application within the national legal orders.

The approach taken by Germany is, per se, in conformity with its obligations under international law. However, the rank thus accorded to the ECHR has several drawbacks, at least in theory, compared to a scenario in which the ECHR had a higher rank. With the rank of a federal statute,

---

[3] Gesetz über die Konvention zum Schutze der Menschenrechte und Grundfreiheiten vom 7. August 1952, BGBl. (Federal Law Gazette) II, pp. 685–700.

[4] Pursuant to the announcement of 15 December 1953, BGBl 1954 II p. 14; see BVerfGE 128, 326 (367) with further references. For the approval of additional protocols, see, in particular, Bekanntmachung der Neufassung der Konvention vom 4. November 1950 zum Schutz der Menschenrechte und Grundfreiheiten, 22 October 2010, BGBl 2010 II, pp. 1198–228; Gesetz zu dem Protokoll Nr. 15 vom 24. Juni 2013 zur Änderung der Konvention zum Schutz der Menschenrechte und Grundfreiheiten, 2 December 2014, BGBl 2014 II pp. 1034–37; the most recent Protocol No. 16 to the ECHR has not been signed by Germany (as of 31 December 2021), according to the database provided by the Council of Europe, available at https://www.coe.int).

[5] An English translation of the Grundgesetz is available at https://www.gesetze-im-internet.de/englisch_gg/englisch_gg.html (translation by C. Tomuschat et al.); see C. Tomuschat, 'The Effects of Judgments of the European Court of Human Rights According to the German Constitutional Court' (2010) 11 *German Law Journal* 513, 518; D. Grimm et al., 'European Constitutionalism and the German Basic Law' in A. Albi and S. Bardutzky (eds), *National Constitutions in European and Global Governance: Democracy, Rights, the Rule of Law*, pp. 407, 484, point out that there are no provisions as to the rank of international treaties in the domestic legal order, and that it is, therefore, up to the legislature to determine their rank; see T. Giegerich, 'Wirkung und Rang der EMRK in den Rechtsordnungen der Mitgliedstaaten' in O. Dörr, R. Grote and T. Marauhn (eds), *EMRK/GG*, 2nd ed., Mohr Siebeck, Tübingen 2013, para. 47 n. 135 for further references. Furthermore, see T. Giegerich, 'Wirkung und Rang der EMRK in den Rechtsordnungen der Mitgliedstaaten' in O. Dörr, R. Grote and T. Marauhn (eds), *EMRK/GG*, 2nd ed., Mohr Siebeck, Tübingen 2013, para. 45 n. 130; and R. Geiger, *Staatsrecht III*, 7th ed., C.H. Beck, München 2018, §36 for further references on the theoretical discussion as to how the ECHR is integrated into German law – by an act of transformation, implementation, incorporation or reference.

[6] *Pacta sunt servanda*, see Art. 26 of the Vienna Convention on the Law of Treaties.

[7] C. Tomuschat, 'The Effects of Judgments of the European Court of Human Rights According to the German Constitutional Court' (2010) 11 *German Law Journal* 513, 517–18.

the ECHR ranks below the constitution, but above the laws of the *Länder*, Art. 31 GG, and secondary legislation (Rechtsverordnung and Satzung).[8] With regard to the relationship between other federal statutes and the ECHR, *lex posterior derogat legi priori* applies. While the ECHR takes precedence over previous laws, the ECHR guarantees may, in theory, be abrogated by newer ordinary statutes, even though no instance of this happening can be identified.[9] Notably, the legislator is only presumed to have deviated from obligations under public international law if they have made explicit their intent to do so.[10]

As the ECHR lacks constitutional rank, fewer safeguards apply against ECHR violations.[11] A constitutional complaint cannot be filed with the Bundesverfassungsgericht (Federal Constitutional Court – BVerfG) based solely on an allegation that rights under the ECHR have been violated. The pertinent provision of Art. 93 para. 1 no. 4a GG refers only to violations of rights under the GG, not the ECHR. All these aspects contribute to a lingering risk that Germany might violate its obligations under the ECHR.[12]

1.2. WHY NOT ACCORD A HIGHER FORMAL RANK TO THE ECHR? ROADS NOT TAKEN[13]

Various suggestions have been made as to how the ECHR might be accorded a higher rank in the German legal system, thus ranking above statutory law, and on the same level as the constitution, or even above it. However, none of these have ultimately been accepted.

---

[8] T. Giegerich, 'Wirkung und Rang der EMRK in den Rechtsordnungen der Mitgliedstaaten' in O. Dörr, R. Grote and T. Marauhn (eds), *EMRK/GG*, 2nd ed., Mohr Siebeck, Tübingen 2013, para. 47.

[9] Ibid; A. Nussberger, 'The European Court of Human Rights and the German Federal Constitutional Court', https://www.cak.cz/assets/pro-advokaty/mezinarodni-vztahy/the-echr-and-the-german-constitutional-court_angelika-nussberger.pdf, 3; C. Tomuschat, 'The Effects of Judgments of the European Court of Human Rights According to the German Constitutional Court' (2010) 11 *German Law Journal* 513, 517. But see BVerfGE 141, 1, stating that treaty overrides by national statutory law are permissible under the GG (the matter underlying this case related to a double taxation treaty).

[10] BVerfGE 74, 358 (370); see also the aforementioned decision BVerfGE 141, 1, for an instance of an actual treaty override.

[11] T. Giegerich, 'Wirkung und Rang der EMRK in den Rechtsordnungen der Mitgliedstaaten' in O. Dörr, R. Grote and T. Marauhn (eds), *EMRK/GG*, 2nd ed., Mohr Siebeck, Tübingen 2013, para. 48.

[12] Ibid., para. 49.

[13] See, generally, ibid., paras. 51 *et seq.*

1.2.1. The ECHR and its Institutions as an International Organisation in the Sense of Art. 24 GG?

According to Art. 24 GG, the federation may transfer sovereign powers to international organisations. If (the system of) the ECHR were understood as such an international organisation, it might claim primacy over German national law. However, it is hard to argue that a sufficient transfer of sovereign powers has taken place with the adoption of the ECHR, particularly if one were to compare it with the European Union. The ECHR does not claim primacy of application,[14] and European Court of Human Rights (ECtHR) decisions are binding only at the level of public international law, not on an intrastate level. ECtHR decisions do not annul national judgments.[15] Hence, the ECHR can hardly be understood, currently, as an international organisation under Art. 24 GG.[16]

1.2.2. ECHR Rules as General Rules of International Law According to Art. 25 GG

According to Art. 25 GG, the general rules of international law shall take precedence over the laws and directly create rights and duties for the inhabitants of the federal territory. The exact meaning of the provision is under debate, but it is safe to say the general rules of international law would take precedence over German statutory law.[17]

Hence, under this provision, the ECHR would take precedence over statutory law if it was understood as part of the general rules of international law.[18] This would be the case if rules in the ECHR were also rules of customary international law. This, in turn, would require the ECHR to be supported by a general acceptance within the international community. However, the

---

[14] Ibid., para. 52, with further references, and para. 53 on the relevance of the *Pershing* decision of the BVerfG (BVerfGE 90, 286 (346–47)).
[15] Ibid., para. 52.
[16] See also R. STREINZ, 'Art. 24 GG' in M. SACHS (ed), *Grundgesetz*, 9th ed., C.H. Beck, München 2021, para. 31a.
[17] T. GIEGERICH, 'Wirkung und Rang der EMRK in den Rechtsordnungen der Mitgliedstaaten' in O. DÖRR, R. GROTE and T. MARAUHN (eds), *EMRK/GG*, 2nd ed., Mohr Siebeck, Tübingen 2013, paras. 54–61.
[18] On the term 'general rules of international law', see, e.g. A. ENGEL, 'Staatenimmunität in der Rechtsprechung des Bundesverfassungsgerichts' in D. MÜLLER and L. DITTRICH (eds), *Linien der Rechtsprechung des Bundesverfassungsgerichts*, vol. 6, De Gruyter, Berlin 2022 (forthcoming), pp. 412–17.

ECHR would only be part of a regional customary international law,[19] if at all, not part of global customary international law, as it is not supported by a general acceptance in its entirety.[20] There is some debate as to whether regional customary international law could still be applicable via Art. 25 GG, but the BVerfG has not (yet) subscribed to this view.[21]

1.2.3. *The ECHR as Part of the Constitution (Art. 1 Para. 2 GG or the Rule of Law According to Art. 20 Para. 3 GG)*

Another avenue to incorporate the ECHR into the German legal system would be to construe it as part of the constitution. Two provisions of the GG could lend themselves as bridges to that result. One would be Art. 20 para. 3, under which the ECHR could be understood as part of the rule of law. Art. 20 para. 3 GG explicitly addresses aspects of the rule of law, and falls within the umbrella of the eternity clause (Art. 79 para. 3 GG), which prohibits fundamental changes to key provisions. Hence, understanding the ECHR as part of the national rule of law might even activate this constitutional threshold.[22] However, the BVerfG has, so far, stopped short of accepting a full incorporation of the ECHR into the national rule of law.[23] Rather, it has only drawn, from Art. 20 para. 3 GG, a duty to consider the ECHR (which will be discussed in more detail in section 2 below).

Alternatively, one might refer to Art. 1 para. 2 GG.[24] According to this provision, the German people acknowledge inviolable and inalienable human rights as the basis of every community, of peace, and of justice in the world. However, the BVerfG has not, so far, understood this

---

[19] See UN Draft conclusions on identification of customary international law, with commentaries, A/73/10, 2018, available at https://legal.un.org/ilc/texts/instruments/english/commentaries/1_13_2018.pdf, Conclusion 16.

[20] See also R. STREINZ, 'Art. 25 GG' in M. SACHS (ed), *Grundgesetz*, 9th ed., C.H. Beck, München 2021, paras. 68–69.

[21] See BVerfGE 95, 96 (129), with further references; T. GIEGERICH, 'Wirkung und Rang der EMRK in den Rechtsordnungen der Mitgliedstaaten' in O. DÖRR, R. GROTE and T. MARAUHN (eds), *EMRK/GG*, 2nd ed., Mohr Siebeck, Tübingen 2013, paras. 57–61, with further references.

[22] T. GIEGERICH, 'Wirkung und Rang der EMRK in den Rechtsordnungen der Mitgliedstaaten' in O. DÖRR, R. GROTE and T. MARAUHN (eds), *EMRK/GG*, 2nd ed., Mohr Siebeck, Tübingen 2013, paras. 62–70.

[23] See BVerfGE 148, 296 (342, 352).

[24] See also T. GIEGERICH, 'Wirkung und Rang der EMRK in den Rechtsordnungen der Mitgliedstaaten' in O. DÖRR, R. GROTE and T. MARAUHN (eds), *EMRK/GG*, 2nd ed., Mohr Siebeck, Tübingen 2013, paras. 80–82; F.C. MAYER, 'Einleitung' in U. KARPENSTEIN and F.C. MAYER, *Konvention zum Schutz der Menschenrechte und Grundfreiheiten*, 3rd ed., C.H. Beck, München 2022, paras. 103–04.

provision as referring to human rights outside of the GG, in the sense of a full incorporation.[25] Rather, it calls Art. 1 para. 2 GG a 'non-binding programmatic statement'.[26]

2. THE RELEVANCE OF THE ECHR FOR THE INTERPRETATION OF GERMAN LAW: QUALITATIVE REMARKS

While formally ranked as statutory law, the ECHR is accorded a higher de facto rank.[27] Scholars have gone so far as to surmise that a higher formal rank might not even make a significant difference to the outcome of cases, given the de facto importance of the ECHR.[28]

Thus, there is more to the relevance of the ECHR for the interpretation of German Law than is generally the case with statutory law. The ECHR is not simply understood as a federal statute, but as being of eminent importance for the understanding of the Basic Law, which is accorded supremacy over parliamentary statutes.[29] Hence, the risk of conflicts with the Convention is mitigated.[30]

---

[25] BVerfGE 128, 326 (369), with further references; J. GRIEBEL, 'Europäische Grundrechte als Prüfungsmaßstab der Verfassungsbeschwerde' [2014] *Deutsches Verwaltungsblatt* 204, 209–10.

[26] BVerfGE 128, 326 (369), with further references; see also P.M. HUBER, 'Die Einwirkungen des Unionsrechts und der EMRK auf das Grundgesetz' in H.-J. BLANKE, S. MAGIERA, J.C. PIELOW and A. WEBER (eds), *Verfassungsentwicklungen im Vergleich – Italien 1947 – Deutschland 1949 – Spanien 1978*, Duncker & Humblot, Berlin 2021, p. 178.

[27] C. GRABENWARTER and K. PABEL, *EMRK*, 7th ed., C.H. Beck, München 2021, §3 paras. 10–11; J. GRIEBEL, 'Europäische Grundrechte als Prüfungsmaßstab der Verfassungsbeschwerde' [2014] *Deutsches Verwaltungsblatt* 204, 209–10; F.C. MAYER, 'Einleitung' in U. KARPENSTEIN and F.C. MAYER, *Konvention zum Schutz der Menschenrechte und Grundfreiheiten*, 3rd ed., C.H. Beck, München 2022, para. 77.

[28] J. GRIEBEL, 'Europäische Grundrechte als Prüfungsmaßstab der Verfassungsbeschwerde' [2014] *Deutsches Verwaltungsblatt* 204, 210.

[29] F. HOFFMEISTER, 'Germany: Status of European Convention on Human Rights in domestic law' (2006) 4 *International Journal of Constitutional Law* 723, 728.

[30] T. GIEGERICH, 'Wirkung und Rang der EMRK in den Rechtsordnungen der Mitgliedstaaten' in O. DÖRR, R. GROTE and T. MARAUHN (eds), *EMRK/GG*, 2nd ed., Mohr Siebeck, Tübingen 2013, para. 49; J. GRIEBEL 'Europäische Grundrechte als Prüfungsmaßstab der Verfassungsbeschwerde' [2014] *Deutsches Verwaltungsblatt* 204, 207.

This de facto importance of the ECHR has developed over time. Put briefly, the practical relevance of the ECHR has risen 'extraordinarily'.[31] In early pertinent cases, in the 1950s, German courts pointed out why the ECHR did not apply to the facts of the case,[32] why it had not been violated,[33] or that ECHR guarantees did not extend further than basic rights under the GG.[34] Subsequent cases demonstrated a slight shift in tone. In several cases from the 1960s to the 1980s, the BVerfG saw the ECHR and the GG as aligned in their respective relevant aspects,[35] or pointed to the ECHR as enshrining relevant legal values (in particular, the presumption of innocence).[36] A 1987 decision on the presumption of innocence then pointed out that the ECHR was to be taken into account when interpreting the GG.[37] This jurisprudence was affirmed and further developed in cases in 1990 (presumption of innnocence),[38] 2004 (*Görgülü* – respect for family life),[39] 2008 (*Caroline of Monaco III* – respect for private life)[40] and 2011 (preventive detention),[41] and, finally, in 2018 (ban on strike action for civil servants).[42]

2.1. CURRENT APPROACH

In its 2018 decision on a ban on strike action for civil servants, the BVerfG laid out in detail its current understanding of the role of the ECHR in the German legal system.[43]

---

[31] T. GIEGERICH, 'Wirkung und Rang der EMRK in den Rechtsordnungen der Mitgliedstaaten' in O. DÖRR, R. GROTE and T. MARAUHN (eds), *EMRK/GG*, 2nd ed., Mohr Siebeck, Tübingen 2013, para. 45, with further references.
[32] BVerwGE 5, 153, para. 50; Oberverwaltungsgericht für das Land Nordrhein-Westfalen [1956] *Deutsches Verwaltungsblatt* 524; Staatsgerichtshof des Landes Hessen, 11 May 1956 – P.St. 191, juris.
[33] See, in particular, the infamous decision BVerfGE 6, 389 (441) on §§175, 175a StGB (Criminal Code), which provisions made homosexual acts between men a crime.
[34] BVerfGE 9, 36, 39.
[35] BVerfGE 27, 71 (82); BVerfGE 31, 58 (67–68).
[36] BVerfGE 20, 162 (207–08); BVerfGE 31, 58 (67–68); BVerfGE 35, 202 (232).
[37] BVerfGE 74, 358 (370).
[38] BVerfGE 82, 106 (114); BVerfGE 83, 119 (128).
[39] BVerfGE 111, 307 (316–17, 329).
[40] BVerfGE 120, 180 (200–01).
[41] BVerfGE 128, 326 (367–68).
[42] BVerfGE 148, 296 (350–56, paras. 126–35).
[43] BVerfGE 148, 296 (the following quotations refer to the translation provided by the BVerfG on its website www.bverfg.de); on the decision, see, in more detail, the chapter by G. BUCHHOLTZ, 'The Impact of the European Convention on Human Rights on

With regard to the matter at hand, there were (arguably) pertinent judgments by the ECtHR from cases involving Turkey.[44] Thus, the BVerfG had to grapple with the question of the relevance of the ECHR and ECtHR judgments. Again, the court affirmed its jurisprudence, which accords the ECHR the formal rank of statutory law, only to then elaborate on the de facto importance of the ECHR in the interpretation of the GG: 'While the European Convention on Human Rights ranks as statutory federal law and is therefore below constitutional rank … it must be taken into account when interpreting fundamental rights and the constitutional principles of the rule of law'.[45]

Thus, the ECHR and judgments of the ECtHR 'serve … as guidelines for the interpretation of the content and scope of fundamental rights and constitutional principles of the rule of law'.[46] As these, in turn, shape the interpretation of German law, the ECHR and the case law of the ECtHR become relevant for the German legal system generally, even if they are not directly applicable, but act only as guidelines for interpretation.

2.2. FOUNDATIONS FOR THE CURRENT APPROACH IN THE BASIC LAW

The BVerfG provides a two-prong rationale for this approach: 'This significance of the European Convention on Human Rights and thus also of the case-law of the European Court of Human Rights is based on the Constitution's openness to international law and its substantive focus on human rights'.[47]

While the openness of the Basic Law to international law is evidenced in Art. 59 para. 2 GG – and also in Art. 25 GG – Art. 1 para. 2 GG expresses the substantive orientation of the Basic Law to human rights. These articles, when combined, allow for the ECHR and the case law of the ECtHR to become guidelines for constitutional and statutory interpretation.

German Labour Law: A Special Focus on Collective Labour Law', section 4, in this volume.
[44] *Demir and Baykara v. Turkey*, no. 34503/97, §85, ECtHR 12 November 2008; *Enerji Yapi-Yol Sen v. Turquie*, no. 68959/01, §24, ECtHR 21 April 2009.
[45] BVerfGE 148, 296 (350, para. 126).
[46] BVerfGE 148, 296 (351, para. 128).
[47] BVerfGE 148, 296 (351, para. 128).

2.3. ADAPTATION: FOCUS ON OUTCOMES, NOT ON UNDERLYING CONCEPTS

The relevance of the ECHR for the interpretation of German law is marked by a focus on outcomes, not on underlying concepts:[48]

> Using them [i.e. the European Convention on Human Rights and the case-law of the European Court of Human Rights] as guidelines for interpretation does not require that the statements of the Basic Law and those of the European Convention on Human Rights be schematically aligned or completely harmonised, but that the values be included.[49]

And furthermore:

> The human rights content of the relevant international treaty must be 'adapted' to the context of the receiving constitutional system in an active process (of acknowledgment).[50]

This cautious approach is well aligned with the fact that the ECHR does not impose the way that it should be implemented in the Contracting States. Viewing its adaptation as an active process of acknowledgement gives leeway to courts to find a way to carefully integrate the values enshrined in the ECHR into the German legal system, avoiding any possible friction. At a minimum, the relevant fundamental rights of the GG can be read in close connection with the guarantee of the rule of law and the primacy of the law, thus creating a link to the ECHR.[51]

2.4. RELEVANCE OF ECtHR JUDGMENTS

The interpretation of the ECHR by the ECtHR must be taken into account, too.[52] For specific cases decided by the ECtHR, the binding force of ECtHR

---

[48] BVerfGE 148, 296 (353, para. 131); see also the ECtHR decisions *Swedish Engine Drivers' Union v. Sweden*, no. 5614/72, §50, ECtHR 6 February 1976; *James et al. v. UK*, no. 8793/79, §84, ECtHR 21 February 1986; *Observer and Guardian v. UK*, no. 13585/88, §76, ECtHR 26 November 1991.
[49] BVerfGE 148, 296 (350, para. 126).
[50] BVerfGE 148, 296 (353–54, para. 131).
[51] BVerfGE 111, 307 (329–30); F.C. Mayer, 'Einleitung' in U. Karpenstein and F.C. Mayer, *Konvention zum Schutz der Menschenrechte und Grundfreiheiten*, 3rd ed., C.H. Beck, München 2022, paras. 80–86.
[52] BVerfGE 148, 296 (350, para. 126).

judgments is directly required by Art. 46 ECHR. The BVerfG has also spelt out that lower courts (and other state bodies) are directly bound by ECtHR judgments. It had occasion to do so in the infamous case of *Görgülü*, which related to the protection for private and family life, specifically concerning a father's right of contact with his child, in which a lower court showed resistance to accepting and adapting to ECtHR decisions regarding that very case. According to the BVerfG, within their jurisdiction, and without violating the binding effect of statute and law (Art. 20 para. 3 GG), courts even have a 'duty to take into account a judgment that relates to a case already decided by them if they preside over a retrial of the matter in a procedurally admissible manner and are able to take the judgment into account without a violation of substantive law'.[53]

While, for cases other than those specified above, the jurisprudence of the ECtHR is not binding at a public international law level, it still has a factual function of direction and guidance. There have been high-profile instances illustrating both ways in which ECtHR decisions have relevance. While in *Görgülü*, the BVerfG held that a lower court was under an obligation to take into account the pertinent ECtHR decision,[54] in *Caroline of Monaco III*, the ECtHR decision exercised a factual function.[55]

Again, this relevance does not translate into a requirement to follow pertinent judgments word by word, but rather to adapt them to the surrounding legal environment:

> the case-law of the European Court of Human Rights must be integrated as carefully as possible into the existing, dogmatically differentiated national legal system ... aspects considered by the European Court of Human Rights in its weighing of interests may also be included in the constitutional review of proportionality.[56]

The second part of this quotation makes clear that the considerations of the ECtHR may exert influence on, and be considered at, more than one stage of judicial reasoning. They may also be relevant in a proportionality review, as a later stage of review.[57]

---

[53] BVerfGE 111, 307 (316).
[54] BVerfGE 111, 307 (330–32).
[55] BVerfGE 120, 180 (200–01).
[56] BVerfGE 148, 296 (355–56, para. 135).
[57] For an example, see BVerfGE 128, 326 (391–99) ('the weight of the affected concerns ... is also reinforced by the principles of the European Convention on Human Rights', 391).

2.5. LIMITATIONS

However, there are limitations on the influence of the ECHR within the German legal system, even where the ECHR applies, and there is conclusive case law of the ECtHR.

A first (theoretical) boundary requires that the influence of the ECHR must not lead to 'restricting or lowering the protection of fundamental rights under the Basic Law'.[58] This safeguard has, so far, remained a theoretical one, as the ECHR itself explicitly states, in Art. 53, that '[n]othing in this Convention shall be construed as limiting or derogating from any of the human rights and fundamental freedoms which may be ensured under the laws of any High Contracting Party'. Still, the BVerfG has pointed out that this boundary deserves particular attention in multipolar fundamental rights relationships; that is, when granting more liberty to one party means reducing another party's liberty.[59] Taken strictly, this would leave little leeway to national courts in private law matters, where they have to strike a balance between the rights of the parties involved, and thus conflicts between national courts and the ECtHR could easily arise.[60] Scholars have, therefore, suggested that, in such cases, the ECtHR should only provide minimum standards. Thus, German courts would be left with a 'corridor' of potential decisions within these minimum standards set by the ECHR, and would still be free in their decisions as to how exactly to balance the conflicting fundamental rights involved.[61]

As a second, somewhat related, boundary, despite the openness of the GG to international law, the legislature may have to decline to observe international treaty law in exceptional cases, particularly if this is the

---

[58] BVerfGE 148, 296 (351, para. 128).
[59] BVerfGE 148, 296 (355, para. 134).
[60] M. FORNASIER, 'Europäische Menschenrechtskonvention' in U. PREIS and A. SAGAN (eds), *Europäisches Arbeitsrecht*, 2nd ed., Otto Schmidt, Köln 2019, para. 4.31.
[61] M. FORNASIER, 'Europäische Menschenrechtskonvention' in U. PREIS and A. SAGAN (eds), *Europäisches Arbeitsrecht*, 2nd ed., Otto Schmidt, Köln 2019, para. 4.32; G. LÜBBE-WOLFF, 'Der Grundrechtsschutz nach der Europäischen Menschenrechtskonvention bei konfligierenden Individualrechten – Plädoyer für eine Korridor-Lösung' in M. HOCHHUTH (ed), *Nachdenken über Staat und Recht. Kolloquium zum 60. Geburtstag von Dietrich Murswiek*, Duncker & Humblot, Berlin 2010, pp. 193–209; F.C. MAYER, 'Einleitung' in U. KARPENSTEIN and F.C. MAYER, *Konvention zum Schutz der Menschenrechte und Grundfreiheiten*, 3rd ed., C.H. Beck, München 2022, paras. 107–09.

only way to avert a violation of fundamental constitutional principles: 'Where it is methodologically untenable or incompatible with the Basic Law to include values of the European Convention on Human Rights, the Constitution's openness to international law is limited.'[62]

This limitation concerns possible violations of German constitutional provisions that are in clear opposition to the ECHR – in particular, fundamental rights of third parties, or the eternity clause in Art. 79 para. 3 GG – and of statutory law which is in clear opposition to the ECHR; that is, cases in which the German legislator has expressed the clear intention to deviate from the Convention. So far, no such conflicts have arisen with regard to the ECHR.[63]

A limitation that may be of more practical relevance concerns cases beyond the scope of Art. 46 ECHR; that is, cases where ECtHR judgments are not binding. Here, German courts have more leeway:

> Beyond Art. 46 ECHR, special importance must be attached to the specific context of the decision by the European Court of Human Rights when interpreting the Basic Law.[64]

And furthermore:

> [T]aking account of the case-law of the European Court of Human Rights primarily means to identify statements regarding principal values enshrined in the Convention and address them ... the specific facts of the decided case and its background (in terms of legal culture) must be included as well as possible specific particularities of the German legal order.[65]

Domestic courts have to consider the specific facts of the case decided by the ECtHR, as well as the background of the case, and also possible specific particularities of the German legal order. These aspects allow for distinctions to be made between the decisions of the ECtHR and of domestic courts, and thus may curtail the relevance of the ECHR and its interpretation by the ECtHR.

---

[62] BVerfGE 148, 296 (350, para. 126).
[63] T. GIEGERICH, 'Wirkung und Rang der EMRK in den Rechtsordnungen der Mitgliedstaaten' in O. DÖRR, R. GROTE and T. MARAUHN (eds), *EMRK/GG*, 2nd ed., Mohr Siebeck, Tübingen 2013, para. 49.
[64] BVerfGE 148, 296 (350, para. 126).
[65] BVerfGE 148, 296 (354, para. 132).

2.6. APPLICATION OF EU FUNDAMENTAL RIGHTS AND THE ECHR

German courts may also apply EU fundamental rights as their main standard of review, as recently decided by the BVerfG.[66] For legal issues fully determined by EU law, EU fundamental rights (rather than fundamental rights under the GG) act as the relevant standard for review. The ECHR and ECtHR judgments thus become relevant via another route, as German courts must take them into account when interpreting EU fundamental rights:

> When interpreting the fundamental rights of the Charter of Fundamental Rights of the European Union, both the human rights of the European Convention on Human Rights as they are specified by the European Court of Human Rights and the fundamental rights as they are reflected in common constitutional traditions and shaped by the constitutional and supreme courts of the Member States must be taken into account.[67]

This statement affirms the importance of the ECHR for the interpretation of the EU Charter of Fundamental Rights (CFR), which is also acknowledged in the Charter: according to Art. 52, para. 3 CFR, the meaning and scope of rights contained in the Charter shall be the same as in the corresponding rights laid down by the ECHR. Thus, the weight of the ECHR, in this context, can be compared to EU primary law, and is much higher than in a purely national context.[68]

2.7. BRINGING AN ECHR VIOLATION BEFORE THE COURTS

The mainly indirect relevance of the ECHR within the German legal system is reflected in the ways that an ECHR violation can be brought before the courts. The ECtHR remains the sole institution with jurisdiction for individual complaints based on an allegation of an infringement of the ECHR. Notably, ECtHR judgments do not have direct effect in Germany

---

[66] BVerfGE 152, 216; BVerfGE 156, 182.
[67] BVerfGE 156, 182 (Ls. 2 = headnote 2).
[68] M. FORNASIER, 'Europäische Menschenrechtskonvention' in U. PREIS and A. SAGAN (eds), *Europäisches Arbeitsrecht*, 2nd ed., Otto Schmidt, Köln 2019, para. 4.33.

(nor in other Member States, for that matter),[69] and Germany has not (yet) signed the additional Protocol No. 16 which establishes preliminary reference proceedings before the ECtHR.[70] However, an individual can file an individual application before the ECtHR, according to Art. 34 ECHR,[71] as introduced in its current form by the 11th protocol to the ECHR, which entered into force on 1 November 1998.[72]

As regards the situation within Germany, a constitutional complaint cannot be filed with the BVerfG based *solely* on the allegation that rights under the ECHR have been violated, as these are not listed in Art. 93 para. 1 no. 4a GG as rights based upon the violation of which a constitutional complaint can be filed.[73] However, a constitutional complaint can be filed based on an allegation that rights under the GG (or the CFR) – to be interpreted in accordance with the ECHR – have been violated.[74] Such an allegation might even be implicit in a complaint against the violation of an ECHR guarantee that runs parallel to a fundamental right contained in the Basic Law.[75] Additionally, a constitutional complaint can be filed based on

---

[69] D. GRIMM et al., 'European Constitutionalism and the German Basic Law' in A. ALBI and S. BARDUTZKY (eds), *National Constitutions in European and Global Governance: Democracy, Rights, the Rule of Law*, 407, 487.

[70] Protocol No. 16 to the Convention for the Protection of Human Rights and Fundamental Freedoms (CETS No. 214), 2 October 2013, status as of 15 December 2021, see the database available at https://www.coe.int/en/web/conventions/; see also C. TOMUSCHAT, 'The Effects of Judgments of the European Court of Human Rights According to the German Constitutional Court' (2010) 11 *German Law Journal* 513, 519.

[71] See C. TOMUSCHAT, 'The Effects of Judgments of the European Court of Human Rights According to the German Constitutional Court' (2010) 11 *German Law Journal* 513 (referring to Art. 25 ECHR): the 'declaration under Article 25 ECHR was made on 5 July 1955. On that day, the individual application came into force since the applicable threshold of six States had been reached (Sweden, Ireland, Denmark, Iceland, Belgium, and the Federal Republic of Germany)'.

[72] Protocol No. 11 to the Convention for the Protection of Human Rights and Fundamental Freedoms, restructuring the control machinery established thereby (ETS No. 155), 11 May 1994, available at https://www.coe.int/en/web/conventions. For details of the individual complaint procedure before the ECHR, see F.C. MAYER, 'Einleitung' in U. KARPENSTEIN and F.C. MAYER, *Konvention zum Schutz der Menschenrechte und Grundfreiheiten*, 3rd ed., C.H. Beck, München 2022, paras. 31–44.

[73] BVerfGE 148, 296 (342, para. 109).

[74] BVerfGE 148, 296 (342, para. 109); T. GIEGERICH, 'Wirkung und Rang der EMRK in den Rechtsordnungen der Mitgliedstaaten' in O. DÖRR, R. GROTE and T. MARAUHN (eds), *EMRK/GG*, 2nd ed., Mohr Siebeck, Tübingen 2013, para. 48.

[75] BVerfGE 111, 307 (329–30); T. GIEGERICH, 'Wirkung und Rang der EMRK in den Rechtsordnungen der Mitgliedstaaten' in O. DÖRR, R. GROTE and T. MARAUHN (eds), *EMRK/GG*, 2nd ed., Mohr Siebeck, Tübingen 2013, para. 48.

an allegation the ECHR has been applied in an arbitrary manner, which would entail a violation of Art. 3 GG (prohibition of arbitrary action).[76]

2.8. OBSERVATIONS ON THE ECHR IN ACTION

How has the approach described above played out? One might venture to say that friction has been limited. This stands to reason, as parallels between fundamental rights in the GG (Arts. 1 to 19), and the guarantees set forth in ECHR, facilitate compliance;[77] even where they are not precisely aligned, ECHR guarantees can be read into fundamental rights contained in the Basic Law.[78] Moreover, the constitutional complaint before the German Federal Constitutional Court also acts as an effective safeguard against human rights violations.[79] If incompatibilies have arisen, these have mainly been due to the way that the law has been applied in specific cases, and not to statutory law itself.[80]

Still, one can identify areas in which the ECHR has had particular influence on the interpretation of the Basic Law.[81] The main examples of these would be procedural rights (Arts. 5 to 7 ECHR, influencing the constitutional principle of the rule of law); the presumption of innocence;[82]

---

[76] BVerfGE 74, 102 (128); T. GIEGERICH, 'Wirkung und Rang der EMRK in den Rechtsordnungen der Mitgliedstaaten' in O. DÖRR, R. GROTE and T. MARAUHN (eds), *EMRK/GG*, 2nd ed., Mohr Siebeck, Tübingen 2013, para. 48.

[77] C. TOMUSCHAT, 'The Effects of Judgments of the European Court of Human Rights According to the German Constitutional Court' (2010) 11 *German Law Journal* 513, 514–15; see, e.g. BVerfGE 151, 101 (125–26, para. 58).

[78] J. GRIEBEL, 'Europäische Grundrechte als Prüfungsmaßstab der Verfassungsbeschwerde' [2014] *Deutsches Verwaltungsblatt* 204, 207.

[79] C. TOMUSCHAT, 'The Effects of Judgments of the European Court of Human Rights According to the German Constitutional Court' (2010) 11 *German Law Journal* 513, 515.

[80] A. NUSSBERGER, 'The European Court of Human Rights and the German Federal Constitutional Court', https://www.cak.cz/assets/pro-advokaty/mezinarodni-vztahy/the-echr-and-the-german-constitutional-court_angelika-nussberger.pdf, 4.

[81] See also P.M. HUBER, 'Die Einwirkungen des Unionsrechts und der EMRK auf das Grundgesetz' in H.-J. BLANKE, S. MAGIERA, J.C. PIELOW and A. WEBER (eds), *Verfassungsentwicklungen im Vergleich – Italien 1947 – Deutschland 1949 – Spanien 1978*, Duncker & Humblot, Berlin 2021, pp. 180–82.

[82] See C. TOMUSCHAT, 'The Effects of Judgments of the European Court of Human Rights According to the German Constitutional Court' (2010) 11 *German Law Journal* 513, 519; but, notably, in a dissenting opinion in a decision on the presumption of innocence in 1990, Justice Mahrenholz argued that the relevant ECtHR case law was inconsistent and, thus, inconclusive: 'It is impossible to find a clear line [in the pertinent ECtHR jurisprudence]' (BVerfGE 82, 106 (122–23)).

rights of persons in detention;[83] the functioning of justice (trial within a reasonable time);[84] and the protection of the privacy of public figures, and the right to respect for private and family life, as per Art. 8 ECHR (see, in particular, the BVerfG decisions *Görgülü*[85] and *Caroline of Monaco III*).[86]

Still, it is hard to make broad general qualitative statements about the influence that the ECHR has in practical terms. Its relevance varies between individual cases, and needs specific scrutiny. For example, in the aforementioned case on the ban on strike action for civil servants, the BVerfG acknowledged that there were ECtHR judgments giving directions which seemingly opposed the ban. However, the BVerfG proceeded to find no relevant conflict with these judgments:

> When taking into consideration the decisions' essential principal values, a conflict between German law and the European Convention on Human Rights can presently not be established … with regard to the particularities of the German system of career civil service, the Senate finds that the requirements to restrict the right to strike stipulated in Art. 11 para. 2 ECHR would also be met.[87]

Hence, even for cases with a very thorough discussion of the role of the ECHR, and of specific guarantees, the relevance of the ECHR depends on the specific circumstances of the case.

3. QUANTITATIVE REMARKS

Whereas the following chapters of this book will explore qualitative aspects further, and in more detail, this chapter concludes with quantitative remarks to shed further light on the relevance of the ECHR in German

---

[83] BVerfGE 128, 326 (366–403).
[84] See C. TOMUSCHAT, 'The Effects of Judgments of the European Court of Human Rights According to the German Constitutional Court' (2010) 11 *German Law Journal* 513, 517, with further references.
[85] BVerfGE 111, 307.
[86] BVerfGE 120, 180; C. TOMUSCHAT, 'The Effects of Judgments of the European Court of Human Rights According to the German Constitutional Court' (2010) 11 *German Law Journal* 513, 522, with references to comments by Justices; See also P.M. HUBER, 'Die Einwirkungen des Unionsrechts und der EMRK auf das Grundgesetz' in H.-J. BLANKE, S. MAGIERA, J.C. PIELOW and A. WEBER (eds), *Verfassungsentwicklungen im Vergleich – Italien 1947 – Deutschland 1949 – Spanien 1978*, Duncker & Humblot, Berlin 2021, p. 180.
[87] BVerfGE 148, 296 (373–74, para. 163).

Law: it presents statistics on how often German court decisions include a reference to the ECHR.[88] Thus, this final part is a descriptive and explorative study,[89] and intends to give an idea about the overall relevance of the ECHR for court decisions, and how this has developed over time. In accordance with the general theme of the book, special attention is devoted to decisions in civil law, and in employment law.

3.1. DATA AND METHODOLOGY

This section adopted the following approach: using the decisions available in the juris database[90] (December 2021) as data, and the search and filter tools provided by juris, it counted decisions by German courts with

---

[88] For statistics on cases before the ECtHR, see https://www.echr.coe.int/Pages/home.aspx?p=reports, and, specifically on individual complaints before the ECtHR, J. MEYER-LADEWIG and M. NETTESHEIM, 'Einleitung' in J. MEYER-LADEWIG, M. NETTESHEIM and S. VON RAUMER (eds), *EMRK*, 4th ed., Nomos, Baden-Baden 2017, para. 60; for quantitative studies of ECtHR jurisprudence, see Y. LUPU, 'Precedent in International Courts: A Network Analysis of Case Citations by the European Court of Human Rights' (2012) 42 *British Journal of Political Science* 413; M.L. CHRISTENSEN, H.P. OLSEN and F. TARISSAN, 'Identification of Case Content with Quantitative Network Analysis: An Example from the ECtHR' in F. BEX and S. VILLATA (eds), *Legal Knowledge and Information Systems*, IOS Press, Amsterdam 2016, p. 53; U. ŠADL and H.P. OLSEN, 'Can Quantitative Methods Complement Doctrinal Legal Studies? Using Citation Network and Corpus Linguistic Analysis to Understand International Courts' (2017) 30 *Leiden Journal of International Law* 327; for a quantitative study of references to the jurisprudence of the ECtHR by the International Criminal Tribunal for the former Yugoslavia (ICTY), see F. SAUERWEIN, 'Beyond Anecdotal Reference: A Quantitative Assessment of ICTY References to the Jurisprudence of the ECtHR' in P. LOBBA and T. MARINIELLO (eds), *Judicial Dialogue on Human Rights*, Brill, Leiden 2017, p. 109; for further examples of quantitative studies of jurisprudence, see, e.g. A. FLECKNER, 'Anlegermitverschulden vor dem Bankensenat – Eine quantitative juristische Studie' in S. GRUNDMANN, H. MERKT and P.O. MÜLBERT (eds), *Festschrift für Klaus J. Hopt zum 80. Geburtstag am 24. August 2020*, De Gruyter, Berlin 2020, p. 256, and the further examples mentioned in n. 9 of the article.
[89] See C. COUPETTE and A. FLECKNER, 'Quantitative Rechtswissenschaft' [2018] *Juristenzeitung* 379, 380; H. HAMANN, *Evidenzbasierte Jurisprudenz*, Mohr Siebeck, Tübingen 2014, pp. 87–88.
[90] For a discussion of other potential sources (e.g. the competing database beck-online, websites of federal courts or direct requests to the relevant courts), see C. COUPETTE and A. FLECKNER, 'Quantitative Rechtswissenschaft' [2018] *Juristenzeitung* 379, 380–82, and also A. FLECKNER, 'Anlegermitverschulden vor dem Bankensenat – Eine quantitative juristische Studie' in S. GRUNDMANN, H. MERKT and P.O. MÜLBERT (eds), *Festschrift für Klaus J. Hopt zum 80. Geburtstag am 24. August 2020*, De Gruyter, Berlin 2020, p. 256.

textual references to the ECHR (that is, decisions that explicitly mention the ECHR) that appeared in said database. Based on these numbers, it calculated the percentages of those decisions with a textual reference to the ECHR, as compared to all decisions by the same court(s) that were available in the database.

This data has been collected for German courts overall, i.e. all judgments to which juris has assigned the labels 'Arbeitsgerichtsbarkeit' (employment tribunals[91]), 'Finanzgerichtsbarkeit' (tax courts), 'ordentliche Gerichtsbarkeit' ('ordinary jurisdiction', i.e. civil and criminal courts), 'Sozialgerichtsbarkeit' (social courts), 'Verfassungsgerichtsbarkeit' (constitutional courts) and 'Verwaltungsgerichtsbarkeit' (administrative courts), thus excluding only the label 'Europäische Gerichte' (European Courts).[92] These labels were combined with the labels – in the field 'Regionen' (regions) – of 'Bund' (Federation) and 'Länder' (states), thus excluding judgments from courts of the German Democratic Republic (GDR)[93] and foreign judgments, for example from Austria. Subsets for specific federal courts were applied too, corresponding to the general theme of this book: for the Federal Constitutional Court (BVerfG), for the senates of the Federal Court of Justice (Bundesgerichtshof – BGH) handling civil law matters (Zivilsenate),[94] and for the Federal Employment Tribunal (Bundesarbeitsgericht – BAG).

---

[91] For the English translation of terms related to the field of 'Arbeitsrecht', this chapter follows the usage of the ECtHR, as e.g. in *Schüth v. Germany*, no. 1620/03, ECtHR 23 September 2010.

[92] Using the labels assigned by juris seemed to be the best approximation to the body of German court judgments provided by juris. However, this approach might entail a certain degree of error, as it is not clear whether all labels for courts have been assigned correctly.

[93] Judgments from GDR courts are not considered, as the GDR had not acceded to the ECHR: see C. TOMUSCHAT, 'The Effects of Judgments of the European Court of Human Rights According to the German Constitutional Court' (2010) 11 *German Law Journal* 513, 513–14.

[94] Using the court categories 'BGH Zivilsenat', 'BGH Großer Senat für Zivilsachen' (Grand Civil Panel) and 'BGH Vereinigte Große Senate' (United Grand Panels) in juris. This way, joint panels were included, but senates for criminal law and further senates for specific subject matters were excluded, see https://www.bundesgerichtshof.de/EN/TheCourt/AllocationJurisdiction/allocationJurisdiction_node.html and https://www.bundesgerichtshof.de/DE/DasGericht/Geschaeftsverteilung/SachlicheZustaendigkeit/WeitereSenate/weitereSenate_node.html. The Gemeinsamer Senat der Obersten Gerichtshöfe des Bundes (Joint Panel of the Federal Supreme Courts), which is also staffed by judges from other federal supreme courts, was not included either. For the period under discussion, juris lists 43 decisions of this body, of which none make a textual reference to the ECHR.

The data was collected on a per year basis, for the period between 1 January 1953 (year of entry into force of the ECHR)[95] and 31 December 2020 (the end of the last full year before this data was collected).[96]

In total, the database provided 1,422,823 decisions matching these initial selection criteria. The number of cases per year varied from 1,464 in 1953 to 46,349 in 2007.

Within this dataset, the decisions that make textual references to the ECHR were counted, using the tools provided by juris. To do this, using the juris search bar, the judgments were filtered for those that contained the terms 'Europäische(n) Menschenrechtskonvention' or 'EMRK', and 'Konvention zum Schutz(e) der Menschenrechte' or 'MRK', with the variations indicated by using brackets.[97] While for the earliest years, 1953 and 1954, not a single decision matched these search terms, numbers rose to as high as 2,240 decisions by German courts overall, in 2017.

The subsequent analysis calculates the percentages of decisions that make textual references to the ECHR, within the overall number of decisions for given time periods, and in specific courts.

3.2. CAVEATS

Before moving on to the results, several limitations are worth mentioning. Most importantly, the juris database does not report all cases that have been decided by the German courts. The number of cases available in the database is particularly low for the early years of the time period under consideration (while from 1953 to 1962, juris provided 36,778 decisions

---

[95] The ECtHR was established in 1959 (see A. NUSSBERGER, 'The European Court of Human Rights and the German Federal Constitutional Court', https://www.cak.cz/assets/pro-advokaty/mezinarodni-vztahy/the-echr-and-the-german-constitutional-court_angelika-nussberger.pdf), but individual cases show the ECHR was discussed by German courts even before then: see, e.g. BVerfGE 9, 36.

[96] On a note of caution, it is not quite clear what percentage of decisions for a given year are added to the database later, and after what amount of time no (or almost no) further decisions from that year will be added.

[97] For details of the search tools within juris, see https://www.juris.de/jportal/portal/page/fshelp.psml?cmsuri=/hilfe/de/r3/suche_1/allgemeines_2/suche.jsp. For a more refined approach using downloaded versions of relevant judgments for further analysis (based on a former interface of the juris database), see C. COUPETTE, Juristische Netzwerkforschung, Mohr Siebeck, Tübingen 2019, pp. 236 et seq.

matching the initial criteria, it provided 391,161 decisions for the period from 2011 to 2020).[98] This particularly applies to decisions of the lower courts: these end up in the database only if they have been specifically selected by the courts, or if they have been published elsewhere.[99] Calculating the percentage of decisions with a reference to the ECHR among all decisions listed in juris may mitigate this concern. However, the de facto criteria that lead to a decision being listed in juris might mean that the more important and contentious cases end up in the database. Hence, there is a possibility that a reference to the ECHR makes it more likely that a decision will be included. Still, the (absolute and relative) numbers of cases with textual references to the ECHR may hint at the influence of the ECHR in the German legal system; tendencies and relative changes may become visible.

The calculation of percentages presupposes that each decision is listed only once in the database. No instance of a decision being listed multiple times could be identified, so this seems plausible. However, this was not checked systematically.

Moreover, while the search strings were selected with an eye on the language employed by courts in pertinent decisions, they might still be under-inclusive and not cover all references to the ECHR. At the same time, they might also be over-inclusive, and also count decisions that refer only to literature on the ECHR, and not to the ECHR itself. Judging from samples, the risk of over-inclusion seems negligible, however.

As this study uses labels and tools provided by juris, all errors in the database will be carried over to the results presented here. While the data in juris can generally be expected to be correct,[100] and small samples of data were checked, this remains a potential source of errors (these could

---

[98] H. HAMANN, 'Der blinde Fleck der deutschen Rechtswissenschaft – Zur digitalen Verfügbarkeit instanzgerichtlicher Rechtsprechung' [2021] Juristenzeitung 656; and C. COUPETTE and A. FLECKNER, 'Quantitative Rechtswissenschaft' [2018] Juristenzeitung 379, 381, who even point out that only 21.7% of the cases before the XIth Senate of the Bundesgerichtshof that were resolved between 2006 and 2016 are documented in the juris database; for more background, see M. HEESE, 'Veröffentlichung gerichtlicher Entscheidungen im Zeitalter der Digitalisierung' in C. ALTHAMMER and C. SCHÄRTL (eds), *Dogmatik als Fundament für Forschung und Lehre, Festschrift für Herbert Roth*, Mohr Siebeck, Tübingen 2021, pp. 293–340.

[99] C. COUPETTE and A. FLECKNER, 'Quantitative Rechtswissenschaft' [2018] *Juristenzeitung* 379, 381, fn. 17.

[100] Judging, inter alia, from the author's experience of working with the database over a longer period of time.

not be ruled out within a reasonable amount of time, given that the initial data collected consisted of more than a million judgments).

Aside from this, as a general remark, numbers have a limited meaning. A quantitative approach may not adequately reflect the complexity of the legal question at hand.[101] In particular, a simple count of textual references does not tell us what stance the various decisions took with regard to the ECHR. The ECHR may even have been mentioned only as part of a party's pleadings.[102] The ambition of these remarks is correspondingly modest. They are meant as an additional contribution to an overall picture of the ECHR within the German legal system, and can give us an idea of how often German courts have grappled with the ECHR.

The study employs a simple technique, using a simple count and not counting the number of citations *within* a case. Hence, it makes no distinction as to how often a specific decision makes reference to the ECHR, which might have provided an indication of the depth in which the ECHR was discussed.[103]

3.3. QUANTITATIVE OBSERVATIONS

The following table shows the results for German courts overall, the BVerfG, the civil senates of the BGH, and the BAG. For each of these courts, or group of courts, the first column lists the total number of decisions available for a given year, the second column lists the absolute number of decisions with a textual reference to the ECHR, and the third column provides the percentage thus calculated.

---

[101] For a more thorough discussion, see M. SIEMS, 'Numerical Comparative Law: Do We Need Statistical Evidence in Order to Reduce Complexity?' (2005) 13 *Cardozo Journal of International and Comparative Law* 521; and also C. COUPETTE and A. FLECKNER, 'Quantitative Rechtswissenschaft' [2018] *Juristenzeitung* 379, 389; H. HAMANN, *Evidenzbasierte Jurisprudenz*, Mohr Siebeck, Tübingen 2014, pp. 14–15.

[102] See, e.g. BVerfG, 8 August 2021 – 2 BvR 171/20.

[103] See also C. COUPETTE and A. FLECKNER, 'Quantitative Rechtswissenschaft' [2018] *Juristenzeitung* 379, 384, who point out the approach adopted here is used fairly frequently; see, further, M. SIEMS, 'Citation Patterns of the German Federal Supreme Court and the Court of Appeal of England and Wales?' (2010) 21 *King's Law Journal* 152, 154.

Table 1. Total numbers of decisions and absolute and relative numbers of decisions with a textual reference to the ECHR

year	German courts overall			BVerfG			BGH civil senates			BAG		
	total	ECHR	%	total	ECHR	%	total	ECHR	%	total	ECHR	%
1953	1464	0	0.0%	44	0	0.0%	485	0	0.0%	0	0	0.0%
1954	2546	1	0.0%	24	1	4.2%	476	0	0.0%	80	0	0.0%
1955	3209	4	0.1%	22	0	0.0%	476	0	0.0%	128	0	0.0%
1956	3157	2	0.1%	24	0	0.0%	551	0	0.0%	178	0	0.0%
1957	3440	4	0.1%	49	2	4.1%	661	0	0.0%	221	0	0.0%
1958	3971	3	0.1%	61	1	1.6%	655	0	0.0%	225	0	0.0%
1959	4156	2	0.0%	51	0	0.0%	607	0	0.0%	163	0	0.0%
1960	4885	3	0.1%	65	0	0.0%	757	0	0.0%	279	0	0.0%
1961	4990	4	0.1%	59	0	0.0%	708	0	0.0%	225	0	0.0%
1962	4960	5	0.1%	65	2	3.1%	695	0	0.0%	172	0	0.0%
1963	5081	6	0.1%	78	2	2.6%	719	0	0.0%	182	0	0.0%
1964	5251	10	0.2%	54	1	1.9%	650	1	0.2%	154	0	0.0%
1965	5860	8	0.1%	67	2	3.0%	655	0	0.0%	163	0	0.0%
1966	6248	14	0.2%	52	4	7.7%	722	3	0.4%	157	0	0.0%
1967	6382	8	0.1%	101	1	1.0%	795	1	0.1%	153	0	0.0%
1968	6273	7	0.1%	92	2	2.2%	642	0	0.0%	151	1	0.7%
1969	6379	5	0.1%	143	1	0.7%	675	0	0.0%	177	1	0.6%
1970	6187	4	0.1%	122	0	0.0%	599	1	0.2%	156	0	0.0%
1971	6092	14	0.2%	116	2	1.7%	670	1	0.1%	156	0	0.0%
1972	7049	5	0.1%	110	0	0.0%	664	0	0.0%	199	0	0.0%
1973	7219	14	0.2%	125	6	4.8%	652	1	0.2%	201	0	0.0%
1974	7137	10	0.1%	106	1	0.9%	649	0	0.0%	201	0	0.0%

(continued)

Table 1 continued

year	German courts overall			BVerfG			BGH civil senates			BAG		
	total	ECHR	%	total	ECHR	%	total	ECHR	%	total	ECHR	%
1975	7329	13	0.2%	129	3	2.3%	669	1	0.1%	200	0	0.0%
1976	8612	10	0.1%	133	2	1.5%	708	0	0.0%	183	0	0.0%
1977	9997	13	0.1%	160	2	1.3%	714	1	0.1%	183	0	0.0%
1978	11540	11	0.1%	174	1	0.6%	775	0	0.0%	215	0	0.0%
1979	12265	13	0.1%	165	1	0.6%	712	0	0.0%	216	0	0.0%
1980	13466	22	0.2%	156	2	1.3%	794	2	0.3%	487	2	0.4%
1981	14893	15	0.1%	200	2	1.0%	850	0	0.0%	490	0	0.0%
1982	15080	24	0.2%	235	1	0.4%	867	0	0.0%	632	0	0.0%
1983	15755	21	0.1%	217	5	2.3%	842	0	0.0%	726	0	0.0%
1984	15640	13	0.1%	243	1	0.4%	883	0	0.0%	669	0	0.0%
1985	15613	17	0.1%	184	3	1.6%	890	0	0.0%	563	0	0.0%
1986	16762	29	0.2%	183	5	2.7%	939	1	0.1%	620	0	0.0%
1987	18279	32	0.2%	210	6	2.9%	914	0	0.0%	689	1	0.1%
1988	19206	29	0.2%	200	2	1.0%	914	0	0.0%	661	1	0.2%
1989	19547	46	0.2%	287	5	1.7%	1020	1	0.1%	587	0	0.0%
1990	18870	49	0.3%	326	5	1.5%	989	0	0.0%	553	0	0.0%
1991	18819	60	0.3%	306	7	2.3%	919	0	0.0%	538	0	0.0%
1992	20577	64	0.3%	360	9	2.5%	857	0	0.0%	561	0	0.0%
1993	21903	94	0.4%	414	10	2.4%	821	2	0.2%	587	0	0.0%
1994	23226	180	0.8%	374	5	1.3%	823	0	0.0%	669	4	0.6%
1995	24567	305	1.2%	333	10	3.0%	832	1	0.1%	732	1	0.1%
1996	25323	306	1.2%	337	9	2.7%	818	2	0.2%	719	1	0.1%

The ECHR in the German Legal System

Year												
1997	28677	439	1.5%	319	4	1.3%	861	1	0.1%	665	1	0.2%
1998	30835	624	2.0%	354	6	1.7%	790	3	0.4%	699	0	0.0%
1999	31125	523	1.7%	419	6	1.4%	782	1	0.1%	595	2	0.3%
2000	37527	1194	3.2%	453	9	2.0%	1067	1	0.1%	627	0	0.0%
2001	37274	844	2.3%	481	16	3.3%	1033	1	0.1%	569	1	0.2%
2002	39444	840	2.1%	481	14	2.9%	1207	5	0.4%	607	2	0.3%
2003	39983	729	1.8%	417	15	3.6%	1487	3	0.2%	579	0	0.0%
2004	40905	817	2.0%	497	19	3.8%	1654	5	0.3%	519	0	0.0%
2005	42327	760	1.8%	458	20	4.4%	1780	16	0.9%	544	1	0.2%
2006	45537	960	2.1%	648	20	3.1%	1899	5	0.3%	583	3	0.5%
2007	46349	906	2.0%	649	28	4.3%	2047	12	0.6%	673	3	0.4%
2008	45081	858	1.9%	574	28	4.9%	2265	17	0.8%	602	1	0.2%
2009	43417	781	1.8%	550	20	3.6%	2133	14	0.7%	650	6	0.9%
2010	43976	986	2.2%	499	21	4.2%	2230	29	1.3%	698	3	0.4%
2011	43704	1108	2.5%	444	17	3.8%	2347	79	3.4%	603	3	0.5%
2012	42213	1134	2.7%	394	28	7.1%	2195	87	4.0%	642	8	1.2%
2013	40186	1330	3.3%	330	33	10.0%	1965	73	3.7%	593	3	0.5%
2014	39519	1629	4.1%	425	36	8.5%	1809	47	2.6%	556	6	1.1%
2015	39328	1737	4.4%	446	42	9.4%	1804	19	1.1%	553	4	0.7%
2016	39451	1798	4.6%	525	38	7.2%	1960	29	1.5%	501	11	2.2%
2017	39007	2240	5.7%	493	33	6.7%	1756	33	1.9%	542	7	1.3%
2018	36172	2192	6.1%	470	43	9.1%	1619	39	2.4%	411	9	2.2%
2019	35400	2087	5.9%	439	36	8.2%	1377	30	2.2%	435	10	2.3%
2020	36181	2045	5.7%	679	44	6.5%	1795	25	1.4%	271	3	1.1%

Source: Compiled by the author from data available in juris.

If we plot the results for the share of decisions with a textual reference to the ECHR for each year in a diagram, and add a moving average (for a five-year-period), we get the following figures:

Figure 1. Decisions of German courts with a textual reference to the ECHR

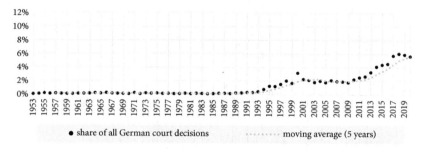

Figure 2. Decisions of the BVerfG with a textual reference to the ECHR

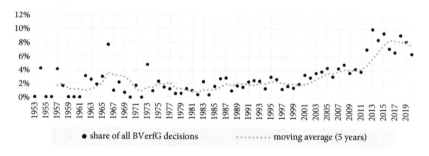

Figure 3. Decisions of the civil senates of the BGH with a textual reference to the ECHR

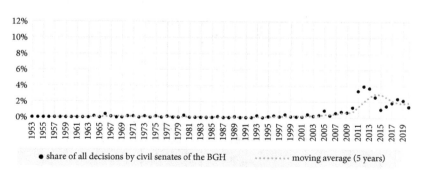

Figure 4. Decisions of the BAG with a textual reference to the ECHR

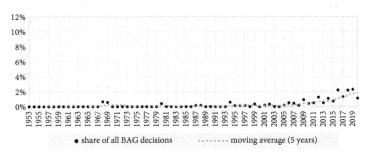

Putting all values and moving averages together yields the following two figures:

Figure 5. Decisions with a textual reference to the ECHR

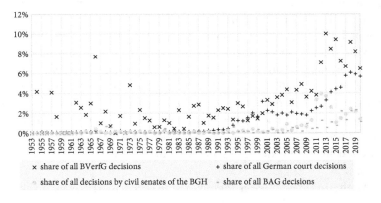

Figure 6. Decisions with a textual reference to the ECHR – moving averages (5 years)

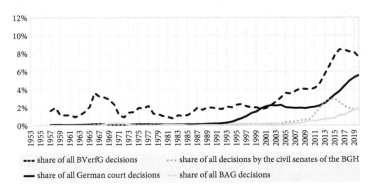

For German courts overall, the *absolute number* of decisions with a textual reference to the ECHR remained fairly low for several decades, spiking to 10 for the first time in 1964, above 20 for the first time in 1980 (22), above 50 in 1991 (60), and then increasing at a rapid pace to 180 in 1994, and to 1,194 in 2000, and then above 2,000 for the last four years considered. The *relative number* of decisions with a textual reference to the ECHR shows a similar, if slower movement: it remained between 0.0% and 0.2% from 1953 to 1989, and has remained above that level since then, rising to 1.2% in 1995, spiking from 1.7% in 1999 to 3.2% in 2000, and then slumping back to 2.3% in 2001. Between 2009 and 2018, the share rose steadily, from 1.8% to 6.1%. Since 2017, the share has consistently been equal to or above 5.7%.

While the overall tendency is similar for all courts, several variations stand out. Among all the subsets considered, the share of decisions with a textual reference to the ECHR has almost consistently been the highest for the BVerfG (with brief exceptions until the early 1970s, and for the period from 1997 to 2000, when the share was higher for German courts overall, but still lower for the civil senates of the BGH and the BAG). The absolute number of pertinent decisions by the civil senates of the BGH and the BAG, respectively, first exceeded 3 in 2002 for the civil senates of the BGH, and in 1994 for the BAG. Since then, the corresponding share of decisions with a textual reference to the ECHR has almost consistently been lower for the civil senates of the BGH and the BAG than for German courts overall (with the exception of the years from 2011 to 2013, when the share was higher for the civil senates of the BGH than for German courts overall).[104]

As the number of decisions by the BVerfG in the juris database is very low in the early years of the period (below 100 up until 1967), even single decisions containing a reference to the ECHR cause spikes in the relative numbers (most drastically in 1954, when one pertinent decision accounted for 4.2% of the 24 available decisions, and also in 1966, when 4 pertinent decisions amounted to 7.7% of the available decisions). The absolute number of BVerfG decisions with a textual reference to the ECHR increased to a two-digit number in 1993, and has remained above 14 since

---

[104] While this study focuses on the selected courts, it is worth mentioning that, of the 915 decisions by the Bundesverwaltungsgericht (Federal Administrative Court – BVerwG) issued in 2019, and available in juris, 81 make a textual reference to the ECHR (8.9%). Moreover, since 2017, the pertinent share for BVerwG decisions has consistently been higher than for German courts overall.

2001. The number for the BVerfG reached an all-time high in 2013 at 10.0%, and has moved down from there, in a zigzag line, to 6.5%.

For the civil senates of the BGH, more decisions were reported in juris for every single year, compared with the number of reported decisions by the BVerfG, and the absolute number of decisions with a textual reference to the ECHR remained below 10 up until 2005 (corresponding to 0.6% of the decisions made in 2004 or 2005). The sharpest rise took place between 2009 (14 decisions with a textual reference to the ECHR/0.7%) and 2012 (87/4.0%). Since then, the numbers have – with ups and downs during the intervening period – decreased to 25/1.4%.

The absolute number of BAG decisions with a textual reference to the ECHR has remained very low (peaking at 11, in 2016). While the relative number showed a general upward tendency, it remained below 1% up until 2012, and was often the lowest among the subsets considered.

Finally, if, for the sake of comparison, the corresponding shares of decisions of German courts overall with a textual reference to the GG, or to the CFR,[105] are collected and plotted in the same graphs as Figures 5 and 6,[106] we get:

Figure 7. Decisions with a textual reference to the ECHR/GG/CFR

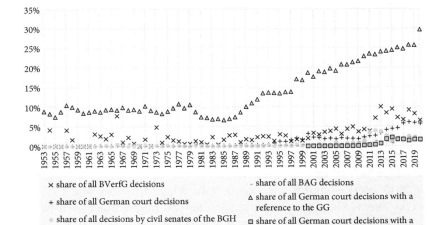

× share of all BVerfG decisions
+ share of all German court decisions
• share of all decisions by civil senates of the BGH
- share of all BAG decisions
△ share of all German court decisions with a reference to the GG
▫ share of all German court decisions with a reference to the CFR (2000–2020)

---

[105] As yielded by the search strings 'Grundgesetz', 'Grundgesetzes' and 'GG', and 'Grundrechtecharta', 'Grundrechte-Charta', 'Charta der Grundrechte', 'EuGrCh' and 'EUGrdRCh' (data on file with the author).
[106] References to the CFR are only plotted from 2000 onwards, in which year the CFR was proclaimed, and the pertinent number first exceeded 0.

Figure 8. Decisions with a textual reference to the ECHR/GG/CFR – moving averages (5 years)

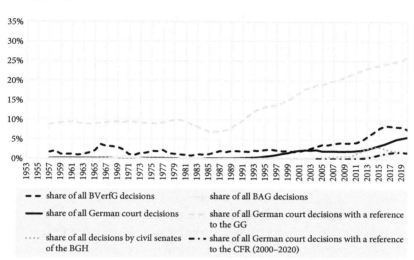

- – share of all BVerfG decisions
- share of all German court decisions
- ···· share of all decisions by civil senates of the BGH
- share of all BAG decisions
- share of all German court decisions with a reference to the GG
- – ·· share of all German court decisions with a reference to the CFR (2000–2020)

Source: All figures produced by the author.

These figures show that the German courts, overall, have consistently made more textual references to the GG than to the ECHR, while references to the CFR by German courts overall have remained at a fairly low level, similar to the numbers of textual references to the ECHR by the BAG.

3.4. DISCUSSION

Speaking in broad terms, the number of German court decisions with a textual reference to the ECHR has shown an upward tendency over time, even if, in the last few years, numbers have gone down again. In particular, the relative number of BVerfG decisions with a textual reference to the ECHR, which seldom exceeded 3.0% for decades, but went up as far as 10% in 2013, bears witness to the recently gained high relevance of the ECHR in the German legal system: parties and lawyers might raise ECHR-based arguments in expectation that these will be considered by the court, and courts might engage with the ECHR, as they acknowledge its importance for handling legal matters before them.[107]

---

[107] See also P.M. HUBER, 'Die Einwirkungen des Unionsrechts und der EMRK auf das Grundgesetz' in H.-J. BLANKE, S. MAGIERA, J.C. PIELOW and A. WEBER (eds), *Verfassungsentwicklungen im Vergleich – Italien 1947 – Deutschland 1949 – Spanien 1978*, Duncker & Humblot, Berlin 2021, p. 178; F.C. MAYER, 'Einleitung' in

The general upward tendency and its dynamics align with national and international developments. On a national level, landmark decisions by the BVerfG on the relationship between the ECHR and national law were issued in 1987, 1990, 2004, 2008 and 2011.[108] Following the larger number of these respective years, the numbers of decisions by German courts overall which referenced the ECHR rose (with the exceptions of 2004 and 2005 as well as 2008 and 2009. These exceptions are qualified in that there is a rise between the numbers for 2004 and 2006, and for 2008 and 2010). Hence, there might be an underlying connection, in that landmark cases may have generated a greater awareness of the relevance of the ECHR, among litigants as well as among judges. While these cases, such as *Caroline of Monaco III*,[109] may, at first glance, seem mainly to influence a specific area of the law, such as personality rights, they might still contribute significantly to the overall picture and numbers.

On an international level, the introduction of the individual complaint before the ECtHR in its current form, in 1998, might also have contributed to a growing number of textual references to the ECHR in German court decisions; lawyers might have resorted to the ECHR knowing that they might eventually bring a case before the ECtHR (or might at least threaten to do so), and courts might have considered the influence of the ECHR in light of this.

Finally, in keeping with the general theme of this book, a closer look at civil law and employment law cases: the share of cases with a textual reference to the ECHR is lower for the civil senates of the BGH and BAG than for the BVerfG, and, mostly, than for the German courts overall. This does not come as a surprise, as the matters before the former courts are between private parties, so the relevance of rights enshrined in the ECHR is not as obvious as in other constellations of cases.[110] Still, even for these subject matters, the relevance of the ECHR has risen to new highs over the last two decades. Thus, at the very least, these numbers can be taken as an invitation to explore in further detail the role of the ECHR in the German legal system for specific areas and questions.

---

[108] U. KARPENSTEIN and F.C. MAYER, *Konvention zum Schutz der Menschenrechte und Grundfreiheiten*, 3rd ed., C.H. Beck, München 2022, paras. 69–70.
See section 2 above.
[109] BVerfGE, 120, 180; for a deeper analysis and context see the chapter by K. DE LA DURANTAYE, 'Shaping the Right to Privacy: The Interplay between Karlsruhe, Strasbourg, and Luxembourg', in this volume.
[110] But see section 2.5 above, and nn. 60 and 61.

THE ROLE OF THE ITALIAN COURTS IN THE EFFECTIVE IMPLEMENTATION OF THE EUROPEAN CONVENTION ON HUMAN RIGHTS

Introductory Remarks

Laura VAGNI

1. Premise 43
2. The Interpretation in Conformity with the European Convention: The Italian Doctrine of Consolidated Case Law 46
3. The Lack of Ratification of Protocol 16 to the Convention by Italy 50
   3.1. The First Grand Chamber's Advisory Opinion and its Influence on Italian Case Law 52
   3.2. The Decisions of the Court of Cassation and of the Constitutional Court 55
4. Lights and Shadows in the Effective Implementation of the European Convention 59

1. PREMISE

The European Court of Human Rights (ECtHR) has always referred to the European Convention on Human Rights (ECHR) as a living instrument which must be interpreted in light of present-day conditions. According to the evolutive doctrine adopted by the Court, national judges, who are clearly closer to the needs of citizens, and the facts of cases dealing with national law, make a major contribution to the implementation of the Convention.[1] In fact, national courts are European human rights judges

---

[1] Among the extensive literature on the issue, see E. BJORGE, *Domestic Application of the ECHR: Courts as Faithful Trustees*, OUP, Oxford 2015, p. 131.

in their respective countries, and 'are best placed to act as ambassadors of the Court's case law in the Contracting States'.[2]

The role of national judges is not a passive one. They are not the mere recipients of the Strasbourg Court's interpretation; rather, they have an active role, based on a critical function that is exercised, on the one hand, by conformity with the ECtHR case law and, on the other, by the identification of national peculiarities under the doctrine of the margin of appreciation.[3] Thus, national judges are identified, in the research, as the key actors for a point of equilibrium between the international and national dimensions of human rights, which constitutes the principal engine of the formation of human rights law. This process is described through expressions which have, today, entered the vocabulary of legal scholars, such as 'dialogue' among the courts, and 'shared responsibility' (of international and national judges) for the effective implementation of Convention rights.

The relationship between the ECtHR and the national courts is shaped by the principle of subsidiarity that permeates the whole system of the Convention, although this principle was not expressly mentioned in the 1950 text.[4]

---

[2] J. LAFRANQUE, 'Dialogue between judges. Implementation of the judgments of the European Court of Human Rights: a shared judicial responsibility?', Strasbourg, 31 January 2014, p. 9, <https://www.echr.coe.int/Documents/Dialogue_2014_ENG.pdf>. According to the principle of primarity, the primary responsibility for the effective protection of Convention rights lies with the national authorities. For a general introduction to the issue, see J. GERARDS, *General Principles of the European Convention of Human Rights*, CUP, Cambridge 2019, p. 3 and references *ivi*.

[3] For the first references to the margin of appreciation doctrine, see J. GERARDS, above n. 2, p. 160; J. GERARDS, 'The European Court of Human Rights and the National Courts: Giving Shape to the Notion of "Shared Responsibility"' in J. GERARDS and J. FLEUREN, *Implementation of the European Convention of Human Rights and of the judgments of the ECtHR in national case-law: A comparative Analysis*, Intersentia, Cambridge 2014, p. 13.

[4] In fact, the principle of subsidiarity is reflected in various ways in the text of the Convention. Thus, Art. 1, Art. 13 and Art. 35 have been considered the normative basis for the recognition of the principle. On the issue *ex multis*, see J. CHRISTOFFERSEN, *Fair Balance: Proportionality, Subsidiarity and Primarity in the European Convention on Human Rights*, Martinus Nijhoff, Laiden/Boston 2009; A. MOWBRAY, 'Subsidiarity and the European Convention on Human Rights' (2015) 15(2) *Human Rights Law Review* 313. The ECtHR, interpreting Arts. 1, 13 and 35 jointly, has recognised the principle of subsidiarity since the case *'Relating to certain aspects of the laws on the use of languages in education in Belgium' v. Belgium*, nos. 1474/62; 1677/62; 1691/62; 1769/63; 1994/63; 2126/64, §10, ECtHR 1968: 'the Court cannot disregard those legal and factual features which characterise the life of the society in the State which, as a Contracting Party, has to answer for the measure in dispute. In so doing it cannot

The principle of subsidiarity has two different senses: the first is a procedural meaning, and concerns the rule of the exhaustion of domestic remedies; the second sense is a substantive one, implying that it is the task of national courts to interpret domestic law, ensuring the rights and liberties provided by the Convention.[5]

The recent entry into force of Protocol 15 to the Convention highlights the centrality of the principle of subsidiarity in the European Convention system.[6] Protocol 15, among other things, added a new recital at the end of the Preamble to the Convention:

> Affirming that the High Contracting Parties, in accordance with the principle of subsidiarity, have the primary responsibility to secure the rights and freedoms defined in this Convention and the Protocols thereto, and that in doing so they enjoy a margin of appreciation, subject to the supervisory jurisdiction of the European Court of Human Rights established by this Convention.[7]

The modified Preamble was welcomed by some scholars as a further implementation of the role of domestic courts in the European Convention system.[8] In this context, the application and interpretation of Convention rights by national courts are the main mechanisms for ensuring the effectiveness of the Convention.

---

assume the role of the competent national authorities, for it would thereby lose sight of the subsidiary nature of the international machinery of collective enforcement established by the Convention.' Cf. also *Kudła v. Poland*, no. 30210/96, §152, ECtHR 26 October 2000; *Cocchierella v. Italy*, no. 64886/01, §79, ECtHR, Grand Chamber, 29 March 2006; *De Souza Ribeiro v. France*, no. 22689/07, ECtHR 13 December 2012.

[5] H. PETZOLD, 'The Convention and the Principle of Subsidiarity' in R. MACDONALD, F. MATSCHER and H. PETZOLD (eds), *The European System for the Protection of Human Rights*, Martinus Nijhoff, Dordrecht 1993, p. 60. On the principle of subsidiarity and its correlation with international human rights law, see P.G. CAROZZA, 'Subsidiarity as a Structural Principle of International Human Rights Law' (2003) 97 *American Journal of International Law* 38.

[6] Protocol no. 15 amending the Convention for the Protection of Human Rights and Fundamental Freedoms (CETS No. 213), Strasbourg, 24 June 2013, entry into force 1 August 2021. The Protocol was ratified by Italy through the L. 15 January 2021, no. 11, GU 10.02. 2021, no. 34.

[7] Ibid.

[8] See, on this point, Cassese, who observes that we should not accept a meaning of subsidiarity that leads to the revival of the protection of national rights against the obligations accepted with the signing of the Convention: S. CASSESE, 'Ruling Indirectly Judicial Subsidiarity in the ECtHR' in *Subsidiarity: a two-sided coin? Dialogue between Judges 2015*, seminar organised by the ECtHR, Strasbourg, 30 January 2015, p. 17 <https://images.irpa.eu/wp-content/uploads/2011/10/Subsidiarity-a-two-sided-coin_1.pdf>.

2. THE INTERPRETATION IN CONFORMITY WITH THE EUROPEAN CONVENTION: THE ITALIAN DOCTRINE OF CONSOLIDATED CASE LAW

In the Italian system, the application of the Convention by ordinary judges, and the duty of those judges to conform to the ECtHR case law, have been at the centre of a wide debate, the milestones of which have been established by various judgments given by the Italian Constitutional Court.

It is outside the aims of this work to describe the development of Constitutional case law and the academic debate on this issue. I will limit myself to assuming the recognition of the Conventional Articles as interposed rules, established by the twin judgments of the Italian Constitutional Court in 2007, as a point of departure for formulating a few remarks on the role of national courts in implementing the ECHR.[9] This task is performed within the limits of the duties derived from Art. 101 and Art. 117 of the Constitution. According to the former Article, the Italian judge is subject to legislation and has to obey it; at the same time, on the basis of Art. 117, the judge cannot ignore the case law of the ECtHR, especially when the interpretation of the European Court is based on well-established case law.

The interpretation of national law in conformity with the European Convention is subordinated to the primary duty of the judge to adopt a constitutionally oriented interpretation. In fact, the Constitution has an 'axiological primacy' with respect to the European Convention.[10]

---

[9] Const. Court, 24 October 2007, no. 348 and no. 349, GU 31.10.2007, no. 42. Among the extensive literature on the issue, see, for the first references in English, F. BIONDI DAL MONTE and F. FONTANELLI, 'The Decisions No. 348 and 349/2007 of the Italian Constitutional Court: The Efficacy of the European Convention in the Italian Legal System' (2008) 7 *German Law Journal* 889; O. POLLICINO, 'Italy: Constitutional Court at the Crossroads between Constitutional Parochialism and Co-Operative Constitutionalism. Judgments No. 348 and 349 of 22 and 24 October 2007' (2008) 4 *European Constitutional Law Review* 363; D. TEGA, 'The Constitutional Background of 2007 Revolution. The Jurisprudence of the Constitutional Court' in G. REPETTO (ed), *The Constitutional Relevance of the ECHR in Domestic and European Law: An Italian Perspective*, Intersentia, Cambridge 2013, p. 25; V. BARSOTTI, P. CAROZZA, M. CARTABIA and S. SIMONCINI, *Italian Constitutional Justice in Global Context*, OUP, Oxford 2016, p. 222.

[10] Cf. R. SABATO, 'The Experience of Italy' in A. MÜLLER (ed), *Judicial Dialogue and Human Rights*, CUP, Cambridge 2017, pp. 267, 273. For a comparative perspective, see the remarks by E. CALZOLAIO, 'National Judges and Strasbourg Case Law: Comparative Reflections about the Italian Experience' in M. ANDENAS and D. FAIRGRIEVE (eds), *Courts and Comparative Law*, OUP, Oxford 2015, pp. 177, 183.

The Strasbourg judgments themselves need to be interpreted in conformity with the Constitution; among the different potential meanings of a Strasbourg judgment, the interpreter has to choose a meaning that can be reconciled with the Constitution, or is, at least, not in contrast with it. The Constitutional Court confirmed this approach in judgment no. 49 of 2015, stating that, except in the case of pilot judgments, the judge is obliged to accommodate the interpretation of national law to Strasbourg case law only where there is consolidated law on the question, while there is no obligation to do so in cases involving rulings that do not express a final position.[11] The Constitutional Court described the ordinary judge as holding the balance between autonomous interpretation and the duty to cooperate in ensuring that the meaning of the fundamental rights ceases to be a matter of dispute.[12]

The case referred to above dealt with the Italian institution of confiscation on the grounds of unlawful land development, and its compatibility with Arts. 7 ECHR and 1 of the first Protocol to the Convention, following the judgment *Varvara v. Italy*, where the ECtHR found a violation of both of these Articles by the Italian State.[13] In particular, one main problem was the specific nature of the Italian confiscation on the grounds of unlawful land development, which, being an administrative measure, does not respect the requirements established by Art. 7 ECHR in declaring an

---

[11] Const. Court, 14 January 2015, no. 49, GU 1.04.2015, no.13, §6.1, English translation available at <https://www.cortecostituzionale.it/documenti/download/doc/recent_judgments/S49_2015_en.pdf>: 'The canons of interpretation in accordance with constitutional law and the ECHR must in fact be applied also to the judgments of the Strasbourg Court when it is not possible to infer directly from them – inter alia for the reasons set out below – the effective principle of law which the Strasbourg court sought to assert in order to resolve the specific case (see Judgment no. 236 of 2011). In such situations, which are not common but are nonetheless possible, when confronted with a range of meanings potentially compatible with the signifier, the interpreting body is required to situate the individual ruling within the continuous flow of case law from the European Court in order to infer a meaning from the ruling that can be reconciled with that case law, and which does not under any circumstances violate the Constitution.' Cf. R. BIFULCO and D. PARIS, 'The Italian Constitutional Court' in A.V. BOGDANDY, P.M. HUBER and C. GRABENWARTER (eds), *Constitutional Adjudication: Institutions*, vol. III, 3rd ed., OUP, Oxford 2020, pp. 447, 501.

[12] Cost. Court, 14 January 2015, no. 49, above n. 11, §7: 'This interpretative equilibrium ... must be coordinated with Art 102(2) of the Constitution within the synthesis between the interpretative autonomy of the ordinary courts and their duty to cooperate in ensuring that the meaning of the fundamental rights ceases to be a matter of dispute.'

[13] *Varvara v. Italy*, no. 17475/2009, ECtHR 29 October 2013. The Italian confiscation was at the centre of a set of judgments by the European Court: see, previously, *Sud Fondi srl and Others v. Italy*, no. 75909/01, ECtHR 20 January 2009.

individual or juridical person guilty of a criminal offence.[14] For example, Italian confiscation is applicable by the judge even without a formal conviction, owing to the expiry of statutory time limits.

The doctrine of consolidated case law by the Constitutional Court, therefore, emerged in a context where the Court distinguished the nature and meaning of Italian confiscation from the concept of 'penalty' accepted at international level. The Constitutional Court gave evidence of the particular nature of Italian confiscation that could not be included indiscriminately within the definition of 'criminal penalty', and resisted an interpretation by the ECtHR that risked nullifying the application of domestic law on confiscation. Accordingly, the Court stated that the *Varvara* case was not an expression of a consolidated interpretation within European case law, and that the Italian judge was not obliged to conform to it.

The distinction between consolidated and non-consolidated case law is often difficult to trace. In judgment no. 49 of 2015, the Constitutional Court underlined some points to guide a judge in the process of discernment: the creativity of the principle asserted, compared with the traditional approach of European case law; an inner conflict within the jurisprudence of the ECtHR; the presence of dissenting opinions, especially if they are grounded on robust reasoning; the delivery of the judgment by a Chamber, and not by the Grand Chamber, of the ECtHR; and the fact that some specific features of Italian law were not contemplated in the judgment.[15] The Court stated that:

> When all or some of these signs are apparent, as established in a judgment which cannot disregard the specific features of each individual case, there is no reason to require the ordinary courts to use the interpretation chosen by the Strasbourg Court in order to resolve a particular dispute, unless it relates to a 'pilot judgment' in a strict sense.[16]

The doctrine of consolidated case law, however, was disowned by the ECtHR. In the judgment *GIEM v. Italy*, the Grand Chamber stated that, 'the Court would emphasise that its judgments all have the same legal value. Their binding nature and interpretative authority cannot therefore depend on the formation by which they were rendered.'[17] This case, once

---

[14] Cf. M. SIMONATO, 'Confiscation and fundamental rights across criminal and non-criminal domains' (2017) 18 *ERA Forum* 365.
[15] Const. Court, 14 January 2015, no. 49, above n. 11, §7.
[16] Ibid.
[17] *G.I. E.M. s.r.l. and Others v. Italy*, nos. 1828/06 34163/07 19029/11, §252, ECtHR, Grand Chamber, 28 June 2018; see I. MOTOC and M. VOLIKAS, 'The dialogue between

again, concerned Italian confiscation. The European Court this time partially accepted the Italian approach: the Grand Chamber affirmed that confiscation presumes the presence of the objective and subjective (mental element) requirements to be applied, in conformity with Art. 7 ECHR, but it admitted the application of confiscation without a formal conviction.

Finally, the case law on confiscation on the grounds of unlawful site development is an example of the mutual influence of international and domestic case law on human rights. This dynamic was analysed in the *GIEM* case, where the majority of the opinions focused on the importance of a dialogue between national and international courts for the formation of human rights law.[18] In this context, two main approaches emerged: a universal approach, viewing national differences as a risk for fragmentation; and another approach, attributing a significant role to the national jurisprudence in the definition of the meaning and nature of international rules. Adhering to the latter view, Judge Motoc, significantly, affirmed that:

> As European Judges, we look at the dialogue between judges from our own perspective, that of the application of the European Convention of Human Rights. But to avoid reverting to a monologue, we need to understand the national authorities and sometimes, as Churchill supposedly once said, 'courage is what it takes to stand up and speak; courage is also what it takes to sit down and listen'.[19]

After the *GIEM* case, the distinction between consolidated and non-consolidated case law remained at the centre of the Italian debate, and the doctrine of consolidated case law continued to be applied. Even recently, the United Sections of the Court of Cassation, in deciding a case concerning external cooperation in criminal organisations, applied the doctrine, and stated that the judge does not have a duty to conform with the non-consolidated case law of the ECtHR.[20] Nevertheless, the judge has the autonomy to orient national law to ECtHR case law by interpretation, respecting the limits of constitutional conformity. Within these parameters,

---

the ECHR and the Italian Constitutional Court' in R. CHENAL et al. (eds), *Intersecting Views on National and International Human Rights Protection*, Liber Amicorum *Guido Raimondi*, Wolf Legal Publishers, Chicago 2019, p. 603.

[18] On the importance of a comparative law perspective in this regard, see L. VAGNI, 'The relationship between Human Rights and Property and the need for comparison in International Law' (2019) 54 *Questions of International Law* 51, 59.
[19] *G.I.E.M. srl and Others v. Italy*, above n. 17, §72.
[20] Cass. Pen., Sez. Un., 24 October 2019, no. 8544, (2020) 6 *Cassazione Penale* 2259.

since the twin judgments of the Constitutional Court in 2007, the proactive role of the Italian courts in the implementation of human rights into domestic law has grown exponentially. Sometimes, judges have anticipated legislative reforms through an evolutive interpretation of national legislation, or have even taken real leaps forward in the implementation of the Convention.

3. THE LACK OF RATIFICATION OF PROTOCOL 16 TO THE CONVENTION BY ITALY

The recent approval of Protocol 16 to the ECHR is another important mechanism for aiding the domestic courts in their effective implementation of the ECHR.[21]

The Protocol, which came into force on 1 August 2018, allows the highest courts and tribunals of the Contracting Parties to 'request the Court to give advisory opinions on questions of principle relating to the interpretation or application of the rights and freedoms defined in the Convention or the protocols thereto'.[22]

In line with the principle of subsidiarity, an advisory opinion of the ECtHR is not formally binding, even on the requesting court.[23] The non-binding nature of the opinion does not affect the right of a party to

---

[21] Protocol 16 to the Convention for the Protection of Human Rights and Fundamental Freedoms (CETS no. 214), entry into force 1 August 2018, Art. 1. On the basis of Protocol 11 to the Convention, the Strasbourg Court could give advisory opinions on legal questions concerning the interpretation of the Convention, at the request of the Committee of Ministers, however it should not deal with any question relating to the content or scope of the rights or freedoms defined in Section I of the Convention and the Protocols thereto, which are at the heart of the Convention; see Art. 47 of the Protocol 11 to the Convention for the Protection of Human Rights and Fundamental Freedoms (CETS no. 155), entry into force 11 April 1994. Cf. J. GERARDS, 'Advisory Opinions, Preliminary Rulings, and the new Protocol no. 16 to the European Convention of Human Rights. A Comparative and Critical Appraisal' (2014) 21 *Maastricht Journal* 648; L.A. SICILIANOS, 'L'élargissement de la compétence consultative de la Cour européenne des droits de l'homme. A' propos du Protocole n. 16 à la Convention européenne des droits de l'homme?' (2014) 1 *Revue Trimestrielle des Droit de l'Homme* 9; S. O'LEARY and T. EICKE, 'Some Reflections on Protocol 16' (2018) 3 *European Human Right Law Review* 220.

[22] Protocol 16 to the Convention for the Protection of Human Rights and Fundamental Freedoms, above n. 21, Art. 1.

[23] For the different opinions on the non-binding nature of the advisory opinions by the Grand Chamber see *Reflection Paper on the proposal to extend the Court's advisory jurisdiction*, §§42–44 <https://www.echr.coe.int/Documents/2013_Courts_advisory_jurisdiction_ENG.pdf>.

bring the case before the European Court, after the exhaustion of domestic remedies.

The Italian State has not yet ratified Protocol 16. In 2018, the Italian government presented a bill for the ratification of both Protocols 15 and 16 to the Convention.[24] Art. 3 of the bill established, on the basis of Art. 10 of Protocol 16, that the highest courts and tribunals, which would be allowed to submit a request for an opinion to the Strasbourg court, were the Court of Cassation, the Council of State (highest tribunal for administrative law matters), the Court of Accounts (Corte dei Conti), and the Council for the Administrative Jurisdiction of the Region of Sicily. The Constitutional Court was not included in the list, however the third paragraph of Art. 3 provided that the Constitutional Court could amend its regulation in order to establish the application of Protocol 16. Therefore, the bill gave the Constitutional Court freedom of choice regarding the application of the Protocol.

The Articles of the bill relating to the ratification of Protocol 16, however, were separated, and on 30 September 2015, Parliament approved the law ratifying Protocol 15, which came into force on 11 February 2021.[25]

Currently, it is quite difficult to predict whether, and when, the Italian Parliament will ratify Protocol 16. Therefore, Italian courts cannot submit a request for an advisory opinion to the Grand Chamber. Nevertheless, the submission of requests by the courts of other Contracting Parties undeniably impacts on the implementation of the Convention within the Italian system.

An example of this dynamic can be found in the recent Italian case law concerning the recognition of the legal parental relationship between a

---

[24] In the XVII Legislature, a first bill was presented (C. 2801, available at <http://www.senato.it/leg/17/BGT/Schede/Ddliter/45139.htm>). This bill was never approved by the Senate. In the XVIII legislature, two bills that reproduced the first bill were presented: C. 1124, introduced by the Government, and C. 35. Cf. E. CRIVELLI, 'The Italian Debate about the Ratification of Protocol 16' (2020) 4 *Eurojus* 371.

[25] L. no. 11, 15 January 2021, GU 10.02.2021, no. 34, in force the day after. The problem that led to the separation of the ratification of Protocols 15 and 16 was a concern related mainly to the erosion of the role of the High Italian Courts and the principles of the Italian system. On the challenge that Protocol 16 could represent for the Constitutional Court's autonomy, see the comparative remarks in M. DICOSOLA, C. FASONE and I. SPIGNO, 'The Prospective Role of Constitutional Courts in the Advisory Opinion Mechanism before the European Court of Human Rights: A First Comparative Assessment with the European Union and the Inter-American System' (2015) 16(6) *German Law Journal* 1387; on the Italian lack of ratification of Protocol 16, see, for the first references in English, the critical commentary by E. LAMARQUE, 'The Failure by Italy to Ratify Protocol no. 16 to the ECHR' (2021) 1(1) *The Italian Review of International and Comparative Law* 159.

child born through surrogate motherhood and the intended parent, which will be analysed in section 3.2. It shows the influence of the first advisory opinion by the Grand Chamber on the interpretation of domestic law by the Court of Cassation, and also the potential contribution of Protocol 16 to the implementation of Convention rights in non-Contracting States.

3.1. THE FIRST GRAND CHAMBER'S ADVISORY OPINION AND ITS INFLUENCE ON ITALIAN CASE LAW

On 19 April 2019, the Grand Chamber delivered its first advisory opinion on the basis of Protocol 16, requested by the French Court of Cassation.[26] The opinion concerned the recognition, in domestic law, of a legal parent–child relationship between a child born through a gestational surrogacy arrangement abroad and the intended mother.[27]

---

[26] *Advisory opinion concerning the recognition in domestic law of a legal parent-child relationship between a child born through a gestational surrogacy arrangement abroad and the intended mother*, requested by the French Court of Cassation, no. P16-2018-001, ECtHR, Grand Chamber, 10 April 2019. The Grand Chamber delivered four other advisory opinions: no. P16-2019-001, ECtHR, Grand Chamber, 29 May 2020, requested by the Armenian Constitutional Court; no. P16-2020-002, ECtHR, Grand Chamber, 8 April 2022, requested by the Lithuanian Supreme Administrative Court; no. P16-2021-001, ECtHR, Grand Chamber, 26 April 2022, requested by the Court of Cassation of Armenia; no. P16-2021-002, ECtHR, Grand Chamber, 13 July 2022, requested by the French Conseil d'État; the ECtHR, sitting as a panel of the Grand Chamber, under Art. 2(1) of Protocol 16, decided not to accept the request for an advisory opinion by the Supreme Court of the Slovak Republic, no. P16-2020-001, 14 December 2020.

[27] The French case law on the issue was revised after the judgments *Mennesson v. France*, no. 65192/11, ECtHR 26 June 2014 and *Labassee v. France*, no. 65941/11, ECtHR 26 June 2014, both concerning the refusal to register birth certificates recognising the intended father as the legal parent of a child born through gestational surrogacy, on the basis of French legislation. Indeed, after the Strasbourg judgments, the intended father of the child, where he is also the biological father, may be registered as the legal parent of a child born through gestational surrogacy. The new interpretation by the Court of Cassation was introduced by a set of decisions in 2015: see Civ., 1re, 5 July 2017, no. 15-28-597; no. 16-16-901; no. 16-16-455 and no.16-20-052, where the Court established the principle of a partial registration of the birth, designating the intended father as legal parent where he is also the child's biological father, but refusing the recognition of the intended mother as the legal mother. Following the European Court judgment in the *Mennesson* case, the French Court of Cassation re-examined this issue. In the course of this proceeding, the request for an advisory opinion from the Grand Chamber was formulated. Cf. H. HURPY, 'La judiciarisation par défaut du lien de filiation des enfants nés d'une GPA transfrontière avec le mère d'intention' (2019) 631 *Revue de l'Union Européenne* 486; M. PICCHI, 'Surrogate

The Court of Cassation submitted two questions to the Grand Chamber. French law recognises the intended father as having the status of legal parent when he is also the biological father of a child, whereas it prohibits the registration, as legal parent, of the intended mother of a child born through gestational surrogacy. The Court of Cassation inquired whether the refusal to enter an intended mother in the birth register consisted in a State Party overstepping its margin of appreciation under Art. 8 ECHR. Moreover, in the event of an affirmative answer, the Court of Cassation asked whether the possibility of the intended mother adopting the child of her spouse, the biological father, would be a means of establishing the legal mother–child relationship, in compliance with the requirements of Art. 8 ECHR.

In the advisory opinion, the Grand Chamber underlined the differences between Contracting Parties in the prohibition of surrogate motherhood, and in the recognition of a legal relationship between the child and the intended parent.[28] Moreover, the procedures for establishing a legal parent–child relationship in such cases varies from state to state, and there are sometimes also different procedures available in the same state. On this issue, there is, therefore, a margin of appreciation for States Parties.

In the Court's answer, two factors assumed particular weight: the child's best interests – which is a paramount value whenever the situation of a child is at issue – and the scope of the margin of appreciation available to the States Parties.

The lack of recognition of the legal relationship between a child and an intended mother has a negative impact on several aspects of the child's right to respect for his or her private life. The Court accepted that the best interests of the child do not merely reside in the protection of the right to a private and personal life, but also include other components that are not necessarily in favour of a recognition of a legal relationship between a child and an intended parent. However, from the principle of the best interests of the child is derived the importance of the legal identification of the persons responsible for raising him or her, meeting his or her needs, and ensuring

---

Motherhood: Protecting the Best Interests of the Child in Light of Recent Case Law' (2019) 3(3) *Peace Human Rights Governance* 307.

[28] The Grand Chamber undertook a comparative law survey covering the States Parties, from which it emerged that surrogacy arrangements were permitted in 9 of these 43 states, were tolerated in a further 10 states, and were prohibited, either explicitly or implicitly, in the other 24 States Parties. Consequently, the registration of a foreign birth certificate recognising a legal parent–child relationship is admitted in 16 of the 19 states where surrogacy is permitted or tolerated: *Advisory opinion*, ECtHR, Grand Chamber, 29 April 2019, above n. 26, §22.

his or her welfare, as well as the possibility for a child to live and develop in a stable environment. Consequently, the Court stated that:

> the general and absolute impossibility of obtaining recognition of the relationship between a child born through a surrogacy arrangement entered into abroad and the intended mother is incompatible with the child's best interests, which require at a minimum that each situation be examined in the light of the particular circumstances of the case.[29]

States' margin of appreciation on the question should be wide, due to the absence of a consensus on the issue of surrogacy; nevertheless, where a particularly important facet of an individual's identity is at stake, such as where the legal parent–child relationship is concerned, the margin allowed to the state is normally restricted.[30] In a situation where a father has a biological link with the child, the right to respect for the private life of a child born abroad through a gestational surrogacy arrangement requires that domestic law provides a possibility of recognition of a legal parent–child relationship with the intended mother, who is registered abroad as the legal mother. This recognition appears even more necessary when the child was conceived using the eggs of the intended mother. The Court affirmed that this assertion does not place any obligation on the state to recognise ab initio a legal relationship between a child and an intended mother, but it should at least do so when the parental relationship has become a practical reality.[31] It is within the margin of appreciation of the state to establish when, and through what procedures, to recognise a legal relationship between a child and an intended mother. One possible solution is the adoption of the child by the intended mother.

---

[29] *Advisory opinion*, ECtHR, Grand Chamber, 19 April 2019, above n. 26, §42.
[30] Ibid., §44.
[31] Note that the French Court of Cassation complied with the advisory opinion of the Grand Chamber: see Cass. Civ., *Ass. Plén*, 4 October 2019, no. 10-19053, §6. See also Cass. Civ., 1ère, 18 December 2019, no. 19-11815 and no. 18-12327, where the Court recognised a legal parent–child relationship between a child born through surrogate motherhood and the intended non-biological father. After the recent approval of the Loi relative à la bioéthique, 2 August 2021, no. 2021–1017, JORF 3.09.2021, no. 0178, Art. 47 code civil was reformed. The Article, in contrast with the recent Cassation case law, requires judicial control of the birth certificate 'que cet acte est irrégulier, falsifié ou que les faits qui y sont déclarés ne correspondent pas à la réalité. Celle-ci est appréciée au regard de la loi française'. Cf. S. PICHARD, 'La Transcription totale des actes étrangers des enfants nés d'une GPA: un schisme antre loi and jurisprudence' (2020) 7 *Requeil Dalloz* 426; A. KARILA-DANZIGER and F.G. JOLY, 'Transcription à l'état civil français des actes de naissance étrangers dresses dans le cadre d'une GPA, «Fin de partie»' (2021) 11 *AJ Famille* 582.

The importance of the advisory opinion for the enhancement of the interaction between the ECtHR and the national courts in the development of human rights law was underlined by the Grand Chamber itself in the preliminary considerations of the opinion.[32] In more recent cases, the ECtHR expressly referred to the advisory opinion given on request by the French Court of Cassation and followed the same approach in deciding cases concerning the recognition of a legal parent–child relationship between children born abroad as the result of a surrogacy agreement and the intended parents.[33] Thus, the advisory opinion given by the Court is intended to have effects beyond the application of Protocol 16 and its entry into force in the States Parties.

These considerations have a counterpart in a question of constitutionality raised by the Italian Court of Cassation in 2020,[34] concerning the recognition of a legal relationship between an intended father and a child born through gestational surrogacy, where the intended father is married to the biological father. In that case, the Court of Cassation analysed, in depth, the advisory opinion issued by the Grand Chamber on request of the French Court of Cassation, and found an insoluble conflict between Art. 8 ECHR, in light of the advisory opinion, and the national law prohibiting the registration of an intended parent as legal parent of a child born through gestational surrogacy.

3.2. THE DECISIONS OF THE COURT OF CASSATION AND OF THE CONSTITUTIONAL COURT

The case brought before the Italian Court of Cassation concerned the registration of the birth of a child born through surrogate motherhood. The child was the son of two homosexual partners who had married in Canada, and recorded their union in the Italian Register of Civil Unions. The partners asked the competent officer to register the birth of the child, stating both partners to be legal parents, but the officer refused to make the registration.

---

[32] *Advisory opinion*, ECtHR, Grand Chamber, 19 April 2019, above n. 26, §§25–26. On the basis of Art. 3 of Protocol 16, written observations were submitted to the Court by some non-governmental organisations and also by the governments of the United Kingdom, the Czech Republic and Ireland.

[33] *Affaire D v. France*, no. 11288/18, §21, ECtHR 16 July 2020; *D.B. and Others v. Switzerland*, nos. 58817/15 and 58252/15, §79, ECtHR 22 November 2022; *Case of K.K. and Others v. Denmark*, no. 25212/21, §15, ECtHR 2 December 2022.

[34] Cass. Civ., Sez. I, no. 8325, 29 April 2020, (2020) 3 *Diritto di famiglia e delle persone*, II, 960.

Italian law does not allow an intended parent without a biological relationship to a child to be recorded as the legal parent of that child. In fact, Art. 12, paragraph 6 of the law on medically assisted reproduction expressly prohibits human reproduction through surrogate motherhood.[35] Moreover, Art. 18 of the DPR no. 396 of 2000 prohibits the registration of acts of civil status that are in conflict with public policy.[36] On the basis of this legislation, a consolidated interpretation of the Court of Cassation stated that the lack of recognition of the intended parent as the legal parent derives from the prohibition of surrogate motherhood.[37]

Conversely, the Court of Appeal of Venice had decided the case in favour of the partners, establishing that the request for registration of the intended parent as the legal parent was not in conflict with international public policy.[38] According to the Court, the meaning of public policy should be interpreted in light of the protection of the best interests of the child, in conformity with Strasbourg case law.

The Court of Cassation had to evaluate whether the decision of the Court of Appeal of Venice was in conflict with the law. Its attention was focused on a previous judgment of the United Sections of the Court of Cassation, stating that the execution of a foreign judicial order concerning the recognition of the legal relationship between a child and an intended parent was in conflict with the principle of public policy.[39] Thus, the recognition conflicted with the prohibition of surrogate motherhood, which protected fundamental values such as the dignity of the woman and the institution of adoption. These values, according to a reasonable balance established by the legislator, and not amendable by the judge, prevailed over the interests of the minor.[40]

---

[35] L. no. 40, 19 February 2004, *Norme in materia di procreazione medicalmente assistita*, GU 24.02.2004, no. 45.

[36] DPR no. 396, 3 November 2000, *Regolamento per la revisione e semplificazione dell'ordinamento dello strato civile, a norma dell'art. 2, comma 12, della legge 15 maggio 1197, n. 127*, GU 30.12.2000, no. 303 (suppl. ord.).

[37] For an analysis of the main questions on this issue, in English, see I. KRIARIM and A VALONGO, 'International Issues Regarding Surrogacy' (2016) 2 *The Italian Law Journal* 331.

[38] Court of Appeal of Venice, Ord., sez. III, 16 July 2018, (2019) 1 *Diritto di famiglia e delle persone*, I, 149.

[39] Cass. Civ., Sez. Un., 8 May 2019, no. 12193, (2019) 6 *Il Foro Italiano*, I, c. 2003. See the commentary by F. MARONGIU BUOINAIUTI, 'Recognition in Italy of Filiation Established Abroad by Surrogate Motherhood, between Transnational Continuity of Personal Status and Public Policy' (2019) 11(2) *Cuadernos de Derecho Transnacional* 294.

[40] Ibid., the Court added that an intended parent can have access to adoption for particular cases, on the basis of Art. 44 of the L. no. 184 of 1983, *Disciplina dell'adozione*

It is worth mentioning that the judgment of the United Sections curbed the leap forward made by some national judges who, while stressing the use of conforming interpretation with the ECtHR case law, admitted the registration of an intended parent as the legal parent in the Italian civil status records.[41] The United Sections, therefore, had achieved a difficult equilibrium between the duty to respect legislation and the implementation of Convention rights into the Italian system.

This equilibrium was revised by the order of the Court of Cassation in the case under judgment, which departed from the interpretation of the United Sections. The Court raised a question of constitutionality on the basis of Art. 117 of the Italian Constitution, underlining the conflict between consolidated Italian case law and Art. 8 ECHR.

In general, the Court of Cassation is not obliged to conform to its previous consolidated case law.[42] However, Art. 374 of the Italian Code of Civil Procedure states that, if the single section of the Court of Cassation does not agree with the principle of law pronounced by the United Sections, it can refer to the United Sections, by way of a reasoned order, the decision on the appeal.[43] In fact, the options at the disposal of a single section of the Court of Cassation are not limited to conformation with the United Sections interpretation, or the referral of the decision to the United sections. There exists a third way – a last resort – namely the question of constitutionality; the Court decided to take this approach in this case.[44]

---

e dell'affidamento dei minori, GU 17.05.1983, no. 133. See the interpretation by Cost. Court., 23 February 2022, no. 79, GU 30.3.2022, no. 13, where the Court declared Art. 55 of L. n. 184 of 1983 incompatible with Arts. 3, 31 and 117 of the Constitution, in so far as it rules out that adoption in special cases can give rise to any civil relationship between the adopted child and the adoptive parent's relatives; see the commentary by E. CRIVELLI, 'La Corte costituzionale garantisce i rapporti di parentela a tutti i minori adottati: nota alla sentenza n. 79 del 2022' (2022) 5 *Osservatorio Costituzionale* 1.

[41] The more favourable approach to the recognition of a legal parent–child relationship in similar cases was also followed by the Cass. Civ., sez. I, 21 June 2016, no. 19599, see F. MARONGIU BUOINAIUTI, 'Recognition in Italy of Filiation Established Abroad by Surrogate Motherhood, between Transnational Continuity of Personal Status and Public Policy', above n. 39, 296.

[42] On this point, Cass. Civ., Sez. I, no. 8325, 29 April 2020, above n. 34, referred to the Const. Court, 13 November 1997, no. 350, GU 26.11.1997, no. 48.

[43] Cf. S. GROSSI and M.C. PAGNI (eds), *Commentary on the Italian Code of Civil Procedure*, OUP, Oxford 2010, p. 306; L. BACCAGLINI, G. DI PAOLO and F. CORTESE, 'The value of Judicial precedent in the Italian Legal System' (2016) 7(1) *Civil Procedure Review* 3, at 21. A United Sections judgment, indeed, roots the case law on a question, in order to assure the certainty of law and its uniform application in the territory of the state.

[44] Cf. Const. Court, 22 January 2015, no. 3, GU 28.1.2015, no. 4; see the commentary by M. CAREDDA, 'Quando "reinterpretare" dovrebbe equivalere ad "accogliere"' (2015) 1 *Giurisprudenza Costituzionale* 30.

In the decision of 2020, the Court of Cassation affirmed that an advisory opinion from the Grand Chamber is an abstract opinion by the European Court which has the aim of clarifying the content of Convention rights and preventing their violation. In this light, a general and abstract limitation of rights concerning the personal identity of a child is incompatible with the Convention: the lack of recognition of the status filiationis is to be evaluated on a case-by-case basis.[45] On the contrary, the United Sections judgment of the Court of Cassation assumed that the best interests of the child can always be restricted in favour of the protection of public policy. Finally, the Court of Cassation underlined the conflict between the consolidated Italian case law, based on the United Sections judgment, and Art. 8 ECHR, according to the advisory opinion of the Grand Chamber.

The Constitutional Court declared admissible the question in judgment no. 33 of 2021, which established, in particular, that the obligation of a single section of the Court of Cassation to conform with the interpretation of the United Sections concerns the interpretation of law, and not its compatibility with the Constitution.[46] The latter question is within the competence of any court which has the authority to raise a question of constitutionality, without consulting any of the other high-level courts beforehand. The non-binding nature of the advisory opinion of the Grand Chamber – underlined by the Constitutional Court – does not preclude the admissibility of a question of constitutionality, but it is very important to understand the correct interpretation of the Convention rights.[47]

Finally, the Constitutional Court confirmed the value attributed by the Court of Cassation to a non-binding opinion of the Grand Chamber for the interpretation of domestic legislation, and accepted that a conflict between Italian legislation, as interpreted in consolidated case law, and a Convention right, as interpreted by the Strasbourg Court, could be the basis for a question of constitutionality. The Constitutional Court, however, did not declare the unconstitutionality of Art. 12, Law no. 40 of 2004, stating that the protection of the interests of the child born through surrogate motherhood is, in the first instance, within the authority of the legislator. Within the margin of appreciation of the states, there are different options compatible with the European Convention. The choice among the different compatible solutions is at the discretion of the legislator.

---

[45] Cass. Civ., Sez. I, 29 April 2020, no. 8325, above n. 34.
[46] Const. Court, 9 March 2021, no. 33, GU 3.03.2021 n. 9, §3.2.
[47] Ibid.

At the end of 2022, the United Sections of the Italian Court of Cassation dealt with the same question again, referring to the decision of the Constitutional Court mentioned above, confirming the conflict between the surrogate motherhood and the principle of public policy.[48] Therefore, an intended parent of a child born through surrogate motherhood cannot be registered as the legal parent in the Italian civil status records. However, the Court, in light of the principle of the best interests of the child, recognised that, in such cases, the child can be adopted by the intended parent.[49] In adopting this approach, the Court focused on the notion of international public policy and highlighted that it includes, primarily, the values of the Italian Constitution, but also the shared values of the international community. In this respect, the ECtHR case law, subsequent to the advisory opinion delivered by the Grand Chamber in response to the request from the French Court of Cassation, was deeply considered.

In conclusion, the decisions of the Court of Cassation and the Constitutional Court, concerning the recognition of a legal parent–child relationship between children born abroad as the result of a surrogacy agreement and the intended parents, clearly show the influence of the non-binding advisory opinions of the Grand Chamber on the effective implementation of the ECHR into the Italian legal system.

4. LIGHTS AND SHADOWS IN THE EFFECTIVE IMPLEMENTATION OF THE EUROPEAN CONVENTION

The principle of solidarity that permeates the entire system of the ECHR, as now expressly recognised by the Preamble to the Convention, highlights the paramount role of national courts in ensuring the effective implementation of the ECHR, and the development of human rights law. This role has been further emphasised after the entry into force of

---

[48] Cass. Civ., Sez. Un., 30 December 2022, no. 38162; the question was referred to the United Sections by Cass. Civ., Sez. I, ord., 21 January 2022, n. 1842; see the commentary by A.M. PINELLI, 'Le persistenti ragioni del divieto di maternità surrogata e il problema della tutela di colui che nasce dalla pratica illecita. In attesa della pronuncia delle Sezioni Unite' (2022) 12 *Famiglia e diritto* 1175; A FEDERICO, 'La "maternità surrogata" ritorna alle Sezioni Unite' (2022) 5 *Nuova Giurisprudenza Civile Commentata* 1047.

[49] On the basis of L. no. 184 of 1983, allowing the adoption for particular cases, as interpreted by the Constitutional Court in judgment n. 79 of 2022, above n. 40.

Protocol 16 to the Convention, independently of its ratification by a State Party, as the recent Italian case law on the status of a child born through surrogate motherhood shows.

However, the effective implementation of the European Convention by the Italian courts is still hampered by some obstacles. The lack of ratification of Protocol 16 certainly prevents Italy's highest courts from directly consulting the Grand Chamber. Therefore, an advisory opinion will be requested by courts within the framework of a foreign legal system, and the opinion itself, although formulated in abstract terms, will be delivered with the addressee in mind. The contribution of the Italian courts to the formation of human rights case law at international level could be weakened as a result.[50]

Until recently, another obstacle to the full conformation of Italian courts decisions with Strasbourg case law was due to the impossibility of protecting the injured person by restitutio in integrum, beyond the limit of res judicata.

This problem was analysed by the Committee of Ministers of the Council of Europe, in a Recommendation of 2000, which stated that 'in exceptional circumstances the re-examination of a case or a reopening of proceedings has proved the most efficient, if not the only, means of achieving *restitutio in integrum*'.[51]

There is no obligation for a Contracting Party to guarantee a re-examination of the case, as full compensation for the injured party could also be achieved through the application of different measures. However, the Council invited the states to ensure that their legal systems made it possible for injured parties to achieve restitutio in integrum.

Some Member States followed this Recommendation by introducing a new reason for reviewing res judicata in civil matters, on the basis of an ascertained violation, by the state, of the ECHR.

In Germany, for example, paragraph 580 no. 8 of the German Code of Civil Procedure (ZPO) provides that:

> An action for retrial of the case may be brought ... [w]here the European Court of Human Rights has established that the European Convention for the

---

[50] Cf. E. LAMARQUE, 'The Failure by Italy to Ratify Protocol no. 16 to the ECHR' (2021) 1(1) *The Italian Review of International and Comparative Law* 159.

[51] Recommendation of the Committee of Ministers to Member States, R (2000) 2, *on the re-examination or reopening of certain cases at domestic level following judgements of the European Court of Human Rights*: <https://search.coe.int/cm/Pages/result_details.aspx?ObjectID=09000016805e2f06>.

Protection of Human Rights and Fundamental Freedoms or its protocols have been violated, and where the judgment is based on this violation.[52]

A partially different approach to the restitutio in integrum was followed in the French system. Art. 452-1 of the Code de l'organisation judiciaire allows the re-examination of cases involving civil matters (*réexamenen matière civil*) only where the case concerns the legal status of a person, and the just satisfaction of the injured person (Art. 41 ECHR) does not put an end to the violation ascertained by the ECHR against France.[53] In this way, the French state finds a balance between the values protected by the doctrine of res judicata, especially the certainty of rights and the interests of third parties in good faith, and the effective implementation of the Convention rights.

In the Italian system, the opportunity to review res judicata in civil matters, following a judgment by the Strasbourg Court finding a violation of Convention rights by Italy, was not recognised until recently due to the absence of a legislative basis.[54] Consequently, the remedy of restitutio in integrum was precluded for injured parties. Again, the ECtHR judgments did not affect res judicata in similar cases decided by Italian courts, requiring the injured party to take his or her case to the Strasbourg Court, as the only option to obtain compensation for damages (Art. 41, on just satisfaction), if the time limit for doing so had not lapsed. The result was a less effective application of Art. 46 of the Convention, which sets out the obligation on Contracting States to abide by the Court's judgments.[55]

---

[52] §580 *Zivilprozessordnung*, translated by Samson-Übersetzungen GmbH, Dr Carmen von Schöning <https://www.gesetze-im-internet.de/englisch_zpo/index.html#gl_p2206>.

[53] Loi 18.11.2016, no. 2016–1547, JORF 19.11.2016, no. 0269.

[54] On the contrary, the review of a final criminal judgment, as a consequence of a violation of the ECHR established by the ECtHR for the same case, is recognised, on the basis of Art. 630 of the Code of Criminal Proceeding. See Const. Court, 4 April 2011, n. 113, in GU 13.04.2011, no. 16. For an analysis of the Italian approach in comparative perspective, see. V. SCIARABBA, *Il Giudicato e la CEDU*, Cedam, Padova 2012. A more recent interpretation of the Court of Cassation extended the use of the remedy to similar criminal cases, other than that to which the relevant Strasbourg Court is applied. See, on the matter, and on the recent Italian case law on the effects of a Strasbourg judgment finding a violation of the Convention on final administrative and civil judgments, C. PETTA, 'Res Iudicata in breach of the ECHR: The Italian Constitutional Court Point of View' (2018) *The Italian Law Journal* 225; F.M. BUONAIUTI, 'The Effects of Judgments of The European Court of Human Rights on the Final Decisions of Domestic Courts: Recent Developments in the Italian Case Law' (2019) 28(1) *The Italian Yearbook of International Law Online* 159.

[55] According to the interpretation of Art. 46 by the Strasbourg Court, the Contracting Parties are under an obligation not only to pay the applicant the sums awarded by

A recent reform of the Code of Civil Procedure has partially filled the regulatory gap that had existed, introducing Art. 391-quarter. The Article regulates the revocation of a final judgment in civil matters, when the ECtHR has established that the judgment conflicts with ECHR or its Protocols. The final judgment can be revoked only when the violation of the ECHR concerns the legal status of a person and the just satisfaction of the injured person (Art. 41 ECHR) has not adequately remedied the violation ascertained.[56] Along these lines, the remedy of restitution in integrum is admitted in civil matters. Thus, the interpretation of Art. 391-quater by Italian courts will certainly play an important role in moving forward with the effective implementation of the ECHR into Italian private law and in lighting a path where some shadows still exist.

---

way of just satisfaction, but also to take individual measures in domestic laws to put an end to the violation found by the Court, and to redress its effects; cf., lastly, *Ilgar Mammadov v. Azerbaijan*, Grand Chamber, no. 15171/13, §147 ECtHR 29 May 2019. On the issue, see ECtHR, *Guide on Article 46 of the European Convention of Human Rights: Binding force and execution of judgements*, updated on 30 April 2021 <https://www.echr.coe.int/Documents/Guide_Art_46_ENG.pdf>.

[56] D. Lgs. 10 October 2022, n. 149, Art. 3(28), letter o; Art. 35, emended by L. 29 December 2022, n. 197, Art. 1(380), established the entry into force of Art. 391-quarter on 28 February 2023. Art. 391-quarter provides that the appeal for revocation must be filed within 60 days from the communication or the publication of the ECtHR's judgment. The revocation of the judgment does not affect the rights of bona fide third parties, who were not parties in the proceeding before ECtHR.

PART II
FAMILY LAW

PARENTAL AUTONOMY AND CHILD PROTECTION MEASURES

Procedural and Substantive Standards

Konrad DUDEN

1. Introduction 65
2. The ECtHR Case Law: *Wetjen* and *Tlapak* 67
3. Procedural Standards 70
   3.1. Right to be Involved 71
   3.2. Length of Proceedings 73
4. Substantive Standards 76
   4.1. Proportionality of Family Separation 76
      4.1.1. The Standard of Proportionality 77
      4.1.2. Margin of Appreciation 78
      4.1.3. Proportionality in *Tlapak* and *Wetjen* 79
   4.2. Religious Freedom and Child Protection Measures 81
5. Influence of National Constitutional Law 82
6. Conclusion 84

1. INTRODUCTION

Article 8(1) of the European Convention on Human Rights (ECHR) grants the right to respect for one's private and family life. Parents are given the right to decide autonomously on how to bring up their children and how to educate them. In this regard, Article 8(1) ECHR is complemented by Article 2 Protocol 1 to the Convention, which obliges the Contracting States to respect the right of parents to ensure, for their children, an education in conformity with the parents' religious and philosophical convictions.[1]

---

[1] *Catan and others v. Moldova and Russia*, nos. 43370/04, 8252/05 and 18454/06, ECtHR 19 October 2012, para. 138; *Kjeldsen, Busk Madsen and Pedersen v. Denmark*, nos. 5095/71, 5920/72 and 5926/72, ECtHR 7 December 1976, para. 52.

Parents' autonomy in raising their children, however, faces its limits in the children's rights to physical and psychological integrity. If their integrity is threatened by how their parents raise them, the Contracting States have a positive obligation to intervene in order to protect the children from their own parents.[2] Such measures can be necessary when parents are unable, or unwilling, to provide their children with a family life that respects the children's rights and best interests. Accordingly, child protection measures can range from supportive measures that aid the parents in raising their child, to coercive measures enacted against the will of the parents.

If other measures fail, states can partially or fully withdraw parents' custody over their children, and transfer the children into the care of family members, foster parents or other institutions. Such a family separation constitutes a grave interference with the respect for one's family life, as protected by Article 8(1) ECHR. Like any other interference with Article 8(1) ECHR, such a family separation can only be justified under the conditions set out in Article 8(2) ECHR.[3] This latter provision states that interferences by a public authority in the right to respect for one's family life have to be in accordance with the law, and have to be necessary in a democratic society for the protection of certain interests, including the protection of the rights and freedoms of others.

The jurisprudence of the European Court of Human Rights (ECtHR) has spelt out these general conditions in detail for cases of family separation, and has established strict standards. In what follows, some of the standards set by the ECtHR will be highlighted, and how German law implements these standards will be analysed.

Two ECtHR decisions from 2018 will be used to illustrate the standards set by the ECtHR (section 2). The judgments relate to children who were brought up in the religious community of the 'the Twelve Tribes', and who were subsequently separated from their families by German authorities because the courts and authorities were convinced that the children were being subjected to systematic corporal punishment as an educational tool. These cases are particularly insightful: on the one hand, the reason for separating the families is easy to explain, and will intuitively convince many readers of the necessity of family separation – as it did the ECtHR,

---

[2] *Bevacqua and S. v. Bulgaria*, no. 71127/01, ECtHR 12 June 2008, para. 65; *M. and M. v. Croatia*, no. 10161/13, ECtHR 3 September 2015, para. 136.

[3] *Elsholz v. Germany*, no. 25735/94, ECtHR 13 July 2000, paras. 46 *et seq.*; *K. and T. v. Finland*, no. 25702/94, ECtHR 12 July 2001, para. 152.

in the end. However, even seemingly extreme cases require a cautious and differentiated assessment when considering the importance of parental autonomy in child-rearing, and the high threshold for a family separation. In its decisions, the ECtHR was, therefore, very careful to reiterate and apply the standards that have to be met in order to justify such a separation. The decisions, therefore, serve as a pointed illustration of the standards set by the ECtHR in relation to family separations.

In its case law, the ECtHR establishes both procedural (section 3) and substantive (section 4) standards, which German law generally complies with. The reasoning behind these standards reflects a general observation regarding the case law of the ECtHR that is also highlighted in other contributions in this volume,[4] namely the interdependency of procedural and substantive standards. Procedural standards indirectly protect substantive interests. Conversely, the application of substantive standards is based on the presumption that certain procedural standards have been met. In cases of family separation, this interplay of procedural and substantive standards is particularly clear.

The case law on family separation highlights another general issue: the specificity of the influence of ECtHR case law on national law (section 5). Similarly to the ECtHR, the German Federal Constitutional Court also has very strict jurisprudence on the compatibility of family separation with fundamental rights. In many cases, the specific influence of the ECHR on national family law cannot, therefore, be distinguished from the influence of human and fundamental rights generally.

2. THE ECtHR CASE LAW: *WETJEN* AND *TLAPAK*

The two cases used here to illustrate the ECtHR case law on family separation are *Wetjen and others v. Germany*[5] and *Tlapak and others v. Germany*.[6] Both cases relate to the same set of facts. However, they differ in relation to the nature of the national proceedings that led to the separation of the families. *Wetjen* relates to preliminary proceedings, whereas *Tlapak* relates to main proceedings.

---

[4] Cf. the chapter by M. FORNASIER, 'Harmonisation through the Back Door? The Impact of the European Convention on Human Rights on National Private Law', in this volume.
[5] *Wetjen and others v. Germany*, nos. 68125/14 and 72204/14, ECtHR 22 March 2018.
[6] *Tlapak and others v. Germany*, nos. 11308/16 and 11344/16, ECtHR 22 March 2018.

The cases involve the religious community of 'the Twelve Tribes'. This is a close-knit religious community which, at the time, had congregations in Germany, in the Bavarian villages of Klosterzimmern and Wörnitz.[7] In 2012, the press reported on the mistreatment of children living in these communities. The media coverage showed that parents and other authority figures in the communities, such as teachers, used systemic corporal punishment as an aid in the education of the children. This related, in particular, to the practice of caning, i.e. beating the child with a wooden stick.[8] A reporter had documented several instances of such corporal punishment with a hidden camera, and in August 2013 the video was sent to the local youth offices, as well as to the family courts.[9]

A couple of weeks later, in September 2013, the family courts in Ansbach and Nördlingen made preliminary orders regarding the children living in both local 'Twelve Tribes' communities.[10] The courts transferred some of the parents' custody rights to the youth office, including the right to decide where the children should live.[11] The family courts argued that these steps were necessary because there was a reasonable likelihood that the children would otherwise be subject to corporal punishment. The family courts based their decisions on the above-mentioned video, and on statements made by several former members of the religious community.[12] Most of the children were first taken into state care, and later placed in foster families. Some children were, however, returned to

---

[7] *Wetjen and others v. Germany*, nos. 68125/14 and 72204/14, ECtHR 22 March 2018, para. 6.

[8] *Tlapak and others v. Germany*, nos. 11308/16 and 11344/16, ECtHR 22 March 2018, para. 7; *Wetjen and others v. Germany*, nos. 68125/14 and 72204/14, ECtHR 22 March 2018, para. 7; OLG Nürnberg, 11.6.2015, 9 UF 1430/14, juris-database, para. 7.

[9] *Tlapak and others v. Germany*, nos. 11308/16 and 11344/16, ECtHR 22 March 2018, para. 9; *Wetjen and others v. Germany*, nos. 68125/14 and 72204/14, ECtHR 22 March 2018, para. 9.

[10] The decisions were not published; see, for a summary, OLG Nürnberg, 11.06.2015, 9 UF 1430/14, juris-database, paras. 6–7; and *Tlapak and others v. Germany*, nos. 11308/16 and 11344/16, ECtHR 22 March 2018, para. 10; *Wetjen and others v. Germany*, nos. 68125/14 and 72204/14, ECtHR 22 March 2018, para. 11.

[11] *Tlapak and others v. Germany*, nos. 11308/16 and 11344/16, ECtHR 22 March 2018, para. 10; *Wetjen and others v. Germany*, nos. 68125/14 and 72204/14, ECtHR 22 March 2018, paras. 11–12; OLG Nürnberg, 11.06.2015, 9 UF 1430/14, juris-database, para. 6.

[12] *Tlapak and others v. Germany*, nos. 11308/16 and 11344/16, ECtHR 22 March 2018, para. 10; *Wetjen and others v. Germany*, nos. 68125/14 and 72204/14, ECtHR 22 March 2018, para. 11; OLG Nürnberg, 11.06.2015, 9 UF 1430/14, juris-database, para. 7.

their parents, for instance because they were too young, or too old, to be subjected to corporal punishment under the religious tenets of the 'Twelve Tribes'.[13]

The ECtHR decisions relate to various children that remained separated from their parents. Regarding these children, the preliminary orders by the family courts were generally[14] upheld by the family courts in Ansbach[15] and Nördlingen,[16] as well as by the respective courts of appeal in Nuremberg and Munich.[17] In *Tlapak*, the orders were issued and reviewed both during preliminary proceedings, and in the main proceedings that occurred subsequently.[18] In *Wetjen*, only preliminary proceedings took place.[19] In both cases, the decisions were appealed to the German Federal Constitutional Court, which did not admit the constitutional complaints in either case,[20] thus opening up the path to the Strasbourg Court.

---

[13] *Tlapak and others v. Germany*, nos. 11308/16 and 11344/16, ECtHR 22 March 2018, paras. 10–13; *Wetjen and others v. Germany*, nos. 68125/14 and 72204/14, ECtHR 22 March 2018, paras. 14 and 21.

[14] *Tlapak and others v. Germany*, nos. 11308/16 and 11344/16, ECtHR 22 March 2018, paras. 20 and 44: one child, who was only one year old at the time, was returned to their parents; *Wetjen and others v. Germany*, nos. 68125/14 and 72204/14, ECtHR 22 March 2018, para. 21: one child who was too old to be subject to corporal punishment was returned to their parents.

[15] Cf. *Tlapak and others v. Germany*, nos. 11308/16 and 11344/16, ECtHR 22 March 2018, paras. 16 and 19. The decisions were not published; cf., for a summary, OLG Nürnberg, 11.06.2015, 9 UF 1430/14, juris-database, paras. 16 *et seq.*

[16] *Wetjen and others v. Germany*, nos. 68125/14 and 72204/14, ECtHR 22 March 2018, paras. 16 and 21. The decisions were not published.

[17] OLG Nürnberg, 11.06.2015, 9 UF 1430/14, juris-database; cf. *Tlapak and others v. Germany*, nos. 11308/16 and 11344/16, ECtHR 22 March 2018, paras. 17, 20, 32 *et seq.* and 43 *et seq.* Other decisions by the Nuremberg Court of Appeal (two decisions on 02.12.2013 and one decision on 27.05.2015, case no. 9 UF 1549/14; cf. *Tlapak and others v. Germany*, nos. 11308/16 and 11344/16, ECtHR 22 March 2018, paras. 17, 20 and 32; OLG Nürnberg, 11.06.2015, FamRZ 2015, 1908, 1908), as well as decisions by the Munich Court of Appeal (cf. *Wetjen and others v. Germany*, nos. 68125/14 and 72204/14, ECtHR 22 March 2018, paras. 18 and 23), were not published.

[18] *Tlapak and others v. Germany*, nos. 11308/16 and 11344/16, ECtHR 22 March 2018, paras. 16 *et seq.* and 22 *et seq.*

[19] *Wetjen and others v. Germany*, nos. 68125/14 and 72204/14, ECtHR 22 March 2018, paras. 15 *et seq.*

[20] Federal Constitutional Court, 05.05.2014, case no. 1 BvR 770/14 and 1 BvR 959/14 – not published (cf. *Wetjen and others v. Germany*, nos. 68125/14 and 72204/14, ECtHR 22 March 2018, paras. 19 and 24); Federal Constitutional Court, 16.08.2015, case no. 1 BvR 1467/15 and 1 BvR 1589/15 – not published (cf. *Tlapak and others v. Germany*, nos. 11308/16 and 11344/16, ECtHR 22 March 2018, paras. 35 and 49).

In both cases, the ECtHR saw no violation of Article 8 ECHR. It did find interferences with Article 8(1) ECHR;[21] however, the justification for these interferences met the standards of Article 8(2) ECHR.[22] The ECtHR concluded that the national courts had carried out fair proceedings, and had issued well-reasoned decisions that gave 'relevant and sufficient' reasons for withdrawing part of the parental authority. The decisions by the national courts showed that the courts had struck a balance, between the interests of the parents and those of the children, that did not fall outside of the margin of appreciation that the ECtHR grants to the national authorities.[23] In reaching this result, the court reiterated several procedural and substantive standards that both national authorities and national law have to fulfil.

3. PROCEDURAL STANDARDS

In relation to procedural standards, the ECtHR started by highlighting the procedural autonomy of the contracting states. It emphasised that Article 8 ECHR contains no explicit procedural requirements.[24] It does, however, implicitly create procedural standards, i.e. standards for the procedure which the public authorities, and in particular the courts, of a Contracting State have to follow when taking or upholding measures that interfere with a substantive right protected under the ECHR: in this case, the right to respect for one's family life under Article 8(1) ECHR. Only if these procedural standards are met can the decision to separate children from their parents be compatible with Article 8(2) ECHR.

---

[21] *Tlapak and others v. Germany*, nos. 11308/16 and 11344/16, ECtHR 22 March 2018, para. 76; *Wetjen and others v. Germany*, nos. 68125/14 and 72204/14, ECtHR 22 March 2018, para. 63.

[22] *Tlapak and others v. Germany*, nos. 11308/16 and 11344/16, ECtHR 22 March 2018, paras. 100–01; *Wetjen and others v. Germany*, nos. 68125/14 and 72204/14, ECtHR 22 March 2018, paras. 86–87.

[23] *Tlapak and others v. Germany*, nos. 11308/16 and 11344/16, ECtHR 22 March 2018, para. 100; *Wetjen and others v. Germany*, nos. 68125/14 and 72204/14, ECtHR 22 March 2018, para. 86.

[24] *Tlapak and others v. Germany*, nos. 11308/16 and 11344/16, ECtHR 22 March 2018, para. 83; *Wetjen and others v. Germany*, nos. 68125/14 and 72204/14, ECtHR 22 March 2018, para. 70.

3.1. RIGHT TO BE INVOLVED

In deducing the procedural standards, the ECtHR started from a very broad claim: 'the decision-making process involved in [separating children and their parents] must be fair and such as to afford due respect to the interests safeguarded by Article 8'.[25] The factual basis for child protection measures must be thoroughly investigated before a court may separate a family.

A national court – and subsequently the ECtHR – can determine whether the family separation is justified under Article 8(2) ECHR only if it has ascertained and taken into account the interests of all persons whose rights will be affected by its decision.[26] This, in turn, is only possible if the court engages with the family members. Article 8 ECHR, thus, leads to a right for affected family members to be involved in the proceedings.

German national law complies with this standard set by the ECtHR.[27] German procedural law protects the right to be involved, in the Act on Proceedings in Family Matters.[28] In proceedings in parent and child matters, the family courts have to hear the parents and children, according to sections 159 and 160 of this Act.[29] When the Act on Proceedings in Family Matters came into force in 2009, sections 159 and 160 replaced similar provisions in the previous Act on procedural rules for proceedings in family matters.[30] However, the wording was strengthened by the reform, in order to highlight the importance, and the mandatory nature, of hearing the child and parents during proceedings.[31]

---

[25] *Tlapak and others v. Germany*, nos. 11308/16 and 11344/16, ECtHR 22 March 2018, paras. 83 and 92; *Wetjen and others v. Germany*, nos. 68125/14 and 72204/14, ECtHR 22 March 2018, para. 70.

[26] *Tlapak and others v. Germany*, nos. 11308/16 and 11344/16, ECtHR 22 March 2018, para. 83; *Wetjen and others v. Germany*, nos. 68125/14 and 72204/14, ECtHR 22 March 2018, para. 70; J. MEYER-LADEWIG and M. NETTESHEIM, in J. MEYER-LADEWIG et al. (eds), *EMRK – Europäische Menschenrechtskovention*, 4th ed., Nomos, Baden-Baden 2017, Art. 8, paras. 73 and 120.

[27] Cf. D. WACHE, 'Note on ECtHR, *Wetjen and others v. Germany*, 22.03.2018', *NZFam* 2018, 455, 459.

[28] Gesetz über das Verfahren in Familiensachen und in den Angelegenheiten der freiwilligen Gerichtsbarkeit (FamFG) of 17.12.2008, BGBl. 2008 I 2586, last changed by Art. 5 Gesetz zum Ausbau des elektronischen Rechtsverkehrs mit den Gerichten und zur Änd. weiterer Vorschriften of 05.10.2021, BGBl. 2001 I 4607.

[29] Cf. S. HAMMER, in H. PRÜTTING and T. HELMS (eds), *FamFG*, 5th ed., Otto Schmidt, Cologne 2020, §159 FamFG, paras. 1–2 and §160 FamFG, paras. 1–3.

[30] S. 50a and 50b FGG (Act on Matters of Non-contentious Jurisdiction: Gesetz über die Angelegenheiten der freiwilligen Gerichtsbarkeit).

[31] Deutscher Bundestag, 07.09.2007, BT-Drs. 16/6308, 240.

In relation to child protection matters, section 157 of the Act on Proceedings in Family Matters adds another layer to the engagement with families, in addition to hearing the parents and children during proceedings. Section 157 obliges the court to discuss early on with the parents – and, wherever possible, with the children – how a threat to the child's best interests can be met, particularly through public agencies, and ideally without the need for coercive child protection measures.

This engagement with the parties under section 157 is distinct from the general duty to hear the parties under sections 159 and 160.[32] While the latter provisions aim at collecting the facts necessary to decide the case and grant a protection order, section 157 of the Act is meant to encourage a more open discussion with the parties as to how the threat to the child's best interests can be avoided without the need for a protection order.[33]

According to section 157, the court should also highlight the possible consequences of the parents not accepting the necessary assistance. In this sense, the provision is meant to enable the court to better understand the situation of the child, and to encourage cooperation by parents, in order to avoid coercive child protection measures.[34] It is meant to provide guidance and supervision for the parents even if there is not yet any danger to the best interests of the child.[35] On a procedural level, the provision creates a hurdle that has to be overcome before coercive measures can be enacted, thus providing that such measures should be issued only where necessary. Apart from promoting the procedural right to be heard, the provision, therefore, also helps to ensure that coercive child protection measures remain proportional.[36]

The requirement to involve the parties affected was fulfilled by the German courts in the specific cases of *Wetjen* and *Tlapak*.[37] In both

---

[32] Ibid., 237; S. Hammer, in H. Prütting and T. Helms (eds), *FamFG*, 5th ed., Otto Schmidt, Cologne 2020, §160 FamFG, para. 3.

[33] E. Schumann, in T. Rauscher (ed), *Münchener Kommentar zum FamFG*, 3rd ed., C.H. Beck, Munich 2018, §157 FamFG, paras. 1–2; S. Hammer, in H. Prütting and T. Helms (eds), *FamFG*, 5th ed., Otto Schmidt, Cologne 2020, §157 FamFG, para. 2 and §160 FamFG, para. 3.

[34] Deutscher Bundestag, 07.09.2007, BT-Drs. 16/6308, 237; S. Hammer, in H. Prütting and T. Helms (eds), *FamFG*, 5th ed., Otto Schmidt, Cologne 2020, §157 FamFG, para. 2; E. Schumann, in T. Rauscher (ed), *Münchener Kommentar zum FamFG*, 3rd ed., C.H. Beck, Munich 2018, §157 FamFG, para. 1.

[35] E. Schumann, in T. Rauscher (ed), *Münchener Kommentar zum FamFG*, 3rd ed., C.H. Beck, Munich 2018, §157 FamFG, para. 3.

[36] Cf., on the requirement of proportionality, *infra* at section 4.1.

[37] *Tlapak and others v. Germany*, nos. 11308/16 and 11344/16, ECtHR 22 March 2018, paras. 93 and 96; *Wetjen and others v. Germany*, nos. 68125/14 and 72204/14, ECtHR 22 March 2018, para. 80.

cases, the courts heard the parents, the children and their guardians *ad litem*.[38] During the main proceedings in *Tlapak*, the national court also commissioned an expert opinion from a psychologist.[39] In each of the cases, one child was not heard. However, the ECtHR accepted this omission because in both cases those children were only around two years old when the court of appeal decided the case.[40]

3.2. LENGTH OF PROCEEDINGS

In *Tlapak* and *Wetjen*, the ECtHR reiterated another procedural standard of particular importance in parent and child matters: the demand for effective and speedy proceedings. The court emphasised that ineffective and delayed custody proceedings can give rise to a breach of Article 8.[41] Here, again, the procedural safeguard ultimately serves the substantive protection granted by Article 8; the reason for this is the normative force that the factual developments exert in custody proceedings. When a child is taken from parents and transferred to state care, or to a foster family, that child is likely to develop a bond with its new primary caregiver. The longer the separation continues, the stronger this bond will become. And as that bond grows, the best interests of the child can increasingly favour the child remaining with its new primary caregiver. With time, it becomes less likely that the child will be returned to their parents. Long proceedings can, therefore, effectively deprive parents of their rights under Article 8.[42] In these cases – as the saying goes – justice delayed is truly justice denied.[43]

---

[38] *Tlapak and others v. Germany*, nos. 11308/16 and 11344/16, ECtHR 22 March 2018, para. 93; *Wetjen and others v. Germany*, nos. 68125/14 and 72204/14, ECtHR 22 March 2018, paras. 80–81; cf. OLG Nürnberg, 11.06.2015, 9 UF 1430/14, juris-database, paras. 10–11.

[39] *Tlapak and others v. Germany*, nos. 11308/16 and 11344/16, ECtHR 22 March 2018, para. 94.

[40] *Tlapak and others v. Germany*, nos. 11308/16 and 11344/16, ECtHR 22 March 2018, para. 93; *Wetjen and others v. Germany*, nos. 68125/14 and 72204/14, ECtHR 22 March 2018, paras. 15 *et seq.* and 81.

[41] *Tlapak and others v. Germany*, nos. 11308/16 and 11344/16, ECtHR 22 March 2018, para. 65.

[42] *Kuppinger v. Germany*, no. 62198/11, ECtHR, 15 January 2015, para. 102; *Kuppinger v. Germany*, no. 41599/09, ECtHR, 21 April 2011, para. 45; *K. and T. v. Finland*, no. 25702/94, ECtHR 12 July 2001, para. 155; *Kutzner v. Germany*, no. 46544/99, ECtHR 26 February 2002, para. 67; *Süss v. Germany*, no. 40324/98, ECtHR 10 November 2005, para. 100; *Ignaccolo-Zenide v. Romania*, no. 31679/96, ECtHR 25 January 2000, para. 102.

[43] Cf. Deutscher Bundestag, 06.07.2016, BT-Drs. 18/9092, 19; E. SCHUMANN, in T. RAUSCHER (ed), *Münchener Kommentar zum FamFG*, 3rd ed., C.H. Beck, Munich 2018, §155b FamFG, para. 1.

German law, in principle, also demands expedited proceedings in child protection matters. Section 155(1) of the Act on Proceedings in Family Matters expressly states that such matters 'shall have priority and the proceedings shall be handled in an expedited manner'.[44] The legislator expressly intended for these proceedings to be expedited, even at the expense of other proceedings lodged with the court.[45]

If the parties think that proceedings are not moving fast enough, sections 155b and 155c of the Act give them remedies to force the court to expedite its proceedings.[46] The provisions serve to ensure the effectiveness of section 155 of the Act on Proceedings in Family Matters,[47] and thus the right to a speedy trial as required by the ECtHR. In fact, these provisions are a clear example of the influence of the ECtHR case law on German law. They were enacted in 2016 as a direct and explicit response to the ECtHR decision in *Kuppinger v. Germany*.[48]

In this case, the applicant, Mr Kuppinger, had sued in a national court to be granted contact rights to see his son. The national proceedings in the German district court lasted for several years.[49] In the context of these national proceedings, the ECtHR intervened with several decisions. In a first decision in 2011, the ECtHR held the length of the proceedings to be a violation of the applicant's right to a trial within a reasonable time under Article 6(1) ECHR.[50] It also found a violation of the right to an effective remedy, as protected under Article 13 ECHR, because there was no remedy for the applicant to expedite the proceedings or to receive adequate redress for delays that had already occurred.[51]

---

[44] Cf. S. Hammer, in H. Prütting and T. Helms (eds), *FamFG*, 5th ed., Otto Schmidt, Cologne 2020, §155 FamFG, paras. 14 *et seq.*

[45] Deutscher Bundestag, 07.09.2007, BT-Drs. 16/6308, 235.

[46] S. Hammer, in H. Prütting and T. Helms (eds), *FamFG*, 5th ed., Otto Schmidt, Cologne 2020, §155b FamFG, paras. 1–2.

[47] E. Schumann, in T. Rauscher (ed), *Münchener Kommentar zum FamFG*, 3rd ed., C.H. Beck, Munich 2018, §155b FamFG, para. 1.

[48] Deutscher Bundestag, 06.7.2016, BT-Drs. 18/9092, 15; E. Schumann, in T. Rauscher (ed), *Münchener Kommentar zum FamFG*, 3rd ed., C.H. Beck, Munich 2018, §155b FamFG, para. 2; S. Hammer, in H. Prütting and T. Helms (eds), *FamFG*, 5th ed., Otto Schmidt, Cologne 2020, §155b FamFG, para. 1.

[49] *Kuppinger v. Germany*, no. 62198/11, ECtHR 15 January 2015, paras. 5–8.

[50] *Kuppinger v. Germany*, no. 41599/09, ECtHR 21 April 2011, paras. 44 and 51; *Kuppinger v. Germany*, no. 62198/11, ECtHR 15 January 2015, para. 8.

[51] *Kuppinger v. Germany*, no. 41599/09, ECtHR 21 April 2011, para. 56; cf. *Kuppinger v. Germany*, no. 62198/11, ECtHR 15 January 2015, para. 8; cf. *Sürmeli v. Germany*, no. 75529/01, ECtHR 8 June 2006, paras. 115–17; *Rumpf v. Germany*, no. 46344/06, ECtHR 2 September 2010, paras. 51 and 64–70.

In 2015, while the proceedings continued in Germany, the ECtHR issued another ruling.[52] This is the decision which led to the introduction of sections 155b and 155c of the German Act on Proceedings in Family Matters. In the 2015 ruling, the ECtHR found a violation of Article 13 in conjunction with Article 8 ECHR, because, even after the first ECtHR decision in this case, German law had still not established an effective remedy against lengthy proceedings. This is because German law only permitted financial compensation *ex post*, and did not grant a remedy to expedite a decision by the court *ex ante*, in order to avoid excessively long proceedings.[53]

While remedies for infringements of rights are generally considered sufficiently effective by the ECtHR if they either prevent a violation, or provide adequate compensation for a violation that has already occurred, the court applies a more rigid approach in relation to proceedings whose length has a clear impact on the family life of the applicant[54] – as was the case in *Kuppinger*.[55] In such a case, an effective remedy had to be both preventive and compensatory. Because of the importance of a speedy decision for the substantive protection of the right to respect for one's family life, a merely compensatory remedy would not suffice as an appropriate measure to ensure protection under Article 8.[56] The Court, therefore, held that German law, at the time, was only effective in relation to compensatory and not preventative relief.[57] There had, therefore, been a violation of Article 13 in conjunction with Article 8 ECHR;[58] this led to the introduction of the above-mentioned preventative remedies in sections 155b and 155c of the Act on Proceedings in Family Matters.

Returning to the specific cases of *Tlapak* and *Wetjen*, a mixed picture emerges. In both cases, the parties had argued that the proceedings were unreasonably long.[59] In *Wetjen*, this claim related to preliminary proceedings.[60] The German government acknowledged that those

---

[52] *Kuppinger v. Germany*, no. 62198/11, ECtHR 15 January 2015.
[53] Ibid., paras. 136 *et seq*.
[54] *Macready v. Czech Republic*, nos. 4824/06 and 15512/08, ECtHR 22 April 2010, para. 48; *Bergmann v. Czech Republic*, no. 8857/08, ECtHR 27 October 2011, paras. 45–46.
[55] *Kuppinger v. Germany*, no. 62198/11, ECtHR 15 January 2015, paras. 137 *et seq*.
[56] Ibid., para. 137.
[57] Ibid., paras. 139 *et seq*.
[58] Ibid., para. 145.
[59] *Tlapak and others v. Germany*, nos. 11308/16 and 11344/16, ECtHR 22 March 2018, para. 64; *Wetjen and others v. Germany*, nos. 68125/14 and 72204/14, ECtHR 22 March 2018, para. 44.
[60] *Wetjen and others v. Germany*, nos. 68125/14 and 72204/14, ECtHR 22 March 2018, para. 44.

proceedings had taken too long.⁶¹ In *Tlapak*, on the other hand, it was the length of the main proceedings that was being criticised. Here, however, the ECtHR found the claim to be manifestly ill-founded, and rejected its admissibility according to Article 35(3)(a) and (4) ECHR.⁶² The proceedings across three instances – the family court, Court of Appeal and Federal Constitutional Court – had taken only one year and eleven months. Of the different courts, the family court took the longest to reach a decision. Here, however, the duration of the proceedings was attributed to the fact that an expert opinion had been commissioned, and that this opinion had needed to be supplemented, because of criticism by the parties.⁶³ Therefore, the ECtHR accepted the length of the proceedings.

4. SUBSTANTIVE STANDARDS

In its case law on family separation, the ECtHR also applies a variety of substantive standards, i.e. standards the public authorities have to meet in order for their actions to be compatible with the substance of the right protected under Article 8 ECHR: the right to respect for one's private and family life. Two substantive standards will be discussed below. The first is the requirement of proportionality. This requirement involves particular urgency and complexity in cases of family separation because of the multitude of stakeholders and the gravity of the potential interferences in their rights. A second substantive standard mapped out by the ECtHR, in *Tlapak* and *Wetjen*, relates to the importance of parents' religious freedom in raising their children, and its interplay with the protection of parental autonomy as part of Article 8 ECHR.

4.1. PROPORTIONALITY OF FAMILY SEPARATION

An interference in the right to respect for one's private and family life is only permissible under Article 8(2) ECHR if it is 'in accordance with the law', pursues a legitimate aim, and can be regarded as 'necessary in a democratic

---

61   Ibid., paras. 45–48.
62   *Tlapak and others v. Germany*, nos. 11308/16 and 11344/16, ECtHR 22 March 2018, para. 66.
63   Ibid.

society'. The separation of children from their parents, therefore, only complies with Article 8 ECHR if this measure is proportionate.[64]

4.1.1. The Standard of Proportionality

Separating a family and taking children into care is a very serious interference with the life of that family, and with the family members' right to respect for their family life. Such a step should, therefore, only be taken as a last resort.[65] To determine whether such a separation is necessary, a fair balance has to be struck between the children's interests and those of their parents.[66] In finding this balance, the best interests of the children have to be given particular importance, and may override the interests of their parents.[67] In principle, children should stay with their families unless their families are particularly unfit.[68] It is not enough to show that another family environment would be more beneficial to the upbringing of the child.[69] If possible, the separation should only be temporary, and the goal should be to reunite the children with their parents.[70]

---

[64] *Elsholz v. Germany*, no. 25735/94, ECtHR 13 July 2000, paras. 48–50; *K. and T. v. Finland*, no. 25702/94, ECtHR 12 July 2001, para. 154; *Neulinger and Shuruk v. Switzerland*, no. 41615/07, ECtHR 6 July 2010, para. 134; *Tlapak and others v. Germany*, nos. 11308/16 and 11344/16, ECtHR 22 March 2018, paras. 76, 92 and 97; *Wetjen and others v. Germany*, nos. 68125/14 and 72204/14, ECtHR 22 March 2018, paras. 63, 79 and 84; cf. also OLG Nürnberg, 11.06.2015, 9 UF 1430/14, juris-database, para. 70; cf. C. DRAGHICI, *The Legitimacy of Family Rights in Strasbourg Case Law: 'Living Instrument' or Extinguished Sovereignty?*, Hart, Oxford 2017, pp. 316 et seq.

[65] *Gnahoré v. France*, no. 40031/98, ECtHR 19 September 2000, para. 59; *Neulinger and Shuruk v. Switzerland*, no. 41615/07, ECtHR 6 July 2010, para. 136; *Tlapak and others v. Germany*, nos. 11308/16 and 11344/16, ECtHR 22 March 2018, para. 97; *Wetjen and others v. Germany*, nos. 68125/14 and 72204/14, ECtHR 22 March 2018, para. 84.

[66] *Elsholz v. Germany*, no. 25735/94, ECtHR 13 July 2000, para. 50; *Neulinger and Shuruk v. Switzerland*, no. 41615/07, ECtHR 6 July 2010, para. 134; *Tlapak and others v. Germany*, nos. 11308/16 and 11344/16, ECtHR 22 March 2018, para. 81; *Wetjen and others v. Germany*, nos. 68125/14 and 72204/14, ECtHR 22 March 2018, para. 68.

[67] Ibid.

[68] *Gnahoré v. France*, no. 40031/98, ECtHR 19 September 2000, para. 59; *Neulinger and Shuruk v. Switzerland*, no. 41615/07, ECtHR 6 July 2010, para. 136; *Tlapak and others v. Germany*, nos. 11308/16 and 11344/16, ECtHR 22 March 2018, para. 82; *Wetjen and others v. Germany*, nos. 68125/14 and 72204/14, ECtHR 22 March 2018, para. 69.

[69] *K. and T. v. Finland*, no. 25702/94, ECtHR 12 July 2001, para. 173; *Kutzner v. Germany*, no. 46544/99, ECtHR 26 February 2002, para. 69; *Tlapak and others v. Germany*, nos. 11308/16 and 11344/16, ECtHR 22 March 2018, para. 82; *Wetjen and others v. Germany*, nos. 68125/14 and 72204/14, ECtHR 22 March 2018, para. 69.

[70] *Gnahoré v. France*, no. 40031/98, ECtHR 19 September 2000, para. 59; *K. and T. v. Finland*, no. 25702/94, ECtHR 12 July 2001, para. 155; *Neulinger and Shuruk v. Switzerland*, no. 41615/07, ECtHR 6 July 2010, para. 136; C. DRAGHICI, *The Legitimacy*

Here, again, German family law contains a provision that mirrors this standard. Section 1666 Bürgerliches Gesetzbuch (BGB)[71] sets out the general substantive requirements for court-ordered child protection measures. These range from mandatory public support measures to the partial or complete withdrawal of parental custody, which can ultimately lead to the separation of the family. Section 1666(1) BGB institutes the requirement of proportionality for all such measures, because it only permits measures 'necessary to avert the danger' to the child.[72] Additionally, section 1666a BGB[73] supplements this general provision. It explicitly reinforces that the 'separation of the child from its parental family [is] admissible only if the danger cannot be countered in another way'. This provision was expressly introduced in order to underline the requirement of proportionality in relation to family separation, and to highlight its importance.[74]

On the procedural side, proportionality is reinforced by the above-mentioned section 157 of the Act on Proceedings in Family Matters, according to which the court should discuss, with the parents and the child, how a danger to the best interests of the child should be handled. This provision is meant to encourage cooperation from parents, in order to avoid coercive child protection measures.[75] It thus flags coercive measures, including family separation, as a step which should be taken only if absolutely necessary.

4.1.2. Margin of Appreciation

When assessing the proportionality of family separations, the ECtHR affords national authorities a wide margin of appreciation.[76] For instance, the ECtHR does not take into account whether a child protection measure

---

of Family Rights in Strasbourg Case Law: 'Living Instrument' or Extinguished Sovereignty?, Hart, Oxford 2017, p. 320.

[71] For a translation, see *Tlapak and others v. Germany*, nos. 11308/16 and 11344/16, ECtHR 22 March 2018, para. 55.
[72] Deutscher Bundestag, 27.04.1979, BT-Drs. 8/2788, 59.
[73] For a translation, see *Tlapak and others v. Germany*, nos. 11308/16 and 11344/16, ECtHR 22 March 2018, para. 56.
[74] Deutscher Bundestag, 27.04.1979, BT-Drs. 8/2788, 59–60; I. Götz, in J. Ellenberg et al., *Grüneberg – Bürgerliches Gesetzbuch mit Nebengesetzen*, 81st ed., C.H. Beck, Munich 2022, §1666a BGB, para. 1.
[75] E. Schumann, in T. Rauscher (ed), *Münchener Kommentar zum FamFG*, 3rd ed., C.H. Beck, Munich 2018, §157 FamFG, para. 1.
[76] *Elsholz v. Germany*, no. 25735/94, ECtHR 13 July 2000, paras. 48–50; *K. and T. v. Finland*, no. 25702/94, ECtHR 12 July 2001, paras. 154–55; *Neulinger and Shuruk*

different from the one instituted by the responding state might have been better suited to furthering the interests of the child. The court only examines whether the measure that was taken was proportionate.[77] Neither does it consider whether other Contracting States take a different approach and strike a different balance between the interests of the child and those of the parents. The ECtHR justifies this wide margin of appreciation with the argument that the national authorities have direct contact with all persons concerned,[78] and so are much better positioned to determine whether the welfare of a child is being endangered, and whether a specific protection measure is necessary to confront that danger.

The assumption that national authorities are better equipped to assess the situation of a family assumes, in turn, that the national authorities have granted, to all parties involved, a hearing to determine their interests. The procedural right to be involved in the proceedings ultimately justifies the wide margin of appreciation. Again, the close connection between the procedural standards set forth by the ECtHR and the substantive protection granted by Article 8 becomes apparent.

4.1.3. Proportionality in Tlapak and Wetjen

In the specific cases of *Tlapak* and *Wetjen*, the ECtHR accepted that there were 'relevant and sufficient' reasons to separate the children from their parents, and that the balance struck by the national courts did not fall outside of the margin of appreciation.[79] The national courts had conducted fair proceedings,[80] and had justified their decisions in extensive judgments. They gave detailed reasons why no alternative solution would have been available.[81] The courts had considered each child individually, and had

---

v. Switzerland, no. 41615/07, ECtHR 6 July 2010, para. 134; J. MEYER-LADEWIG and M. NETTESHEIM, in J. MEYER-LADEWIG et al. (eds), *EMRK – Europäische Menschenrechtskovention*, 4th ed., Nomos, Baden-Baden 2017, Art. 8, paras. 111–12.

[77] *Elsholz v. Germany*, no. 25735/94, ECtHR 13 July 2000, para. 48; *K. and T. v. Finland*, no. 25702/94, ECtHR 12 July 2001, para. 154.

[78] Ibid.; *Kutzner v. Germany*, no. 46544/99, ECtHR 26 February 2002, para. 65; *Tlapak and others v. Germany*, nos. 11308/16 and 11344/16, ECtHR 22 March 2018, para. 84; *Wetjen and others v. Germany*, nos. 68125/14 and 72204/14, ECtHR 22 March 2018, para. 71.

[79] *Tlapak and others v. Germany*, nos. 11308/16 and 11344/16, ECtHR 22 March 2018, para. 100; *Wetjen and others v. Germany*, nos. 68125/14 and 72204/14, ECtHR 22 March 2018, para. 86.

[80] Ibid.

[81] *Tlapak and others v. Germany*, nos. 11308/16 and 11344/16, ECtHR 22 March 2018, para. 98; *Wetjen and others v. Germany*, nos. 68125/14 and 72204/14, ECtHR 22 March 2018, para. 85.

refrained from generalisations. Specifically, the courts had assessed, for each child, based on his or her age, whether there was a real and imminent risk of corporal punishment.[82]

Even in the court hearings, the parents had defended their approach to parenting. They considered corporal punishment to be a legitimate part of child-rearing. The national courts could, therefore, assume that corporal punishment would continue. The discussion thus turned to the question of the extent to which corporal punishment could justify a family separation. Here, the ECtHR agreed with the national courts. While isolated or minor incidents of corporal punishment might not necessarily justify a family separation,[83] the systemic and continued use of such measures, as had taken place in the 'Twelve Tribes' communities, constituted a form of institutionalised violence, and crossed the relevant threshold justifying a separation.[84] Parents have no right to use measures that harm their children's health or their development.[85] The national courts pointed out that German law, in section 1631(2) BGB, declares that children have a right to a non-violent upbringing.[86] The ECtHR added that systemic corporal punishment can constitute 'inhuman or degrading treatment or punishment', as prohibited by Article 3 ECHR.[87]

In their decisions, both the national courts and the ECtHR also considered that the separation of the families created its own challenges in relation to the children's welfare.[88] These challenges were, however, outweighed by the constant threat of corporal punishment that the children

---

[82] *Tlapak and others v. Germany*, nos. 11308/16 and 11344/16, ECtHR 22 March 2018, para. 97; *Wetjen and others v. Germany*, nos. 68125/14 and 72204/14, ECtHR 22 March 2018, para. 84.

[83] Cf. D. WACHE, 'Note on ECtHR, *Wetjen and others v. Germany*, 22.03.2018', NZFam 2018, 455, 458–59.

[84] *Tlapak and others v. Germany*, nos. 11308/16 and 11344/16, ECtHR 22 March 2018, paras. 91 and 98; *Wetjen and others v. Germany*, nos. 68125/14 and 72204/14, ECtHR 22 March 2018, paras. 78 and 85.

[85] *Neulinger and Shuruk v. Switzerland*, no. 41615/07, ECtHR 6 July 2010, para. 136; *Elsholz v. Germany*, no. 25735/94, ECtHR 13 July 2000, para. 50; *Tlapak and others v. Germany*, nos. 11308/16 and 11344/16, ECtHR 22 March 2018, para. 82; *Wetjen and others v. Germany*, nos. 68125/14 and 72204/14, ECtHR 22 March 2018, para. 69.

[86] For a translation, see *Tlapak and others v. Germany*, nos. 11308/16 and 11344/16, ECtHR 22 March 2018, para. 54.

[87] Ibid., paras. 85–89; *Wetjen and others v. Germany*, nos. 68125/14 and 72204/14, ECtHR 22 March 2018, paras. 72–76.

[88] OLG Nürnberg, 11.06.2015, 9 UF 1430/14, juris-database, paras. 168 *et seq.*; *Wetjen and others v. Germany*, nos. 68125/14 and 72204/14, ECtHR 22 March 2018, paras. 69 and 75 *et seq.*; *Tlapak and others v. Germany*, nos. 11308/16 and 11344/16, ECtHR 22 March 2018, paras. 82 and 88 *et seq.*

faced in their everyday lives. Ultimately, the ECtHR, therefore, held that family separation remained within the wide margin of appreciation granted to the Contracting States. There was, therefore, no violation of Article 8 ECHR.

4.2. RELIGIOUS FREEDOM AND CHILD PROTECTION MEASURES

A second substantive standard, set out by the ECtHR in *Tlapak* and *Wetjen*, addresses the relationship of religious freedom and child protection measures. The parents in *Tlapak* and *Wetjen* had argued that their religious beliefs were the real reason why their parental rights had been withdrawn, and that they had been prevented from raising their children in accordance with their faith.[89] To prevent family separation, they would have had to abandon their parenting practices. This, they argued, would have been equivalent to abandoning their religious beliefs,[90] because they saw those parenting practices as rooted in their faith. The parents could first claim protection, of course, under Article 9 ECHR, which protects their ability to live according to their faith. Additionally, and more specifically, however, Article 2 of the First Protocol to the Convention protects the parents' right to ensure an education in conformity with their own religious convictions.

These rights of parents end, however, where children may be exposed to dangerous practices, or to physical or psychological harm.[91] Even religious practices within a family can, thus, be a reason to trigger child protection measures.[92] Yet, as the ECtHR points out, there is a clear distinction. Only genuine threats to the welfare of a child can justify child protection measures. Religious practices that do not actually threaten the welfare of a child must not be used as a pretext to interfere with the practice

---

[89] *Tlapak and others v. Germany*, nos. 11308/16 and 11344/16, ECtHR 22 March 2018, para. 64; *Wetjen and others v. Germany*, nos. 68125/14 and 72204/14, ECtHR 22 March 2018, paras. 44 and 59.

[90] *Tlapak and others v. Germany*, nos. 11308/16 and 11344/16, ECtHR 22 March 2018, para. 69.

[91] *Vojnity v. Hungary*, no. 29617/07, ECtHR 12 February 2013, para. 37; Ibid., para. 79; *Wetjen and others v. Germany*, nos. 68125/14 and 72204/14, ECtHR 22 March 2018, para. 66.

[92] D. WACHE, 'Note on ECtHR, *Wetjen and others v. Germany*, 22.03.2018', *NZFam* 2018, 455, 459.

of a particular religion. Furthermore, the threat to the welfare of the child has to be demonstrated specifically in any given case. There must not be generalised attributions based on the faith of parents.

In the specific cases of *Tlapak* and *Wetjen*, the national courts followed these guideposts. While these courts did mention the religion of the parents, the ECtHR was convinced that they had based their decisions to take the children into custody on the real likelihood of corporal punishment being inflicted on each specific child.[93] It was not the courts, but the parents, that had established the connection between their religious beliefs and the practice of caning, by justifying their parental practices with quotes from the Bible, and with their religious views.[94]

5. INFLUENCE OF NATIONAL CONSTITUTIONAL LAW

As has been demonstrated, the introduction, in sections 155b *et seq.* of the Act on Proceedings in Family Matters, of a legal remedy to pre-emptively expedite proceedings in certain parent and child matters, including family separation, shows the specific influence of the ECHR on German law. However, outside of such specific instances, general inferences about the influence of the ECHR on German family law are less clear. One reason for this is that the German Federal Constitutional Court also has a very strict jurisprudence regarding family separations.

This jurisprudence is based on Article 6 of the Basic Law. Its paragraph 1 protects marriage and family. Paragraph 2, sentence 1 establishes the care and upbringing of children as the 'natural right' of parents, and as 'a duty primarily incumbent upon them'. Paragraph 2, sentence 2, conversely, obliges the state to watch over the parents in their performance of this duty. Paragraph 3 determines that children may only be separated from their families against the will of their parents 'pursuant to a law and only if the parents or guardians fail in their duties or the children are otherwise in danger of serious neglect'.

---

[93] *Tlapak and others v. Germany*, nos. 11308/16 and 11344/16, ECtHR 22 March 2018, para. 80; *Wetjen and others v. Germany*, nos. 68125/14 and 72204/14, ECtHR 22 March 2018, para. 67; cf. OLG Nürnberg, 11.06.2015, 9 UF 1430/14, juris-database, paras. 69 *et seq.*

[94] Ibid.; cf. OLG Nürnberg, 11.06.2015, 9 UF 1430/14, juris-database, para. 7.

Based on these provisions, the Constitutional Court has established strict standards for family separations.[95] The starting point of their analysis is a distinction between child protection measures that lead to a family separation, and measures that do not lead to such a separation.[96] If there is no separation, the Court will apply only a deferential scrutiny.[97] If such a separation has taken place, however, the court will apply close scrutiny, and carefully analyse whether there has been strict compliance with the principle of proportionality.[98] Because of the gravity of a family separation, the Court even goes expressly beyond its normal focus on the outer constitutional limits of the application of family law, and also assesses errors in the application of the specific provisions of substantive family law.[99]

Regarding the proportionality of a separation, the court has highlighted that it is not enough that the child might receive a better upbringing in another family. Instead, a family separation is only permissible if remaining in the child's own family would create a substantial and lasting threat to the physical or psychological welfare of the child.[100] Similarly to the ECtHR, the Constitutional Court will review the reasoning of the decision by the family court. In particular, it requires that the threat to the child's best welfare and the proportionality of the adopted measure are both well reasoned in the judgment.[101] The reasoning has to show that the court was aware of the high constitutional threshold for family

---

[95] Cf. G. BRITZ, 'Kindesgrundrechte und Elterngrundrecht: Fremdunterbringung von Kindern in der verfassungsgerichtlichen Kontrolle', *FamRZ* 2015, 793, *passim*; S. SÖPPER, 'Note on BVerfG, 13.07.2017', *NZFam* 2017, 795, 799.

[96] Cf. BVerfG, 14.09.2021, *NZFam* 2021, 953, para. 55.

[97] BVerfG, 14.09.2021, *NZFam* 2021, 953, para. 55.

[98] BVerfG, 10.09.2009, *FamRZ* 2009, 1897, 1897; BVerfG, 20.06.2011, *FamRZ* 2012, 433, 433; BVerfG, 28.02.2012, *FamRZ* 2012, 1127, 1128; BVerfG, 07.04.2014, *FamRZ* 2014, 907, 908–09; BVerfG, 22.05.2014, *FamRZ* 2014, 1266, 1268; BVerfG, 13.07.2017, *FamRZ* 2017, 1577, 1578.

[99] BVerfG, 28.02.2012, *FamRZ* 2012, 1127, 1128; BVerfG, 07.04.2014, *FamRZ* 2014, 907, 909; BVerfG, 22.05.2014, *FamRZ* 2014, 1266, 1268; BVerfG, 13.07.2017, *FamRZ* 2017, 1577, 1579: cf. G. BRITZ, 'Kindesgrundrechte und Elterngrundrecht: Fremdunterbringung von Kindern in der verfassungsgerichtlichen Kontrolle', *FamRZ* 2015, 793, 796.

[100] BVerfG, 10.09.2009, *FamRZ* 2009, 1897, 1897; BVerfG, 07.04.2014, *FamRZ* 2014, 907, 908; BVerfG, 22.05.2014, *FamRZ* 2014, 1266, 1268; BVerfG, 13.07.2017, *FamRZ* 2017, 1577, 1578–79.

[101] BVerfG, 28.02.2012, *FamRZ* 2012, 1127, 1128–30; BVerfG, 07.04.2014, *FamRZ* 2014, 907, 908; BVerfG, 13.07.2017, *FamRZ* 2017, 1577, 1579; G. BRITZ, 'Kindesgrundrechte und Elterngrundrecht: Fremdunterbringung von Kindern in der verfassungsgerichtlichen Kontrolle', *FamRZ* 2015, 793, 796–97.

separation measures.¹⁰² Furthermore, the Constitutional Court demands a careful determination of the facts of a case,¹⁰³ and, at the same time, underlines the need for speedy proceedings in matters of family separation.¹⁰⁴ Here, again, the Constitutional Court takes an approach similar to that of the ECtHR. And, like the ECtHR, the Constitutional Court justifies the procedural standard through the influence that the lapse of time plays on the substantive protection of parental rights.¹⁰⁵

The Constitutional Court draws standards from Article 6 of the Basic Law that are similar to, and sometimes even more demanding than, those established by the ECtHR. This observation underlines the influence of fundamental rights on private law generally, but also raises uncertainty about the specific influence of the ECHR on national private law.

Where the national Constitutional Court already ensures a high level of protection for a fundamental right, there is no room for the ECtHR to exercise a noticeable influence. National measures intended to bring national family law into line with national fundamental rights often also ensure a compatibility with the ECHR, and render recourse to European human rights protection unnecessary. Conversely, if the case law of national courts is lacking in certain areas, and falls outside the margin of appreciation, the ECHR will intervene and show its specific value as a tool of minimum harmonisation. An example of this dynamic is the introduction of sections 155b and 155c of the German Act on Proceedings in Family Matters, as occurred after the ECtHR decision in *Kuppinger*.¹⁰⁶

6. CONCLUSION

The separation of children from their families constitutes a serious interference with the parents' right to respect for their family life. The ECtHR has, therefore, established clear standards for when such a

---

[102] BVerfG, 10.09.2009, *FamRZ* 2009, 1897, 1898; BVerfG, 28.02.2012, *FamRZ* 2012, 1127, 1128–29; G. BRITZ, 'Kindesgrundrechte und Elterngrundrecht: Fremdunterbringung von Kindern in der verfassungsgerichtlichen Kontrolle', *FamRZ* 2015, 793, 797.

[103] BVerfG, 10.09.2009, *FamRZ* 2009, 1897, 1898; BVerfG, 07.04.2014, *FamRZ* 2014, 907, 908; BVerfG, 25.04.2015, *FamRZ* 2015, 1093, 1094; BVerfG, 13.07.2017, *FamRZ* 2017, 1577, 1579; cf. S. SÖPPER, 'Note on BVerfG, 13.07.2017', *NZFam* 2017, 795, 799.

[104] BVerfG, 11.12.2000, *NJW* 2001, 961, 961–62.

[105] BVerfG, 06.05.1997, *FamRZ* 1997, 871, 873; BVerfG, 11.12.2000, *NJW* 2001, 961, 961–62; BVerfG, 07.04.2014, *FamRZ* 2014, 907, 909; BVerfG, 25.04.2015, *FamRZ* 2015, 1093, 1095–96.

[106] Cf. *supra* at section 3.2.

separation is justified, according to Article 8 ECHR. The standards relate to procedural and substantive considerations. The *Tlapak* and *Wetjen* cases highlight four standards in particular: on the substantive side, there is the requirement of proportionality and the importance of upholding parents' religious freedom. Regarding the procedure, the right to be involved in the proceedings, and the importance of effective and timely proceedings, are paramount. Although these standards relate to procedure, they also serve, ultimately, to ensure the substantive protection granted by Article 8 ECHR. In this sense, the jurisprudence of the ECtHR in relation to family separations is emblematic of a general approach which is also highlighted in other contributions to this volume.[107]

Overall, it has been shown that German law, in principle, fulfils the above-specified standards established by the ECtHR. Where the standards of protection in German law were previously lower, reforms of national law have promoted the compliance of such law with the ECHR. In some instances, developments have been driven more by the Federal Constitutional Court than by the ECtHR. In other instances, however, changes to national law were specifically triggered by the case law of the ECtHR, after the Federal Constitutional Court had found that German law adequately protected fundamental rights as conceived nationally. This was the case, for instance, in relation to the introduction of sections 155b and 155c of the German Act on Proceedings in Family Matters, which give parties a remedy to preventatively expedite proceedings, instead of only to ask for compensation, following proceedings that took too long.

Here, the specific influence of the ECtHR becomes apparent, not as a vanguard of a European human rights-based private law, but in bringing up the rear, and helping to ensure that no national private law falls too far below a common minimum standard.

---

[107] Cf. the chapter by M. FORNASIER, 'Harmonisation through the Back Door? The Impact of the European Convention on Human Rights on National Private Law', in this volume.

THE STATUS OF BIOLOGICAL FATHERS

An Example for the Impact of the European Convention on Human Rights on National Family Law

Anatol Dutta

1. Introduction 87
2. Biological Fathers and Legal Fatherhood 89
3. Easier Access to Legal Fatherhood for Biological Fathers
   Required? 92
4. At Least Some Parental Rights for the Biological Father? 95
5. The Impact on National Family Law 96
6. Conclusion 97

1. INTRODUCTION

The European Convention on Human Rights (ECHR or the Convention) and the European Court of Human Rights (ECtHR) have a huge impact on the development of family law within the Member States. Traces of the Strasbourg Court's case law can be found in all corners of this area of law. It is, even for interested family lawyers, who keep pace with the press releases of the Court on a regular basis, rather difficult to fully appreciate all of its family law-related decisions. These decisions often concern rather complex details of national family law; and it requires some effort to understand whether a certain decision also has influence for one's own legal system, for example when deciding – as the editor of a national family law journal – whether a decision on the family law of another Member State of the Council of Europe should be published. If it is decided that a decision should be published in the journal, this requires it to be translated and edited in order to make it digestible for the domestic audience, especially for practitioners.[1] Hence, the rich case law is not always easily accessible, and case reports are essential.[2]

As it is difficult to provide a comprehensive overview of the family law impact of the ECHR,[3] this chapter will provide a sketch of the influence of the Convention on the development (and maybe even modernisation) of one small area of national family law: the legal status of biological fathers, which is rather weak in most jurisdictions, at least in cases where there is also a social father who, at the same time, enjoys legal fatherhood, in particular as the husband of the mother. Such cases are not uncommon: they encompass scenarios where married mothers have conceived a child outside marriage, but also scenarios where the relationship between the mother and the father broke up before the child was born, and the mother has found another partner who has assumed the role of father – a social father – to the child. Cases of sperm donation also fall into this category, where the social father did not contribute his gametes, which originated instead from a (known or anonymous) donor as the biological father. The biological father is often regarded by the mother and her partner as an intruder endangering the peace of the social family.

Hence, all these cases have in common the fact that parenthood is split, because biological and social fatherhood are separate from one another as the biological and social fathers are two different persons. Split parenthood, in general, is one of the challenges faced by modern family law. The diversity of family models, the recognition of same-sex parents and, in particular, the advent of assisted reproductive technology, have increasingly led to families where more than two persons (mother and father) are biological, social or intended parents. 'Intended parents' are persons who plan procreation without being fully

---

[1] See, just as two recent examples, the publication of *Valdís Fjölnisdóttir and others v. Iceland*, no. 71552/17, ECtHR 18 May 2021, in *FamRZ* 2021, 1206, with case note by C. von Bary; and *Abdi Ibrahim v. Norway*, no. 15379/16, ECtHR 10 December 2021, in *FamRZ* 2022, 289, with case note by A. Botthof.

[2] Such as those provided for the German-speaking family law community by R. Uerpmann-Wittzack and A. Prechtl, 'Rechtsprechung des Europäischen Gerichtshofs für Menschenrechte zum Familienrecht seit Ende 2016', *FamRZ* 2020, 469, and by R. Uerpmann-Wittzack, 'Rechtsprechung des Europäischen Gerichtshofs für Menschenrechte zum Familienrecht seit 2014', *FamRZ* 2016, 1897.

[3] A fairly recent overview can be found in W. Pintens, 'Familienrecht und Rechtsvergleichung in der Rechtsprechung des Europäischen Gerichtshofes für Menschenrechte', *FamRZ* 2016, 341.

biological parents, for example the partner of the mother, in cases of a sperm donation; or the commissioning parents, in cases of surrogacy (of course, here the commissioning parents can also be genetic parents, if their cell material is used). Martin Löhnig put it quite illustratively in the title of his small monograph: *in the past parents had many children – today children have many parents*.[4] There is some truth in this aphorism, especially regarding the current discussion on legal parenthood. This is – for the non-family lawyers – the wider landscape from which one scenario has been chosen here: the merely biological father – a case of split parenthood – which has probably always existed in human history, where fathers have been social fathers despite 'their' children originating from the sperm of another man.

2. BIOLOGICAL FATHERS AND LEGAL FATHERHOOD

First, the biological father has a weak position in cases of split parenthood. In most jurisdictions, biological factors have little significance for the attribution of legal fatherhood (or legal co-motherhood, as a growing number of the Member State legal systems – Belgium, Spain, Austria, England and Wales, and the Netherlands – have opened up the second parent position to a co-mother who is determined by similar criteria as a legal father). Legal fatherhood (and, if recognised, legal co-motherhood) is based on marriage with the mother. The spouse of the mother (motherhood is mainly determined by biological factors, the giving birth of the child, see, for example, §1591 of the German Bürgerliche Gesetzbuch (BGB)) is the legal father or legal co-mother of the child. In some legal systems, such as that of Germany (as per §1592 No. 1 of the BGB), the legal fatherhood of the mother's husband is established *ex lege*. In other jurisdictions, such as Italy, the fatherhood of the husband is the legal presumption which has to be established by certification in the civil status registers (see Articles 231 and 236 of the Italian Codice civile).

Legal fatherhood (or legal co-motherhood) can, however, also be created voluntarily through the mother and the father (or co-mother) exercising private autonomy: parenthood by recognition is widely accepted, based on

---

[4] M Löhnig, *Früher hatten Eltern viele Kinder – heute haben Kinder viele Eltern – Zum Wandel des Familienbildes unserer Rechtsordnung*, Nomos, Baden-Baden 2015.

a declaration of the second parent with consent of the mother (see §§1592 No. 2, 1594 *et seq.* of the BGB, or Articles 250 *et seq.* of the Codice civile). The biological truth of the declaration is, in most jurisdictions, irrelevant for establishing the legal parenthood of the recognising person in the first place. Under German law, only if the recognition of fatherhood was made vexatiously – for example, in order to establish, through legal fatherhood, an immigration status, or German nationality – might the biological truth of the recognition be a legal issue. The BGB, in §1597a (5), clarifies that a recognition of fatherhood cannot be abusive if the recognised person is the biological father of the child. Hence, merely social fatherhood does not suffice as a basis for legal fatherhood, in this context.

Only in the absence of a legal father (or co-mother), based on marriage or recognition, can legal fatherhood be established by a court decision based solely on biological factors. §§1592 No. 3, 1600d of the BGB, and Article 269 of the Codice civile, enable courts to confer legal fatherhood on the person who is the biological father of the child.

Hence, apart from this last scenario, biological fatherhood and legal parenthood may be separate from one another. Furthermore, the access of the biological father to the initial attribution of legal fatherhood is mainly controlled autonomously by the mother (and her partner, as the potential legal father or co-mother), who can establish the legal parenthood (or co-motherhood) of her partner through marriage or recognition. Insofar as the mother's decision is not subject to any judicial control, neither biological factors nor the best interests of the child play any role in the attribution of fatherhood.

However, biological factors are not only irrelevant for the initial attribution of fatherhood at the time of the child's birth. Later in the child's life, the biological father also has limited access to legal fatherhood where this would be against the intentions of the mother and her partner. The second parent position besides the mother is restricted, in almost all legal systems, to one person: the father (or the co-mother). Hence, establishing legal fatherhood requires the biological father first to challenge the legal fatherhood (or co-motherhood) based on marriage or recognition. Most jurisdictions provide mechanisms to challenge such legal fatherhood (or co-motherhood) through court proceedings. However, the right of the biological father to challenge the legal fatherhood (or co-motherhood) is often limited, if it exists at all: in Germany, this right of the biological father was introduced only after a decision of the Bundesverfassungsgericht (the German Federal Constitutional Court), which, in 2003, held that the Grundgesetz (the German constitution), *in concreto* the protection of parental rights, according to its Article 6(2), requires a procedure to establish legal fatherhood against the intentions of the mother.[5] Some legal systems still exclude any right for the biological father to challenge such legal fatherhood, for example in Hungary,[6] and in the Netherlands.[7] In Italy, the biological father, at a minimum, cannot challenge the fatherhood of the mother's husband (see Article 243-bis of the Codice civile). Some systems do not limit the right to challenge the fatherhood at all, for example Norway[8] or Romania.[9]

What are the hurdles that the biological father needs to overcome in order to successfully challenge the legal parenthood of the father, or the co-mother, in order to establish his own legal fatherhood?

Under German law, only 'natural' biological fathers have the right to challenge a legal fatherhood through court proceedings. The right to challenge fatherhood is restricted, by §1600 (1) No. 2 of the BGB, to the *'Mann, der an Eides statt versichert, der Mutter des Kindes während der Empfängniszeit beigewohnt zu haben'*. The potential biological father has to affirm, in a formal affidavit, that he has *'beigewohnt'* the mother during the period of conception. The verb *'beiwohnen'* is rather strange; even German native speakers will not understand this term, although it is the traditional word for having sexual intercourse. Hence, the merely biological father has to affirm that he had sexual intercourse with the mother, in order to challenge the legal fatherhood, for example, of the mother's husband. The German Bundesgerichtshof has, however, taken a rather liberal view towards the concept of *'beiwohnen'*. The Court of Justice has held that, except in cases of anonymous sperm donation, self-insemination with sperm acquired privately, with the consent of the sperm donor, can be qualified as *'beiwohnen'*.[10] Hence, biological fathers who have privately donated their sperm to the mother (and her partner) are qualified to challenge the legal fatherhood of the partner.

Furthermore, there are time limits for exercising the right to challenge the parenthood of another person who is not the biological father. Under German law, the biological father has to start such proceedings within

---

5	BVerfG 9 April 2003 – 1 BvR 1493/96 and 1724/01, *FamRZ* 2003, 816; the German legislator reacted by means of the Gesetz zur Änderung der Vorschriften über die Anfechtung der Vaterschaft of 23 April 2004, *BGBl.* 2004 I p. 598, which changed §1600 (1) No. 2 and (2) of the Bürgerliche Gesetzbuch.
6	See §4:109 of the Hungarian Polgári Törvénykönyv.
7	See Articles 1:200, 1:205 of the Dutch Burgerlijk Wetboek.
8	See §6 of the Norwegian Lov om barn og foreldre.
9	See Article 421 of the Romanian Codul civil.
10	BGH 15 May 2013 – XII ZR 49/11, *FamRZ* 2013, 1209, 1210.

two years after he obtains knowledge of the facts which speak against the fatherhood being challenged (§1600b (1) of the BGB).

Finally, and foremost, German law protects legal fatherhood if it coincides with social fatherhood; according to §1600 (2) of the BGB, the biological father cannot challenge the legal fatherhood if the legal father is, at the same time, the social father. The law excludes his right to challenge legal fatherhood if there is a social and family relationship – a *'sozial-familiäre Beziehung'* – between the legal father and the child, which is assumed, inter alia, if the mother and the legal father are married to one another (see §1600 (3) of the BGB). As it is mainly the mother and her partner who decide whether such a *'sozial-familiäre Beziehung'* exists, and whether it is only to be presumed due to marriage, once again legal fatherhood, or the continuation thereof, is mainly controlled by the mother and her partner. This fact is in slight contradiction to the policy decisions reflected in adoption law, where, in most jurisdictions, the biological parents can only be deprived of their legal parenthood if they agree to the adoption, and if the legal parenthood of the adopting person serves the best interest of the child.[11] Furthermore, it is rather arbitrary that the social and family relationship between the legal father and the child at the point in time when the right to challenge the fatherhood is exercised is decisive; if that relationship later ceases, the right to challenge the fatherhood might be time-barred (cf. §1600b (1) of the BGB).

3. EASIER ACCESS TO LEGAL FATHERHOOD FOR BIOLOGICAL FATHERS REQUIRED?

What is the position of the ECHR on this weak status of biological (but non-social) fathers? Should they have easier access to legal fatherhood in the event that another man is the social father of the child?

In a number of decisions in cases from Germany and Bulgaria, the Strasbourg Court has stressed that Article 8 of the Convention also protects the merely biological father; the protection of the biological father's private life is affected if national family law restricts his access to the legal parenthood of a child, even if he has no social and family relationship with

---

[11] T. HELMS, *Rechtliche, biologische und soziale Elternschaft – Herausforderungen durch neue Familienformen, Gutachten F zum 71. Deutscher Juristentag*, CH Beck, Munich 2016, p. 44 *et seq.*; see also D. COESTER-WALTJEN, 'Statusrechtliche Folgen der Stärkung der Rechte der nichtehelichen Väter', *FamRZ* 2013, 1693, 1698.

the child.[12] The cases decided by the ECtHR, to date, have all been quite similar: in *Ahrens v. Germany*, for example, the applicant was the biological father of the child. At the time the child was conceived, the mother lived in a relationship with another man, who recognised, with the consent of the mother, his legal fatherhood of the child. The mother and her partner lived with the child in a social family. As a consequence, under German law the applicant could not challenge the legal fatherhood, although he declared that he was in an intimate relationship with the mother at the time of conception. Although the German courts were provided with the results of a blood test which showed that the applicant was the biological father, they came to the conclusion that the applicant was not in a position to challenge the legal fatherhood, because there was a social and family relationship between the legal father and the child, and, as already shown, under German law the right of the putative biological father to challenge legal fatherhood is precluded by such a relationship.

Although the biological father is protected under Article 8(1) of the Convention, a restriction of his access to fatherhood can be 'necessary in a democratic society', according to Article 8(2) of the Convention, and therefore justified. At least in principle, according to the Strasbourg Court, the Council of Europe Member States can protect the 'enduring social family unit'[13] between the mother, child and legal father (and probably also a legal co-mother) against the interests of the biological father. Ultimately, the ECtHR has avoided giving a clear answer on how this conflict has to be solved in general, because there is no consensus within the Member States as to the status of the biological father in the event of the social fatherhood of another man. The Court instead requires a balancing of the interests (notably those of the child) in each individual case.[14] Hence, the protection afforded by Article 8(1) of the Convention is more procedural in nature. A denial of legal parenthood to a biological father can be justified if all interests have been duly considered. Against this background, the Court

---

12   See, e.g. *Ahrens v. Germany*, no. 45071/09, ECtHR 22 March 2012, §60; *Kautzor v. Germany*, no. 23338/09, ECtHR 22 March 2012, §62; *Adebowale v. Germany*, no. 546/10, ECtHR 2 December 2014, §21; *L.D. and P.K. v. Bulgaria*, nos. 7949/11 and 45522/13, ECtHR 8 December 2016, §56; *Koychev v. Bulgaria*, no. 32495/15, ECtHR 13 October 2020, §44; see also *Koppikar v. Germany*, no. 11858/10, ECtHR 11 December 2012.

13   *Ahrens v. Germany*, no. 45071/09, ECtHR 22 March 2012, §77.

14   See *Ahrens v. Germany*, no. 45071/09, ECtHR 22 March 2012, §§63 *et seq.*; *Kautzor v. Germany*, no. 23338/09, ECtHR 22 March 2012, §§65 *et seq.*; *Adebowale v. Germany*, no. 546/10, ECtHR 2 December 2014, §§24 *et seq.*; *Markgraf v. Germany*, no. 42719/14, ECtHR 10 March 2015, §§23 *et seq.*; *L.D. and P.K. v. Bulgaria*, nos. 7949/11 and 45522/13, ECtHR 8 December 2016, §§63 *et seq.*; *Koychev v. Bulgaria*, no. 32495/15, ECtHR 13 October 2020, §§56 *et seq.*

has held that the German courts, at least, have balanced these interests within their margin of discretion.[15] In the Bulgarian cases, the Court held that denying the biological father a right to challenge the legal fatherhood of another man violated Article 8 of the Convention, but did not ultimately decide the case, because the Bulgarian courts had not established the necessary facts.[16] Hence, some of the strict limits of the biological father's right to challenge legal fatherhood can only justified with difficulty. For example, as has already been seen, the best interest of the child is irrelevant under German law, in this context, and the focus lies only on the existence of a social and family relationship between the legal father and the child. The doubts over whether the restrictions on a biological father's ability to challenge the legal parenthood of another man are in line with Article 8 of the Convention have led to a discussion over the reform of German family law,[17] but the legislator has not, so far, taken any action.

The national legislators could, indeed, be much more generous in granting access to legal parenthood to the merely biological father, as has also been stressed by the Strasbourg Court. In *Mandet v. France*,[18] the Court confirmed that even a challenge to the legal father's position without a time limit or any further conditions – as was available under the (old) French law, in relation to the recognition of fatherhood – was not a violation of the family or private life of the merely social father, the child and the mother. In this French case, a child had been born shortly after the mother's divorce. Her former husband recognised his fatherhood of the child, thus establishing legal parenthood. The legal parents remarried (with different partners) a couple of years later. Nevertheless, another man applied to the French courts challenging the recognition of fatherhood made by the legal father, the former husband of the mother, and seeking to have his own fatherhood established. In the end, the French courts set aside the recognition of fatherhood and held that the other man was the father of the child. The mother, her husband and the child were all of the opinion that their right to family life, according to Article 8 of the Convention, had been violated.

---

[15] *Ahrens v. Germany*, no. 45071/09, ECtHR 22 March 2012, §79; *Kautzor v. Germany*, no. 23338/09, ECtHR 22 March 2012, §82; *Adebowale v. Germany*, no. 546/10, ECtHR 2 December 2014, §25; cf. also *Koppikar v. Germany*, no. 11858/10, ECtHR 11 December 2012; *Hülsmann v. Germany*, no. 33375/03, ECtHR 18 March 2008.

[16] *L.D. and P.K. v. Bulgaria*, nos. 7949/11 and 45522/13, ECtHR 8 December 2016, §75; *Koychev v. Bulgaria*, no. 32495/15, ECtHR 13 October 2020, §67.

[17] See, e.g. the conclusions of R. Frank, 'Art. 8 EMRK und die Anfechtung wahrheitswidriger Vaterschaftsanerkennungen durch den biologischen Vater (§1600 Abs. 2 BGB)', *FamRZ* 2021, 1081, 1084 *et seq.*

[18] *Mandet v. France*, no. 30955/12, ECtHR 14 January 2016.

This argument was rejected by the ECtHR: the interests, especially those of the child, had been duly considered by the French courts. In particular, the social and family life between the mother, her husband and the child was not affected by vesting legal fatherhood in the biological father.[19]

4. AT LEAST SOME PARENTAL RIGHTS FOR THE BIOLOGICAL FATHER?

Apart from the question whether the biological father has a human right to better access to legal fatherhood (in particular, by reducing the restrictions on his right to challenge the legal fatherhood of the mother's partner), there is also a second issue where the ECtHR has strengthened the position of biological fathers: should biological, but non-legal, fathers have at least some parental rights?

In *Anayo v. Germany*[20] and *Schneider v. Germany*,[21] the Strasbourg Court clarified that Article 8 ECHR can be violated if the biological father has no parental rights at all.[22] The facts of these cases, especially those of *Anayo v. Germany*, were rather remarkable. The applicant in *Anayo*, a Nigerian national, had been in a relationship with a married woman, who already had three children with her husband. Four months after the end of this extramarital relationship, the woman gave birth to twins, the applicant being the biological father. The mother brought the twins up, together with her husband, who was their legal father under German law, based on his marriage to the mother. Neither legal parent allowed the applicant to have any contact with the twins. The German courts decided that the applicant was not entitled to access under the relevant provisions of German law. On the one hand, the applicant was not a legal parent to the children, which alone could be a basis for access rights under §1684 of the BGB. On the other hand, he had, thus far, not borne any responsibility for the children, and thus had no social and family relationship with them. Therefore, the applicant did not fulfil the requirements necessary for a third person other than the legal parents (with whom the children had close ties) to be entitled to access to the children, according to §1685 (2) of the BGB.

---

[19] Ibid., §§57 *et seq.*
[20] *Anayo v. Germany*, no. 20578/07, ECtHR 21 December 2010.
[21] *Schneider v. Germany*, no. 17080/07, ECtHR 15 September 2011.
[22] See also *Koppikar v. Germany*, no. 11858/10, ECtHR 11 December 2012; *Hülsmann v. Germany*, no. 33375/03, ECtHR 18 March 2008; *Adebowale v. Germany*, no. 546/10, ECtHR 2 December 2014, §23.

The ECtHR, on the other hand, stressed that Article 8 of the Convention also protects an intended family life between a biological father and his children. Accordingly, Article 8 ECHR would be violated if all access rights were denied to the biological father, without considering the best interest of the children.

5. THE IMPACT ON NATIONAL FAMILY LAW

Anayo v. Germany and *Schneider v. Germany* had a considerable impact on German family law. The German legislator reacted by introducing a new provision: §1686a of the BGB, which grants access rights to a biological father: (1) who has shown serious interest in the child; and (2) if the access serves the best interest of the child. This new concept introduced an element of multiparentality into German law, as it allows more than two persons to be equipped with parental rights. The new §1686a of the BGB was criticised for introducing a 'fatherhood-lite': parental rights for the biological father without corresponding duties, an idea which is alien to the current German child law system.[23] However, the case law of the ECtHR and the new §1686a of the BGB have triggered a new academic discussion on multiparentality in German family law.[24]

Of course, the new access right for biological, but non-legal, fathers gives rise to many new and difficult questions: for example, how should the best interest of the child be assessed when deciding on the

---

[23] L.M. PESCHEL-GUTZEIT, 'Der doppelte Vater – Kritische Überlegungen zum Gesetz zur Stärkung der Rechte des leiblichen, nicht rechtlichen Vaters', *NJW* 2013, 2465.

[24] See, e.g. B. HEIDERHOFF, 'Kann ein Kind mehrere Väter haben?', *FamRZ* 2008, 1901, 1904 *et seq.*; B. HEIDERHOFF, 'Herausforderungen durch neue Familienformen – Zeit für ein Umdenken', *NJW* 2016, 2629, 2631 *et seq.*; M. COESTER, 'Reformen im Kindschaftsrecht', *Brühler Schriften zum Familienrecht* 18 (2014), 43, 51 *et seq.*; I. PLETTENBERG, *Vater, Vater, Mutter, Kind – Ein Plädoyer für die rechtliche Mehrelternschaft*, Mohr Siebeck, Tübingen 2016; T. HELMS, 'Wieviele Eltern verträgt ein Kind? Mehrelternfamilien aus rechtlicher Sicht'; A. RÖTHEL, 'Wieviele Eltern verträgt ein Kind? Konzepte für originäre Mehr-Elternschaft'; and S. WALPER, 'Wieviele Eltern verträgt ein Kind? Mehrelternfamilien aus sozialwissenschaftlicher Sicht', all in K. LUGANI and P.M. HUBER (eds), *Moderne Familienformen – Symposium zum 75. Geburtstag von Michael Coester*, De Gruyter, Berlin 2018, pp. 125 *et seq.*; pp. 129 *et seq.*; pp. 143 *et seq.*; A. SANDERS, *Mehrelternschaft*, Mohr Siebeck, Tübingen 2018. See also J. SCHERPE, 'Breaking the existing paradigms of parent-child relationships' in G. DOUGLAS, M. MURCH and V. STEPHENS (eds), *International and National Perspectives on Child and Family Law: Essays in Honour of Nigel Lowe*, Intersentia, Cambridge 2018, pp. 343 *et seq.*; I. BOONE, 'Co-parenting before conception – The Low Countries' approach to intentional multi-parent families', *Family & Law*, February 2018.

access rights of the biological father, based on §1686a of the BGB? In a spectacular follow-up decision to *Anayo v. Germany*, the German Bundesgerichtshof came to the conclusion that the court can only assess the best interests of children regarding access for their biological father if the children – in this case, the twins – know that their legal father is not their biological father.[25] The Court of Justice held that parental truth ousts the parental responsibility of the legal parents, and that, in a worst-case scenario, the court itself would have to inform the children about their true biological fatherhood. Does §1686a of the BGB apply to other cases of multiparentality as well? The Bundesgerichtshof recently confirmed that private sperm donors in co-motherhood cases can also claim access rights, even they have agreed to the child being adopted.[26] Why should §1686a of the BGB only give access rights to biological, but non-legal fathers, and why not also to biological, but non-legal mothers? A split parentage can also arise on the maternal side: in surrogacy cases, if the applicable law allocates legal parentage to the intended mother, i.e. the commissioning mother. However, this is rather rare, at least in Europe. Some German literature claims that the surrogate mother, as the biological mother, also has access rights, based on §1686a of the BGB, applied by analogy.[27] Finally, should intended parents who are not legal parents also be able to claim access? §1686a of the BGB is silent on this point, but the ECtHR has also stressed the rights of intended parents.[28]

6. CONCLUSION

The small sketch has shown that the case law of the ECtHR has contributed to the discussion on split parenthood in national family law. Apart from granting access rights to biological and non-legal parents, however, the jurisprudence has not yet triggered legislative reforms, because the Strasbourg Court has restricted itself to clarifying the guidelines, and not deciding on the abstract rules in the Member States. Hence, the role of the ECHR in this field is more that of a catalyst fuelling the general and necessary discussion on how family law should deal with split parenthood, where the biological, social and intended parents of a child are different persons.

---

[25] BGH 5 October 2016 – XII ZB 280/15, *FamRZ* 2016, 2082.
[26] BGH 16 June 2021 – XII ZB 58/20, *FamRZ* 2021, 1375.
[27] M. LÖHNIG, 'Die leibliche, nicht rechtliche Mutter', *FamRZ* 2015, 806.
[28] *Honner v. France*, no. 19511/16, ECtHR 12 November 2020.

SHAPING NEW FAMILIES

Same-Sex Couples' Rights in the Dialogue between the Courts

Maria Gabriella STANZIONE

1. The Role of the ECtHR in the Recognition of Same-Sex Couples' Right to Family Life 99
2. Legal Recognition of Same-Sex Couples in Europe: The Comparatist's Laboratory. 105
3. Some Conclusions. 113

1. THE ROLE OF THE ECtHR IN THE RECOGNITION OF SAME-SEX COUPLES' RIGHT TO FAMILY LIFE

In the current cultural scenario, a wide-ranging debate has developed regarding the legal recognition of same-sex couples. This topic is crucial not only for the rights and principles at stake, which range from self-determination, equality and human dignity, to personal identity and family life, but also since it can be an effective tool for the comparatist who is attempting to assess the velocity of interaction – to use the words of Constantinesco[1] – between society and the law, the relationship between the social transformations, and the reactions of the legal system, whether necessary or solicited.[2]

---

[1] This reference is to his renowned essay on comparative law: L.J. CONSTANTINESCO, *Traité de droit comparé, t. II, La méthode comparative*, Librairie générale de droit et de jurisprudence, Paris 1974.

[2] See I. CURRY-SUMNER, 'Same-Sex Relationships in a European Perspective' in J.M. SCHERPE (ed), *European Family Law*, vol. III, Edward Elgar Publishing, Cheltenham 2016, pp. 116–45; J. MILES, 'Unmarried Cohabitation in a European Perspective', ibid., pp. 82–115; K. BOELE-WOELKI and A. FUCHS (eds), *Legal Recognition of Same-Sex Relationships in Europe: National, Cross-border and European Perspectives*, 3rd ed., Intersentia, Cambridge 2017.

The possible protection is grounded in a twofold foundation: on the one hand, a stable life-sharing communion can arise between same-sex persons based on the existence of a relationship grounded in affection, assistance and solidarity, identical to that between persons of a different sex and, therefore, likely to pose problems similar to those commonly faced by opposite-sex partners. On the other hand, the failure to protect these relationships results in unlawful discrimination based on sexual orientation, which is expressly prohibited, not only by national constitutions, but also by Article 21 of the Charter of Fundamental Rights of the European Union.

In this respect, national and supranational courts have played, and still play, a pivotal role in the removal of various forms of discrimination against same-sex couples, in order to recognise specific legal situations, in particular in those jurisdictions which lack a regulation, but also in those where situations of inequality based on sexual orientation still persist, despite the existence of a legislative solution – or, in some cases, because of it.

The judgments of the European Court of Human Rights (ECtHR) push hard in this direction by upholding an evolutive interpretation of the notions of family life, protection of privacy, and so on, as well as by enhancing the principle of non-discrimination pursuant to Articles 14 and 8 of the European Convention on Human Rights (ECHR). The path that has led to such interpretation has been gradual, and starts from the landmark decision *Marckx v. Belgium*,[3] in which the Strasbourg Court showed the ability to stimulate and guide the profound transformations which went on to shape family law over recent decades, on the basis of the principles of equality, democracy and non-discrimination.[4]

The key concept is that of family life, recognised and protected, of itself, simply because of its existence, regardless of whether or not it has been formalised. Hence, there is a 'family' where there is a relationship between partners, or between parents and children, which is considered worthy of protection. From this perspective, non-marital families fall under the remit of legal protection: opposite-sex and same-sex families; single-, double- or multi-parent families; and families where a child's relationship with a stepparent assumes relevance, regardless of the lack of existence

---

[3] *Marckx v. Belgium*, no. 6833/74, ECtHR 13 June 1979.
[4] Among others, see M.-T. MEULDERS-KLEIN, 'Internationalisation des droits de l'Homme et évolution du droit de la famille: un voyage sans destination?' in F. DEKEUWER-DÉFOSSEZ (ed), *Internationalisation des droits de l'Homme et évolution du droit de la famille*, Actes du Colloque du Laboratoire d'études et de recherches appliquées au droit privé, Université Lille II, L.G.D.J., 1996, pp. 180–213.

of a blood bond, but grounded instead on an emotional–educational relationship to be preserved in the interest of the child.[5]

This complex and controversial process of change found a significant point of arrival in the European Charter, with a clear discontinuity from the ECHR. Overturning the previous order, Article 9 of the Charter establishes, indeed, that 'the right to marry and the right to found a family shall be guaranteed in accordance with the national laws governing the exercise of these rights'. The distinction between the 'right to marry' and the right 'to found a family' is not arbitrary, but was consciously introduced for the purpose of fully recognising 'non-traditional families'.

Moreover, comparison of this provision with the literal content of Article 12 ECHR reveals another substantial difference. The latter provision states that 'men and women of marriageable age have the right to marry and to found a family, according to the national laws governing the exercise of this right'. On the one hand, there is a reference to 'men and women', which disappears in the Charter; and, on the other, while the Convention recognises only one right 'to marry and found a family' – as though it were a hendiadys – the Charter, enacted 50 years later, mentions two distinct and independent rights: the right to marry and the right to found a family.[6]

The traditional construction of the family has been shaken to its foundations: there no longer exists an acknowledged model, with traditional heterosexual marriage recognised by law, and an exception – civil partnerships – accessible to same-sex couples.

From this perspective, the Charter, and the evolutive interpretation of Article 12 ECHR upheld by the Strasbourg Court, mirror the deep social and cultural changes which have unfolded over recent decades.

---

[5] For a comprehensive analysis on this matter, see M.G. STANZIONE, *Filiazione e genitorialità. Il problema del terzo genitore*, Giappichelli, Torino 2010.

[6] In another seminal decision, *Goodwin v. United Kingdom*, the ECtHR found no justification for excluding a transgender person from enjoying the right to marry under any circumstances, despite there not being any European consensus on the matter, considering that the terms used by Article 12 ECHR, which referred to the right of a man and woman to marry, no longer had to be understood as determining gender by purely biological criteria. In that context, the Court noted that there had been major social changes in the institution of marriage since the adoption of the Convention. Furthermore, it referred to Article 9 of the Charter, which departed from the wording of Article 12 ECHR. Finally, the Court noted that there was widespread acceptance of the marriage of transsexuals in their assigned gender. In conclusion, the Court found that the impossibility of a post-operative transsexual marrying in her assigned gender violated Article 12 ECHR. See *Goodwin v. United Kingdom*, no. 28957/95, ECtHR 11 July 2002.

In just over 30 years, in fact, an increasing number of legal systems have begun to allow marriage for same-sex couples, or have recognised a form of registered partnership or de facto relationship.[7] Nevertheless, it is important to take into account the diversity of the contexts, to avoid the risk of limiting the analysis to one dimension alone, since even in Europe, particularly in Eastern and South-Eastern Europe, there are still jurisdictions where there is no legal recognition of same-sex relationships, or where homosexuality continues to be stigmatised, or even punished as a crime.[8]

In this respect, from its very first decisions on the matter, the ECtHR has taken a strict position on the issue of discrimination on grounds of sexual orientation, requiring 'particularly serious reasons' to justify differential treatment based on sexual orientation.[9]

---

[7] As of June 2021, 16 Contracting States to the Convention legally recognise and perform same-sex marriages: Austria, Belgium, Denmark, Finland, France, Germany, Iceland, Ireland, Luxembourg, Malta, Netherlands, Norway, Portugal, Spain, Sweden and the United Kingdom. Additionally, 14 Contracting States legally recognise some form of civil union for same-sex couples: Andorra, Croatia, Cyprus, the Czech Republic, Estonia, Greece, Hungary, Italy, Liechtenstein, Monaco, Montenegro (the relevant legislation entered in force in July 2021), San Marino, Slovenia and Switzerland.

[8] See S. KRALJIĆ, 'Same-Sex Partnerships in Eastern Europe: Marriage, Registration or No Regulation?' in K. BOELE-WOELKI and A. FUCHS (eds), *Legal Recognition of Same-Sex Relationships in Europe: National, Cross-border and European Perspectives*, 3rd ed., Intersentia, Cambridge 2017, pp. 55–76. See also the recent decision *Fedotova and Others v. Russia*, no. 40792/10, ECtHR 2021. In this case, the applicants were three same-sex couples whose intention to marry notices had been rejected by the Russian authorities. The applicants complained that there had been a violation of Article 8 alone, and Article 14 in conjunction with Article 8 of the ECHR, as due to their sexual orientation, they 'had no means of securing a legal basis for their relationship as [it] was impossible for them to enter into marriage'. Moreover, they 'had no other possibility to gain formal acknowledgment for their relationship'. The judges confirmed the general principles, from *Schalk and Kopf* and *Vallianatos*, that same-sex couples 'are in a relevantly similar situation to a different-sex couple as regards their need for formal acknowledgment and protection of their relationship', holding that 'as regards same-sex couples, the Court has already held that they are just as capable as different-sex couples of entering into committed relationships. They are in a relevantly similar situation to a different-sex couple as regards their need for formal acknowledgment and protection of their relationship.' Eventually, the Court held that the refusal to recognise same-sex couples 'creates a conflict between the social reality of the applicants who live in committed relationships based on mutual affection, and the law, which fails to protect the most regular of "needs" arising in the context of a same-sex couple. That conflict can result in serious daily obstacles for same-sex couples.'

[9] For a comprehensive analysis on the matter, see J. SCHERPE, 'Legal Recognition of Same-Sex Couples in Europe and the Role of the European Court of Human Rights' (2013) 10 *The Equal Rights Review* 83–96.

The enhancement of the non-discrimination principle is the solution chosen by the ECtHR to answer the claim for legal recognition of same-sex relationships, in particular by recognising, for the first time, in the historic *Schalk and Kopf v. Austria* decision, that same-sex couples enjoy the right to respect for family life.[10] Thus, the Court has overturned its previous case law, which merely recognised same-sex couples' right to respect for private life, stating that it encompassed the right to establish and develop relationships with other persons. Indeed, in *Mata Estevez v. Spain*, the ECtHR, on the one hand, acknowledged that 'the applicant's emotional and sexual relationship related to his private life within the meaning of Art. 8 §1 of the Convention',[11] but, on the other hand, held that:

> as regards establishing whether the decision in question concerns the sphere of 'family life' within the meaning of Article 8 §1 of the Convention, the Court reiterates that, according to the established case-law of the Convention institutions, long-term homosexual relationships between two men do not fall within the scope of the right to respect for family life protected by Article 8 of the Convention ... The Court considers that, despite the growing tendency in a number of European States towards the legal and judicial recognition of stable de facto partnerships between homosexuals, this is, given the existence of little common ground between the contracting States, an area in which they still enjoy a wide margin of appreciation.

A decade later, the Court expressed its *revirement* on this question in *Schalk and Kopf v. Austria*, in which the applicants' complaints concerned the discrimination arising from their being denied the opportunity to marry, or to have their relationship otherwise recognised by the legal system:

> The Court notes that since 2001, when the decision in *Mata Estevez* was given, a rapid evolution of social attitudes towards same-sex couples has taken place in many member States. Since then, a considerable number of member States have afforded legal recognition to same-sex couples ... Certain provisions of European Union law also reflect a growing tendency to include same-sex couples in the notion of 'family'. In view of this evolution, the Court considers it artificial to maintain the view that, in contrast to a different-sex couple, a same-sex couple cannot enjoy 'family life' for the purposes of Article 8. Consequently, the relationship of the applicants, a cohabiting same-sex couple living in a stable *de facto* partnership, falls within the notion of 'family life',

---

[10] *Schalck and Kopf v. Austria*, no. 30141/04, ECtHR 24 June 2010.
[11] See *Mata Estevez v. Spain*, no. 56501/00, ECtHR 10 May 2001.

just as the relationship of a different-sex couple in the same situation would. The Court therefore concludes that the facts of the present case fall within the notion of 'private life' as well as 'family life' within the meaning of Article 8. Consequently, Article 14 taken in conjunction with Article 8 of the Convention applies.

Here, the ECtHR utilised the tools of the European consensus, and of the margin of appreciation, in a twofold manner.[12] The Court had to determine whether the Austrian legislator should have provided the applicants with an alternative means of legal recognition for their partnership. Having noted the rapidly developing European consensus which had emerged over the previous decade, but that there was not yet a majority of states providing for legal recognition of same-sex couples, the Court considered the area in question to be one of evolving rights, with no established consensus, where states enjoyed a margin of appreciation in the timing of the introduction of legislative changes. Thus, the Court concluded that, though the Austrian legislator had not been in the vanguard, they could not be reproached for not having introduced the Registered Partnership Act any earlier than 2010.

---

[12] On the debated question of the relationship between the doctrine of the margin of appreciation and the European consensus, see E. BENVENISTI, 'Margin of Appreciation, Consensus, and Universal Standards' (1999) 31 *Journal of International Law and Politics* 843–54; E. BREMS, *Human Rights: Universality and Diversity*, Martinus Nijhoff Publishers, The Hague/Boston/London 2001; K. DZEHTSIAROU, *European Consensus and the Legitimacy of the European Court of Human Rights*, CUP, Cambridge 2015, pp. 132 *et seq.*; J. GERARDS, 'Pluralism, Deference and the Margin of Appreciation Doctrine' (2011) 17 *European Law Journal* 80–120; G. REPETTO, *Argomenti comparativi e diritti fondamentali in Europa. Teorie dell'interpretazione e giurisprudenza sovranazionale*, Jovene, Napoli 2011; P. KAPOTAS and V. TZEVELEKOS, *Building Consensus on European Consensus: Judicial Interpretation of Human Rights in Europe and Beyond*, CUP, Cambridge 2019; E. KASTANAS, *Unité et Diversité: Notions Autonomes et Marge d'Appréciation des États dans la Jurisprudence de la Cour Européenne des Droits de L'Homme*, coll. 'Organisation internationale et relations internationals', Bruylant, Bruxelles 1996; G. LETSAS, 'Two Concepts of the Margin of Appreciation' (2006) 26 *Oxford Journal of Legal Studies* 705–32; D. PEAT, *Comparative Reasoning in International Courts and Tribunals*, CUP, Cambridge 2019, pp. 140–77; E. POLGARI, 'European Consensus: A Conservative and a Dynamic Force in European Human Rights Jurisprudence' (2017) 12 *ICL Journal* 59–84; N. VOGIATZIS, 'The Relationship Between European Consensus, the Margin of Appreciation and the Legitimacy of the Strasbourg Court' (2019) 25 *European Public Law* 445–80. See also E. BRIBOSIA, I. RORIVE and L. VAN DEN EYNDE, 'Same-Sex Marriage: Building an Argument before the European Court of Human Rights in Light of the US Experience' (2014) 32 *Berkeley Journal of International Law* 1–43; L. HODSON, 'A Marriage by Any Other Name? *Schalk and Kopf v Austria*' (2011) 11 *Human Rights Law Review* 170–79, 177.

On the other hand, the argument of 'little common ground' between the Contracting States, concerning access to marriage, was the way chosen by the judges to justify the refusal to recognise the existence of an obligation to grant same-sex couples the right to marry.[13] In particular, the Court observed that 'marriage has deep-rooted social and cultural connotations which may differ largely from one society to another'. And reiterated that it: 'must not rush to substitute its own judgment in place of that of the national authorities, who are best placed to assess and respond to the needs of society'.

Although the Court rejected the applicants' complaints, its inclusion, in the judgment, of same-sex couples in the notion of family life has a historic relevance. It has been said that there is no doubt that, after Schalk and Kopf, 'complete non-recognition of same-sex couples [was] no longer a viable option',[14] as shown, some years later, by the cases of *Vallianatos v. Greece*[15] and *Oliari and Others v. Italy*,[16] which fostered the adoption of measures of recognition by the legislators.[17]

2. LEGAL RECOGNITION OF SAME-SEX COUPLES IN EUROPE: THE COMPARATIST'S LABORATORY

The above-mentioned decisions and pieces of legislation can be regarded as the principal steps in an ideal itinerary towards the legal recognition of same-sex couples. In this perspective we can affirm that a global dialogue between the various actors has taken place, and is still developing, with national and supranational courts playing a primary role. This dialogue has contributed to – and in some cases has determined – an increased recognition of same-sex couples' rights at the national level.

---

[13] See, among others, L. HODSON, 'A Marriage by Any Other Name? *Schalk and Kopf v Austria*' (2011) 11 *Human Rights L. Rev.* 170–79, 177.
[14] J. SCHERPE, above n. 9, 102.
[15] *Vallianatos and Others v. Greece*, nos. 29381/09 and 32684/09, ECtHR 7 November 2013.
[16] *Oliari and Others v. Italy*, nos. 18766/11 and 36030/11, ECtHR 21 July 2015.
[17] Greece has recognised same-sex cohabitation agreements, which provide several of the rights and benefits of marriage. Legislation allowing such unions has been approved by the Hellenic Parliament on 23 December 2015. On 11 May 2016, the Italian Parliament approved its very first Act on civil unions, Law no. 76 of 2016: Regolamentazione delle unioni civili tra persone dello stesso sesso e disciplina delle convivenze.

In 2009, with its judgment no. 359, the Portuguese Tribunal Constitucional legally recognised same-sex couples, arguing against the crystallisation of the concept of marriage, and endorsing an evolutive interpretation of the Portuguese Constitution through the modification of the legal system by the legislator.[18]

After this decision, the Portuguese Parliament passed a law amending Article 1577 of the civil code, deleting any reference to 'wife' and 'husband', and adopting the expression 'two individuals' instead; in 2010, the Parliament recognised same-sex marriage.

In 2012, with decision n. 198, the Spanish Tribunal Constitucional confirmed the full legitimacy of the Spanish law on same-sex marriage, grounding it on the interpretation of Article 32 of the Spanish Constitution, which granted men and women the right to get married.[19]

It is important to stress that the Court adopted a gender-neutral definition of marriage, talking about an:

> affective unit that generates a bond, or a form of mutual assistance between two persons that hold the same *status* within this institution and who voluntarily decide to join together to establish a shared family life plan.

Particularly significant in this decision is the use of comparative law for contextualising the notion of marriage, and – to quote the Court – in order to:

> determine whether the possibility of homosexual marriage, is, in society today, something that renders marriage unrecognisable or, on the contrary, whether it falls within the portrayed remit of marriage as an institution.

After an extensive analysis, the judges concluded that:

> the institution of marriage, as a partnership between two persons irrespective of their sexual orientation, is being gradually laid down, as evidenced by ascertained steps taken in comparative law and European human rights law with respect to the acknowledgement of marriage between same-sex couples. This progress indicates that there is a new 'image' of marriage, gradually becoming more common, which allows us to interpret the idea of marriage, from the point of view of Western comparative law, as a plural conception.

---

[18] Tribunal Constitucional de Portugal, Acórdão n.º 359/2009, publicado no Diário da República, 2.ª série, n.º 214, de 4 de Novembro de 2009.

[19] Tribunal Constitucional de España, Sentencia 198/2011, de 13 de diciembre, (BOE núm. 9, de 11 de enero de 2012).

Moreover, in its decision no. 669 of 2013, the French Conseil Constitutionnel recognised the compatibility of the French law providing for same-sex marriage with the Constitution.[20] In particular, the judges held that the existence of references to 'husband' and 'wife' in various laws did not allow the conclusion that heterosexual marriage was a 'principle recognised by the laws of the Republic'. Hence, the Court stated firmly that 'the objection alleging that marriage is "naturally" the union of a man and a woman must in any case be rejected'.

The historic decision of the Italian Corte Costituzionale n. 138/2010,[21] despite not showing the same openness,[22] recognised the constitutional relevance of same-sex unions, understood as being the stable cohabitation of two individuals of the same sex, by qualifying them as *'formazioni sociali'* – the social groupings protected by Article 2 of the Italian Constitution – meaning that such couples must be granted the

---

[20] Conseil Constitutionnel, Décision n° 2013-669 DC du 17 mai 2013.

[21] Corte Costituzionale, 14 aprile 2010, n. 138. The referring courts were the Tribunal of Venice and the Court of Appeal of Trento. Afterwards, the Court of Appeal of Florence and the Tribunal of Ferrara raised similar questions: see decisions 276/2010 and 4/2010 of the Italian Constitutional Court.

[22] The Court considered that it was true that the concepts of family and marriage could not be deemed to have 'crystallised' at the moment when the Constitution came into effect, given that constitutional principles must be interpreted bearing in mind changes in the legal order, and the evolution of society and its customs. Nevertheless, such an interpretation could not be extended to the point where it affected the very essence of legal norms, modifying them in such a way as to include phenomena and problems which had not been considered in any way when the Constitution was enacted. In fact, it appeared from the preparatory work to the Constitution that the question of homosexual unions had not been debated by the assembly, despite the fact that homosexuality was not unknown. In drafting Article 29 of the Constitution, the assembly had discussed an institution with a precise form, and an articulate discipline provided for by the Civil Code. Thus, in the absence of any such reference to homosexual unions, it must inevitably be concluded that what had been considered was the notion of marriage as defined in the Civil Code, which came into effect in 1942, and which, at the time, established (and continues to establish) that spouses had to be of the opposite sex. Therefore, the meaning of this constitutional precept could not be altered by a creative interpretation. In consequence, the constitutional norm did not extend to homosexual unions, and was intended to refer to marriage in its traditional sense. Lastly, the Court considered that, in respect of Article 3 of the Constitution regarding the principle of equality, the relevant legislation did not create unreasonable discrimination, given that homosexual unions could not be considered as equivalent to marriage. Even Article 12 ECHR and Article 9 of the Charter of Fundamental Rights did not require full equality between homosexual unions and marriages between a man and a woman, as this was a matter of parliamentary discretion to be regulated by national law, as evidenced by the different approaches existing in Europe.

fundamental right to live out their situation freely, and to obtain legal recognition.[23]

The Constitutional Court considered Article 2 of the Italian Constitution, which provided that the Republic recognises and guarantees the inviolable rights of the person, as an individual, and in social groups where personality is expressed, as well as the duties of political, economic and social solidarity, from which there could be no derogation. It noted that, by 'social group', one had to understand any form of community, simple or complex, that was intended to enable and encourage the free development of any individual by means of relationships. Such a notion included homosexual unions, understood as a stable cohabitation of two people of the same sex, who have a fundamental right to freely express their personalities in a couple, obtaining – in time, and subject to the means and limits set by law – juridical recognition of the relevant rights and duties.

This recognition, which necessarily requires general legal regulation aimed at setting out the rights and duties of the partners in a couple, could be achieved through ways other than making the institution of marriage available to homosexual couples. As shown by the different systems operating in different European countries, the question of the type of recognition was to be left to regulation by Parliament, in the exercise of its full discretion.

However, the Constitutional Court held that it was for the legislator to determine the forms of guarantees and recognition for such unions, while the Court retained the ability to intervene in order to protect specific situations. The judges clarified that, without prejudice to Parliament's discretion, the Constitutional Court could intervene, according to the

---

[23] The notion of *'formazione sociale'* being extended to same-sex unions has been endorsed by three Supreme Courts: the ECtHR, the Italian Constitutional Court and the Italian Court of Cassation. In general, in the Italian legal system, the courts have intervened several times by recognising the legal effectiveness of the relationship between persons of the same sex under specific circumstances. A ruling by the Tribunal of Rome equated, for the purposes of subletting a property, same-sex cohabitation *more uxorio* to opposite-sex cohabitation. Furthermore, the Tribunal of Florence placed a relationship between two persons of the same sex in the category of a de facto family, and consequently applied the principle – generally recognised in circumstances of cohabitation *more uxorio* – according to which welfare services and donations spontaneously given qualify as natural obligations, and are, therefore, not repeatable. At the base of these decisions lies the conviction that a same-sex cohabitation relationship corresponds to the essential elements of the marital relationship, which can be identified in the existence of a stable emotional bond that includes the mutual willingness to entertain sexual relations, all included in a relational situation in which there are attitudes of mutual assistance and solidarity.

principle of equality, in specific situations relating to a homosexual couple's fundamental rights, where the same treatment of married couples and homosexual couples was called for; in such cases, it would assess the reasonableness of the measures enacted by the legislator.

The Italian Court of Cassation expanded on the reasoning of the Italian Constitutional Court, in its judgment no. 4184 of 15 March 2012, by referring to the ECtHR interpretation that conceded that the right to marry enshrined in Article 12 ECHR cannot 'in all circumstances be limited to marriage between two persons of the opposite sex'.[24]

The decision concerned two Italian citizens of the same sex who had married in the Netherlands, and who had challenged the refusal of the Italian authorities to register their marriage in the civil status record on the ground of its 'non-configurability as a marriage'. The Court of Cassation concluded that the claimants had no right to register their marriage, not because it did not exist, or that it was invalid, but because of its inability to produce any legal effect in the Italian order. It further held that persons of the same sex living together in a stable relationship had the right to respect for their private and family life, under Article 8 of the European Convention; therefore, in the exercise of the right to freely live in accordance with their inviolable status as a couple, they could bring an action before a court to claim, in specific situations related to their fundamental rights, the same treatment as that afforded by law to married couples.

Although the Italian Supreme Court upheld the refusal to register the marriage officiated abroad, it stated that there was no inherent problem of public policy, in light of the ECtHR's requirements, and the current state of public opinion. The rejection was, rather, grounded on the circumstance that same-sex marriage has no equivalent in Italian law, and thus cannot be recognised for the purpose of acquiring legal effects. There being no constitutional obstacle to such recognition, the Court concluded that the

---

[24] Corte di Cassazione, 15 marzo 2012, n. 4184, *Il Foro Italiano*, vol. 135, no. 10. More recently, in a case concerning the refusal to issue marriage banns to a same-sex couple who had so requested, the Court of Cassation rejected the claimants' request (Corte di Cassazione, 09 febbraio 2015, n. 2400). Having considered recent domestic and international case law, it concluded that, while same-sex couples had to be protected under Article 2 of the Italian Constitution, and that it was for the legislature to take action to ensure the recognition of unions between such couples, the absence of same-sex marriage was not incompatible with the applicable domestic and international system of human rights. Accordingly, the lack of same-sex marriage could not amount to discriminatory treatment: the problem in the current legal system revolved around the fact that there was no other available form of union, apart from marriage, either for heterosexual or homosexual couples. However, it noted that the court could not establish, through jurisprudence, matters which went beyond its competence.

Parliament was free to pass a statute legalising same-sex marriages, and that, in any event, same-sex couples were provided, under the Constitution, with the right to enjoy family life in a non-discriminatory way, quite apart from the legal recognition.

At that time, Italy was the only nation among the so-called 'mature democracies' not to have provided any protection or form of recognition for same-sex couples,[25] leaving such protection up to judges on a case-by-case basis.[26] Pleas to the legislator remained unheeded until 2016,[27] when the controversial law on the so-called civil unions entered into force.[28]

---

[25] Nevertheless, some Italian cities had established registers of 'civil unions' between unmarried persons, regardless of whether they were of the same sex or of different sexes: among others, the cities of Empoli, Pisa, Milan, Florence and Naples. However, the registration of such 'civil unions' in these registers had a merely symbolic value.

[26] In a case before the Tribunal of Reggio Emilia, the claimants (a same-sex couple) had not requested the tribunal to recognise their marriage entered into in Spain, but to recognise their right to family life in Italy, on the basis that, as a result of the marriage, they were related. The Tribunal of Reggio Emilia, by means of an ordinance of 13 February 2012, in light of the EU directives and their transposition into Italian law, as well as the EU Charter of Fundamental Rights, considered that such a marriage was valid for the purposes of obtaining a residence permit in Italy. In the judgment of the Tribunal of Grosseto of 3 April 2014, delivered by a court of first instance, it was held that refusal to register a foreign marriage was unlawful. The court thus ordered the competent public authority to proceed with registration of the marriage. While the order was being executed, the case was appealed against by the state. By a judgment of 19 September 2014, the Court of Appeal of Florence, having detected a procedural error, quashed the first-instance decision and remitted the case to the Tribunal of Grosseto.

[27] In a report of 2013, Professor F. Gallo, at the time President of the Constitutional Court, stated: 'Dialogue is sometimes more difficult with the Constitutional Court's natural interlocutor. This is particularly so in cases where it solicits the legislature to modify a legal norm which it considered to be in contrast with the Constitution. Such requests are not to be underestimated. They constitute, in fact, the only means available to the Constitutional Court to oblige the legislative organs to eliminate any situation which is not compatible with the Constitution, and which, albeit identified by the Constitutional Court, does not lead to a pronouncement of anti-constitutionality. ... A request of this type which remained unheeded was that made in judgment no. 138/10, which, while finding the fact that a marriage could only be contracted by persons of a different sex to be constitutional[ly] compliant, also affirmed that same-sex couples had a fundamental right to obtain legal recognition, with the relevant rights and duties, of their union. It left it to Parliament to provide for such regulation, by the means and within the limits deemed appropriate.'

[28] On 11 May 2016, the Italian Parliament approved its very first Act on civil unions, Law no. 76 of 2016: Regolamentazione delle unioni civili tra persone dello stesso sesso e disciplina delle convivenze. This statute gives same-sex couples and heterosexual unmarried cohabiting couples some kind of legal recognition. For same-sex couples,

The inertia of the legislator led to the *Oliari* judgment, in which the ECtHR went beyond its previous findings, stating that Italy, at the date of the decision, had failed to comply with its positive obligation to ensure respect for the applicants' private and family life,[29] in particular through the provision of a legal framework allowing them to have their relationship recognised and protected under domestic law.[30] It is important, in this regard, to highlight the use of comparative law reasoning by the ECtHR,[31] focusing not only on European legal systems, but also encompassing the US Supreme Court's decision of 2015 in the

---

the law grants legal recognition of their unions, and makes several references to the rules on marriage in the Italian Civil Code. However, parental rights are absent from the legislation: adoption and second-parent adoption are not permitted. Cohabiting couples are defined as relationships of two persons of a different sex, over the age of 18, that are not bound by any link of kinship, adoption, wedlock or civil union. According to Law no. 40 of 2004 on medically-assisted procreation techniques, homosexual people cannot have access to artificial procreation and surrogacy; in the latter case, this prohibition applies to heterosexual couples as well.

[29] The Court observes that, 'while the Government is usually better placed to assess community interests, in the present case the Italian legislature seems not to have attached particular importance to the indications set out by the national community, including the general Italian population and the highest judicial authorities in Italy. The Court notes that in Italy the need to recognise and protect such relationships has been given a high profile by the highest judicial authorities, including the Constitutional Court and the Court of Cassation. Reference is made particularly to the judgment of the Constitutional Court no. 138/10 in the first two applicant[s]' case, the findings of which were reiterated in a series of subsequent judgments in the following years ... In such cases, the Constitutional Court, notably and repeatedly called for a juridical recognition of the relevant rights and duties of homosexual unions ... a measure which could only be put in place by Parliament'. Cf. *Oliari and Others v. Italy*, nos. 18766/11 and 36030/11, ECHR 21 July 2015, paras. 179–80. Regarding the matter of cohabiting couples *more uxorio*, such protection has always been derived from Article 2 of the Italian Constitution, as interpreted in various court judgments over the years (post-1988). In more recent years (2012 onwards), domestic judgments have also considered cohabiting same-sex couples as deserving such protection.

[30] The Court reiterated that 'it ha[d] already held that same-sex couples are just as capable as different-sex couples of entering into stable, committed relationships, and that they are in a relevantly similar situation to a different-sex couple as regards their need for legal recognition and protection of their relationship ... It follows that the Court has already acknowledged that same-sex couples are in need of legal recognition and protection of their relationship'. Cf. *Oliari and Others v. Italy*, nos. 18766/11 and 36030/11, ECHR 21 July 2015, para. 165.

[31] F. Viglione, 'Comparative Law at the European Court of Human Rights: Does Context Still Matter?', in this volume.

case of *Obergefell et al. v. Hodges*, in which the right to same-sex marriage for US citizens was fully recognised.[32]

Furthermore, references to the aforementioned Italian judgments on the status of same-sex couples took on decisive relevance in founding this decision, thereby also establishing a seminal dialogue with the domestic courts.

---

[32] *Obergefell v. Hodges, Director, Ohio Department of Health et al*, 135 S. Ct. 2584 (2015). On 26 July 2015, the Supreme Court of the United States held that same-sex couples may exercise the fundamental right to marry in all US states, and that there was no lawful basis for a state to refuse to recognise a lawful same-sex marriage performed in another state on the ground of its same-sex character. The petitioners had claimed that the respondent state officials had violated the Fourteenth Amendment by denying them the right to marry, or to have a marriage lawfully performed in another state given full recognition. The Supreme Court held that that the laws being challenged burdened the liberty of same-sex couples, and abridged central precepts of equality. It considered that the marriage laws enforced by the respondents were unequal, as same-sex couples were denied all the benefits afforded to opposite-sex couples, and were barred from exercising a fundamental right. This denial, to same-sex couples, of the right to marry, caused a grave and continuing harm, and the imposition of this disability on gay people and lesbians served to disrespect and subordinate them. Indeed, the Equal Protection Clause, like the Due Process Clause, prohibited this unjustified infringement of the fundamental right to marry. These considerations led to the conclusion that the right to marry was a fundamental right inherent in the liberty of the person, and under the Due Process and Equal Protection Clauses of the Fourteenth Amendment, couples of the same sex may not be deprived of that right and that liberty. The Supreme Court thus held that same-sex couples may exercise the fundamental right to marry. Having noted that substantial attention had been devoted to the question by various actors in society, and that, according to the US constitutional system, individuals need not await legislative action before asserting a fundamental right, it considered that, were the Supreme Court to stay its hand and allow slower, case-by-case determination of the required availability of specific public benefits to same-sex couples, it would still deny gay people and lesbians many rights and responsibilities intertwined with marriage. Lastly, noting that many states already allowed same-sex marriages, and that hundreds of thousands of these marriages had already occurred, it opined that the disruption caused by the prohibition on recognition was significant and ever-growing. Thus, the Supreme Court also found that there was no lawful basis for a state to refuse to recognise a lawful same-sex marriage performed in another state. This case is of immeasurable importance since, by constitutionally legitimising same-sex marriage, it has effectively invalidated all the state norms, constitutional and otherwise, which, over the years, have been introduced by limiting access to the institution of marriage to opposite-sex couples only. Furthermore, it represents a great victory in the battles against all forms of homophobic discrimination, as well as fostering a strengthening of the fundamental rights of the person, including the choice of marriage, with all the legal consequences that derive from it in matters of property, succession, tax law, social policy, and so on. For a commentary on the case, see J.M. BALKIN, '*Obergefell v. Hodges*: A Critical Introduction' in J.M. BALKIN (ed), *What Obergefell v. Hodges Should Have Said: The Nation's Top Legal Experts Rewrite America's Same-Sex Marriage Decision*, Yale University Press, New Haven 2020, pp. 3–70; and A. SPERTI, 'La sentenza

3. SOME CONCLUSIONS

In light of this brief overview, it seems possible to confirm the opinion held by the majority of European family law scholars: namely that there exists a tendency towards approximation of national legislation on same-sex relationships – a 'continuing international movement towards legal recognition', to use the ECtHR's words.[33]

This phenomenon can be traced back to the so-called cross-fertilisation among anomalous sources of legal production:[34] the law deriving in some way from the Council of Europe; that of the European Union; the conventional or jurisprudential law of the supranational courts; and even comparative law that, in a European dimension, has finally emerged as a source of law.[35]

The relationships between the various European legal orders, whether national or supranational, cannot be reduced to hierarchical or horizontal ones. They are much more complex and rely on dialogue: that is, on exchanges and reciprocal influences. The approximation mentioned above seems to have taken place in compliance with the diversity of traditional approaches to the subject, but certainly follows the path of coordination; of standardisation, caused by private international law; and of harmonisation, on the basis of the fundamental principles of freedom and equality.

Obergefell v. Hodges e lo storico riconoscimento del diritto al matrimonio per le coppie same-sex negli Stati Uniti. Introduzione al focus' (2015) 2 *Genius* 6–17.

[33] *Oliari v. Italy*, no. 18766/11 and 36030/11, ECHR 21 July 2015, para. 178.

[34] See W. SANDHOLTZ, 'Human Rights Courts and Global Constitutionalism: Coordination Through Judicial Dialogue' (2020) 10(3) *Global Constitutionalism* 439–64; D. KOSAŘ and L. LIXINSKI, 'Domestic Judicial Design by International Human Rights Courts' (2015) 109(4) *American Journal of International Law* 713–60.

[35] See, among others, V. GREMENTIERI, 'Comparative Law and Human Rights in Europe' in A.M. RABELLO (ed), *European Legal Traditions and Israel*, The Hebrew University of Jerusalem, Jerusalem 1994, p. 375; T. KOOPMANS, 'Comparative Law and the Courts' (1996) 45 *Int'l & Comp. L. Quarterly* 545–56; U. DROBNIG and S. VAN ERP, *The Use of Comparative Law by Courts*, XIVth International Congress of Comparative Law, Kluwer Law International, The Hague 1999; B. MARKESINIS and J. FEDTKE, 'The Judge as Comparatist' (2005) 80 *Tulane Law Review* 11–167; C.L. ROZAKIS, 'The European Judge as Comparatist' (2005) 80 *Tulane Law Review* 257–79; G.F. FERRARI and A. GAMBARO, *Corti nazionali e comparazione giuridica*, Esi, Napoli 2006; T.H. BINGHAM, *Widening Horizons: The Influence of Comparative Law and International Law on Domestic Law*, CUP, Cambridge 2010; M. BOBEK, *Comparative Reasoning in European Supreme Courts*, OUP, Oxford 2013; M. GELTER and M. SIEMS, 'Citations to Foreign Courts. Illegitimate and Superfluous, or Unavoidable? Evidence from Europe' (2014) 62 *Am. J. Comp. Law* 35–85; M. ANDENAS and D. FAIRGRIEVE (eds), *Courts and Comparative Law*, OUP, Oxford 2015; N. VOGIATZIS, 'The Relationship

This was the perspective indicated by the Italian Court of Cassation when interpreting the notion of international public policy, and which was used to finally reject the construction of public policy entirely grounded in a literal interpretation of the mandatory rules.[36] The Court's reasoning took inspiration from the traditional notion of international public policy, which diverges from domestic public policy. On the basis of a consolidated doctrinal and jurisprudential orientation, the Court not only affirms the historicity of the former notion, but refers it to a perspective in which the national legal system is located – in accordance with Articles 10, 11 and 117, paragraph 1, of the Italian Constitution[37] – within a larger community of a supranational nature, which is expressed through shared principles, and not necessarily translated into internal rules.

If this perspective is correct, then it would probably be possible to argue that it no longer makes much sense to distinguish between internal and international order, since both have been merged into a single notion that could be precisely defined as 'constitutional public policy'.[38]

Such a notion is rightly understood by the Italian Supreme Court as:

> the set of fundamental principles characterizing the internal legal system in a given historical period, inspired by the needs of protection of fundamental rights, needs common to the various legal systems and placed at a higher level than the ordinary legislation.[39]

Hence, if it is true that the Court's scrutiny for compliance with the supreme principles of the constitutional order can be ascribed to the implementation

---

Between European Consensus, the Margin of Appreciation and the Legitimacy of the Strasbourg Court' (2019) 25 *European Public Law* 445–80.

[36] Let me refer here to my essay, M.G. STANZIONE, 'Ordine pubblico costituzionale e status filiationis in Italia e negli ordinamenti europei: la normativa e l'esperienza giurisprudenziale', in *Comparazione e diritto civile*, www.comparazionedirittocivile, 2016, pp. 1–58.

[37] Article 10 of the Italian Constitution establishes that 'the Italian legal system conforms to the generally recognised principles of international law'. Article 11 states that 'Italy agrees, on conditions of equality with other States, to the limitations of sovereignty that may be necessary to a world order ensuring peace and justice among the Nations.' Article 117 requires that 'legislative powers shall be vested in the State and the Regions in compliance with the Constitution and with the constraints deriving from EU legislation and international obligations.'

[38] This is the viewpoint of P. PERLINGIERI, fully expressed in *Il diritto civile nella legalità costituzionale secondo il sistema italo-comunitario delle fonti*, vol. I, ESI, Naples 2006, in particular at p. 77.

[39] Corte di Cassazione, 15 marzo 2012, n. 4184, *Il Foro Italiano*, vol. 135, no. 10.

of national order, it is equally true that this order contributes to forming the supranational one, and endorses, in a reciprocal way, its fundamental choices through adherence to the founding Treaties and the Charter of Fundamental Rights of the European Union, as well as, and above all, to the ECHR.[40]

---

[40] On 5 June 2018 the Court of Justice of the European Union issued a landmark decision against Romania, recognising that the term 'spouse' includes same-sex spouses under EU freedom of movements law. The judgment meant that all EU countries must treat same-sex couples in the same way as different-sex couples when they exercise their right to free movement. Years later, Romania is still not complying with the judgment, the couple's marriage has not been recognised and Clai Hamilton is unable to apply for residency. The couple was forced to turn to the ECtHR for redress. See CJEU Case-673/16, *Relu Adrian Coman and Others v. Inspectoratul General pentru Imigrări and Ministerul Afacerilor Interne*, ECLI:EU:C:2018:385.

PART III
RIGHT TO PRIVACY AND DATA PROTECTION

SHAPING THE RIGHT TO PRIVACY

The Interplay between Karlsruhe, Strasbourg, and Luxembourg

Katharina DE LA DURANTAYE

1. Introduction 119
2. The Baseline: The *von Hannover* Cases 120
3. The 'Right to be Forgotten': Shaping the Future, Shaping the Past 125
   3.1. The *Sedlmayr* Cases in Germany 125
   3.2. The CJEU's Judgment in *Google Spain*. 126
   3.3. The ECtHR's Judgment in *M.L. and W.W. v. Germany* 127
   3.4. The Federal Constitutional Court's Order in *Right to be Forgotten I* 129
   3.5. The ECtHR's Judgment in *Hurbain v. Belgium*............. 131
4. Connecting the Dots 135

1. INTRODUCTION

The contours of the right to privacy in Germany are very much determined by case law. The European Court of Human Rights (ECtHR) has significantly and visibly shaped that right. Its decision in one of a set of cases involving Caroline de Monaco/Caroline von Hannover famously led German Courts to change their course. This chapter will briefly recount these iconic developments from the beginning of the 21st century, and will sketch out how the courts interacted with one another back then.[1] The events concerned traditional, physical media publications.

---

[1] For a more in-depth analysis of this judicial dialogue, see R. KRÄMER and J. MÄRTEN, 'Der Dialog der Gerichte – Die Fortentwicklung des Persönlichkeitsschutzes im europäischen Mehrebenenrechtsverbund' (2015) *Europarecht* 169; S. MÜLLER-RIEMENSCHNEIDER, *Pressefreiheit und Persönlichkeitsschutz*, Kovac, Hamburg 2013. See also L.R. GLAS, *The Theory, Potential and Practice of Procedural Dialogue in the European Convention on Human Rights System*, Intersentia, Cambridge 2016.

Nowadays, the media landscape is more complex, and the number of players has grown. The same is true for the number of courts involved. We have witnessed this over the past few years, as European Courts have dealt with the so-called 'right to be forgotten'. Within a period of only a few years, the ECtHR, the Court of Justice of the European Union (CJEU), and the German Federal Constitutional Court (Bundesverfassungsgericht) all dealt with cases concerning the said right. The way in which the courts interacted with one another will be at the centre of this chapter. I will show how the three courts shaped the right, and demonstrate that the courts' interactions differed from the classical one, which was on display in the *von Hannover* cases.

2. THE BASELINE: THE *VON HANNOVER* CASES

The highest German courts are proud and rather self-confident. Like many of their counterparts in other countries, they can, at times, be somewhat stubborn, and not too eager to change their course. However, when it came to the right to privacy, the ECtHR forced both the German Federal Constitutional Court and the Federal Court of Justice (Bundesgerichtshof) to do just that. It did so as part of a set of cases which established a dedicated line of sorts between Karlsruhe, where the Federal Constitutional Court and the Federal Court of Justice are located, and the ECtHR in Strasbourg.[2]

In 1999, the Federal Constitutional Court upheld a decision by the Federal Court of Justice.[3] It had declared image reporting in the tabloid press on Caroline von Hannover, then known as Caroline de Monaco, to be legal.[4] Consequently, von Hannover filed an individual application (Article 34 ECHR) with the ECtHR, thereby making use of a procedural tool which had only been introduced, in this form, the year before (1998).[5] In fact, she was the first individual to do so.

---

[2] The cases concerning Caroline von Hannover, and their aftermath, contributed to the spike in references to the ECtHR's case law which Andreas Engel identified in his chapter, 'The European Convention on Human Rights in the German Legal System: A Qualitative and Quantitative Introduction', in this volume.

[3] BGH, 19.12.1995, *Caroline von Monaco II*, VI ZR 15/95.

[4] BVerfG, 15.12.1999, *Caroline von Monaco*, 1 BvR 653/96.

[5] Initially, the individual application fell under the ambit of Article 25 ECHR. Individuals had to petition the European Commission of Human Rights, which could hear the case only if the Contracting Party against which the complaint had been lodged had declared that it recognises the competence of the Commission to receive such petitions.

In a judgment that would later be called *von Hannover I*, the ECtHR's Third Section unanimously held that the Federal Constitutional Court's ruling violated Article 8 ECHR because it had not struck a fair balance between the competing interests of von Hannover, on one hand, and society, on the other hand.[6] The ECtHR established that:

> [A] fundamental distinction needs to be made between reporting facts – even controversial ones – capable of contributing to a debate in a democratic society relating to politicians in the exercise of their functions, for example, and reporting details of the private life of an individual who ... does not exercise official functions.[7]

It further held that the 'decisive factor in balancing the protection of private life against freedom of expression should lie in the contribution that the published photos and articles make to a debate of general interest'.[8]

The ECtHR did not limit itself to establishing the factors which national courts have to consider when balancing the competing interests at stake. Notably, it prescribed the result which the German courts had to reach in their balancing exercise. In particular, the ECtHR took issue with the established German concept that a 'figure of contemporary society par excellence' (*'absolute Person der Zeitgeschichte'*) enjoys:

> protection of her private life ... outside her home ... only if she was in a secluded place out of the public eye to which persons retire, 'with the objectively recognisable aim of being alone and where, confident of being alone, they behave in a manner in which they would not behave in public'.[9]

While said concept 'could conceivably be appropriate for politicians exercising official functions', it was not legitimate for someone like von Hannover. She, the court stated, was of interest to the public (only) because

---

As to the 11th Protocol, which reformed the initial Articles 19–51, see V. SCHLETTE, 'Das neue Rechtsschutzsystem der Europäischen Menschenrechtskonvention. Zur Reform des Kontrollmechanismus durch das 11. Protokoll' (1996) *Zeitschrift für ausländisches öffentliches Recht und Völkerrecht* 905, 914–34; A. DRZEMCZEWSKI and J. MEYER-LADEWIG, 'Grundzüge des neuen EMRK-Kontrollmechanismus nach dem am 11.5.1994 unterzeichneten Reform-Protokoll (Nr. 11)' (1994) *Europäische Grundrechtezeitschrift* 317.

6   *Von Hannover v. Germany I*, no. 59320/00, ECtHR (Third Section) 24 June 2004. Two judges provided concurring opinions.
7   Ibid., para. 63.
8   Ibid., para. 76.
9   Ibid., para. 54.

she was a member of Monaco's reigning family, and was not a public official of that principality.[10] Consequently, the ECtHR held, the Federal Constitutional Court had wrongly applied the national statute upon which it had based its judgment.[11]

The ECtHR's judgment led to a public outcry in Germany. Media companies published whole-page advertisements in newspapers asking the German government to seek redress under Article 43 ECHR.[12] Academics were up in arms as well. One of the multiple points of criticism which they brought forward[13] was that Strasbourg had not sufficiently taken into account the wide margin of appreciation which national courts enjoy when applying the ECHR, especially since the case concerned positive obligations in an area of law with a fairly low level of harmonisation among Convention States.[14]

The Federal Constitutional Court was also displeased. Its president at the time, Hans-Jürgen Papier, gave multiple newspaper interviews. In one of these, he stated that the constitution would 'not abstain from having the last say as a sign of national sovereignty'.[15] This formulation is similar to the one which the court itself chose. Seizing the first opportunity to make a point, in *Görgülü*, a case that did not involve von Hannover, the Federal Constitutional Court stated that:

> The Basic Law aims to integrate Germany into the legal community of peaceful and free states, but does not waive the sovereignty contained in the last

---

[10] Ibid., para. 72.
[11] Ibid., para. 72.
[12] These advertisements appeared in multiple newspapers on 30 August 2004. See A. OHLY, 'Harmonisierung des Persönlichkeitsrechts durch den Europäischen Gerichtshof für Menschenrechte? Rechtsvergleichende Anmerkungen zum Urteil in der Sache von Hannover/Deutschland' (2004) *GRUR International* 902.
[13] For an overview, see G. ZAGOURAS, 'Bildnisschutz und Privatsphäre im europäischen und nationalen Kontext – Das Springreiter-Urteil des BGH vor dem Hintergrund der Caroline-Entscheidung des EGMR' (2004) *Archiv für Presserecht* 509–10.
[14] See C. GRABENWARTER, '*Schutz der Privatsphäre versus Pressefreiheit*: Europäische Korrektur des deutschen Sonderweges?' (2004) *Zeitschrift für das gesamte Medienrecht: Archiv für Presserecht* 309, 315; A. OHLY, above n. 12, 911.
[15] Frankfurter Allgemeine Zeitung, 09.12.2004, p. 5 ('verzichtet nicht auf das letzte Wort als Ausdruck staatlicher Souveränität'). After some criticism, his language became more conciliatory. In DIE ZEIT, Nr. 25/2005, p. 9, Papier underlined that the relationship between the Federal Constitutional Court, the Federal Court of Justice and ECtHR 'should be informed by mutual consideration and cooperation. One cannot simply say: "One or the other has the last say".' ('sollte von gegenseitiger Rücksichtnahme und Kooperation geprägt sein. Man kann nicht einfach sagen: "Der eine oder der andere hat das letzte Wort"'). For more on this, see M. HERTIG RANDALL, 'Der grundrechtliche Dialog der Gerichte in Europa' (2014) *Europäische Grundrechte-Zeitschrift* 5, 16–18.

instance in the German constitution. There is therefore no contradiction with the aim of commitment to international law if the legislature, exceptionally, does not comply with the law of international agreements, provided this is the only way in which a violation of fundamental principles of the constitution can be averted.

The Basic Law is intended to achieve comprehensive commitment to international law, cross-border cooperation and political integration in a gradually developing international community of democratic states under the rule of law. However, it does not seek a submission to non-German acts of sovereignty that is removed from every constitutional limit and control.[16]

The court stressed that judgments of the ECtHR were not binding. They had to be 'take[n] into account' ('Berücksichtigung') as 'part of a methodologically justifiable interpretation of the law' ('im Rahmen methodisch vertretbarer Gesetzesauslegung').[17] The court pointed out that the schematic enforcement of a decision by the ECtHR could, if contradictory to higher-ranking law, violate fundamental rights and the rule of law. It continued by referencing *von Hannover I*, thereby indicating the reasons for its forceful statement:

> Individual application proceedings under Article 34 of the Convention before the EC[t]HR are intended to decide specific individual cases in the two-party relationship between the complainant and the state party ... The decisions of the EC[t]HR may encounter national partial systems of law shaped by a complex system of case-law. In the German legal system, this may happen in particular ... in the law on the protection of personality (on this, see, recently, EC[t]HR ... – *von Hannover v. Germany* ...), in which conflicting fundamental rights are balanced by the creation of groups of cases and graduated legal consequences. It is the task of the domestic courts to integrate a decision of the EC[t]HR into the relevant partial legal area of the national legal system, because it cannot be the desired result of the international-law basis nor express the will of the EC[t]HR for the EC[t]HR through its decisions itself to undertake directly any necessary adjustments within a domestic partial legal system.[18]

The Federal Constitutional Court thus stressed that national courts such as itself enjoyed a wide margin of appreciation. Judgments by the ECtHR only had indirect effects.

---

[16] BVerfG, 14.10.2004, *Görgülü*, 2 BvR 1481/04, paras. 35–36 (official English translation).
[17] Ibid., para. 47 (official English translation).
[18] Ibid., para. 58 (official English translation).

And yet, despite all the criticism, German courts actively changed course to accommodate the ECtHR's concerns. The Federal Court of Justice stopped using the concept that there are 'figures of contemporary society par excellence' *('absolute Person der Zeitgeschichte')*. Instead, the court established a new test, according to which the balancing depends on whether the image in question portrays an 'important event for contemporary society' *('Ereignis von zeitgeschichtlicher Bedeutung')*.[19] The person in question's fame and notoriety became but one (important) factor to be taken into account. The Federal Constitutional Court upheld this new practice.[20] In doing so, it struck a more conciliatory tone than it had in *Görgülü*:

> In domestic law, the [European] Convention [on Human Rights] has the rank of ordinary federal law … [T]he guarantees of the Convention and the case-law of the European Court of Human Rights serve as guidelines for interpretation for determining the content and scope of fundamental rights, provided this does not restrict or lower the level of fundamental rights protection afforded under the Basic Law, which is not intended by the Convention (cf. Art. 53 of the Convention).[21]

Von Hannover again filed an individual application with the ECtHR. Strasbourg declared that the new reasoning of the Federal Constitutional Court was in line with Article 8 ECHR.[22]

The conversation between the ECtHR, the Federal Constitutional Court and the Federal Court of Justice was a traditional and fairly straightforward one. The partners in that conversation were not completely in synch; the national courts were not too happy with the homework that the Strasbourg court gave them, but they did modify their line of reasoning, and the ECtHR accepted that change as sufficient.

---

[19] BGH, 06.03.2007, *Abgestuftes Schutzkonzept*, VI ZR 13/06; BGH, 06.03.2007, *Winterurlaub*, VI ZR 51/06 and VI ZR 52/06; BGH, 01.07.2008, *Urlaubsfoto von Caroline*, VI ZR 67/08.

[20] BVerfG, 26.02.2008, *Caroline von Hannover*, 1 BvR 1602/07, 1606/07 and 1626/07. See also BVerfG, 24.09.2009, 1 BvR 2678/08.

[21] BVerfG, 26.02.2008, *Caroline von Hannover*, 1 BvR 1602/07, 1606/07 and 1626/07, para. 52 (official English translation).

[22] *Von Hannover v. Germany II*, no. 40660/08 and 60641/08, ECtHR (Grand Chamber) 7 February 2012; *von Hannover v. Germany III*, no. 8772/10 ECtHR (Fifth Section) 19 September 2013.

3. THE 'RIGHT TO BE FORGOTTEN': SHAPING THE FUTURE, SHAPING THE PAST

Over the past few years, we have witnessed a different set of illustrious cases concerning the right to privacy as enshrined in Article 8 ECHR. These cases were brought by individuals who claimed their 'right to be forgotten'. The life stories of these people all contained some kind of event which did not give a very favourable impression of them. They may have been convicted of a crime or gone bankrupt, or there may have been something else in their life that did not make them look good and which had been the subject of news articles where they had been identified by name. In the analogue age, finding such stories once they no longer constituted news was not an easy task. One had to physically go to the archive of the relevant news organisation and retrieve the relevant page (or a microfiche/microfilm thereof). In most cases, one could only obtain the story if one knew what one was looking for.

Nowadays, press archives are available online. Some archives require registration or are hidden behind a paywall, but many of them are openly accessible. Articles in these archives are not only much easier to access than they used to be; they are also much easier to find. Search engines point their users to such articles even when the user does not know that the article exists and/or that the events described therein took place, merely because he or she conducted a general online search by typing in a person's name.

Because of this, people who want to distance themselves from newsworthy events in their past have a much harder time doing so than they would have had twenty years ago. In order to freely shape their future, they might have to hide or even reshape their past. While, in the analogue world, they would have had to sue the media company which had published the article, nowadays, they have two possible paths they can take: they can sue the media company which runs the online archive, and/or the operator of the search engine – usually Google. A relationship which used to be bilateral has thus become triangular: it involves the media company, the search engine operator and the individual who was the subject of the media report.

3.1. THE *SEDLMAYR* CASES IN GERMANY

In Germany, the initial set of cases on online press archives fall under the heading *Sedlmayr*. The two applicants, brothers M.L. and W.W., had been convicted, in 1993, for the murder of Bavarian actor Walter Sedlmayr two years earlier. The brothers had maintained their innocence, and had taken every possible legal avenue to try and overturn the verdict, to no avail. In addition, they had launched a publicity campaign. The media had reported on the murder itself, and on the initial trial, as well as on the legal battles that followed. On multiple occasions, the brothers had contacted the media, and had actively asked to be interviewed. The media reports and/or transcripts of these interviews became part of multiple online press archives.

Shortly before their release from prison in 2007, the brothers sued the media companies and asked that the reports be anonymised. The cases went all the way up to the Federal Court of Justice which, unlike the lower courts,[23] decided that the press was not prohibited from making the reports and transcripts available.[24] It held that the freedom of the press outweighed the brothers' personality rights. When the Federal Constitutional Court decided not to entertain the brothers' constitutional complaints, they filed multiple applications to the ECtHR.

3.2. THE CJEU's JUDGMENT IN *GOOGLE SPAIN*

While the *Sedlmayr* cases were pending in Strasbourg, the CJEU issued a judgment, on a request for a preliminary ruling by a Spanish court, which made quite an impact.[25] It, too, concerned the 'right to be forgotten'. However, there was one important difference: while the brothers in the *Sedlmayr* cases had sued the media companies, the plaintiff in the Spanish case had sued both the media company and Google.

On the orders of the Spanish authorities, a Spanish newspaper had printed two announcements stating that real estate belonging to the plaintiff was being put to a forced sale because the plaintiff had accumulated social security debt. These announcements later became part of the newspaper's online archive. The Spanish court had asked the CJEU for a preliminary ruling on Google's obligations under European data protection law.[26]

---

[23] LG Hamburg, 29.02.2008, 324 O 459/07; LG Hamburg, 29.02.2008, 324 O 469/07; OLG Hamburg, 29.07.2008, 7 U 30/08; OLG Hamburg, 29.07.2008, 7 U 31/08.
[24] BGH, 15.12.2009, *Online-Archiv*, VI ZR 227/08 and VI ZR 228/08; BGH, 09.02.2010, *Spiegel-Dossier*, VI ZR 243/08 and 244/08; BGH, 20.04.2010, VI ZR 245/08 und VI ZR 246/08.
[25] CJEU Case C-131/12, *Google Spain*, ECLI:EU:C:2014:317.
[26] At the time, what was at stake were Google's obligations under Articles 12 and 14 of the Data Protection Directive (Directive 95/46/EC). Today, the case would centre

Shaping the Right to Privacy

The court held the following:

> [P]rocessing of personal data ... by the operator of a search engine ... enables any internet user to obtain through the list of results a structured overview of the information relating to that individual ... information which potentially concerns a vast number of aspects of his private life and which, without the search engine, could not have been interconnected or could have been only with great difficulty.[27]

> [T]he outcome of the weighing of the interests at issue ... may differ according to whether the processing carried out by the operator of a search engine or that carried out by the publisher of the web page is at issue, given that, first, the legitimate interests justifying the processing may be different and, second, the consequences of the processing for the data subject, and in particular, for his private life, are not necessarily the same.[28]

> [H]aving regard to ... the fact that its initial publication had taken place 16 years earlier, the data subject establishes a right that that information should no longer be linked to his name by means of such a list.[29]

Hence, the CJEU not only stressed that it is search engines which enable personal profiles of individuals to be created with great ease. It also indicated that the interests of search engine operators might be different, and less weighty than those of press publishers who, unlike Google, can claim freedom of the press, and whose online archives would, without (external) search engines, only provide information to those who specifically looked for it. Finally, the court indicated that the passing of time was a factor to be taken into account.

3.3. THE ECtHR's JUDGMENT IN *M.L. AND W.W. v. GERMANY*

In 2018, four years after the CJEU had rendered its decision in *Google Spain*, the ECtHR's Fifth Section decided the *Sedlmayr* case, *M.L. and W.W. v. Germany*.[30] The court did not find a violation of Article 8 ECHR.

---

around Article 17 GDPR (Regulation (EU) 2016/679), which is explicitly dedicated to the 'right to be forgotten'.
[27] CJEU Case C-131/12, *Google Spain*, ECLI:EU:C:2014:317, para. 80.
[28] Ibid., para. 86.
[29] Ibid., para. 98.
[30] *M.L. and W.W. v. Germany*, no. 60798/10 and 65599/10, ECtHR (Fifth Section) 28 June 2018.

What is interesting about the case, however, is not so much its outcome but the long *obiter dictum* which the court provided at the start of its judgment. The judges did not begin their legal analysis by applying the principles which they had developed in prior case law to the decisions rendered by the German courts in the case at hand. Neither did they examine the function of online press archives, who were the defendants in the set of cases that had led to the individual application which the ECtHR was ruling upon. Instead, the judges chose to dedicate their introductory remarks to the role which search engines play in disseminating the information contained in such archives: '[I]t is primarily because of search engines that the information on the applicants held by the media outlets concerned can easily be found by Internet users.'[31]

The court made explicit reference to the CJEU's decision in *Google Spain*, and restated all of that court's core arguments.[32] It pointed to the 'amplifying effect' of search engines, and to the fact that search engines conduct a different (and less protected) kind of business than press companies. The work of the media, the ECtHR held, is at 'the heart of what freedom of expression is intended to protect', while search engines help find any available information on a person and connect it in such a way that a personal profile can be formed. Consequently, the ECtHR concluded, 'obligations of search engines ... may differ from those of the entity which originally published the information'.[33]

In so many words, the court seems to be inviting individuals who did not like being found in a press archive to hold Google accountable. According to the court, Google's case is much weaker than that of a press company; search engines are deemed to be dangerous amplifiers. Requiring them to delist a search entry is presented as a much less restrictive means of protecting the right to privacy than asking a press company to change the content of its archive.

The ECtHR also noted that the balance of interests may change over time:

> [A]fter a certain period of time has lapsed and, in particular, as their release from prison approaches, persons who have been convicted have an interest in no longer being confronted with their acts, with a view to their reintegration in society ... Likewise, the public's interest as regards criminal

---

[31] Ibid., para. 97.
[32] Ibid.
[33] Ibid.

proceedings will vary in degree, as it may evolve during the course of the proceedings.[34]

The idea that the public's interest in obtaining information about a certain event may decrease over time, while the interest of the individual not to be associated with his or her past deeds may increase, had also been on display in *Google Spain*. However, in this passage, the ECtHR was more explicit and elaborate than the CJEU had been.

3.4. THE FEDERAL CONSTITUTIONAL COURT'S ORDER IN *RIGHT TO BE FORGOTTEN I*

It is this last aspect, the importance of time as a factor, which was front and centre in a seminal case which the Federal Constitutional Court decided the following year (2019).[35] Again, the applicant was a person who had been convicted of a crime. This time, the crime consisted of murdering two people on board a yacht called *Apollonia*. Neither the victims nor the perpetrator had been known to the public before the crime had taken place, and the claimant had not thrust himself into public discourse afterwards.

Nevertheless, there was newspaper reporting on the crime, in which the claimant's full name was mentioned. These reports had become part of a media company's online archive. The archive was openly accessible, without any restrictions. The claimant had sued the media company and had tried to get his name erased from the archive. The lower courts had all ruled in his favour. The Federal Court of Justice, by contrast, had denied his claim, in 2013.[36] It had based its ruling partially on the ECtHR's decision in *Axel Springer v. Germany*, yet another controversial German case involving the balance between the right to privacy and the freedom of the press.[37] That case had been decided the year before; *M.L. and W.W. v. Germany* was still pending.

The Federal Constitutional Court famously overturned the Court of Justice's decision. It stated that: 'The possibility for matters to be forgotten forms part of the temporal dimension of freedom. This applies

---

[34] Ibid., para. 100.
[35] BVerfG, 06.11.2019, *Right to be forgotten I*, 1 BvR 16/13.
[36] BGH, 13.11.2012, *Apollonia-Prozess*, VI ZR 330/11.
[37] *Axel Springer v. Deutschland*, no. 39954/08, ECtHR (Grand Chamber) 7 February 2012.

in particular with regard to the objective of reintegrating offenders [into society].'[38] This statement is very much in line with what the ECtHR had said in *M.L. and W.W. v. Germany*, and what the CJEU had alluded to in *Google Spain*. It is no wonder, then, that the Federal Constitutional Court made explicit reference to both the Strasbourg and the Luxembourg courts.[39] It stressed that all three courts were aligned on this topic:

> The inclusion of time as a factor in the assessment of the constitutional requirements for the dissemination of information has arisen as a development resulting from the exchange about fundamental rights in Europe.[40]

Similarly, when explaining why, and how, the Federal Court of Justice had failed to grant the passing of time the importance it deserved, the Federal Constitutional Court again made ample reference to the ECtHR's decision in *M.L. and W.W. v. Germany*.[41] The same was true when the court examined the constitutional weight of documenting past articles online, in full and without alterations.[42] The court stressed that online press archives were essential for communicative as well as for research purposes. Both the press and the public at large, the court held, have a constitutionally protected, significant interest in press articles being accessible on the Internet as a resource for factual research on specific events. By contrast, the court granted lesser weight to the interest in using such archives as sources for general research on specific people (by googling them). The court therefore deemed it relevant to determine whether media outlets have the technical means to block search engines from finding individual articles.

The court continued its analysis of *M.L. and W.W. v. Germany* by pointing to several differences in fact: M.L. and W.W. had launched a public campaign to raise awareness, they had actively contacted the press,

---

[38] BVerfG, 06.11.2019, *Right to be forgotten I*, 1 BvR 16/13, para. 105 (official English translation). The original German text reads as follows: 'Die Möglichkeit des Vergessens gehört zur Zeitlichkeit der Freiheit. Dies gilt nicht zuletzt im Blick auf das Ziel der Wiedereingliederung von Straftätern [in die Gesellschaft].'
[39] Ibid., paras. 100, 106.
[40] Ibid., para. 106 (official English translation). The original German text reads as follows: 'Die Einstellung des Zeitfaktors in die Beurteilung der verfassungsmäßigen Anforderungen an die Verbreitung von Informationen stellt sich als Teil einer Entwicklung im Austausch der europäischen Grundrechtsentwicklung dar.'
[41] Ibid., paras. 106, 111, 113, 118.
[42] Ibid., paras. 130, 144.

and the news reports in question had been hidden behind a paywall, or had been accessible only to subscribers.[43] By contrast, in *The right to be forgotten I*, none of the people involved had been famous. Even after the crime, none of them had sought the limelight. In addition, the articles on them had been freely accessible.

The Federal Constitutional Court thus put much emphasis on the specifics of the two cases. It urged the Federal Court of Justice to consider all the aspects which the Strasbourg Court had deemed relevant. In doing so, the court exercised a practice which Andreas Engel analyses in his chapter of this book: the Federal Court of Justice limited the binding effect of the ECtHR judgment by granting much importance to the specifics of the case at hand. The more important these details are, the narrower the judgment's scope of application.[44]

Finally, the Federal Constitutional Court seized the opportunity to once again emphasise that Convention States enjoy a wide margin of appreciation. It pointed out that the ECtHR, in *M.L. and W.W. v. Germany*, had reiterated that, as long as Convention States take all relevant factors into account, 'strong reasons are required if it is to substitute its view for that of the domestic courts'.[45] The German court thus was well aware that the ECtHR had, in *M.L. and W.W. v. Germany*, formulated its role in a much more modest way than it had in *von Hannover I*. And yet, while the Federal Constitutional Court stressed that its analysis of the so-called right to be forgotten was in alignment with that of the ECtHR, it felt compelled to underline its own independence once more.

3.5. THE ECtHR's JUDGMENT IN *HURBAIN v. BELGIUM*

The ECtHR's Third Section reemphasised the broad margin of appreciation which national courts enjoy in a case which it decided in June 2021.[46] There, the applicant, Patrick Hurbain, was a publisher whose newspaper had, in 1994, reported on a car accident which had left two people dead and three people injured. In the report, the full name of

---

[43] Ibid., para. 151.
[44] See the chapter by A. ENGEL, 'The European Convention on Human Rights in the German Legal System: A Qualitative and Quantitative Introduction', in this volume.
[45] *M.L. and W.W. v. Germany*, no. 60798/10 and 65599/10, ECtHR (Fifth Section) 28 June 2018, para. 94.
[46] *Hurbain v. Belgium*, no. 57292/16, ECtHR (Third Section) 22 June 2021.

the driver (G) who had caused the accident was disclosed. The article was freely available in the newspaper's online press archive, and could be picked up by search engines. Belgian courts had found a violation of G's 'right to be forgotten', as enshrined in Article 8 ECHR, and had ordered the newspaper to anonymise the article.

Hurbain claimed that this violated Article 10 of the Convention. The majority of the ECtHR's Third Section was not convinced. It held that the Belgian courts had given relevant and sufficient reasons for their decisions: they had adequately taken the passage of time into consideration, and the required anonymisation of the article was a very effective means of safeguarding G's rights, and one which had left the archive intact. As such, the ECtHR held this approach to be 'proportionate to the legitimate aim pursued [G's right to privacy] and as striking a fair balance between the competing rights at stake'.[47]

The ECtHR ended its judgment by stating that the media companies were under no obligation to continuously check their archives, but that their obligations only kicked in once they had received an 'express request' for anonymisation.[48] While thus setting some outer limits, the court gave much leeway to Convention States. It conducted a merely procedural review of the Belgian case law. This approach was also on display in other judgments analysed in this book.[49]

The court's decision was rendered six to one. The dissenting judge, Darian Pavli from Albania, criticised that the majority had relied on the criteria it had established in *von Hannover I*.[50] Furthermore, he argued that the court had not sufficiently taken the role of search engines into account. Pavli believed that, while the majority had extensively analysed the CJEU's decision in *Google Spain*, it had failed to draw the right conclusions. In his opinion:

> It is important to consider the case at hand in the context of the emerging European consensus on balancing private and public interests in cases involving

---

[47] Ibid., para. 132.
[48] Ibid., para. 134.
[49] See the chapters by A. DUTTA, 'The Status of Biological Fathers: An Example for the Impact of the European Convention on Human Rights on National Family Law' and K. DUDEN, 'Parental Autonomy and Child Protection Measures: Procedural and Substantive Standards', in this volume. For a deeper analysis of the judgment, see K. DE LA DURANTAYE and CÉLINE M. LALÉ, 'Hurbain v. Belgien: Eine Entscheidung zum Vergessen?' (2022) *Zeitschrift für Europäisches Privatrecht* 660.
[50] *Hurbain v. Belgium*, no. 57292/16, ECtHR (Third Section) 22 June 2021, Dissenting Opinion by Judge Pavli, para. 17.

press archives. An important reference in this regard is the CJEU's ruling in *Google Spain*, to which today's judgment refers extensively.[51]

Pavli considered delisting a web page from name-based search engine results to be a less restrictive remedy than anonymising an entry in an online press archive. The latter could undermine the purpose of the archive to provide a full historical record, and as such, could potentially be dangerous for a democratic society.[52] Like the ECtHR in *M.L. and W.W. v. Germany*, and the CJEU in *Google Spain*, Pavli stressed that the obligations of search engine operators might differ from those of the media. The work of the media lay at the heart of freedom of expression, while search engines facilitated the identification of any available information on a person. In addition, he stressed, search engines have a '*transformational* impact on personal privacy', because they allow users to create '"a complete profile" of a person's life'.[53]

Moreover, Pavli pointed towards the Federal Constitutional Court's judgment in *The right to be forgotten I*. He found it notable because it 'introduced a nuanced methodology for balancing private and public interests in cases concerning digital press archives, with an emphasis on examining all available technical options before resorting to altering the historical records directly'.[54] The majority had not taken into account that media companies could use robot.txt files or similar blockers to prevent search engines from crawling their websites. Pavli took issue with this. According to him, the court should have looked at the whole picture, even though G had chosen not to hold the search engine operator liable, but had limited his claim to the media company.[55] Pavli feared that turning the triangular relationship between the individual, the media company and the search engine operator into a bilateral one might make for simplistic and potentially dangerous solutions. He summarised that the majority had upheld 'domestic decisions that failed to engage in the kind of careful balancing that other national and supranational courts across the continent have sought to develop in this delicate context'.[56]

---

[51] Ibid., para. 8.
[52] Ibid., paras. 1–2, 6.
[53] Ibid., para. 10 (Pavli's emphasis).
[54] Ibid., para. 14.
[55] Ibid., para. 21.
[56] Ibid.

Pavli does have a point. It is striking to see the difference between the court's rulings in *M.L. and W.W. v. Germany* and *Hurbain*. Both involved the 'right to be forgotten', and in both cases the individual had sued the media company, but had refrained from doing the same with Google. And yet, while the court's Fifth Section very eagerly discussed the role of search engine operators, and made a point of examining the full lie of the land, the Third Section confined itself to merely looking at the two players that were parties to the individual lawsuit.

The court's majority might have been moved by the differences in the crimes that had given rise to the initial reporting in *M.L. and W.W. v. Germany* and *Hurbain*. M.L. and W.W. had been convicted of a murder, and thus of an intentional and very grave crime which sparked additional public interest because the victim was a famous actor. By contrast, G had negligently caused a car accident with terrible consequences.[57] There is room for debate as to whether the initial publication of G's full name had been lawful. In granting G the right to have the articles anonymised, both the Belgian courts and the ECtHR may well have forced the publisher to right an old wrong.

Interestingly, the last word on *Hurbain* is still out. In September 2021, Patrick Hurbain requested that the case be referred to the court's Grand Chamber (Article 43, para. 1 ECHR). On 11 October 2021, a panel of five judges of the Grand Chamber decided that the case did indeed meet the requisite threshold of raising a serious question affecting the interpretation or application of the Convention or its Protocols, or a serious issue of general importance (Article 43, para. 2 ECHR). Accordingly, it referred the case to the Grand Chamber. The oral argument was held on 9 March 2022. The judges asked quite a few questions on possible technical avenues for media companies and search engine operators to limit the effects which entries in online press archives may have for a person's right to privacy.[58] However, the judgment is still pending.

---

[57] It is notable, though, that during the oral argument in front of the Grand Chamber on 9 March 2022, Patrick Hurbain's lawyer stressed that G was drunk and drove much faster than allowed. He called him a 'speeder' (*'chauffard'*). Cf. the recording at minute 6:05, https://www.echr.coe.int/Pages/home.aspx?p=hearings&w=5729216_09032022&language=lang&c=&py=2022.

[58] Judges Ranzoni, Pastor Vilanova und Schembri Orland asked questions to that effect. The recording of the entire oral argument is available at https://www.echr.coe.int/Pages/home.aspx?p=hearings&w=5729216_09032022&language=lang&c=&py=2022.

4. CONNECTING THE DOTS

For quite some time, the ECtHR has been influential in shaping the right to privacy in Germany. Its decision in *von Hannover I* sent shock waves through Germany, and led to a paradigmatic shift in its highest courts' jurisprudence.

Over the past few years, the landscape has become more complex. This is true for three main reasons. First, cases where courts have to strike a balance between the rights enshrined in Articles 8 and 10 ECHR now often involve three players. What used to be a bilateral issue between a media company and an individual has become a triangular one: search engines play a seminal role in disseminating personal information contained in press reports. All three players are not always parties to the lawsuit, though. In cases surrounding online press archives, individuals often sue the media company that runs the archive but do not also seek to hold Google accountable. On the surface, these cases look very similar to ones from 20 years ago, because the parties are the same. And yet, there is an elephant in the room. Courts have to decide whether and how to take the third player into account. In doing so, the ECtHR, the CJEU and the Federal Constitutional Court very much look at each other's decisions for inspiration, and are working in conjunction to develop rules for cases concerning the 'right to be forgotten'.

At the same time, differences in attitudes remain, sometimes even within the same court. The Federal Constitutional Court had Google very much on its mind when it decided *Right to be forgotten I*. It ordered German courts to consider technical means of blocking search engines from retrieving (and distributing) personal information when devising possible remedies against operators of online media archives. The goal would be to keep the archive intact, but to ensure that sensitive information would not be accessible by anyone with an Internet connection. The ECtHR's Fifth Section showed the same interest, in *M.L. and W.W. v. Germany*. In *Hurbain*, though, the majority (of the court's Third Section) focused on the bilateral relationship between G and the publishing house. It did not hold that changes to the content of press archives should be the last resort, and that a restriction of access for search engines might be a very effective means of safeguarding the right to privacy, and be less restrictive to the freedom of the press.

Second, while cases against press companies are within the classic domain of privacy, claims against search engine operators in cases concerning the 'right to be forgotten' are positioned at the intersection between privacy and data protection.[59] For the ECtHR's purposes, things do not change that much, since data protection is also covered under Article 8 ECHR. When it comes to the European Union (EU) and its Member States, though, this shift provides for dramatic changes. The regulation of the right to privacy is mostly left to the Member States. Article 7 of the Charter of Fundamental Rights of the European Union (CFREU) grants the right to a private life, but there is no specific EU instrument dedicated to privacy. Consequently, there is virtually no CJEU case law in this area. Meanwhile, data protection is not only part of a different Article of the CFREU (Article 8), but it is also very much harmonised within the EU. This is even more true since the General Data Protection Regulation entered into force in 2018; its Article 17 is specifically dedicated to the 'right to be forgotten'.[60]

Third, because of this high level of harmonisation of data protection within the EU, a new and powerful player has emerged among the courts – the CJEU. It is telling that the CJEU is the only one of the three courts in question to have been confronted with a case on the 'right to be forgotten' where Google was actually a party. Its judgment in *Google Spain* has been very influential, even in cases that did not formally involve search engines. Because the legal framework in which the CJEU operates is much more specific than that of the ECHR, and because the powers it holds are broader, the CJEU's case law on privacy, in the broad sense of the word, will, in all likelihood, grow in importance for the ECtHR, too, even though there is no formal relationship between the two courts. This might make for a more relaxed conversation between the courts. While, in the *von Hannover* cases, the ECtHR and the highest German courts were squabbling about their respective competences and duties, European courts seem more in synch in cases concerning the 'right to be forgotten'. They are all trying to solve a complex puzzle, and seem almost eager to informally pick up clues from one another.

---

[59] For a more profound analysis of the ECtHR's case law on data protection as enshrined in Article 8 ECHR, see the chapter by C. HEINZE and D. EBEL, 'Data Protection in Private Relations and the European Convention on Human Rights', in this volume.

[60] The CJEU already issued multiple judgments concerning that article, most notably, in October 2022, CJEU Case C-129/21, *Proximus*, ECLI:EU:C:2022:833.

DATA PROTECTION IN PRIVATE RELATIONS AND THE EUROPEAN CONVENTION ON HUMAN RIGHTS

Christian Heinze and Dominik Ebel

1. Europeanisation of Data Protection Law...........................138
2. Different Concepts of Data Protection 141
   2.1. Concept of Informational Self-Determination...............142
        2.1.1. Right to Informational Self-Determination..........142
        2.1.2. Delineation from the Right to be Forgotten 143
   2.2. Concept of Private Life 144
        2.2.1. Data Protection as an Emanation of the Right
               to Private Life....................................144
        2.2.2. Public Privacy as Private Life under Art. 8(1)
               ECHR...144
3. Consequences of the Privacy-Based Concept of the ECHR
   for Private Relations..145
   3.1. Consequences for the Scope of Protection..................145
        3.1.1. Informational Self-Determination under
               Art. 8(1) ECHR.....................................146
        3.1.2. Limits of Art. 8(1) ECHR...........................147
        3.1.3. Data Protection and Legal Entities.................147
   3.2. Consequences for Justification............................148
        3.2.1. Three-Step Test 148
        3.2.2. Interference by a Public Authority 149
   3.3. Data Protection in Private Relations as a Positive
        Obligation of the Contracting States......................149
        3.3.1. Positive Obligations Established by the ECtHR......150
        3.3.2. Monitoring of Employee's Internet Use 151
        3.3.3. Video Surveillance of Employees 152
        3.3.4. Registration of Divorce Settlement in Land
               Register...152

4. Conclusion... 153
   4.1. Scope of Application 153
   4.2. Justification... 154
   4.3. Methodological Approach 154
   4.4. Result.. 155

The objective of this chapter is to examine the relevance of the European Convention on Human Rights (ECHR)[1] for data protection in private relations, in comparison to the protection under the General Data Protection Regulation (GDPR).[2] This chapter first puts the ECHR and the GDPR in the context of the Europeanisation of data protection law (section 1). It then discusses the underlying concepts of data protection, namely informational self-determination and the protection of private life, and their roots (section 2). Next, it demonstrates the consequences which result from the ECHR approach for the protection of data in private relations (section 3). Finally, it compares the findings to data protection under the GDPR, and draws conclusions concerning the relevance of the ECHR for data protection in private relations (section 4).

1. EUROPEANISATION OF DATA PROTECTION LAW

The codification of data protection law in Europe began in the 1970s, with the adoption of legislation, by some states, to control the processing of personal information by public and private actors. In 1970, the German State of Hesse passed the world's first[3] data protection law.[4] Later in the 1970s, Sweden, France and Germany[5] enacted the first national data

---

[1] Council of Europe, Convention for the Protection of Human Rights and Fundamental Freedoms, 28 January 1981 (ETS No. 005). The Convention has been amended and supplemented by 16 additional protocols, the latest being Protocol No. 16 (CETS No. 214).

[2] Regulation (EU) 2016/679 of the European Parliament and of the Council of 27 April 2016 on the protection of natural persons with regard to the processing of personal data and on the free movement of such data, and repealing Directive 95/46/EC.

[3] S. BRETTHAUER 'Verfassungsrechtliche Grundlagen, Europäisches und nationales Recht', in L. SPECHT and R. MANTZ (eds), *Handbuch Europäisches und deutsches Datenschutzrecht*, C.H. Beck, Munich 2019, Teil A, §2, para. 3.

[4] Datenschutzgesetz (Hesse Data Protection Act), 7 October 1970, HessGVBl. I, S. 625. The law addressed only data protection in relation to public institutions.

[5] Gesetz zum Schutz vor Mißbrauch personenbezogener Daten bei der Datenverarbeitung (Bundesda-tenschutzgesetz – BDSG) (Federal Data Protection Act), 27 January 1977, BGBl. I, S. 201. The Act was revised in 1990 (BGBl. I, S. 2954), and in 2017 (BGBl. I, 2097).

protection laws. But it was not until 1983 that the Bundesverfassungsgericht (Federal Constitutional Court – BVerfG) developed the fundamental right to informational self-determination under the Grundgesetz (Basic Law for the Federal Republic of Germany – GG),[6] and thus subjected all processing of personal data by public actors to a legal reservation.[7]

The starting point of European data protection law was the Council of Europe Convention 108[8] in 1981, an international agreement on the protection of personal data. Although Convention 108 does not contain any rules on its own enforcement, it must be taken into account when interpreting Art. 8 ECHR.[9] Art. 8(1) ECHR itself does not explicitly guarantee a right to data protection as such, but protects 'the right to respect for private and family life'. However, in 1987, the European Court of Human Rights (ECtHR) found that the right to data protection was an emanation of the right to respect for private life under Art. 8(1) ECHR,[10] although the term 'data protection' was not used in the jurisprudence of the ECtHR.[11]

EU secondary law took up data protection with the Data Protection Directive,[12] which was significantly influenced by the German BDSG,[13] and which entered into force in 1995. The Court of Justice of the European Union (CJEU) developed, from the principles of the

---

[6] BVerfGE 65, 1 = *NJW* 1984, 419 – *Volkszählung*.

[7] K.V. LEWINSKI, 'Rechtsgeschichte des Datenschutzes', in G. RÜPKE, K.V. LEWINSKI and J. ECKARDT (eds), *Datenschutzrecht*, C.H. Beck, Munich 2018, §2, para. 67.

[8] Council of Europe, Convention for the Protection of Individuals with regard to Automatic Processing of Personal Data, 28 January 1981 (ETS No. 108). A modernised version was opened for signature on 10 October 2018: see Council of Europe, Protocol amending the Convention for the Protection of Individuals with regard to Automatic Processing of Personal Data (ETS No. 223).

[9] See R.J. SCHWEIZER, 'Die Rechtsprechung des Europäischen Gerichtshofes für Menschenrechte zum Persönlichkeits- und Datenschutz', *DuD* 2009, 462, 465, with further references; J.P. ALBRECHT and F. JOTZO, *Das neue Datenschutzrecht der EU*, Nomos, Baden-Baden 2017, Teil 1, para. 1.

[10] See *Leander v. Sweden*, no. 9248/81, §48, ECtHR 26 March 1987. In 1982, the ECtHR, in an inadmissible judgment on a compulsory public census, had already held that the requirement to complete a form asking for personal data constituted an interference with Art. 8(1) ECHR: see *X. v. the United Kingdom*, no. 9702/82, D.R. 30, 239 (240–41), ECtHR 6 October 1982 [inadmissible].

[11] S. SCHIEDERMAIR in S. SIMITIS, G. HORNUNG and I. SPIECKER (eds), *Datenschutzrecht*, Nomos, Baden-Baden 2019, Einleitung para. 165.

[12] Directive 95/46/EC of the European Parliament and of the Council of 24 October 1995 on the protection of individuals with regard to the processing of personal data and on the free movement of such data.

[13] K.V. LEWINSKI in H. AUERNHAMMER, *DSGVO/BDSG*, 7th ed., Carl Heymanns, Cologne 2020, Einführung, para. 10.

directive, the fundamental right to data protection under EU law.[14] Initially, in 2000, the CJEU only implicitly referred to this right, and based its argumentation on the general principles of the Member States' national laws.[15] In 2003, the CJEU expressly recognised, for the first time, this fundamental right as a manifestation of the general principles of EU law – referring to Art. 8 ECHR (cf. Art. 6(3) TEU) – and, therefore, as a part of EU primary law.[16] With the enactment of the Charter of Fundamental Rights of the European Union (CFR),[17] the fundamental right to data protection under Art. 8 CFR came into force in 2009, and established this right explicitly as part of EU primary law (Art. 6(1) TEU).[18] In 2016, the GDPR and the Data Protection Law Enforcement Directive[19] replaced the Data Protection Directive in secondary law.

This short sketch illustrates that the fundamental rights to data protection developed by constitutional courts have, since their beginnings, both at national and EU levels, been following legislative guarantees in statutory (secondary) law.[20] Unlike the CJEU and the national constitutional courts, the ECtHR lacks a secondary source of law on the basis of which it could concretise the guarantee under Art. 8 ECHR. It can, however, resort to Convention 108 as a functional, albeit less elaborate, substitute for secondary law sources, in order to further develop the fundamental right to data protection under the ECHR.

---

[14] J.P. ALBRECHT and F. JOTZO, *Das neue Datenschutzrecht der EU*, Nomos, Baden-Baden 2017, Teil 1, para. 2.

[15] CJEU Case C-369/98, *The Queen v. Minister of Agriculture, Fisheries and Food, ex parte Trevor Robert Fisher and Penny Fisher*, ECLI:EU:C:2000:443, paras. 33–34.

[16] CJEU Case C-465/00, *Rechnungshof v. Österreichischer Rundfunk and Others and Christa Neukomm and Joseph Lauermann v. Österreichischer Rundfunk*, ECLI:EU:C:2003:294, paras. 68–69.

[17] Charter of Fundamental Rights of the European Union (2007/C 303/01).

[18] For the interrelationship of the rights to data protection in EU primary law, see S. BRETTHAUER in L. SPECHT and R. MANTZ (eds), *Handbuch Europäisches und deutsches Datenschutzrecht*, C.H. Beck, Munich 2019, Teil A, §2 paras. 51–54.

[19] Directive (EU) 2016/680 of the European Parliament and of the Council of 27 April 2016 on the protection of natural persons with regard to the processing of personal data by competent authorities for the purposes of the prevention, investigation, detection or prosecution of criminal offences or the execution of criminal penalties, and on the free movement of such data, and repealing Council Framework Decision 2008/977/JHA.

[20] N. MARSCH, *Das europäische Datenschutzgrundrecht*, Mohr Siebeck, Tübingen 2018, p. 1.

2. DIFFERENT CONCEPTS OF DATA PROTECTION

EU law and ECHR conceptions of data protection are based on differing concepts, which find their roots in the specific design of their respective regulatory frameworks.

Under the GDPR, data protection law is based on the concept of informational self-determination.[21] This is reflected in the broad definitions of 'personal data' and 'data processing' (see Art. 4 (1) and (2) GDPR), covering all processing of personal data regardless of whether that data is private.[22] The GDPR also contains a general prohibition on the processing of personal data unless permission is granted by law (Arts. 5(1) and 6 GDPR).[23] Besides this, the regulation provides strong rights to data subjects, for example information, access and rectification (Art. 12 *et seq.* GDPR).[24] The obligations stemming from the GDPR are addressed both to public as well as private actors.

Data protection under the ECHR is built on a different premise: the concept of private life. Due to the lack of general rights to freedom or data protection in the ECHR, any form of data protection must be deduced from the right to respect for private and family life stemming from Art. 8 ECHR.[25] In contrast to the approach of the GDPR, the ECHR thus does not contain a general prohibition on the processing of personal data subject to certain exceptions, nor does it contain written rights for the data subject. Furthermore, it is binding only for the Contracting States and actors controlled by them (Art. 1 ECHR).[26] In the

---

[21] For more in-depth remarks on the implications of this concept, see K.V. LEWINSKI in H. AUERNHAMMER, *DSGVO/BDSG*, 7th ed., Carl Heymanns, Cologne 2020, Einführung, paras. 26–29. F. THOUVENIN, 'Informational Self-Determination: A Convincing Rationale for Data Protection Law?' 12 (2021) *JIPITEC* 246, para. 18, finds that the concept has not truly been implemented in the GDPR.

[22] See M. KARG in S. SIMITIS, G. HORNUNG and I. SPIECKER (eds), *Datenschutzrecht*, Nomos, Baden-Baden 2019, Art. 4 Nr. 1 DSGVO, para. 3; A. ROSSNAGEL in S. SIMITIS, G. HORNUNG and I. SPIECKER (eds), *Datenschutzrecht*, Nomos, Baden-Baden 2019, Art. 4 Nr. 2 DSGVO, para. 1.

[23] P. KRAMER in H. AUERNHAMMER, *DSGVO/BDSG*, 7th ed., Carl Heymanns, Cologne 2020, Art. 6 DSG-VO, para. 1.

[24] See R. MANTZ and J. MAROSI 'Vorgaben der Datenschutz-Grundverordnung', in L. SPECHT and R. MANTZ (eds), *Handbuch Europäisches und deutsches Datenschutzrecht*, C.H. Beck, Munich 2019, Teil A, §3, paras. 96–141.

[25] S. BRETTHAUER in L. SPECHT and R. MANTZ (eds), *Handbuch Europäisches und deutsches Datenschutzrecht*, C.H. Beck, Munich 2019, Teil A, §2, para. 39.

[26] J. MEYER-LADEWIG and M. NETTESHEIM in J. MEYER-LADEWIG, M. NETTESHEIM and S.V. RAUMER (eds), *EMRK*, 4th ed., Nomos, Baden-Baden 2017, Art. 1 EMRK, paras. 6–9.

horizontal relationship between private parties, data protection based on Art. 8 ECHR depends on whether the Contracting States are positively obliged to protect privacy between private parties, i.e. obliged to not merely abstain from violations by State organs, but also to make sure that the right to privacy can be effectively enjoyed in private law relations.[27] Thereby, the provision at least indirectly guarantees protection against private data processors. From this point of view, the concept of informational self-determination allows for a more extensive approach to data protection than the concept of private life does.

2.1. CONCEPT OF INFORMATIONAL SELF-DETERMINATION

The concept of informational self-determination was first coined by the BVerfG, and was adopted in 1995 by the Data Protection Directive (see Art. 2 (a) and (b)) as the underlying concept of data protection law in the EU.[28] Since 2016, the concept has been carried forward in EU secondary law, under the GDPR.

2.1.1. Right to Informational Self-Determination

In 1983, the BVerfG, in its *Volkszählung* verdict,[29] derived, for the first time, the fundamental right to informational self-determination from the general freedom of personality under Art. 2(1) GG, in conjunction with the fundamental guarantee of human dignity in Art. 1(1) GG.[30]

The right to informational self-determination empowers the individuals to determine for themselves the disclosure and use of their personal data.[31] The Court concretised the general freedom of personality in the context of personal data. It held that the free development of the

---

[27] Ibid., Art. 8 EMRK, paras. 2 and 5.
[28] See K.V. LEWINSKI in H. AUERNHAMMER, *DSGVO/BDSG*, 7th ed., Carl Heymanns, Cologne 2020, Einführung, paras. 10 and 29. The concept of informational self-determination as the underlying concept of EU data protection law seems to be the prevailing view (see recital 7 GDPR), but it is not undisputed, see F. THOUVENIN, 'Informational Self-Determination: A Convincing Rationale for Data Protection Law?', (2021) *JIPITEC* 246, 248 note 10, 250 note 18 with references.
[29] BVerfGE 65, 1 = *NJW* 1984, 419 – *Volkszählung*.
[30] For a view that is sceptical towards the status of this right as a separate fundamental right, see S. SIMITIS, 'Die informationelle Selbstbestimmung – Grundbedingung einer verfassungskonformen Informationsordnung', *NJW* 1984, 389, 399.
[31] BVerfGE 65, 1, 43 = *NJW* 1984, 419, 421 et seq. – *Volkszählung*.

personality presupposes the protection of the individual against the unlimited collection, storage, use and disclosure of his or her personal data.[32] The Court found that, against the background of modern methods of processing and linking data, based on automatic data processing, there is no longer any data which can be regarded as irrelevant.[33] As a consequence, the scope of protection of the right to informational self-determination is defined broadly. As automatic data processing is often non-transparent for the individual data subject, the fundamental right of informational self-determination also aims to prevent the possible effects of intimidation. The BVerfG found that citizens who are uncertain whether their behaviour will be monitored and stored as information which could potentially be used or passed on might refrain from pursuing a divergent behaviour.[34] With this verdict, the Court established the right to data protection, in the form of informational self-determination, as a fundamental right with a broad scope of protection.

2.1.2. Delineation from the Right to be Forgotten

In 2019, the BVerfG, in *Recht auf Vergessen I*, acknowledged the right to be forgotten as an expression of the general freedom of personality under Art. 2(1) GG in conjunction with Art. 1(1) GG.[35] In this case, the BVerfG drew a distinction between the right to be forgotten (based on the freedom of personality, not on data protection law (see Art. 17 GDPR, which also establishes a right to erasure)) and the right to informational self-determination.[36] The latter protects against the unintentional disclosure of individual data, and especially against its non-transparent processing and use by public actors and private parties.[37] Informational self-determination also offers protection against third parties taking possession of individual data and utilising such data in a non-transparent manner as a means of determining the characteristics, types or profiles of the individual data subjects affected.[38] In contrast, the right to be forgotten, as an emanation of the right to personality, protects against statements affecting personal honour.[39] The need for protection in this context is thus based on the

---

[32] Ibid.
[33] Ibid., 423 – *Volkszählung*.
[34] Ibid., 421 *et seq*. – *Volkszählung*.
[35] BVerfGE 152, 152 = *NJW* 2020, 300 – *Recht auf Vergessen I*.
[36] BVerfGE 152, 152, 192 = *NJW* 2020, 300, 308 – *Recht auf Vergessen I*.
[37] Ibid.
[38] Ibid.
[39] Ibid.

visible dissemination of certain information in the public space that is likely to damage an individual's reputation.[40] In such cases, the nature of the access to the information is only of subordinate importance.[41]

2.2. CONCEPT OF PRIVATE LIFE

The concept of private life as a justification for data protection under Art. 8(1) ECHR was first developed by the ECtHR in 1987, and has been expanded since then.

2.2.1. Data Protection as an Emanation of the Right to Private Life

In the *Leander v. Sweden* judgment of 1987, the ECtHR examined, for the first time, whether the storage and release of information relating to an individual's personal life, by a public authority, constituted an interference falling under Art. 8(1) ECHR.[42] The Court held that the storage in a secret register, by the police, of information on an individual's personal or political background, and the release of such information, coupled with a refusal to allow the individual an opportunity to refute the information, interfered with the individual's right to respect for private life under Art. 8(1) ECHR.[43] On that note, the Court implicitly ruled that data protection is an emanation of the right to respect for private life, according to Art. 8(1) ECHR.

2.2.2. Public Privacy as Private Life under Art. 8(1) ECHR

In 2000, the ECtHR, in the *Rotaru v. Romania* verdict, revisited the scope of protection under Art. 8(1) ECHR, and the distinction between private and public life.[44]

The Court found that information on an individual's public political activities can fall under Art. 8(1) ECHR when systematically collected and stored by public authorities, even if it is public information.[45] This broad notion of private life, which includes public information, is derived from Art. 2 of Convention 108, which defines personal data

---

[40] Ibid.
[41] Ibid.
[42] *Leander v. Sweden*, no. 9248/81, §48, ECtHR 26 March 1987.
[43] Ibid.
[44] *Rotaru v. Romania* [GC], no. 28341/95, §§42–44, ECtHR 4 May 2000.
[45] Ibid., §43.

as any information relating to an identified or identifiable individual. According to this notion of private life, respect for private life also encompasses the right to establish and develop relationships with other individuals.[46] Further, there is no compelling reason to justify excluding activities of a professional or business nature from the notion of private life.[47] The Court thereby found that the public accessibility of certain information does not necessarily preclude Art. 8(1) ECHR from applying. Not only the informational content of personal data, but also the extent and consequences of its processing, are relevant in this context.[48]

3. CONSEQUENCES OF THE PRIVACY-BASED CONCEPT OF THE ECHR FOR PRIVATE RELATIONS

As outlined above, the ECHR is founded on a privacy-based concept. This implies consequences for the scope of its protection, and for the scope of the justifications for data processing, under Art. 8 ECHR, especially in private relations.

3.1. CONSEQUENCES FOR THE SCOPE OF PROTECTION

With regard to the scope of protection under Art. 8 ECHR, the ECtHR seems to adhere to the view that the processing of personal data does not, per se, fall under Art. 8(1) ECHR but, rather, must show a certain link to the individual's private life.[49] In order to determine whether the data in question involves any aspect relating to an individual's private life, it is necessary to assess its nature, the context in which it has been processed and used, and the results derived from it.[50] For example, personal data operations have been found to fall under Art. 8(1) ECHR if the data in

---

[46] Ibid.
[47] Ibid.
[48] N. MARSCH, *Das europäische Datenschutzgrundrecht*, Mohr Siebeck, Tübingen 2018, p. 12; S. DRACKERT, *Die Risiken der Verarbeitung personenbezogener Daten*, Duncker & Humblot, Berlin 2014, p. 69.
[49] See N. MARSCH, *Das europäische Datenschutzgrundrecht*, Mohr Siebeck, Tübingen 2018, p. 15.
[50] *S. and Marper v. the United Kingdom* [GC], nos. 30562/04 and 30566/04, §67, ECtHR 4 December 2008, with further references.

question has been the subject of systematic or permanent recording,[51] if it has been used in a process intended to identify an individual in connection with other personal data,[52] or if it has been published in a manner which exceeds what the data subject could reasonably have expected.[53] Another element in the assessment is whether the individual can reasonably expect protection of his or her private life.[54] Some types of personal data and certain methods of processing are more problematic than others, and may, per se, entail a relevance for private life.[55]

3.1.1. Informational Self-Determination under Art. 8(1) ECHR

While data protection under the ECHR is based on the right to private life, recent case law suggests an approximation to the concept of informational self-determination. In the *Satakunnan Markkinapörssi Oy and Satamedia Oy v. Finland* case, in 2017, the ECtHR ruled for the first time that Art. 8(1) ECHR encompasses the right to a form of informational self-determination.[56] This allows individuals to rely on their right to privacy concerning data which are collected, processed and disseminated collectively, and in such a manner that their right to private life may be engaged.[57] This could indicate a conceptual approximation to the data protection approach under the GDPR, potentially resulting in an expansion of the scope of protection. However, Art. 8(1) ECHR still has important limitations.

---

[51] *Uzun v. Germany*, no. 35623/05, §51, ECtHR 2 September 2010.
[52] *P.G. and J.H. v. the United Kingdom*, no. 44787/98, §38, ECtHR 25 September 2001.
[53] *Peck v. the United Kingdom*, no. 44647/98, §§58–59, ECtHR 28 January 2003; *Perry v. the United Kingdom*, no. 63737/00, §38, ECtHR 17 July 2003.
[54] *Perry v. the United Kingdom*, no. 44647/98, §37, ECtHR 17 July 2003; *Bărbulescu v. Romania* [GC], no. 61496/08, §80, ECtHR 5 September 2017.
[55] See *Z v. Finland*, no. 22009/93, §71, ECtHR 25 February 1997; *Radu v. Republic of Moldova*, no. 50073/07, §27, ECtHR 15 April 2014; *Mockutė v. Lithuania*, no. 66490/09, §§93–95, ECtHR 27 February 2018.
[56] *Satakunnan Markkinapörssi Oy and Satamedia Oy v. Finland* [GC], no. 931/13, §137, ECtHR 27 June 2017. See also J. KÜHLING, M. KLAR and F. SACKMANN (eds), *Datenschutzrecht*, 5th ed., C.F. Müller, Heidelberg 2021, para. 29. Before 2017, scholars predominantly did not recognise the right to informational self-determination under Art. 8(1) ECHR: see N. MARSCH, *Das europäische Datenschutzgrundrecht*, Mohr Siebeck, Tübingen 2018, p. 15 with further references.
[57] *Satakunnan Markkinapörssi Oy and Satamedia Oy v. Finland* [GC], no. 931/13, §137, ECtHR 27 June 2017.

3.1.2. Limits of Art. 8(1) ECHR

In consequence of the necessity for there to be some relation to an individual's private life in the processing of personal data, not all such processing falls within the scope of protection under Art. 8(1) ECHR.

For example, in its 2014 *Cakicisoy and Others v. Cyprus* judgment, the ECtHR held that an interference with an individual's right to private life can be ruled out if the individual concerned consented to the collection of personal data for further processing, and was informed about the purpose of the processing, and the data was actually processed according to the stated purpose.[58] Equally, in *Mehmedovic v. Switzerland*, in 2018, the Court did not find an interference with Art. 8(1) ECHR, on the grounds that the collection of information gathered by coincidence, without relevance for a specific purpose, does not concern an individual's private life.[59] Therefore, consent, by the data subject, to the data processing, or a non-systematic or non-permanent gathering of data, excludes the operation in question from the scope of Art. 8(1) ECHR, due to the lack of a sufficient link to the data subject's private life.

3.1.3. Data Protection and Legal Entities

On the basis of the private life concept of data protection under Art. 8(1) ECHR, the entitled person can not only be a natural person, but also a legal person. In 2008, the ECtHR held, in *Liberty and Others v. United Kingdom*, that the mere statutory option of monitoring a legal entity's communications constitutes an interference with the entity's rights to respect for private life (as well as for its correspondence), under Art. 8(1) ECHR.[60] In the 2013 case of *Bernh Larsen Holding AS and Others v. Norway*, the Court left unanswered the question whether a legal person's obligation to provide a copy of all data on a server in its premises to the tax authorities constituted an interference with its right to respect for private life.[61] However, the Court implied that, under certain circumstances, this obligation could interfere with the entity's private life, and that it already interfered with its home and

---

[58] *Cakicisoy and Others v. Cyprus*, no. 6523/12, §51, ECtHR 23 September 2014.
[59] *Mehmedovic v. Switzerland*, no. 17331/11, §18, ECtHR 11 December 2018.
[60] *Liberty and Others v. the United Kingdom*, no. 58243/00, §§56–57, ECtHR 1 July 2008.
[61] *Bernh Larsen Holding AS and Others v. Norway*, no. 24117/08, §107, ECtHR 14 March 2013.

correspondence.[62] In its *Avilkina and Others v. Russia* judgment of 2013, the ECtHR clarified that it is necessary, under any circumstances, for the legal person, and not only the natural persons associated with that entity, to be directly affected by the measure in question.[63]

3.2. CONSEQUENCES FOR JUSTIFICATION

An interference with private life under Art. 8(1) ECHR, due to the processing of personal data by a public authority, can be justified under Art. 8(2) ECHR if it was lawful, necessary in a democratic society and pursued a legitimate aim. The ECtHR's application of these criteria has been influenced by Art. 5 of Convention 108, which sets outs guidelines for the automatic processing of personal data (especially lawful obtaining and processing (para. (a)) and storing for specified and legitimate purposes and not using in a way incompatible with those purposes (para. (b))).[64]

3.2.1. Three-Step Test

An interference with private life under Art. 8(1) ECHR is lawful if it has a legal basis at national level[65] which is sufficiently clear and foreseeable.[66] As for data protection in private relations, the question arises how to deal with consent to the processing, on one hand, and contractual obligations to condone or perform the processing of data, on the other hand. Informed, unequivocal and voluntary consent may exclude a finding of interference with private life, or may lead to the processing of personal data being considered 'in accordance with the law', within the meaning

---

[62] Ibid., §§106–07.
[63] *Avilkina and Others v. Russia*, no. 1585/09, §59, ECtHR 6 June 2013.
[64] See European Court of Human Rights, *Guide on Case-Law of the Convention – Data Protection*, last updated 31.08.2022, paras. 86 and 96, available at https://www.echr.coe.int/Documents/Guide_Data_protection_ENG.pdf.
[65] For cases in which an interference lacked a legal basis at national level, see *Taylor-Sabori v. the United Kingdom*, no. 47114/99, §§17–19, ECtHR 22 October 2002; *Radu v. the Republic of Moldova*, no. 50073/07, § 31, ECtHR 15 April 2014; *Mockutė v. Lithuania*, no. 66490/09, §§103–04, ECtHR 27 February 2018.
[66] For cases in which the legal basis for an interference was not sufficiently clear or foreseeable, see *Rotaru v. Romania* [GC], no. 28341/95, §§57–62, ECtHR 4 May 2000; *Vukota-Bojić v. Switzerland*, no. 61838/10, §§71–77, ECtHR 18 October 2016; *Ben Faiza v. France*, no. 31446/12, §§58–61, ECtHR 8 February 2018; *Benedik v. Slovenia*, no. 62357/14, §132, ECtHR 24 April 2018.

of Article 8(2).[67] As for data processing permitted by contract, the legal basis for this may either be found in national data protection laws which permit data processing for the purposes of the performance of a contract, or (more problematic) in contract law itself. The interference must pursue a legitimate aim listed in Art. 8(2) ECHR, for example public safety, the economic well-being of the state, or the protection of the rights and freedoms of others. While these aims address concerns that are more public than private in nature, the protection of the rights and freedoms of others, in particular, can become relevant in private relations. An interference is necessary in a democratic society if it meets a pressing social need and is not disproportionate to the legitimate aim pursued.[68]

3.2.2. Interference by a Public Authority

As a consequence of the ECHR being binding for the Contracting States only (Art. 1 ECHR), data protection under Art. 8 ECHR primarily aims to protect individuals against interferences by public authorities (Art. 8(2) ECHR). However, Art. 8 ECHR can also impose positive obligations on the Contracting States, in order to ensure data protection between private individuals.[69]

3.3. DATA PROTECTION IN PRIVATE RELATIONS AS A POSITIVE OBLIGATION OF THE CONTRACTING STATES

An interference with the guarantee of private life under the ECHR, including the protection of personal data, by a public authority, raises the question of a negative obligation of the Contracting State to refrain from interfering. If, however, an individual or private entity processes personal data, the ECHR will not immediately be applicable (Art. 1 ECHR). Rather, the case will be examined from the perspective of the state's positive obligation to protect one private actor from data protection violations

---

[67] See European Court of Human Rights, *Guide on Case-Law of the Convention – Data Protection*, last updated 31.08.2022, paras. 232–241.
[68] *Vicent Del Campo v. Spain*, no. 25527/13, §46, ECtHR 6 November 2018; *Khelili v. Switzerland*, no. 16188/07, §62, ECtHR 18 October 2011; *Z v. Finland*, no. 22009/93, §94, ECtHR 25 February 1997.
[69] See, for the concept of the state's positive obligations, section 3.3 below.

by another private actor.⁷⁰ While the concepts of negative and positive obligations are not further specified in the ECHR, the applicable principles are similar: the competing interests of the individual and the community as a whole must be balanced fairly, subject to the margin of appreciation enjoyed by the state.⁷¹ Where an infringement is particularly grave, the state's margin is, correspondingly, narrowed.⁷² Thus, in serious cases, the state must establish a specific legislative framework covering the particular act, taking into consideration the various interests (e.g. respect to private life) to be protected in this context.⁷³ In less serious cases (for example, monitoring of an employee's Internet use), the state does not always need to set up a specific legal framework, but must in any case ensure that the infringing measures are accompanied by adequate and sufficient (general) safeguards against abuse.⁷⁴

3.3.1. Positive Obligations Established by the ECtHR

In the context of data protection law, the ECtHR has established, inter alia, the following positive obligations of states to protect personal data in private relations: protection of personal data from unauthorised disclosure;⁷⁵ documenting data processing operations;⁷⁶ identification of individuals responsible for data breaches,⁷⁷ and holding them liable for data breaches (depending on the seriousness of interference under criminal or civil law);⁷⁸ as well as access of an individual to his or her personal data.⁷⁹

---

[70] *Craxi v. Italy (no. 2)*, no. 25337/94, §§68–76, ECtHR 17 July 2003; *Alkaya v. Turkey*, no. 42811/06, §32, ECtHR 9 October 2012; *Söderman v. Sweden* [GC], no. 5786/08, §89, ECtHR 12 November 2013; *Bărbulescu v. Romania* [GC], no. 61496/08, §111, ECtHR 5 September 2017; *López Ribalda and Others v. Spain* [GC], nos. 1874/13 and 8567/13, §111, ECtHR 17 October 2019; *Buturugă v. Romania*, no. 56867/15, §§60–63, ECtHR 10 February 2020.

[71] *Bărbulescu v. Romania* [GC], no. 61496/08, §112, ECtHR 5 September 2017; *Liebscher v. Austria*, no. 5434/17, §62, ECtHR 6 April 2021.

[72] See *Mosley v. the United Kingdom*, no. 48009/08, §109, ECtHR 10 May 2011.

[73] See *Söderman v. Sweden* [GC], no. 5786/08, §§80–83, ECtHR 12 November 2013, with examples.

[74] *Bărbulescu v. Romania* [GC], no. 61496/08, §§119–20, ECtHR 5 September 2017.

[75] *I. v. Finland*, no. 20511/03, §38, ECtHR 17 July 2008.

[76] Ibid., §44.

[77] *K.U. v. Finland*, no. 2872/02, §49, ECtHR 2 December 2008.

[78] *Söderman v. Sweden* [GC], no. 5786/08, §117, ECtHR 12 November 2013.

[79] *K.H. and Others v. Slovakia*, no. 32881/04, §46, ECtHR 28 April 2009, with further references.

3.3.2. Monitoring of Employee's Internet Use

In the 2017 case *Bărbulescu v. Romania*, the ECtHR assessed whether the monitoring of an employee's communications, and the inspection of their content by his employer, in the course of his potential dismissal, interfered with Art. 8(1) ECHR.[80] The Court found this to be a fairly minor interference, and thus granted the state a wide margin of appreciation in assessing the need to establish a special legal framework governing the conditions under which an employer may regulate communications of a non-professional nature in the workplace.[81] However, it must be ensured that measures taken by an employer to monitor its employee's communications, irrespective of the scale and duration of these measures, are accompanied by adequate and sufficient safeguards against abuse.[82] The Court found the following factors to be relevant when assessing whether the competing interests of the employee and the employer have been fairly balanced:

- a notice in advance about the monitoring, its implementation and its nature;
- the extent of the monitoring and the degree of intrusion into private life;
- the legitimacy of the reasons for justifying the monitoring measures;
- the existence of less intrusive monitoring methods to pursue the aim;
- the consequences of the monitoring for the employee subjected to it;
- the employer's use of the results of the monitoring (with regard to the employer's aim);
- the provision of adequate safeguards to the employee.[83]

Measured against these criteria, the Court held that the state had failed to meet its positive obligation to weigh the employee's right to respect for his private life against the employer's right to engage in monitoring in order to ensure the smooth running of the company.[84] The domestic courts had failed to determine whether any of the criteria for an adequate and sufficient safeguard had been met.[85] Thus, the Court concluded that there had been a violation of Art. 8 ECHR.

---

[80] *Bărbulescu v. Romania* [GC], no. 61496/08, §§82–141, ECtHR 5 September 2017.
[81] Ibid., §119.
[82] Ibid., §120.
[83] Ibid., §121.
[84] Ibid., §141.
[85] Ibid., §140.

3.3.3. Video Surveillance of Employees

In its 2019 *López Ribalda and Others v. Spain* verdict, the ECtHR held that the (partially non-covert) video surveillance of employees by their employer, in connection with potential dismissal for theft, constituted an interference with private life in the sense of Art. 8(1) ECHR.[86] The Court found this case to concern a positive obligation of the state to ensure respect for the private lives of employees, by striking a fair balance between such interests and the interests of the employer in protecting its property and ensuring the smooth operation of its company.[87] As the interference was regarded as being fairly minor, the state could, within the scope of its margin of appreciation, decide not to create a specific legislative framework.[88] However, it had to ensure that the interfering measures were proportionate and accompanied by adequate and sufficient safeguards against abuse (see the criteria from *Bărbulescu v. Romania*, listed above).[89] In this case, the state had put a legislative framework intended to protect the private lives of employees in place, which provided significant safeguards.[90] Therefore, there had been no violation of Art. 8 ECHR.

In contrast, in *Antović and Mirković v. Montenegro*, in 2017, the Court had found that the non-covert video surveillance of university lecturers while they were teaching – the recordings had been stored for a limited time and could be consulted by the dean – violated the right to respect for private life under Art. 8 ECHR.[91] Even though there was a legal framework to protect the interests of the lecturers, the conditions of these laws had not been met, meaning that the infringement was not lawful, and was unjustified under Art. 8(2) ECHR.[92]

3.3.4. Registration of Divorce Settlement in Land Register

In the 2021 case *Liebscher v. Austria*, the ECtHR held that the obligation to present an entire divorce settlement as a basis for an entry in the land register, and for the settlement to be published in the public document

---

[86] *López Ribalda and Others v. Spain* [GC], nos. 1874/13 and 8567/13, §109, ECtHR 17 October 2019.
[87] Ibid., §118.
[88] Ibid., §113.
[89] Ibid., §§114–16.
[90] Ibid., §§119–37.
[91] *Antović and Mirković v. Montenegro*, no. 70838/13, §§44–45, ECtHR 28 November 2017.
[92] Ibid., §§55–60.

archive, interfered with Art. 8 ECHR.[93] Again, the Court considered the case to concern a positive obligation of the state to guarantee effective respect for private life in private relations.[94] In this case, the national courts had failed to assess the possibility of interpreting the applicable provisions of the domestic Land Register Act in compliance with Art. 8 ECHR.[95] Instead, the court had simply declared that the obligation in question had a clear legal basis under domestic law.[96] As a consequence, there had been a violation of Art. 8 ECHR.

4. CONCLUSION

Following this short sketch of data protection in private relations, under the umbrella of the right to respect for private life in Art. 8(1) ECHR, the findings can be compared with the GDPR, in terms of the scope of application, the justification for interferences and the methodological approach. On this basis, a conclusion as to the relevance of the ECHR for data protection in private relations can be drawn.

4.1. SCOPE OF APPLICATION

Concerning its substantive scope of application, the GDPR is applicable to any form of processing of personal data (Art. 4 (a) and (b)), to the extent that personal data of a natural person is involved.[97] In comparison, Art. 8(1) ECHR applies only where a person's private life is concerned. Thus, data protection differs under the ECHR, and under the GDPR: while the GDPR applies to any form of processing of personal data which needs a justification (consent, legal basis, balancing test: Art. 6 GDPR), Art. 8(1) ECHR applies only where 'private life' is concerned. Even if the definition of 'private life', as concerns the processing of personal data, has been expanded over time, it still does not seem to grant a conclusive form of protection for all personal data. However, most recent judgments

---

[93] *Liebscher v. Austria*, no. 5434/17, §67, ECtHR 6 April 2021.
[94] Ibid., §60.
[95] Ibid., §68.
[96] Ibid., §65.
[97] See Regulation (EU) 2016/679 of the European Parliament and of the Council of 27 April 2016 on the protection of natural persons with regard to the processing of personal data and on the free movement of such data, and repealing Directive 95/46/EC, Recital 14.

referring to 'informational self-determination' seem to indicate that the ECtHR could adopt a broader concept of data protection, although its exact contours are still uncertain. On the other hand, the scope of personal protection is broader under Art. 8 ECHR than it is under the GDPR, as the ECHR provision covers legal persons as well.

4.2. JUSTIFICATION

On the justification side, EU law, in principle, treats public and private actors responsible for handling personal data in the same way. Under the ECHR, the handling of personal data by private actors only infringes Art. 8(1) ECHR where the state has violated its 'positive obligation' to adequately protect privacy between private actors. This test essentially contains two elements:

(1) For serious cases, Contracting States must enact specific protective legislation (very rare, and mostly limited to serious criminal offences).
(2) In other cases, Contracting States enjoy a margin of appreciation. They must, however, ensure that their measures are accompanied by adequate and sufficient safeguards against abuse (see the *Barbulescu* criteria listed in section 3.3.2. above).

As a result, the ECHR provides for a proportionality test based on certain flexible criteria ('structured proportionality'). By contrast, the GDPR defines specific fixed grounds of justification where proportionality is considered as part of a ground of justification ('proportionality within formal grounds of justification').

4.3. METHODOLOGICAL APPROACH

EU law, in particular the fundamental right to data protection, is heavily influenced by secondary law: it displays a certain 'merger' of primary and secondary law. The reason for this seems to be that secondary legislation preceded case law in the development of data protection. The ECHR has, from a doctrinal perspective, no comparable 'secondary law basis' that could influence the interpretation and evolution of Art. 8(1) ECHR. Still, the ECtHR often resorts to Convention 108, the EU Data Protection

Directive, and the GDPR, in its judgments.[98] Differently from the CJEU's approach to interpretation which focuses on the GDPR, the ECtHR uses comparative analysis to a much greater extent,[99] to determine, for example, how Contracting States should approach video surveillance in the workplace. This analysis impacts on the margin of appreciation and the guarantees against abuse.

4.4. RESULT

The contribution of the ECHR to data protection in private relations is less important in EU Member States than in non-Member States. In Member States, the GDPR already offers extensive protection, not only against public authorities, but also in relations between individuals. However, the ECHR is important in at least three respects:

(1) For non-Member States of the EU;[100]
(2) To help determine which elements of data protection are actually part of a fundamental right, and which are only enshrined in secondary law;[101]
(3) As an element of reflection on whether a privacy-based concept or an informational self-determination-based concept (covering all forms of processing of personal data) is better suited to finding an optimal balance between data protection and other interests (for example, in big data or machine learning processes).

---

[98] For a reference to Convention 108, see *Rotaru v. Romania* [GC], no. 28341/95, §43, ECtHR 4 May 2000.

[99] See *López Ribalda and Others v. Spain* [GC], nos. 1874/13 and 8567/13, §§67–70, ECtHR 17 October 2019; *Bărbulescu v. Romania* [GC], no. 61496/08, §§52–54, ECtHR 5 September 2017.

[100] See S. SIMITIS, G. HORNUNG and I. SPIECKER (eds), *Datenschutzrecht*, Nomos, Baden-Baden 2019, Einleitung, para. 117, with an enumeration of said Contracting States.

[101] See S. BRETTHAUER 'Verfassungsrechtliche Grundlagen, Europäisches und nationales Recht', in L. SPECHT and R. MANTZ (eds), *Handbuch Europäisches und deutsches Datenschutzrecht*, C.H. Beck, Munich 2019, Teil A, §2, para. 40; T. KINGREEN in C. CALLIESS and M. RUFFERT (eds), *EUV/AEUV*, 5th ed., C.H. Beck, Munich 2016, Art. 6 EUV, para. 21.

COPYRIGHT AS A FUNDAMENTAL RIGHT AND THE INFLUENCE OF THE CASE LAW OF THE EUROPEAN COURT OF HUMAN RIGHTS AND OF THE EUROPEAN COURT OF JUSTICE

Giovanni Maria Riccio

1. The Confusing Age of Copyright 157
2. Is Copyright a Fundamental Right? 162
3. Copyright as a Fundamental Right in Other International Conventions. 164
4. The Case Law of the ECJ 166
5. The Case Law of the ECtHR 169
6. The 'Propertisation' of Copyright and the Need for a Different Approach 172

1. THE CONFUSING AGE OF COPYRIGHT

Copyright is living through confusing years. This confusion is due to the erosion of a systematic approach to the boundaries of this area and, consequently, to the interests that copyright should protect.

When investigating the relationship between copyright and fundamental rights, the first questions an intellectual property scholar should ask are: what does copyright protect? What are the interests that copyright effectively safeguards? Why should copyright be included in the list of fundamental rights?

Instinctively, it could be argued that copyright should be focused on the development of culture and art. In all the international conventions, and in the recitals of the European Union (EU) directives devoted to copyright, the protection of creativity, art and culture is a common reference, but is it a declamatory or an effective reference? Is it a tinsel to embellish the legislative text or a form of respect towards legal traditions?

The rationale of copyright protection is to be sought at a deeper level, also taking into account the necessity of determining economic incentives for the authors, and for the cultural industry as a whole.[1] This chapter aims to briefly analyse how the economic and moral aspects of copyright affect the attempt to investigate whether copyright is a fundamental right, how systematically copyright is placed among other fundamental rights, and the balance, in cases of conflict, between copyright and other fundamental rights.

The uncertainty of this systematic analysis of copyright and, especially, of its purposes, can be exampled by the examination of the subject matter (i.e. the protected works), and by the list of the categories of works which are included within copyright protection. This aspect differs between different jurisdictions: in some cases, the applicable regulations provide a closed list of works (for example, UK, India, Australia), while in others this list is open, as long as some preconditions are fulfilled (for example, France, Germany, Italy). Apart from this distinction, which reflects the frameworks of the different legal traditions, we are facing the enlargement of copyright boundaries (as well as those in all other sectors of intellectual property). Those boundaries are progressively expanding to include works which have not traditionally been included within the categories of literary, dramatic, musical and artistic works, or, in general, among cultural and artistic works.[2]

Recently, one of the most discussed copyright cases, heard by the European Court of Justice (ECJ), dealt with the copyrightability of a fragrance. Is there any connection between a fragrance and the 'progress of ... useful arts' mentioned in Article 1, clause 8 of the US Constitution, or the 'the Encouragement of Learned Men to Compose and Write useful Books', as affirmed by the Statute of Anne?

Copyright has changed its skin: the protection granted by international conventions, European legislation and national rules has progressively

---

[1] *Mazer v. Stein*, 347 U.S. 201, 219 (1954): 'the economic philosophy behind the clause empowering Congress to grant patents and copyrights is the conviction that encouragement of individual effort by personal gain is the *best* way to advance public welfare through the talents of authors and inventors in "Science and useful Arts"'.

[2] On this aspect, see J. PILA, 'Copyright and Its Categories of Original Works' (2010) 30 *Oxford Journal of Legal Studies* 229.

moved from authors' interests to those of the market. The patrimonialisation of the copyright rules is evident, and does not deal merely with (legitimate) support for the cultural productive chain (i.e. the production of the works), but more deeply with the intimate nature of these rules. Property rules have been chosen as the only legislative way to protect intellectual property in general, and copyright in particular, neglecting other forms of legal protection that could adequately balance the need to ensure incentives for those who create, and guarantees for the public's free access to knowledge.

Moreover, analysis of the EU's copyright legislation over the last few decades, especially in the last 20 years, appears patchy, and often driven by emergency reasons – for example, by new technologies – or by lobbyist pressures.[3] The European legislation on copyright first appeared in the 1990s, with two directives which included software and databases within the spectrum of copyright protection (Directive 91/250/EEC of 14 May 1991 on the legal protection of computer programs, repealed by Directive 2009/24/EC and Directive 96/9/EC on the legal protection of databases), even if these were not directly related with culture and arts, granting protection, in particular, to those making economic investments aimed at composing software and database works. Nevertheless, despite this aspect, these directives were useful for the purpose of globally regulating such works; in recent years, on the other hand, many interventions of the European institutions on copyright seem disarticulated from one another, and neither the Commission nor the Council seem to have a long-term view of the sector's problems, nor of the proper solutions to these problems.

A recent example is Directive no. 2019/790 on copyright and related rights in the Digital Single Market (CDSM), which contains several controversial provisions, such as Article 15 on the protection of press publications concerning online uses. This is one of the most discussed Articles of the directive, and has been implemented differently (and in some cases, imaginatively) by individual Member States; it exemplifies the business-oriented, rather than authors' rights-oriented, approach of the European legislation.

---

[3] The most recent example is the Directive (EU) 2019/790 of the European Parliament and of the Council of 17 April 2019 on copyright and related rights in the Digital Single Market and amending Directives 96/9/EC and 2001/29/EC. See C. ANGELOPOULOS and J.P. QUINTAIS, 'Fixing Copyright Reform. A Better Solution to Online Infringement' (2019) 10 *Journal of Intellectual Property, Information Technology and E-Commerce Law* 147, para. 1.

Starting from these premises, it is difficult even to discuss the inclusion of copyright among the fundamental rights, though the attempt to include copyright (and intellectual property in general) within the fundamental rights is quite recent, and, as will be analysed in further detail later, has not yet been properly categorised.

Copyright is a product of the industrial revolution, and of the creative processes of the cultural industry. Similarly, the rise of copyright law coincided with the processes of urbanisation, and the advent of the bourgeoisie, which became the social class that benefitted most from intellectual works, determining the need for a specific market in these.

As a part of the capitalistic society, copyright plays a fundamental role in the development of the cultural industries, and also as a source of employment, and income of opportunities. At the same time, though, copyright legal regimes may affect the diffusion of knowledge, creating barriers to accessing copyrighted works (such as scientific publications, news publications, software and databases), having a negative impact on the development of the production of new cultural works.

The source of this confusion is also due to the different origins of copyright law in the main different geographical areas (at least those belonging to the so-called Western legal tradition). Thus, it is necessary, albeit briefly, to retrace the philosophical assumptions that differentiate common law and civil law legal systems.

In common law legal systems, the rationale of copyright regulations is based on the social utility of the works, whereby the authors are conceived as producers of wealth for the whole society. Thus, according to the utilitarian theory, copyright is needed in order to guarantee authors with means of sustenance, even in periods during which they are not productive.

Conversely, personalistic theory – which is archetypal of the civil law area – holds that the works are an extension of the author's personality, thereby also protecting the moral rights of the authors themselves. According to this view, copyright aims to allow individuals to express themselves and their thoughts.

A corollary of the utilitarian theory is the labour theory, which is influenced by Lockean positions, according to which copyright is a reward for the time spent by authors on the creation of their works. Furthermore, the purpose of the royalties granted to authors is to guarantee their independence, and thus intellectual property is a way to contribute to the edification of a free culture (free from external influences), from which the entire society may benefit.

The above arguments help in investigating whether copyright is a fundamental right, and, if so, what the theoretical roots are that justify the inclusion of copyright among the fundamental rights.

In this scenario, at least for European law, a watershed was marked by the Lisbon Treaty, which entered into force in 2009, and whose impact will be investigated further later in this chapter. In fact, before this Treaty, the EU had no jurisdiction over copyright law, and decisions of the ECJ were based on Article 30 EC, which allowed an exception to the freedom of circulation of goods and services in the case of industrial property protection.[4]

Similarly, pursuant to Article 345 of the Treaty on the Functioning of European Union (TFEU), '[t]he Treaties shall in no way prejudice the rules in Member States governing the system of property ownership.' Yet the ECJ's forays into the intellectual property law sector have been frequent, and have often contained misinterpretations caused by a merger between common law and civil law traditions, and the use of a polymorphic language which is affected by different legal traditions.[5]

Over the same years, the ECtHR has changed its jurisprudence by admitting that intellectual property, and notably copyright, falls within the scope of Article 10 of the European Convention on Human Rights (ECHR). Also, discussions on copyright as a fundamental right disregard moral interests, taking into consideration only the material interests embodied in copyright. In fact, the present chapter might also lead to a provocatory outcome, concluding that moral rights do not belong to intellectual property law, at least in the context of the fundamental rights.

However, some recent publications, based on extensive interpretation of the ECtHR case law, suggest that moral rights could also be included in the list of fundamental rights (at least in the ECHR context). Other international conventions, although not allowing for direct enforcement, could even be included in the analysis, since these conventions provide protections for intellectual property rights (including copyright) which are not based purely on property rules, but also on liability rules and other rules aimed at ensuring incentives to authors, balancing intellectual property rights with other rights (for example, access to knowledge or information).

---

[4] See A. Lucas-Schloetter, 'Is there a concept of European Copyright Law? History, Evolution, Policies and Politics and the Acquis Communautaire' in I. Stamatoudi and P. Torremans (eds), *EU Copyright Law: A Commentary*, Edward Elgar Publishing, Northampton 2014, pp. 5 *et seq.*

[5] See C. Sganga, *Propertizing European Copyright: History, Challenges and Opportunities*, Edward Elgar Publishing, Northampton 2018, pp. 88 *et seq.*

2. IS COPYRIGHT A FUNDAMENTAL RIGHT?

The assumption that copyright is a fundamental right is often apodictic. Essentially, it can be argued, on the one hand, that copyright is a fundamental right because it is a corollary of another fundamental right (the right to private property). On the other hand, copyright is an expression of the author's personality and could, therefore, be ascribed to free speech, or to speech rights.

This dichotomy could lead to two antithetical answers (private property/free speech), depending on whether the question regarding the underlying basis for copyright as a fundamental right is posed to legal scholars educated within the civil law or the common law traditions; this is only one piece in a more complicated puzzle.

As mentioned above, the utilitarian theory has strongly influenced the private property approach, by pointing out that copyright should be considered as associated with the social utility of the works. In this sense, authors are 'producers' of social wealth, and thus law should essentially guarantee them the means of subsistence, even during periods when they are not productive. On this view, the monopoly power granted to the authors (and to other subjects to whom the rights are transferred) is an incentive to create and innovate, which balances the free access of the public to these resources. According to this first theory, the real question should be 'does copyright maximise public wealth?'.

Theoretically speaking, recognising copyright as a fundamental right should cover the multiple sides of this right, whether economic or personal. In practice, if the legislative sources are always associated with the idea that copyright is only part of a property right, then only the material part of the copyright itself would be fully protected (at least as a fundamental right). May we conclude that the personal aspects of copyright are not fundamental rights, and that this designation exclusively covers the economic aspects?

The two main legislative provisions invoked by scholars when discussing whether copyright can be included in the list of fundamental rights are Article 17(2) of the Charter of Fundamental Rights of the European Union (CFREU), and Article 1, Protocol 1 of the ECHR.

These two legislative backgrounds are different, considering that the ECHR does not contain a specific clause on intellectual property, but the protection of intellectual property (and specifically of copyright) may be found in two places in the ECHR: first, Article 1, Protocol 1 ECHR, which protects intellectual property as a specification of the right to property; second, from another perspective, considering intellectual property to be a constraint on the full application of fundamental rights other than the right to property, such as, for instance, the freedom of expression and information (Article 10 ECHR), the right to privacy (Article 8 ECHR), and the freedom of assembly and association (Article 11 ECHR).

In the CFREU, copyright is a fundamental right under Article 17(2), which laconically states that '[i]ntellectual property shall be protected', bringing intellectual property back into the realm of property rights. This provision has, for a long time, been widely discussed by legal scholars, who have criticised the choice to circumscribe intellectual property (and thus copyright) exclusively within the boundaries of private property,[6] as well as the vagueness of the provision.[7]

Article 17(2) is the result of a lack of uniformity among national legal traditions: the concise and apparently nonsensical formulation of the rule reflects this theoretical fragility, failing to take a position between the proprietary-centric vision of intellectual property, and a vision that emphasises the role of the author and the production of works as an expression of his or her personality. Limiting copyright to the protection spectrum of property law means admitting that copyright is nothing more than a legal mechanism of the capitalist economy, and that the position of authors is subordinate to that of producers; or, if preferred, that the authors are only the last piece of a complex jigsaw.

This conclusion is confirmed by the explanations prepared under the Praesidium of the Convention which drafted the CFREU, which hold that intellectual property is 'one aspect of the right of property'.[8]

---

[6] See ibid.; C. GEIGER, 'Intellectual Property Shall be Protected!? – Article 17(2) of the Charter of Fundamental Rights of the European Union: a Mysterious Provision with an Unclear Scope' (2009) *European Intellectual Property Review* 115.

[7] See J. GRIFFITHS and L. MCDONAGH, 'Fundamental Rights and European IP Law: The Case of Art 17(2) of the EU Charter' in C. GEIGER (ed), *Constructing European Intellectual Property: Achievements and New Perspectives*, Edward Elgar Publishing, Cheltenham, UK/Northampton, MA, US 2013.

[8] Explanations relating to the Charter of Fundamental Rights (2007/C 303/02), Official Journal of the European Union, C 303/17, 14.12.2007.

3. COPYRIGHT AS A FUNDAMENTAL RIGHT IN OTHER INTERNATIONAL CONVENTIONS

Intellectual property is also included in other international conventions, which take different approaches from both the CFREU and the ECHR.[9]

Article 27 of The Universal Declaration of Human Rights (UDHR) states that, '[e]veryone has the right freely to participate in the cultural life of the community, to enjoy the arts and to share in scientific advancement and its benefits'.[10] The second paragraph of the same provision holds that, '[e]veryone has the right to the protection of the moral and material interests resulting from any scientific, literary or artistic production of which he is the author'.[11]

Similarly, the nature of copyright as a fundamental right is also associated with Article 15(1)(c) of the International Covenant on Economic, Social and Cultural Rights of 1966 (ICESCR), where it is recorded that State Parties recognise the right of every person '[t]o benefit from the protection of the moral and material interests resulting from any scientific, literary or artistic production of which he is the author'.

The perspectives of both provisions seem to be centred on the author, who is the owner of the right granted, although the latter provision (Article 15(1)(c)) refers to the 'production' rather than to the 'work', as if to grant protection exclusively to works that are the outcome of industrial cultural production.

In any case, Article 27 UDHR and Article 15 ICESCR subvert the now dominant idea that intellectual property is subordinate to other human (and fundamental) rights,[12] insofar as the comparative parameter is not merely the right to property, but also an aspect of copyright which is not

---

[9] For a complete overview, see P.K. YU, 'Reconceptualizing Intellectual Property Interests in a Human Rights Framework' (2007) 40 *U.C. Davis Law Review* 1039, 1047–52.

[10] Article 27: '1. Everyone has the right freely to participate in the cultural life of the community, to enjoy the arts and to share in scientific advancement and its benefits. 2. Everyone has the right to the protection of the moral and material interests resulting from any scientific, literary or artistic production of which he is the author'.

[11] See F. MACMILLAN, '"Speaking Truth to Power": Copyright and the Control of Speech' in O. POLLICINO, G.M. RICCIO and M. BASSINI (eds), *Copyright and Fundamental Rights in the Digital Age. A Comparative Analysis in Search of a Common Constitutional Ground*, Edward Elgar Publishing, Cheltenham, UK/Northampton, MA, US 2020, p. 23.

[12] L.R. HELFER, 'Toward a Human Rights Framework for Intellectual Property' (2007) 40 *U.C. Davis Law Review* 971.

related to the monopoly structure, nor to the material interests which are protected, from different perspectives, by the CFREU and the ECHR.

Moreover, the insertion of moral interests (which precede the references the material ones, in both of these legal formulas) might suggest a different interpretation of the potential conflicts of intellectual property with other fundamental rights. Moral rights in intellectual property generally have a scope of application which is not limited to, and not necessarily focused on, the dichotomy of private versus public rights, by having an impact which affects copyright rules, and also those rules pertaining to cultural heritage, and to the collective rights of communities.

This interpretation, even if fascinating, does not fit with the intentions of the UDHR (or of the ICESCR): the moral rights protection was a concern of the UDHR's drafters, but was limited to the right of authors to be recognised as the creators of their works, and to object to any distortion, mutilation or other modification which would be prejudicial to their honour and reputation, in line with Article 6*bis* of the Berne Convention.

Moreover, interpretations of these rules seem to confirm this understanding, by latently recognising the supremacy of economic over moral interests. In particular, General Comment 17 of the Committee on Economic, Social and Cultural Rights, although it states that Article 15(1)(c) ICESCR 'safeguards the personal link between authors and their creations and between peoples, communities, or other groups and their collective cultural heritage', contradictorily concludes that 'intellectual property regimes primarily protect business and corporate interests and investments'.[13]

On the other hand, 'material interests', referred to in Article 27 UDHR and Article 15 ICESCR, apparently seem to be compatible with Article 1, Protocol 1 of the Convention, and with Article 17(2) of the CFREU. Probably, as one author argues, these provision do not contain references to the right to property simply because of Cold War politics and the concerns raised by socialist countries,[14] similarly to Article 17 of the UDHR, which uses the term '*own* property' rather than '*private* property'.

However, the same author notes that both Article 27 UDHR and Article 15 ICESCR fit with regimes other than property, such as liability

---

[13] Committee on Economic, Social and Cultural Rights, General Comment 17, the right of everyone to benefit from the protection of the moral and material interests resulting from any scientific, literary or artistic production of which he or she is the author (Article 15, paragraph 1 (c), of the Covenant), UN Doc. E/C.12/GC/17 (12.01.2006).

[14] P.K. Yu, 'Reconceptualizing Intellectual Property Interests in a Human Rights Framework' (2007) 40 *U.C. Davis Law Review* 1039, 1085.

rules, and rules granting rewards and economic benefits to authors.[15] In other words, material rights do not necessarily correspond to property rights, as a material interest can also be acquired in other ways. Consider, for instance, works created by public employees: in many jurisdictions, works (for example, publications) created by employees of public entities are not covered by copyright, even if incentives are provided to their authors (for example, 17 U.S.C. §105 US Copyright Law), or a moral right is granted to them (for example, in Italy). Similarly, in some cases, liability rules may be more effective than proprietary rules in finding a balance between an economic monopoly (a characteristic of copyright regimes) and the need for cultural participation and access to the works.

Thus, copyright is not the only way to ensure incentives for authors; the free-access movement promotes compensation for creators, provided that their works are released under free-use or free-access licences.[16] The exegesis of Article 27 UDHR and Article 15 ICESCR – not mentioning property rules – could be a path to be followed.

4. THE CASE LAW OF THE ECJ

Thus far, national courts have never applied Article 27 UDHR or Article 15 ICESCR; however, as will be scrutinised below, they have frequently adopted the interpretations provided by the ECJ and, albeit more rarely, the ECtHR.

When analysing the case law of the ECJ, and of the ECtHR, a preliminary (and obvious) assumption must be considered. The ECJ has the principal aim of harmonising the laws of each Member State, especially in the field of copyright, where legislative interventions have generally been made through directives, leaving a certain degree of space to individual jurisdictions. Moreover, as stated above, intellectual property was not originally included in the EU's harmonisation purposes. On the other hand, the ECtHR is the judicial body of an international organisation, and its principal purpose is to ensure the correct application of the Convention.

However, there is no doubt that the case law of each court influences that of the other, and that the case law of both courts influences the states

---

[15] Ibid.
[16] See D.L. ZIMMERMAN, 'Authorship Without Ownership: Reconsidering Incentives in a Digital Age' (2003) 52 *DePaul Law Review* 1121, 1126.

belonging to the EU, or which ratified the Convention, even if, because of a language issue (the decisions of the ECtHR are only available in French), the decisions based on the ECtHR are not often referred to by the national courts. However, some scholars have recently demonstrated that this trend is changing, and that lower courts (not surprisingly, especially French-speaking courts) are also increasingly applying these precedents.[17]

The inclusion, in the CFREU, of a reference to intellectual property has reinforced the position of the ECJ, which has frequently invoked the fundamental rights to support its decisions.[18] Often, the reference to fundamental rights, or rather to copyright as a fundamental right, appears to be instrumental in justifying *ex post* a reasoning of the ECJ as long as the conclusions of the rulings of the Court, in this context, have remained unmodified even after the introduction of the Charter of Fundamental Rights.[19]

This chaotic scenario in EU law can be explained by the fragmentation of legislative interventions on copyright by the European institutions, which have often been driven by emergency reasons, or by lobbyist pressures.[20] After the adoption of the CFREU, the ECJ has, as mentioned above, often referred to the fundamental rights in copyright cases; undoubtedly, at least in the ECJ's interpretation, Article 17 CFREU is aimed at protecting property rights.[21]

This assumption was openly affirmed in the *Laserdisken* decision, where the Court stated that the freedom to receive information could

---

[17]   See C. GEIGER and E. IZYUMENKO, *Shaping Intellectual Property Rights Through Human Rights Adjudication: The Example of the European Court of Human Rights*, Center for International Intellectual Property Studies Research Paper No. 2020-02 (2020), fn. 15.

[18]   See C. GEIGER, 'The Role of the Court of Justice of the European Union: Harmonizing, Creating and Sometimes Disrupting Copyright Law in the European Union' in I. STAMATOUDI (ed), *New Developments in EU and International Copyright Law*, Kluwer Law International, Alphen aan den Rijn 2016, p. 444.

[19]   Similarly, M. HUSOVEC, 'The Essence of Intellectual Property Rights Under Article 17(2) of the EU Charter' (2019) 20 *German Law Journal* 840, 849: 'Today's IP case-law of the CJEU is dominated by fundamental rights rhetoric. The number of cases which rely on the fundamental rights – including the right to intellectual property – have risen substantially since the Lisbon Treaty entered into force.'

[20]   See C. ANGELOPOULOS and J.P. QUINTAIS, 'Fixing Copyright Reform. A Better Solution to Online Infringement' (2019) 10 *Journal of Intellectual Property, Information Technology and E-Commerce Law* 147, para 1.

[21]   For further details, see A. STROWEL, 'Copyright strengthened by the Court of Justice interpretation of Article 17(2) of the EU Charter of Fundamental Rights' in O. POLLICINO, G.M. RICCIO and M. BASSINI (eds), *Copyright and Fundamental Rights in the Digital Age. A Comparative Analysis in Search of a Common Constitutional Ground*, Edward Elgar Publishing, Cheltenham, UK/Northampton, MA, US 2020, p. 28.

be limited by intellectual property rights, 'which form part of the right to property'.[22] However, this statement has been widely discussed in the ECJ's decisions, following the approval of the Lisbon Treaty, where judges have been called on to fix a scale of the values and of the rights to be protected, raising the question of balancing copyright (considered as an absolute and granitic right) with other fundamental rights. The ECJ's case law has been decisive in showing how intellectual property (and copyright, in particular) may coexist with other sectors, such as competition law and freedom of expression, although not in drawing the boundaries of the 'mysterious provision'[23] contained in Article 17(2) of the CFREU.

In any case, the ECJ seems never to have changed its position, considering copyright (as a type of intellectual property) exclusively as a patrimonial right, without admitting its personalistic connotations.

This conclusion is evident if we analyse the cases concerning the filtering obligations of Internet service providers, as requested by the copyright holders, and the balance struck by the ECJ in these cases.[24] The cases of *Promusicae* (where the facts of the case occurred before the adoption of Article 17(2)), *Scarlet* and *Netlog* were referred to the ECJ, in order to decide whether an obligation to communicate the personal data of the users of a service infringing the copyright of the claimants (in *Promusicae*), or an obligation to install filtering systems – applied indiscriminately to all users, irrespective of any suspicion of infringing acts (*Scarlet* and *Netlog*) – as a preventive measure, were precluded by EU law.

In *Promusicae*, the ECJ concluded that the EU legal framework – notably the e-Commerce Directive[25] and the InfoSoc Directive[26] – does not require the Member States to lay down an obligation to disclose personal data to ensure effective protection of copyright in the context of civil proceedings. In particular, the decision laid down that Member States,

---

[22] CJEU Case C-479/04, *Laserdisken*, ECLI:EU:C:2006:549, para. 65.
[23] C. GEIGER, above n. 6, 118.
[24] CJEU Case C-275/06, *Productores de Música de España (Promusicae) v. Telefónica de España SAU*, Judgment of 29 January 2008, ECLI:EU:C:2008:54; Case C-70/10, *Scarlet Extended NV v. Belgische Vereniging van Auteurs, Componisten en Uitgevers CVBA (SABAM)* ('*Scarlet*'), Judgment of 24 November 2011, ECLI:EU:C:2011:771; CJEU Case C-360/10, *Belgische Vereniging van Auteurs, Componisten en Uitgevers CVBA (SABAM) v. Netlog NV* ('*Netlog*'), Judgment of 16 February 2012, ECLI:EU:C:2012:85.
[25] Directive 2000/31/EC of the European Parliament and of the Council of 8 June 2000 on certain legal aspects of information society services, in particular electronic commerce, in the Internal Market.
[26] Directive 2001/29/EC of the European Parliament and of the Council of 22 May 2001 on the harmonisation of certain aspects of copyright and related rights in the information society.

when implementing EU directives, must ensure a fair balance between the various fundamental rights protected by the Community legal order.

This fair balance was clarified in the *Scarlet* and *Netlog* decisions, in which the Court held that there was nothing in the EU legislation, or in the ECJ's case law, which considered copyright as inviolable, and, for that reason, absolutely protected. In particular, these rulings emphasised that an obligation imposing the adoption of filtering measures would have caused a systematic scrutiny of the users' personal data, also jeopardising their freedom to receive or impart information, as long as there was a possibility that these filters might not adequately differentiate between unlawful contents and lawful ones.[27]

Thus, the balance among competing rights was recognised in favour of the protection of personal data and freedom of speech, over copyright. This balancing test has since been confirmed in other cases, such as *GS Media*,[28] in which the Court has recognised that the Internet is essential for safeguarding freedom of expression, and that the interests of copyright holders in protecting their intellectual property rights, pursuant to Article 17 of the CFREU, would have to be interpreted in the light of the freedom of expression and information of users, under Article 11 of the CFREU.[29]

5. THE CASE LAW OF THE ECtHR

The discourse on copyright as a fundamental right is possibly even more intricate in the case law of the ECtHR than in that of the ECJ. First, because, as already mentioned, the Convention does not contain any definition of (or reference to) intellectual property as such. Moreover, references to property were only introduced by the First Protocol, in 1953, even if a definition of right to property is still not present.

The ECtHR, since the *Sporrong* case, has been of the opinion that Article 1, Protocol 1 comprises three distinct rules.[30] The first rule, set

---

[27] *Scarlet*, para. 43; *Netlog*, para. 41.
[28] CJEU Case C-160/15, *GS Media BV v. Sanoma Media Netherlands BV and Others*, Judgment of 8 September 2016, ECLI:EU:C:2016:644.
[29] The ECJ has resorted to the same approach in other cases, such as those dealing with the lawfulness of hyperlinks. For further details, see E. ROSATI, 'Linking and Copyright in the Shade of VG Bild-Kunst', (2021) 58 *Common Market Law Review* 1875.
[30] *Sporrong and Lönnroth v. Sweden*, no. 7151/75, ECtHR 18 December 1984, para. 61.

out in the first sentence of the first paragraph, enounces the principle of peaceful enjoyment of property. The second rule, which is in the second sentence of the same paragraph, covers deprivation of possessions. The third rule, contained in the second paragraph of the provision, recognises that states are entitled to control the use of property in accordance with the public interest, by enforcing such laws as they deem necessary for that purpose.

Intellectual property has struggled to be recognised by the ECtHR: all claims based on intellectual property violations were dismissed by the European Commission on Human Rights until 1990, with the decision in the *Smith Kline* case.[31] Only in 2007 did the ECtHR state, for the first time, that the right to property under the ECHR covers the financial interests of intellectual property owners in their inventions, creations and marks.[32]

Here, again, the spectrum of protection is limited to the economic interests of IP (including copyright), without any reference to moral rights. This conclusion, as with the interpretation of Article 17(2) by the ECJ, is even clearer, considering that intellectual property is interpreted in the context of the right to property, and that the non-patrimonial aspects of IP fall outside the jurisdiction of both courts.

The majority of the rulings issued by the ECtHR deal with the potential conflict between Article 1, Protocol 1, and copyright law.

Preliminarily, as highlighted by many legal scholars, it has to be remembered that copyright is affected by a paradox.[33] Copyright is no longer an engine of free expression, nor is it an instrument to empower and improve progress – reflecting the words used by the US Constitution, and by the Statute of Anne, the seminal legislative acts on the protection of intellectual works – copyright, before being considered a fundamental right, could be a limit on the exercise of other fundamental rights, such as freedom of expression.

This outcome was expressed by the ECtHR in *Ashby Donald and others v. France*.[34] This case involved three photographers who were ordered by the French national courts to pay fines for the unauthorised publication of pictures of models during a fashion show, without the permission

---

[31] *Smith Kline and French Laboratories Ltd. v. The Netherlands*, no. 12633/87, Commission decision of 4 October 1990.
[32] *Anheuser-Busch Inc. v. Portugal*, no. 73049/01, ECtHR Grand Chamber Judgment, 11 January 2007.
[33] N.W. NETANEL, *Copyright's Paradox*, OUP, Oxford 2008.
[34] *Ashby Donald and others v. France*, no. 36769/08, ECtHR 10 January 2013.

of the fashion houses who had organised the event. In its ruling, the ECtHR recalled that Article 10 ECHR is applicable to communication by means of the Internet (and thus also to an Internet site), whatever the type of message being conveyed, and even when the objective pursued is lucrative. Furthermore, freedom of expression includes the publication of photographs, and this freedom is subject to exceptions, even if these exceptions must be construed strictly, and the need for any restrictions must be established convincingly. Thus, Article 10 should be accompanied by exceptions, which should be interpreted narrowly, and the need to restrict it must be established in a convincing manner.

Briefly, the ECtHR stated that a restriction of the use of copyrighted works can be regarded as an interference with the right of freedom of expression, and that the infringement of a copyright law provision is not a sufficient justification for restricting this freedom. The Court also held that the ECHR affords state authorities a particularly wide margin of appreciation in the balancing of the competing rights.[35]

The ECtHR also reached the same conclusion in the *Pirate Bay* case.[36] This case concerned the managers of a peer-to-peer platform who had been convicted for their assumed complicity in committing copyright infringements. The peculiarity of the case was that Pirate Bay did not directly host, on its servers, any protected content, limiting its activity to the maintenance and making available of a peer-to-peer file sharing system, through which Internet users could exchange files present on their computers, often including works protected by copyright, without any permission from the holders of the rights.

In the opinion of the Court, Article 10 ECHR covered the right to receive and distribute information and, regarding the instant case, the activities of sharing copyrighted works reproduced in files on the Internet. Further, according to the Court's decision, the national courts had correctly balanced the interests at stake: notably, the protection of copyright, on the one hand, and the right to receive and impart information from or to third parties, on the other.

---

[35] See H.G. RUSE-KHAN, 'Overlaps and conflict norms in human rights law: Approaches of European Courts to Address Intersections with Intellectual Property Rights' in C. GEIGER (ed), *Research Handbook on Human Rights and Intellectual Property*, Edward Elgar Publishing, Cheltenham 2015, p. 20.

[36] Case C-610/15, *Stichting Brein v. Ziggo BV, XS4ALL Internet BV*, Judgment of 14 June 2017, ECLI:EU:C:2017:456.

The ECHR, even if not expressly, contains a link between copyright and Article 8, which deals with privacy and intimate life, concerning the protection of moral rights. Despite the lack of judicial precedents, legal scholars believe that moral rights fall within the material scope of this provision for two reasons:[37] the first is that, in the only case dealing with image rights and trademarks, the reasoning of the Court was in line with moral rights; the second reason relates to the inclusion of moral rights among personality rights,[38] in some states, such as Germany and Italy.

6. THE 'PROPERTISATION' OF COPYRIGHT AND THE NEED FOR A DIFFERENT APPROACH

The previous section underlined how copyright regulations, both at an international and a European level, have emphasised the role of property rules. However, these rules seem not to be the most efficient means of regulating copyright, as they focus exclusively on one face of the dice. Moreover, as stated above, the centralisation of the property aspects of copyright may create conflict with other fundamental rights, even in secondary legislation, through which the weaknesses of the interpretations of both the CFREU and ECHR reverberate.

For instance, the tension between copyright and freedom of expression, and the detachment from the original values of copyright protection, is clearly reflected in Article 15 of the Directive on Copyright in the Digital Single Market (CDSM),[39] which has created a new and disputed ancillary right which benefits press publishers. The principal aim of this rule is to ensure that press publishers receive remuneration in the event of reuse of their publications by Internet operators, notably news aggregators.

---

[37] See J. DREXL, 'Constitutional Protection of Authors' Moral Rights in the European Union – Between Privacy, Property and the Regulation of the Economy' in K.S. ZIEGLER (ed), *Human Rights and Private Law: Privacy as Autonomy*, Hart Publishing, Oxford 2007, pp. 173–74.

[38] C. GEIGER and E. IZYUMENKO, *Shaping Intellectual Property Rights Through Human Rights Adjudication: The Example of the European Court of Human Rights*, Center for International Intellectual Property Studies Research Paper No. 2020-02 (2020).

[39] N.W. NETANEL, *Copyright's Paradox*, OUP, Oxford 2008, p. 6: 'Yet copyright too often stifles criticism, encumbers individual self-expression, and ossifies highly skewed distributions of expressive power. Copyright's speech burdens cut a wide swath, chilling core political speech such as news reporting and political commentary, as well as church dissent, historical scholarship, cultural critique, artistic expression, and daily entertainment. And copyright imposes those speech burdens to a far greater extent than can be justified by applauding its "engine of free expression" role.'

The mechanism adopted in the CDSM has attracted a lot of criticism. As far as this chapter is concerned, the most stinging criticism relates to the difficulties that freelancers, and non-institutional press publishers in general, may encounter in reusing news. In such circumstances, as stated above, copyright could curb the possibility of elaborating press information, and so the new mechanism adopted in the CDSM could be, at the same time, an economic benefit for 'static' information (i.e. the information which has been created by its author) and a disadvantage for the modification and adaptation of existing pieces of information (i.e. news created through access to, and elaboration of, the existing news).

Moreover, the new rules do not affect the quality of information. On the contrary, a paradoxical effect could occur aggregators could use press agencies established outside the territory of the EU – as has already happened after the approval of the Spanish law[40] – to which the directive and individual national transposition laws would not apply.

This aspect is sufficient to demonstrate the inefficiency of Article 15 CDSM in relation to freedom of speech, or at least its absolute indifference to this freedom.

In this author's opinion, a different approach could have been followed, as focusing the copyright debate on property rules may also have a negative effect on lower courts, which, following the analysis of the ECJ and the ECtHR, may limit the scope of copyright protection to material rights, assigning an ancillary, or at least subordinate, role to moral interests.

---

[40] Law 21/2014, of 29 December 2014 which has modified the Spanish Copyright Law.

PART IV
PROCEDURAL LAW

THE RELATIONSHIP BETWEEN ARTICLE 6 OF THE EUROPEAN CONVENTION ON HUMAN RIGHTS AND INTERNATIONAL COMMERCIAL ARBITRATION

Francesca BENATTI

1. Introduction 177
2. Access to Justice 180
3. Independence, Impartiality and Neutrality.................... 183
   3.1. Definition 183
   3.2. Impartiality and Duty of Disclosure 190
4. Conclusion... 194

1. INTRODUCTION

Traditionally,[1] the European Convention on Human Rights (ECHR) has been deemed inapplicable to voluntary arbitration,[2] primarily due to the absence of any reference to arbitration in the preparatory drafts, or in Art. 6 ECHR. However, scholars note, correctly,[3] that this apparent oversight was due to a historical context in which recourse to

---

[1] A. JAKSIC, 'Procedural Guarantees of Human Rights in Arbitration Proceedings – A Still Unsettled Problem?' (2007) 24(2) *Journal of International Arbitration* 159; see also A. SAMUEL, 'Arbitration, Alternative Dispute Resolution Generally and the European Convention on Human Rights' (2004) 21(5) *Journal of International Arbitration* 413.

[2] In cases of compulsory arbitration, the guarantees provided by the ECHR had to be respected. See the debate in C. JARROSSON, 'L'arbitrage et la Convention européenne des droits de l'homme' (1989) *Revue de l'arbitrage* 573.

[3] M. BENEDETTELLI, 'Human rights as a litigation tool in international arbitration: reflecting on the ECHR experience' (2015) 31 *Arbitration International* 631.

commercial arbitration was not so frequent or relevant. Moreover, the legal equivalence of arbitral awards to court judgments (now accepted in all legal systems) invalidates objections based on the difference between a 'tribunal established by law' and an 'arbitral tribunal' founded on an agreement between the parties. The ECHR has stressed that

> the term tribunal in Article 6(1) need not be understood in the sense of a court of the classical type, integrated within the standard judicial apparatus of the country; it may therefore be a body established to determine a limited number of specific questions, provided that it offers the appropriate guarantees.[4]

A static and traditional reading of Art. 6 is, then, at odds with the interpretation of the Convention adopted by the European Court of Human Rights (the Court or ECtHR), which characterises the Convention as a 'living document', in order to enable it to adapt flexibly to new social needs and requirements. Although this view is not without criticism, and may lead to subjective and arbitrary decisions, it appears justified with regard to the extension of Art. 6 to arbitration. Respect for the principles of due process, albeit with some functional differences, must also be guaranteed in such proceedings.[5]

Deweer v. Belgium[6] thus represents a decisive case in which the Court held that the Convention does not prevent parties from waiving their rights to court proceedings through an arbitration clause. And in *Suovaniemi v. Finland*, the Court clarified even more precisely that

> there is no doubt that a voluntary waiver of court proceedings in favour of arbitration is in principle acceptable from the point of view of Art. 6 ... Even so, such a waiver should not necessarily be regarded as a waiver of all rights under Art. 6 ... An unequivocal waiver of Convention rights is valid only to the extent that such a waiver is 'admissible'. It may be admissible for some rights but not for others. A distinction can also be made between different rights guaranteed by Art. 6.[7]

The undeniable advantage of arbitration for the individual, and for the administration of justice, was also recognised.

---

[4] *Lithgow v. United Kingdom*, nos. 9006/80, 9262/81, 9263/81, 9265/81, 9266/81, 9313/81, A 9405/81, ECtHR 8 July 1986.
[5] See K.P. Papanikolaou, 'Arbitration Under the Fair Trial Safeguards of Art. 6 §1 ECHR' in *Essays in Honour of Prof. C. Calavros* (forthcoming); available at https://papers.ssrn.com/sol3/papers.cfm?abstract_id=3567706.
[6] *Deweer v. Belgium*, no. 6903/75, ECtHR 27 February 1980.
[7] *Suovaniemi v. Finland*, no. 31737/96, ECtHR 23 February 1999.

Jurisprudence has, therefore, concentrated, with some fluctuations and ambiguities, on identifying the requirements for the validity of the waiver. First of all, it must represent a free and voluntary decision of the parties. Although this criterion has been variously formulated by the Court,[8] a breach of it has been found only in obvious cases of duress. This is a high standard.

It must, moreover, be an unambiguous waiver, whether expressly worded, or inferred by implication from the text of the contract. In *Tabbane v. Switzerland*, the arbitration clause was deemed adequate to indicate the parties' joint intention to arbitrate the dispute:

> Neither [party] shall have the right to commence or maintain an action in a court of law on any disputed issue arising out of or relating to this agreement or any breach thereof, except for the enforcement of any award rendered as a result of arbitration commenced under this agreement. The award shall be final and binding and neither party shall have the right to appeal such decision to any court.

The waiver must be accompanied by 'minimum guarantees commensurate with its importance'. It was, thus, stated in *Suovaniemi* that,

> considering that throughout the arbitration the Claimants were represented by counsel, the waiver was accompanied by sufficient safeguards commensurate with its importance ... [Moreover] in proceedings before the domestic courts the Claimants had ample opportunity to advance their views, inter alia, as to the circumstances in which the waiver took place in the arbitration proceedings.[9]

Finally, it is required that the dispute may be arbitrable, or in any case that it does not violate a significant public interest. Academic scholarship has highlighted how this assessment concerns not only the subject matter of the dispute, but also the nature of the waiver itself:

> is it not an important public interest that every dispute in a specific jurisdiction be decided by an independent and impartial tribunal and that principles of due process, such as equality of arms, be properly respected? These fundamental rights are too important not to be considered as serving an important public interest.[10]

---

[8] For example, reference has been made to waiver under constraint, and waiver under duress with improper means.
[9] *Suovaniemi v. Finland*, no. 31737/96, ECtHR 23 February 1999.
[10] T. KRUMINS, *Arbitration and Human Rights*, Springer, Cham 2020, p. 89.

The jurisprudential analysis shows a favourable attitude of the Court towards arbitration, balanced, however, by attention to the concrete case, and rigorous analysis of the waiver's validity. The identification of unwaivable[11] rights under Art. 6 is also complex, and must be conducted dynamically. For example, the restrictions imposed during the COVID-19 pandemic, and the consequent use of new technologies to overcome such limits,[12] has prompted courts to question whether due process implies a 'presential procedure'.[13] However, it is noted that, according to the Austrian Supreme Court,

> the use of this videoconferencing technology (which is widely used in court hearings and is recognized worldwide) does not constitute a violation of Article 6 ECHR even if one of the parties does not agree with such a hearing. Indeed, it must also be borne in mind that Article 6 ECHR encompasses not only the right to be heard, but also the right to the provision of justice, which in turn is closely linked to the right to effective judicial protection. In civil rights proceedings, therefore, consideration must be given not only to the parties' right to be heard. The court must also ensure that the parties actually assert their rights or defend themselves. Conducting proceedings by videoconference can save costs and time and thus promote the enforcement of the law and at the same time safeguard the right to be heard. Especially in the case of an imminent halt in the administration of justice during a pandemic, videoconferencing technology offers a possibility covered by the rule of law, to harmoniously combine claims to effective law enforcement and the right to be heard.[14]

2. ACCESS TO JUSTICE

Above all, the relationship between access to justice, established by Art. 6 ECHR, and arbitration remains controversial, to the point of being

---

[11] In *Axelsson v. Sweden*, no. 11960/86, ECtHR 13 July 1990, it was recognised that the right to a public hearing could be waived: 'The public character of court hearings constitutes a fundamental principle enshrined in Article 6(1). Neither the letter nor the spirit of the provision prevents a person from waiving of his own free will, either tacitly or expressly, the entitlement to a public hearing.'

[12] Art. 27 of the Swiss Rules 2021 now establishes that: '2. Any hearings may be held in person or remotely by videoconference or other appropriate means, as decided by the arbitral tribunal after consulting with the parties'.

[13] M. SCHERER, 'Remote Hearings in International Arbitration: An Analytical Framework' (2020) 37(4) *Journal of International Arbitration* 407. D.P. DE MARTINO and K. PLAVEC, 'Has COVID-19 Unlocked Digital Justice? Answers from the World of International Arbitration' (2021) 6(1) *Cambridge Law Review* 45.

[14] OGH, 23 July 2020, Case No. 18 ONc 3/20s.

considered by some academic scholarship as a forced marriage.[15] The issue emerges strongly in cases where the non-payment of costs leads to the suspension of the arbitration procedure, or even to defences being considered the withdrawn. Such consequences, although provided for in many Arbitration Chambers' rules, may represent a violation of both the right to a fair trial, and the right of defence.

The decision of the French Court of Cassation concerning the annulment of the arbitration award in the dispute between Pirelli and LP is emblematic.[16] During the proceedings, LP had gone bankrupt, and was unable to pay the advanced costs under Art. 36.3 of the ICC Rules (2012).[17] Its counterclaims were, therefore, deemed withdrawn. LP sued for the annulment of the award, claiming that its right to access to justice and the principle of equal treatment under Art. 6 ECHR, had been violated. Although LP was not precluded from bringing its claims at a later date, this was only a theoretical possibility, given its financial difficulties. The Paris Court of Appeal ruled in favour of LP, while the Court of Cassation specified that the violation of the right of access to justice exists only if the main claim and counterclaims are so interconnected that they cannot be judged separately.

However, the issue of advanced costs remains controversial. On the one hand, such controversy stems from what the arbitration world has noted as an often strategic or opportunistic use of the refusal to pay, and on the other hand, from a substantial injustice in denying the possibility of bringing claims or raising defences to parties who may find themselves in financial difficulties precisely because of the contract in dispute. Above all, the possibility for a party to act or defend itself in court is a fundamental right which should not depend on their financial conditions.[18] Therefore,

---

[15] J. KUDRNA, 'Arbitration and Right of Access to Justice: Tips for a Successful Marriage', *New York University Journal of International Law and Politics (JILP) Online Forum*, February 2013, available at https://www.nyujilp.org/arbitration-and-right-of-access-to-justice-tips-for-a-successful-marriage/. See also N.F. ŞANLI, 'Party Impecuniosity and International Arbitration: The Interplay between Failure to Pay the Advance Costs and Validity of Arbitration Agreement in International Arbitration' (2020) 40 *Public and Private International Law Bulletin* 573–611.

[16] *Pirelli*, Cour de cassation, 1e civ., 28 March 2013, no. 11-27.770.

[17] The provision is now found in the ICC Rules 2021 and establishes the advanced costs discipline in Art. 37. The text is available at https://iccwbo.org/dispute-resolution-services/arbitration/rules-of-arbitration/#article_37.

[18] A. REINER, 'Impecuniosity of Parties and Its Effects on Arbitration – From the Perspectives of Austrian Law' in German Institution of Arbitration (ed), *Financial Capacity of the Parties: A Condition for the Validity of Arbitration Agreements?*

part of the case law and legal scholarship consider that the hypothesis can be read into Art. II(3) of the New York Convention (NYC), according to which an arbitration agreement is considered substantially invalid if it is 'void, inoperative or incapable of being performed'.[19]

A problematic aspect also arises with regard to the possibility of waiving challenges to the award, provided for in some national laws, and in some arbitration clauses. This issue has been addressed by the ECtHR, with reference to Swiss law, in the *Tabbane* case. Art. 182 of the Federal Act on Private International Law (PILA) states that,

> if none of the parties has their domicile, habitual residence or seat in Switzerland, they may, by a declaration in the arbitration agreement or by subsequent agreement, wholly or partly exclude all appeals against arbitral awards; they may limit such proceedings to one or several of the grounds listed in Article 190 paragraph 2; the right to a review under Article 190a paragraph 1 letter b may not be waived. The agreement requires the form specified in Article 178 paragraph 1. Where the parties have excluded all setting aside proceedings and where the awards are to be enforced in Switzerland, the New York Convention of 10 June 1958 on the Recognition and Enforcement of Foreign Arbitral Awards applies by analogy.

The Court found that Ms Tabbane had freely entered into an agreement provided for in an arbitration clause which expressly excluded, under Art. 192 PILA, the possibility of challenging the award. The legislation appeared justified by the desire to increase the attractiveness and effectiveness of Swiss law, in the context of international arbitration. In addition, it was proportional, because Switzerland's policy interests had been balanced against Ms Tabbane's freedom of contract.

It was noted that the decision did not imply the general validity of exclusion agreements. In this case, the parties were on an equal footing, and the procedure had respected the rules of adversarial proceedings. Moreover, the introduction, by law, of a principle of general non-appealability of awards, without any reservation, does not seem possible.

(Schriftenreihe Der August-Maria- Berges-Stiftung Für Arbitrales Recht, vol. 16), Peter Lang, Frankfurt am Main 2004, p. 41.

[19] G.G.T. JUN, 'An Arbitral Tribunal's Dilemma: The Plea of Financially Impecunious Parties' (2020) 37(4) *Journal of International Arbitration* 479, observes that while impecuniosity should not render an arbitration agreement automatically 'incapable of being performed', an exception should be recognised when the impecuniosity results in a breach of the rules of natural justice.

Indeed, it was pointed out 'that the parties were not obliged under Swiss law to exclude the right to appeal, but could decide on this themselves. Consequently, party autonomy seems to prevail in Strasbourg (at least for now).'[20]

3. INDEPENDENCE, IMPARTIALITY AND NEUTRALITY

3.1. DEFINITION

Art. 6 of the Convention is also relevant with regard to the requirements of independence, neutrality and impartiality of the arbitral tribunal. It is noted that, although these are 'often understood as the same thing under a narrow construct by some commentators, the neutrality of an arbitrator goes much further than the other two concepts'.[21] Impartiality and independence are often used synonymously to reflect the unbiased quality that arbitrators are expected to possess. While often used interchangeably, they are conceptually different albeit linked.[22]

To begin with, neutrality (understood as equidistance in thought and action) is considered, in international arbitration, primarily with regard to the nationality of the panel. It is considered, in fact, that, 'it is because of its supposed implications: by an instinctive reaction, parties will generally assume without much further thought that a prospective arbitrator is likely, or even bound, to share his country's ideology and common values, if any'.[23] It is, therefore, an appearance of neutrality that would be lacking in the hypothesis of common citizenship between one of the parties and the arbitrator. However, the thesis does not appear completely convincing. A first objection resides precisely in the requirement of citizenship, which is not always indicative of particular relationships or commonality between

---

[20] M. KNIGGE and P. RIBBERS, 'Waiver of the Right to Set-Aside Proceedings in Light of Article 6 ECHR: Party-Autonomy on Top?' (2017) 34(5) *Journal of International Arbitration* 775.

[21] G. BERNINI, 'Cultural Neutrality: A Prerequisite to Arbitral Justice' (1989) 10(1) *Michigan Journal of International Law* 39.

[22] R. FEEHILY, 'Neutrality, Independence and Impartiality in International Commercial Arbitration, A Fine Balance in the Quest For Arbitral Justice' (2019) 7(1) *Penn State Journal of Law & International Affairs* 88.

[23] P. LALIVE, 'On the Neutrality of the Arbitrator and of the Place of Arbitration' (1970) *Revue de l'arbitrage* 59.

the arbitrator and the party. Consider the case of a Swiss professional who has studied in, and works in, the United Kingdom. Clearly, the centre of interest is not linked to the country of origin. A second criticism is based on the need for the arbitrator to be familiar with the law applicable to the dispute, which could coincide with that of one of the parties. Especially in an international arbitration, the panel's knowledge of the law is essential to avoid mistakes and misunderstandings, or the application of a generic *lex mercatoria* that has no normative basis. An example would be the case of an arbitration between an English and a French party, in which the applicable law is German law.

Impartiality is the freedom of the arbitrator from bias due to preconceptions about the dispute, or any other reason that may result in them favouring one party over the other.

Independence, on the other hand, reflects the lack of a pre-existing relationship between the arbitrator and the parties.

There are, however, different nuances in national legislation: English law refers to impartiality but not to independence (Arbitration Act 1996, s. 24), whereas Swiss law mentions only independence. This does not necessarily lead to significant differences in practice. The English courts, in fact, consider independence to be a requirement of impartiality.

In an attempt at systematisation, Italian doctrine has distinguished between neutrality and independence, on the one hand, as preventive requirements, abstractly aimed at guaranteeing impartiality; and impartiality (the real, effective one, as a guarantee of results, which must characterise the function), on the other. Only the latter is inescapable and unavailable and, where violated, can lead to serious consequences both for the award and for the arbitrators.[24]

However, this does not make it possible to overcome the difficulty of concretising these requirements in the context of arbitration, as these are determined both by the peculiarities of the procedure itself, and by the multiple perceptions and mentalities of the parties.

It is, first and foremost, undeniable that there is an unresolvable tension between these requirements and the appointment of arbitrators by the parties, which is based on trust; this should not be understood as trust in a decision in one's own favour at any cost, but in competence and capacity leading to a correct solution. This is, moreover, the very

---

[24] C. Spaccapelo, 'Imparzialità, terzietà, neutralità e indipendenza degli arbitri' in D. Mantucci (ed), *Trattato di diritto dell'arbitrato*, vol. III, Edizioni Scientifiche Italiane, Napoli 2021, p. 162.

function of arbitration, and its advantage for the parties over ordinary judicial proceedings. On the other hand, the independence and impartiality of an arbitrator should not be assessed with regard, mainly or exclusively, for contiguity, as it is a matter of mindset, professionalism and intellectual honesty. There is nothing to ensure that an arbitrator, although appointed for the first time by a party, will not seek to secure a privileged relationship by favouring that party. It has been pointed out by a famous lawyer that, 'when I represent a client in an arbitration, what I really look for in an arbitrator chosen by the parties is someone with the greatest predisposition towards my client, but with the least appearance of partiality'.[25] Proceeding from the definition of 'predisposition' as a favourable 'attitude, prevailing tendency or inclination', this term is believed, in arbitration, to indicate a special attention of the arbitrator to the positions of the party that appointed them.[26] This is an unavoidable psychological state for the arbitrator, because of the trust placed in them by the appointing party. Therefore, one might rightly wonder whether such a party may be 'predisposed'[27] towards one party, but not so partial as to raise a 'justifiable doubt'.[28]

---

[25] M. HUNTER, 'Ethics of the International Arbitrator' (1987) 53(4) *Arbitration* 219, 222–224.

[26] D. BISHOP and L. REED, 'Practical Guidelines for Interviewing, Selecting and Challenging Party-Appointed Arbitrators in International Commercial Arbitration' (1998) 14(4) *Arbitration International* 395–430: 'It is also a truism that a party will strive to select an arbitrator who has some inclination or predisposition to favour that party's side of the case such as by sharing the appointing party's legal or cultural background or by holding doctrinal views that, fortuitously, coincide with a party's case.'

[27] Ibid., 405: 'As I see it, party-appointed arbitrators in international controversies perform two principal and overlapping functions. First, I think the presence of a party-appointed arbitrator gives some confidence to counsel who appointed him or her, and through counsel to die party-disputant. At least one of the persons who will decide the case will listen carefully – even sympathetically – to the presentation, and if the arbitrator is well chosen, will study the documents as well, whether or not they would have done so in any case. Thus the presence of a well-chosen party-appointed arbitrator goes a long way toward promising (if not assuring) a fair hearing and a considered decision. Second, in an international case a party-appointed arbitrator serves as a translator. I do not mean just of language, though occasionally that is required as well, as even persons highly skilled in the language of arbitration may be confused by so-called faux amis (false friends) – words that look the same but have different meanings in different languages. I mean rather the translation of legal culture, and not infrequently of the law itself, when matters that are self-evident to lawyers from one country are puzzling to lawyers from another.'

[28] H.-L. YU and L. SHORE, 'Independence, impartiality, and immunity of arbitrators – US and English Perspectives' (2003) 52(4) *International and Comparative Law Quarterly* 935.

An arbitrator's skills and knowledge, then, might justify their repeated appointment.[29] Indeed, unlike a judge, an arbitrator might have such expertise as to make him irreplaceable in certain disputes. As Posner notes:

> The ethical obligations of arbitrators can be understood only by reference to the fundamental differences between the judgment of arbitrators and the judgment of judges and jurors. No one is compelled to arbitrate a commercial dispute unless he has contractually consented to arbitrate. The voluntary nature of commercial arbitration is an important safeguard for the parties that is lacking in the case of courts. Courts are coercive, not voluntary, agencies, and the American people's traditional fear of government oppression has led to a judicial system in which impartiality is privileged over competence. Thus, people who resort to arbitration do so because they prefer a court that is competent on the subject of their dispute to a generalist court with its austere impartiality but limited knowledge of the subject matter … There is a trade-off between impartiality and experience.[30]

At the same time, one must consider how different market actors are characterised by different views of risk aversion and path dependency – in an important dispute, parties and lawyers might reasonably prefer experienced arbitrators to judges.

A further profile of specificity relates to the professional nature of arbitrators. In the majority opinion in *Commonwealth Coatings Corp v. Continental Casualty Co.*,[31] Mr Justice Black, while noting the difference between judges and arbitrators, observed that,

> [i]t is true that arbitrators cannot cut all their ties with the business world, since they are not expected to derive all their income from their work in deciding cases, but we should, if anything, be even more scrupulous in safeguarding the

---

[29] According to the opinion of Mr Justice Leggatt in *Guidant LLC v. Swiss Re International SE* [2016] EWHC 1201, multiple appointments are not a ground upon which disqualification could be sought: 'I accept the submission made by Mr. Tse on behalf of Guidant that the appointment of a common arbitrator does not justify an inference of apparent bias. The fact that the same person has been appointed by Guidant as its arbitrator in the Markel arbitration is not, therefore, a ground on which an application could be made to seek to disqualify him from acting in the Swiss Re arbitrations. Guidant is entitled to choose the same individual as their arbitrator in all three arbitrations, as they have. But conversely Swiss Re, for their part, are in my view reasonably entitled to object to having forced upon them an arbitrator who has already been appointed in the Markel arbitration and about whose involvement in that arbitration they are entitled to feel the concern which I have indicated.'
[30] 714 F.2d 673 (7th Cir. 1983), cert. denied, 464 US 1009 (1983).
[31] 393 US 145 (1968).

impartiality of arbitrators as compared to judges, since the former are entirely free to decide the law as the facts stand and are not subject to appellate review.'[32]

Conversely, the concurring opinion showed concern about losing 'the best and most capable' arbitrators should overly rigid standards be adopted,[33] and, therefore, emphasised that arbitrators are not

> automatically disqualified from doing business with the parties before them if both parties are informed of the report in advance, or if they are unaware of the facts, but the report is trivial ... An arbitrator cannot be expected to 'provide the parties with a complete biography ... of the affairs'.[34]

For instance, in the English system, even with regard to judges, the irrelevance of certain relationships has been affirmed; in fact, it has been stated that:

> it would be dangerous and futile to attempt to define or list the factors which may or may not give rise to a real danger of bias. Everything will depend on the facts, which may include the nature of the question to be decided. We cannot, however, conceive of circumstances in which an objection could validly be based on the religion, ethnic or national origin, sex, age, class, means, or sexual orientation of the judge. Nor, in any case, ordinarily, could an objection be soundly based on the background or social or educational or service or employment history of the judge, nor that of any member of the judge's family; or prior political associations; or membership in social or athletic or charitable organizations; or Masonic associations or previous judicial decisions; or extracurricular statements (whether in textbooks, lectures, speeches, articles, interviews, reports or responses to reference documents); or previous receipt of instructions to act for or against any party, solicitor or advocate in a case before him; or membership of the same Inn, Circuit, Local Law Society or Chambers.[35]

---

[32] Ibid.
[33] Even academic writing might be problematic: '[it is] unlikely albeit not impossible, that the mere writing of academic papers may serve as sole basis to disqualify an arbitrator for an issue conflict, unless a paper specifically related to the facts or the parties in dispute and not only to general legal issues, or if a position has been argued vehemently as means to achieve academic recognition': H. LAL, B. CASEY and L. DEFRANCHI, 'Rethinking Issue Conflicts in International Commercial Arbitration' (2020) 14(1) *Dispute Resolution International* 3, 19.
[34] 393 U.S. 145, 150–52 (1968).
[35] *Locabail (UK) Ltd v. Bayfield Properties Ltd* [2000] QB 451.

The same principle has also been accepted in Italy, where the common affiliation of an arbitrator and a party, to Opus Dei, has not been deemed sufficient for recusal.[36]

In this uncertain context, a key role is played by the International Bar Association (IBA) Guidelines, which reflect trends in the arbitral world, and attempt to balance different interests and perspectives. Since their initial publication, the Guidelines have aspired to find 'broad acceptance within the international arbitration community, and [to] assist parties, practitioners, arbitrators, institutions and tribunals in addressing ... important issues of impartiality and independence'. This position has also been endorsed by the Swiss Federal Supreme Court, which has made it clear that the Guidelines 'constitute a valuable working tool to contribute to the standardization of standards in international arbitration in the area of conflicts of interest', and 'should have an impact on the practice of courts and institutions administering arbitral proceedings'.[37] Academic scholarship has held that they are connoted by a 'soft normativity'.[38]

It is well known that the Guidelines provide not only a general framework but also specific indications. In fact, they distinguish between:

(a) a non-waivable red list, which includes situations that cannot be overcome, even by the consent of the parties;[39]
(b) a waivable red list, including cases where the parties agree to the appointment of an arbitrator by waiving the incompatibility exception;
(c) an orange list, concerning specific situations that could raise doubts about the arbitrator's impartiality and independence. In such circumstances, there is a duty of disclosure, but if an objection is not raised in a timely manner, the appointment of the arbitrator is valid. The assessment of independence and impartiality depends, however, on the specific facts, and not on the failure to comply with the duty of disclosure; and
(d) a green list, which does not give rise to any disclosure obligation.

However, it must be stressed that the IBA Guidelines are not binding, and cannot prevail over national laws. In fact, a Court could declare all or part

---

[36] P. Rescigno, 'Rapporti associativi, indipendenza e ricusazione dell'arbitro (il caso dell'Opus Dei)' *Rivista dell'arbitrato*, 2012, 263.
[37] *Adrian Mutu v. Chelsea Football Club Ltd.*, 28 ASA Bull. 520, 528.
[38] G. Kaufmann-Kohler, 'Soft Law in International Arbitration Codification and Normativity' [2010] *Journal of International Dispute Settlement* 1, 14.
[39] The Non-Waivable Red List includes situations deriving from the overriding principle that no person can be his or her own judge.

of the criteria established therein inapplicable. The decision in *W Ltd. v. M SDN BHD* is significant in this respect. The High Court stated that it had decided

> the outcome of the present case on the basis of English law. It would be possible to simply say that the 2014 IBA Guidelines are not an expression of English law and then not go into any examination of them. However, the present arbitration is international, and the parties often choose English law in an international context. So the role of this Court has an international dimension. I therefore prefer to consider the 2014 IBA Guidelines, as I have done, and explain why I do not think, with respect, that they can still be correct.[40]

In particular, critical aspects were noted in their reasoning, and an automatic application of the IBA Guidelines that disregarded the assessment of the concrete case was rejected.

Parties may also waive the IBA Guidelines in ad hoc arbitrations. In administered arbitrations, however, as has been correctly noted,[41] party autonomy is sacrificed to the prestige and authority of the institution, which can intervene to ensure compliance with the Guidelines. If the parties insist on their choice of arbitrator, the Arbitration Panel may refuse to administer the proceedings. In such a scenario, the parties could agree to transform the administered arbitration into an ad hoc one; otherwise, it is likely that the party in favour of the application of the IBA Guidelines would prevail with regard to the choice of applying them.

Thus, the difficulty of establishing a uniform standard of adjudication is common to all jurisdictions. Justice Black, in *Commonwealth Coatings*, stated that, 'every court authorized by law to try cases and controversies must not only be impartial, but must also avoid the appearance of partiality'. It must, however, be pointed out that the scope of this principle was limited by the concurring opinion of Justice White, which was fundamental to the attainment of a majority, and has been met with greater favour in practice. More specifically, the concurring opinion established a duty of disclosure only where the arbitrator has a substantial interest in a firm which has done more than trivial business with a party, in which case this interest must be disclosed. In concretising the standard of impartiality, US courts look for balanced and reasonable criteria: something more than

---

[40] *W Ltd. v. M SDN BHD* [2016] EWHC 422 (Comm).
[41] V. Di Gravio, 'L'indipendenza dell'arbitro' (2018) *Rivista dell'arbitrato* 195.

'appearance of bias', and less than 'actual bias'.⁴² The formulas employed are diverse, and not always satisfactory. Judge Posner refers to cases in which the arbitrator's relationship with a party is such as to cast serious doubt on their impartiality, while, for Judge Kaufmann, the assumptions must be identified from the perspective of a reasonable person in light of the peculiar business practices and factual variations of each case.⁴³

3.2. IMPARTIALITY AND DUTY OF DISCLOSURE

The notion of impartiality has also been examined recently by the UK Supreme Court, in *Halliburton v. Chubb*,⁴⁴ with regard to both the ability of an arbitrator to accept appointments in proceedings concerning the same, or a similar, issue, with only one party in common, without giving rise to an appearance of partiality, and the duty to disclose it.⁴⁵ English law, too, has alternated between the criteria of 'reasonable suspicion', 'real danger' and 'real possibility' of partiality.

In its reasoning, the Court highlighted that the standard for assessing the impartiality of an arbitrator is objective. Indeed, it must be considered whether the circumstances of the concrete case would, or could, lead an impartial and informed observer,⁴⁶ after examining them, to conclude that there was a real possibility that the arbitrator was not impartial. This assessment must be made with regard to the time of the objection to the arbitrator.

---

[42] H.-L. Yu and L. Shore, 'Independence, impartiality, and immunity of arbitrators – US and English Perspectives' (2003) 52(4) *International and Comparative Law Quarterly* 935, 935.

[43] *Morelite Constr. Corp. v. New York City District Counsel Carpenters Benefit Fund* 48 F.2d 79 (2d Cir. 1984).

[44] *Halliburton Company v. Chubb Bermuda Insurance Ltd (formerly known as Ace Bermuda Insurance Ltd)* [2020] UKSC 48 (Eng.).

[45] M. Konen, 'A New (Deepwater) Horizon For Arbitrator Bias' (2021) *Arbitration Law Review* 11.

[46] *Halliburton*, above n. 44, defines the informed and impartial observer: 'before she takes a balanced approach to any information she is given, she will take the trouble to inform herself on all matters that are relevant. ... She is fair-minded, so she will appreciate that the context forms an important part of the material which she must consider before passing judgment.'

The Court also found a duty of disclosure in cases of apparent bias,[47] based on Art. 33 of the Electricity Arbitration Association (EAA):

> An arbitrator, like a judge, must always be alive to the possibility of apparent bias and of actual but unconscious bias. … One way in which an arbitrator can avoid the appearance of bias is by disclosing matters which could arguably be said to give rise to a real possibility of bias. Such disclosure allows the parties to consider the disclosed circumstances, obtain necessary advice, and decide whether there is a problem with the involvement of the arbitrator in the reference and, if so, whether to object or otherwise to act to mitigate or remove the problem.

Also, in analysing the disclosure duty, the Court rejected automatism, and considered the specific case to be decisive.[48] Indeed, it noted that, while repeated appointment of the same arbitrator may give rise to suspicion,

> in certain types of arbitration, such as maritime, sports or commodities arbitration, it may be the practice to draw arbitrators from a smaller pool of

---

[47] With respect to judges' duty of disclosure, in *Taylor v. Lawrence* [2003] QB 528, it was affirmed that 'a further general comment which we would make, is that judges should be circumspect about declaring the existence of a relationship where there is no real possibility of it being regarded by a fair-minded and informed observer as raising a possibility of bias. If such a relationship is disclosed, it unnecessarily raises an implication that it could affect the judgment and approach of the judge. If this is not the position no purpose is served by mentioning the relationship. On the other hand, if the situation is one where a fair-minded and informed person might regard the judge as biased, it is important that disclosure should be made. If the position is borderline, disclosure should be made because then the judge can consider, having heard the submissions of the parties, whether or not he should withdraw. In other situations disclosure can unnecessarily undermine the litigant's confidence in the judge.' The solution offered for borderline positions is also useful in arbitration.

[48] *Halliburton*, above n. 44, clarifies that, 'the duty of disclosure is a continuing duty and circumstances may change before there is disclosure. Those circumstances may aggravate an existing failure to disclose a matter or, while not expunging such a failure, may render any continuing failure a less potent factor in an assessment of justifiable doubts as to impartiality. For example a scenario might be that (i) an arbitrator accepts an appointment in a reference between A and B; (ii) the arbitrator accepts an appointment in an overlapping reference to which A is not a party but B is, without disclosing the appointment to A in circumstances in which the arbitrator should have disclosed it; (iii) the arbitrator makes an interim determination in the first reference which causes A to question his or her impartiality; (iv) the second reference then does not proceed. The failures to disclose at stages (ii) and (iii) would not be negated by the termination of the second reference, but in assessing the significance of the continuing failures to disclose after stage (iv) to the question of justifiable doubts, the court would have regard to the fact that the second arbitration did not proceed.'

persons. If it is customary and practical in such fields for parties to frequently appoint the same arbitrator in different cases, disclosure of this fact is not required when all parties to the arbitration should be familiar with such custom and practice.

Additionally, the parties themselves may waive the duty of disclosure; but that does not preclude an arbitrator who is in a position of a clear and established form of incompatibility from having a duty to disclose this.

Nonetheless, it should be noted that there are variations and fluctuations in the standards applied in national case law. For example, it is interesting to note the change of direction of the Austrian Supreme Court. In two 2013 decisions, the Court had ruled that an award could be annulled due to the lack of impartiality and independence of the arbitrators only in blatant cases. These decisions, based on reasons of legal certainty and stability, had been widely criticised in legal scholarship. Therefore, starting from the analysis of Art. 6 ECHR, the Court recently ruled that,

> in view of the limited possibility to review the content of an arbitral award, the independence and impartiality of the arbitral tribunal is of particular importance. This is in favour of qualifying the partiality of arbitrators not only in egregious cases, but in general as a lack of impartiality. Legal certainty is not compromised because an action for annulment – apart from criminal conduct of the arbitrator pursuant to §611 para. 2 item 6 in combination with §530 para. 1 item 4 ZPO (§611 para. 4 S 3 ZPO) – is only admissible within three months of the filing of the arbitral award. However, the possibility of an action for annulment does not mean that a party may 'reserve' the right to assert a ground for annulment for this procedural step – depending on the outcome of the arbitration.[49]

The facts on which the action for annulment is based must, therefore, be known only after the award has been filed.

Yet the extent of the duty of disclosure is also complex. One approach considers it sufficient for the potential arbitrator to disclose known causes of conflicts of interest. A second approach would impose a duty to investigate potential circumstances that could give rise to violations of the requirements of independence and impartiality.[50] This should not, however, result in a 'wild goose chase'. Interestingly, the *W Ltd. v. M SDN*

---

[49] OGH, 1 October 2019, Case No. 18 OCg 5/19p.
[50] J. van Haersolte and J. van Hof, 'Impartiality and independence: fundamental and fluid' (2021) 37(3) *Arbitration International* 599.

BHD case mentioned above involved a sole arbitrator who was a partner in a firm which had one of the parties as a major client. As he had little involvement in the activity of the firm, the circumstance was not disclosed. Subsequently, the fact became known, and the two awards made in the proceedings were challenged, under English law, on the grounds of conflict of interest of the sole arbitrator.

In its reasoning, the Court noted[51] that, 'General Standard(6)(a) appropriately states that the arbitrator's relationship with the firm "should be considered in each individual case". And it was realistic when it observed that,

> [t]he fact that the activities of the arbitrator's firm involve one of the parties does not necessarily constitute a source of that conflict … Similarly, if one of the parties is a member of a group with which the arbitrator's firm has a relationship, that fact should be considered in each individual case, but does not necessarily in itself constitute a source of conflict of interest.

The Court's Explanation of General Standard(6)(a) added that,

> in the context of a group of companies, 'because individual agreements on corporate structure vary widely, a general rule is not appropriate. Instead, the particular circumstances of an affiliation with another entity within the same group of companies, and that entity's relationship with the arbitrator's law firm, should be considered in each individual case.' But there is a tension between all of this and General Standard (2)(d) when an affiliate of a party is a client of the arbitrator's firm, because in that situation General Standard (2)(d) and Section 1.4 of the Non-Waivable Red List (with its definition of affiliate) seem to take a different approach than General Standard (6)(a).[52]

While the Court's assertion of the importance of the concrete situation and the avoidance of overly rigid or automatically applicable rules, is correct, the decision is not fully convincing. In the current context, it seems preferable that, before accepting an assignment, a potential arbitrator who is part of a law firm should carry out a serious internal verification of the existence of potential conflicts of interest, without being able, later, to invoke the complexity of the organisation, or the autonomy of different sectors of the firm.

---

[51] The Court refers to Part II of the 2014 IBA Guidelines, under the heading 'Practical Application of the General Standards'.
[52] *W Ltd v. M SDN BHD*, above n. 40.

In US jurisprudence, this position seems to prevail, whereby,

> when an arbitrator has reason to believe that a non-trivial conflict of interest may exist, he must either (1) investigate the conflict (which may disclose information that must be disclosed under the *Commonwealth Coatings*) or (2) disclose his reasons for believing that there may be a conflict and his intention not to investigate.[53]

With this decision, the Court created a duty, on the part of the arbitrator, to act. However, this does not preclude the parties from also investigating, in a thorough and timely manner, possible conflicts of interest of the arbitrator they have appointed. Effective, in this sense, is the choice of the Swiss Federal Supreme Court to impose on the parties a *devoir de curiosité*.[54]

4. CONCLUSION

In this debate, a recent ruling of the ECtHR, in which it once again clarified the requirement of impartiality, is important.[55] In its reasoning, the Court specified that this requirement must be assessed both on the basis of a subjective criterion, which concerns the conduct and beliefs of the arbitrator, and on the basis of an objective criterion, i.e. in light of concrete facts that could give rise to legitimate doubts. It also noted how the point of view of the arbitrator cannot be the determining factor. Indeed,

> what is decisive is whether that fear can be considered objectively justified. In itself, the objective test is functional: for example, professional, financial or personal ties between a judge and a party to a case may give rise to objectively justified doubts as to the impartiality of the court, which therefore does not meet the standard of the Convention under the objective test. It must therefore be decided in each individual case whether the connection in question is of such a nature and degree as to indicate a lack of impartiality on the part of the court. In this respect even appearances can have a certain importance, a principle reflected in the adage justice must not only be done, it must also be seen to be done.

---

[53] *Applied Indus. Materials Corp. v. Ovalar Makine Ticaret Ve Sanayi*, A.S, 492 F.3d 132, 138 (2d Cir. 2007).
[54] TF, judgment TF 4A_110/2012 of 9 October 2012.
[55] *BEG S.P.A. v. Italy*, no. 5312/11, ECtHR 20 May 2021.

This reasoning is interesting in two respects: the first is that the Court elucidated the minimum content of the notions of impartiality and independence. The decision could, therefore, have a harmonising effect on the different requirements of different national systems. The second concerns the Court's development of its case law on arbitration, which is now increasingly incisive; it has, in fact, become an important player in this type of procedure.

It should be noted, however, that although independence, impartiality and neutrality are fundamental, their uncritical and formalistic exaltation hides risks in arbitration, especially at the international level. The actual or apparent distance between professional arbitrators, in fact, determines,

> a sort of 'commonality' of ideas, practices, [and] expectations that they are the only ones to know since they formulate and promote them in deference to the principle of secrecy and trust of their decision. It would be paradoxical, therefore, if a world of 'secrecy' were to develop in this sense, where instead a constant practice aimed at revelation and transparency is required. It is therefore necessary to take this problem to heart with regard to the authority enjoyed by these professional arbitrators. This authority can only be a de facto authority insofar as, with very rare exceptions in arbitration matters, this structure is expressed outside of any hierarchical structure which has always seemed fundamental to ensure true judicial justice.[56]

It is well known that arbitration thrives on unresolved contradictions: it is private justice equated with public justice. Arbitrators are experts who essentially receive professional appointments, but must be impartial and independent. Arbitration chambers have interests that are often in conflict with their functions. These are delicate balances, and the legitimacy of arbitration depends solely on its ability to conform more easily to the expectations of private autonomy, and to guarantee better and more efficient results, than ordinary justice does. The role of the ECtHR is, therefore, proving to be effective in controlling compliance with the fundamental principles of the arbitration process, while at the same time remaining respectful of private autonomy – which is the primary source of the institution of arbitration.

---

[56] G. HORSMANN, 'La fusione della giustizia pubblica e della giustizia privata. L'arbitrato privato/pubblico' (2017) *Contratto e impresa* 1238.

THE EUROPEAN CONVENTION ON HUMAN RIGHTS AND THE PROTECTION OF FOREIGN DIRECT INVESTMENT

The Role of 'Legitimate Expectations'

Giacomo ROJAS ELGUETA[*]

1. Introduction 198
2. The Notion of Investment under IIL and the ECHR 201
   2.1. The Definition of 'Investment' under IIL 201
   2.2. The Definition of 'Possessions' under the ECHR 204
3. The Use of 'Legitimate Expectations' in IIL and the ECHR System 206
   3.1. The Notion of 'Legitimate Expectations' 207
      3.1.1. The Notion of 'Legitimate Expectations' in IIL 207
      3.1.2. The Notion of 'Legitimate Expectations' in the ECHR System 209
   3.2. Are General Provisions, Included in the Host State Regulatory Framework, Sufficient to Create a Legitimate Expectation? 210
      3.2.1. Legitimate Expectations and the General Regulatory Framework in IIL 210
      3.2.2. Legitimate Expectations and the General Regulatory Framework in the ECHR System 212
   3.3. Is it Necessary that Investors Acquire an Established Legal Position, for Legitimate Expectations to Arise? 213
      3.3.1. The Threshold of 'Objective Certainty' under IIL 213

---

[*] The author wishes to thank Ms Benedetta Mauro for her excellent assistance in the research associated with this chapter.

3.3.2. The Threshold of 'Objective Certainty' under the
ECHR 214
3.4. Does the Protection of Legitimate Expectations Imply
that the Host State is Absolutely Precluded from Enacting
Regulatory Changes that are Detrimental to Investors? 216
3.4.1. Balancing Investment Protection and Regulatory
Freedom in IIL. 216
3.4.2. Balancing Investment Protection and Regulatory
Freedom in the ECHR System. 220
4. Conclusions 222

1. INTRODUCTION

In recent years, international law scholarship has started to explore the intersections between human rights law, in particular the European Convention on Human Rights (ECHR or Convention),[1] and the protection of foreign direct investment (FDI).[2]

---

[1] European Convention for the Protection of Human Rights and Fundamental Freedoms, opened for signature 4 November 1950, 213 UNTS 221 (entered into force 3 September 1953) ('ECHR').

[2] Scholarship covering the relationship between the ECHR and the protection of foreign direct investment is rather limited. However, see, in particular, M. FANOU and V.P. TZEVELEKOS, 'The Shared Territory of the ECHR and International Investment Law' in Y. RADI (ed), *Research Handbook on Human Rights and Investment*, Edward Elgar, Cheltenham 2018, pp. 93–136; U. KRIEBAUM, 'Is the European Court of Human Rights an Alternative to Investor-State Arbitration?' in P.M. DUPUY, E.U. PETERSMANN and F. FRANCIONI (eds), *Human Rights in International Investment Law and Arbitration*, OUP, Oxford 2009, pp. 219–45; C. TOMUSCHAT, 'The European Court of Human Rights and Investment Protection' in C. BINDER, U. KRIEBAUM, A. REINISCH and S. WITTICH (eds), *International Investment Law for the 21st Century: Essays in Honour of Christoph Schreuer*, OUP, Oxford 2009, pp. 636–56; C. SCHREUER and U. KRIEBAUM, 'The Concept of Property in Human Rights Law and International Investment Law' in S. BREITENMOSER (ed), *Human Rights, Democracy and the Rule of Law: Liber Amicorum Luzius Wildhaber*, Dike, Zurich 2007, pp. 743–62; Y. RADI, 'The "Human Nature" of International Investment Law' [2013] *Transnational Dispute Management* <https://www.transnational-dispute-management.com/article.asp?key=1928>. See also N. KLEIN, 'Human Rights and International Investment Law: Investment Protection as Human Right?' (2012) 4 *Goettingen Journal of International Law* 199; K.A.N. DUGALL and N.J. DIAMOND, 'Regime Interaction in Investment Arbitration: Crowded Streets; Are Human Rights Law and International Investment Law Good Neighbors?' [2021] *Kluwer Arbitration Blog* <http://arbitrationblog.kluwerarbitration.com/2022/01/12/regime-interaction-in-investment-arbitration-crowded-streets-are-human-rights-law-and-international-investment-law-good-neighbors/>.

Building upon this emerging literature, the objectives of this chapter are twofold: (i) to explore whether the ECHR can play a role in the protection of FDI, and if so, what role; and (ii) to compare the application of the principle of 'legitimate expectations' (as an increasingly relevant doctrine used to decide disputes over investments) in investment arbitral tribunals' awards, and in the European Court of Human Rights (ECtHR) case law.

In broader and simpler terms, this chapter aims to answer the following questions: is FDI a human right protected by the ECHR? And if so, what is the role played by 'legitimate expectations'?

In examining whether, and to what extent, the ECHR grants protection to FDI, it is necessary to contextualise the present analysis against the backdrop of international investment law (IIL), the field of law that governs the relationships between states and foreign investors, and to which foreign investors typically resort when seeking protection for their investments.[3]

As is well known, within the framework of IIL, investment protection is assured by two main pillars: (i) the bilateral (or multilateral) investment treaties (BITs) signed by states for the promotion and protection of foreign investments; and (ii) the Convention on the Settlement of Investment Disputes between States and Nationals and Other States of 1965 (ICSID or Washington Convention).[4]

Since Germany and Pakistan signed the first BIT, in 1959, a total of 2,825 BITs have been signed (2,257 of which are currently in force).[5] Pursuant to BITs, investors from each Contracting State enjoy certain guarantees (in the form of substantive standards of protection) for their investments made in the other Contracting State (i.e. the host state). Also, in case a dispute arises between the foreign investor and the host state, most BITs provide for arbitration as the method to resolve disputes.[6]

---

[3] In general, on international investment law, see, among others, R. DOLZER and C. SCHREUER, *Principles of International Investment Law*, 2nd ed., OUP, Oxford 2012; M. BUNGERBERG, J. GRIEBEL, S. HOBE and A. REINISCH (eds), *International Investment Law: A Handbook*, Bloomsbury Publishing, London 2015; C.L. LIM, J. HO and M. PAPARINSKIS, *International Investment Law and Arbitration: Commentary, Awards and Other Materials*, CUP, Cambridge 2018.

[4] Convention on the Settlement of Investment Disputes Between States and Nationals of Other States, opened for signature 18 March 1965, 575 UNTS 159 (entered into force 14 October 1966).

[5] See <https://investmentpolicy.unctad.org/international-investment-agreements>.

[6] See R. DOLZER and C. SCHREUER, above n. 3, p. 13, p. 257: 'Most investment arbitration cases in recent years have been based on jurisdiction established through BITs. The basic mechanism is the same as in the case of national legislation: the states parties to the BIT offer consent to arbitration to investors who are nationals of the other contracting party. The arbitration agreement is perfected through the acceptance of that offer by an eligible investor.'

The ICSID Convention (a multilateral treaty sponsored by the World Bank and ratified by 155 Contracting States) adds, to the BITs, a procedural framework for dispute settlement. In particular, through the establishment of the International Centre for Settlement of Investment Disputes (ICSID), the ICSID Convention provides a dispute resolution system exclusively aimed at settling disputes between foreign investors and host states, and which accords institutional support to investment arbitration proceedings.[7] Investment arbitration is both a 'first instance' and a final ('last resort') mechanism,[8] which in some respects 'performs the function of judicial review of administrative acts',[9] giving foreign investors the possibility of raising their grievances through this mechanism, rather than before the host state's domestic courts (when they fear that such courts might be biased in favour of the host state).[10]

Differently from IIL and investment arbitration (which protect only foreign investors), the ECHR does not give any relevance to the nationality of the applicant, and any person claiming to be the victim of a violation (by one of the Contracting States) of his or her rights set forth in the Convention can bring a case before the ECtHR.[11] In light of the broad scope of the ECtHR's jurisdiction, it follows that, if it can be established that the ECHR system encompasses the protection of investments, this system may be considered by foreign investors as an alternative mechanism to IIL, for the protection of their FDI.[12]

---

[7] Ibid., pp. 238–39. According to para. 11 of the Report of the Executive Directors on the Convention on the Settlement of Investment Disputes between States and National of Other States 1965: 'The present Convention would offer international methods of settlement designed to take account of the special characteristics of the disputes covered, as well as of the parties to whom it would apply. It would provide facilities for conciliation and arbitration by specially qualified persons of independent judgment carried out according to rules known and accepted in advance by the parties concerned. In particular, it would ensure that once a government or investor had given consent to conciliation or arbitration under the auspices of the Centre, such consent could not be unilaterally withdrawn.' See also L. REED, J. PAULSSON and N. BLACKABY, *Guide to ICSID Arbitration*, 2nd ed., Wolters Kluwer, Alphen aan den Rijn 2011.

[8] See M. FANOU and V.P. TZEVELEKOS, above n. 2, p. 97, where the authors note the difference between investment arbitration and the ECtHR, which is 'a last resort and last word court that cannot be reached unless domestic remedies have been exhausted'.

[9] See ibid.; R. DOLZER and C. SCHREUER, above n. 3, p. 237.

[10] See P. BERNARDINI, 'Investimento straniero e arbitrato' [2017] *Rivista dell'arbitrato* 673, 673–76.

[11] See ECHR, Articles 1 and 34.

[12] See M. FANOU and V.P. TZEVELEKOS, above n. 2, p. 98.

This chapter is structured as follows: section 2 compares the notions of 'investment' under IIL, and of 'possessions' under the ECHR, to examine whether the latter also encompasses FDI. Once it has been established that there is an overlap between the objects of the two regimes, section 3 compares the extent of the protection that each regime accords to FDI. Due to the limited scope of this chapter, this analysis will focus on the use of the doctrine of 'legitimate expectations' by IIL, and by the ECHR. Finally, section 4 offers some conclusions.

2. THE NOTION OF INVESTMENT UNDER IIL AND THE ECHR

In order to examine whether the ECHR system encompasses protection of FDI, it is paramount to first offer a definition of 'investment', under IIL.

Once it has been clarified what an 'investment' is, under IIL, the next question is whether the protection of property provided by Article 1 Protocol 1 to the ECHR can be construed as including 'investments'.

2.1. THE DEFINITION OF 'INVESTMENT' UNDER IIL

Differently from human rights instruments, including the ECHR, IIL does not provide for the protection of 'property', the object of protection being instead the 'investment' (a term that originates from economic terminology, and is not immediately understood as a legal concept).[13]

But when is an 'investment' a 'protected investment' under IIL? Investment arbitral tribunals answer this question by following one of two different approaches:

- A subjective approach that relies only on the will of the States Parties to the BITs (or to multilateral treaties). According to this approach, the only acceptable definition of 'investment' is the one offered in the relevant treaty.
- A 'dual test' approach, which not only looks at whether an investment exists pursuant to the definition offered by the relevant treaty, but also (going beyond the boundaries of the applicable treaty) applies an

---

[13] See R. DOLZER and C. SCHREUER, above n. 3, p. 60.

objective test, according to which an investment must satisfy a series of prongs derived from the economic context.[14]

As to the first approach, it is worth noting that most of the BITs currently in force provide a definition of 'investment'. According to this approach, the meaning of 'investment' must be established by applying the canons of treaty interpretation pursuant to Articles 31 and 32 of the Vienna Convention on the Law of Treaties.[15]

In the event that the investment in question is not included among the protected investments, as defined under the treaty, it follows that consent to arbitrate the dispute arising from that investment is not established, and that the arbitral tribunal, therefore, lacks jurisdiction.[16]

For example, pursuant to Article 1 of the BIT between Italy and Bahrain:

> For the purposes of this Agreement, and unless otherwise stated in this Agreement: 1. The term 'investment' means any kind of property invested, before or after the entry into force of this Agreement, by an investor of a Contracting Party in the territory of the other Contracting Party, in conformity with the laws and regulations of that party, irrespective of the legal form and framework chosen. Without limiting the generality of the foregoing, the term 'investment' comprises in particular, but not exclusively: (a) movable and immovable property as well as any other similar rights, such as mortgages, liens and pledges; (b) shares, debentures, equity holdings or any other instruments of credit, as well as Government and public securities in general; (c) claims to money or any contractual right having an economic value connected with an investment, as well as reinvested incomes and capital gains; (d) copyright, commercial trade marks, patents, industrial designs, and other intellectual and industrial property rights, know-how, trade secrets, trade names and goodwill; and (e) any economic rights accruing by law or by contract and any licence and franchise granted in accordance with the provisions in force on economic activities, including the right to prospect for, extract and exploit natural resources.[17]

---

[14] See C.L. LIM, J. HO and M. PAPARINSKIS, above n. 3, pp. 210–30; R. DOLZER and C. SCHREUER, above n. 3, p. 61.

[15] See C.L. LIM, J. HO and M. PAPARINSKIS, above n. 3, p. 211, where the authors note that, '[a]s different Contracting States can agree on different definitions of protected investments in different investment treaties, a given investment that may qualify for protection under one treaty may not qualify under another.'

[16] Ibid., pp. 210–11.

[17] Agreement between the Government of the Italian Republic and the Government of the Kingdom of Bahrain on the Promotion and Protection of Investments, 29 October 2006,

As to the 'dual test' approach, this is often applied when the investment treaty provides that the Contracting States consent to submit their disputes to ICSID arbitral tribunals.[18]

Pursuant to Article 25 of the ICSID Convention, ICSID arbitral tribunals have jurisdiction only when the legal dispute arises directly out of an 'investment'.[19] In addition to the subjective meaning of 'investment' derived from the relevant treaty, arbitral tribunals that follow this second approach attribute an objective meaning to the term 'investment', under Article 25 of the ICSID Convention.[20]

The most famous test proposed and applied by investment tribunals to determine whether, from an objective perspective, the dispute concerns a protected investment is the so-called *Salini* test, which comprises four prongs. According to the *Salini v. Morocco* tribunal:

> The Tribunal notes that there have been almost no cases where the notion of investment within the meaning of Article 25 of the Convention was raised. However, it would be inaccurate to consider that the requirement that a dispute be 'in direct relation to an investment' is diluted by the consent of the Contracting Parties. To the contrary, ICSID case law and legal authors agree that the investment requirement must be respected as an objective condition of the jurisdiction of the Centre ... The doctrine generally considers that investment infers: *contributions, a certain duration of performance of the contract* and *a participation in the risks of the transaction* ... In reading the Convention's preamble, one may add *the contribution to the economic development of the host State of the investment* as an additional condition. In reality, these various elements may be interdependent. Thus, the risks of the transaction may depend on the contributions and the duration of performance of the contract. As a result, these various criteria should be assessed globally even

---

Article 1 (entered into force 28 June 2009) <https://investmentpolicy.unctad.org/international-investment-agreements/treaty-files/3384/download>. For the scope of this analysis, it is worth noting that, in the most recent model BITs, the expression 'any kind of property' is no longer used, and has been substituted by the expression 'every kind of asset'. See Netherlands Model Investment Agreement, 22 March 2019, Article 1 <https://investmentpolicy.unctad.org/international-investment-agreements/treaty-files/5832/download>.

[18] While the 'dual test' approach is more frequent in ICSID arbitration proceedings, '[a]ttempts at devising an objective meaning of protected investments are not limited to tribunals obliged to apply Article 25(1) of the ICSID Convention. Even tribunals unfettered by Article 25(1) have tried to impart an objective meaning to protected investments.' (see C.L. LIM, J. HO and M. PAPARINSKIS, above n. 3, p. 218).

[19] See L. REED, J. PAULSSON and N. BLACKABY, above n. 7, p. 68; R. DOLZER and C. SCHREUER, above n. 3, p. 61; U. KRIEBAUM, above n. 2, p. 231.

[20] See R. DOLZER and C. SCHREUER, above n. 3, p. 65.

if, for the sake of reasoning, the Tribunal considers them individually here.[21] (emphasis added)

Interestingly, the *Salini* test has been integrated into the definition of 'investment' offered by the most recent BITs.[22] As a result, in those cases where the applicable BIT incorporates the *Salini* test, the distinction between the two approaches illustrated above becomes, in practical terms, irrelevant (given that the objective meaning of 'investment', as conceptualised by the *Salini* test, is incorporated into the subjective will of the BIT's Contracting States).

2.2. THE DEFINITION OF 'POSSESSIONS' UNDER THE ECHR

Differently from the BITs, the ECHR does not refer to 'investments', providing instead, at Article 1, Protocol 1, for the protection of 'possessions'.

Pursuant to Article 1, Protocol 1 (Protection of property), paragraph 1: '*Every natural or legal person is entitled to the peaceful enjoyment of his possessions. No one shall be deprived of his possessions* except in the public

---

[21] *Salini Costruttori S.p.A. and Italstrade S.p.A. v. Kingdom of Morocco* (ICSID Case No. ARB/00/4), Decision on Jurisdiction (23 July 2001), §52. For an analysis of the *Salini* test (and of the case law that followed), see R. DOLZER and C. SCHREUER, above n. 3, pp. 66–76; C.L. LIM, J. HO and M. PAPARINSKIS, above n. 3, pp. 218–30; L. REED, J. PAULSSON and N. BLACKABY, above n. 7, pp. 68–71.

[22] For example, pursuant to the Dutch Model BIT of 2019 (above n. 17): '*For the purposes of this Agreement: (a) "investment" means every kind of asset that has the characteristics of an investment, which includes a certain duration, the commitment of capital or other resources, the expectation of gain or profit, and the assumption of risk.* Forms that an investment may take include: (i) movable and immovable property as well as any other property rights in rem in respect of every kind of asset, such as mortgages, liens and pledges; (ii) rights derived from shares, bonds and other kinds of interests in companies and joint ventures; (iii) claims to money, to other assets or to any contractual performance having an economic value; (iv) rights in the field of intellectual property, technical processes, goodwill and know-how; (v) rights granted under public law or under contract, including rights to prospect, explore, extract and exploit natural resources. "Claims to money" within the meaning of sub (iii) does not include claims to money that arise solely from commercial contracts for the sale of goods or services by a natural or legal in the territory of a Contracting Party to a natural or legal person in the territory of the other Contracting Party, the domestic financing of such contracts, or any related order, judgment, or arbitral award. Returns that are invested shall be treated as investments and any alteration of the form in which assets are invested or reinvested shall not affect their qualification as investments.' (emphasis added).

interest and subject to the conditions provided for by law and by the general principles of international law.' (emphasis added)

In the first place it is worth noting that, while the ECHR does not provide a definition of either 'property' or 'possessions', any notion of these two concepts, within the context of the ECHR, must be found beyond (and independently from) any legal conceptualisation of the Contracting States' domestic law.[23]

The ECtHR has thus interpreted the concept of 'possessions' in a broad manner, encompassing many assets and subjective rights/interests that would also qualify as protected investments under IIL. As clarified in the ECtHR's *Guide on Article 1 of Protocol No. 1 to the European Convention of Human Rights* (Guide on Article 1, Protocol 1):

> The concept of 'possessions' in the first part of Article 1 of Protocol No. 1 is an autonomous one, covering both 'existing possessions' and assets, including claims, in respect of which the applicant can argue that he or she has at least a 'legitimate expectation'. 'Possessions' include rights '*in rem*' and '*in personam*'. The term encompasses immovable and movable property and other proprietary interests. ... *The concept of 'possessions' has an autonomous meaning which is independent from the formal classification in domestic law and is not limited to the ownership of physical goods: certain other rights and interests constituting assets can also be regarded as 'property rights', and thus as 'possessions' for the purposes of this provision.* The issue that needs to be examined in each case is whether the circumstances of the case, considered as a whole, conferred on the applicant *title to a substantive interest* protected by Article 1 of Protocol No. 1.[24] (emphasis added)

---

[23] See C. SCHREUER and U. KRIEBAUM, above n. 2, p. 745; M. FANOU and V.P. TZEVELEKOS, above n. 2, p. 106. On this point, see *Beyeler v. Italy*, no. 33202/96, §100, ECHR 2000-I: 'In that connection the Court points out that *the concept of "possessions" in the first part of Article 1 has an autonomous meaning which is not limited to ownership of physical goods and is independent from the formal classification in domestic law*: certain other rights and interests constituting assets can also be regarded as "property rights", and thus as "possessions" for the purposes of this provision.' (emphasis added). See also M. RUFFERT, 'The Protection of Foreign Direct Investment by the European Convention on Human Rights' (2000) 43 *German Yearbook of International Law* 116, 121: 'It should not be underestimated, however, that the Court aims at an autonomous approach in formulating the Convention's property right guarantee. The very notion of property varies broadly even within the regional sphere of the original signatories of the European Convention on Human Rights; it opens, as has been duly noted, an "abyss" of comparative law. Property does not exist without law, and consequently it is more difficult to be guaranteed where there is no homogeneous legal order.'

[24] Council of Europe/European Court of Human Rights, *Guide on Article 1 of Protocol No. 1 to the European Convention of Human Rights. Protection of Property* (updated on 31 August 2021), p. 7 <https://www.echr.coe.int/Documents/Guide_Art_1_Protocol_1_ENG.pdf>.

As a result of this broad conceptualisation of the term 'possessions', the ECtHR has included within its meaning, among other things:

- Claims and judgments debts
- Company shares and other financial instruments
- Professional clientele
- Business licences
- Future income
- Intellectual property
- Leases on property and housing rights
- Social security benefits/pensions.[25]

In light of the meaning of 'possessions' under the ECHR, as developed by the ECtHR, it is possible to conclude that the protection of property provided by Article 1, Protocol 1 can be construed as including 'investments' and, among them, FDI.[26]

3. THE USE OF 'LEGITIMATE EXPECTATIONS' IN IIL AND THE ECHR SYSTEM

If both IIL and the ECHR protect investments, the next question is whether they offer the same degree of protection.

---

[25] Ibid. See also M. RUFFERT, above n. 23, 142: at 122, the author says: 'The Court has always attributed a broad meaning to these terms containing in substance the right of property. The guarantee of property, whether movable or immovable, is not confined to tangible property in a private law sense, but includes all vested rights bearing an economic value whatsoever. Therefore, rights arising out of contractual obligations, such as a contract for employment or a leasehold contract, are also protected by Article 1 of Protocol No. 1, including intellectual property rights or shares in company as well. Even vested interests that stem from a state concession or license, e.g., permission to sell alcoholic beverages, are within the field of application of the Protocol's guarantee.'

[26] This is also the opinion offered by M. FANOU and V.P. TZEVELEKOS, above n. 2, p. 106. See also M. RUFFERT, above n. 23, 123: 'There is obviously a strong connection between Article 1 of Protocol No. 1 and the protection of FDI: The Convention adopts its notion of property from general Public International Law. Thus it covers what have commonly been held to be property rights. Among these rights that are of utmost importance to FDI are those rights that are granted by the state by means of a concession or license, as are rights arising out of private law contracts in the context of what is summarized under the heading of "creeping expropriation".'

Due to the limited scope (and length) of this chapter, the following analysis focuses on the doctrine of 'legitimate expectations', being an increasingly relevant doctrine used by both investment arbitral tribunals and the ECtHR in deciding cases involving investments.

As is well known, the principle of 'legitimate expectations' is understood to be relevant in circumstances where a public authority contradicts – for example, through a regulatory change – its previous conduct, which had engendered in an individual a reasonable expectation of receiving a certain benefit.[27]

After clarifying the notion of 'legitimate expectations', in IIL and in the ECHR system, respectively, this section will look at how each of the two regimes answers three different questions:

- Are general provisions, included in the host state's regulatory framework, sufficient to create a legitimate expectation?
- Is it necessary that investors acquire an established legal position, for legitimate expectations to arise?
- Does the protection of legitimate expectations imply that the host state is absolutely precluded from enacting regulatory changes that are detrimental to investors?

3.1. THE NOTION OF 'LEGITIMATE EXPECTATIONS'

3.1.1. *The Notion of 'Legitimate Expectations' in IIL*

In IIL, the notion of legitimate expectations is considered a sub-standard of fair and equitable treatment (FET), the most frequently invoked standard of protection in investment treaty disputes.[28]

FET is a very broad and elusive standard, whose meaning depends on the specific circumstances of the case. In general terms, as clarified in *MTD Equity Sdn. Bhd and MTD Chile S.A. v. Republic of Chile*:

> [F]air and equitable treatment should be understood to be treatment in an even-handed and just manner, conducive to fostering the promotion of foreign

---

[27] See M.C. MALAGUTI and G. ROJAS ELGUETA, 'Alcance y fuentes de las expectativas legítimas de los inversores en las sagas de energía renovable españolas e italianas' (2021) 13 *Arbitraje: Revista de arbitraje comercial y de inversiones* 151, 156.

[28] The fact that FET is the most-used standard in investment disputes, and the standard 'with the highest practical relevance' is underlined by R. DOLZER and C. SCHREUER, above n. 3, p. 130.

investment. Its terms are framed as a pro-active statement – 'to promote', 'to create', 'to stimulate', rather than prescriptions for a passive behavior of the State or avoidance of prejudicial conduct to the investors.[29]

In construing and defining the scope of the FET standard, investment arbitral tribunals widely resort to the doctrine of legitimate expectations,[30] whose legal grounds must be sought not in international law, but in domestic legal systems.[31]

According to the arbitral tribunal in *Total S.A. v. Argentine Republic*:

> Since the concept of legitimate expectations is based on the requirement of good faith, one of the general principles referred to in Article 38(1)(c) of the Statute of the International Court of Justice as a source of international law, *the Tribunal believes that a comparative analysis of the protection of legitimate expectations in domestic jurisdictions is justified at this point*. While the scope and legal basis of the principle varies, *it has been recognized lately both in civil law and in common law jurisdictions within well defined limits*.[32] (emphasis added)

In general terms, it is considered 'legitimate' or 'reasonable' for an investor to expect a certain degree of stability and/or consistency in the legal and business environment of the host state in which the investment takes place. In order to be considered legitimate, expectations must be based either

---

[29] *MTD Equity Sdn. Bhd and MTD Chile S.A. v. Republic of Chile* (ICSID Case No. ARB/01/7), Award (25 May 2004), §113.

[30] On the doctrine of 'legitimate expectations', see A. BROWN, *A Theory of Legitimate Expectations for Public Administration*, OUP, Oxford 2017; see also M. POTESTÀ, 'Legitimate Expectations in Investment Treaty Law: Understanding the Roots and the Limits of a Controversial Concept' (2013) 28 *ICSID Review – Foreign Investment Law Journal* 88; J. OSTŘANSKÝ, 'An Exercise in Equivocation: A Critique of Legitimate Expectations as a General Principle of Law under the Fair and Equitable Treatment Standard' in A. GATTINI, A. TANZI and F. FONTANELLI (eds), *General Principles of Law and International Investment Arbitration*, Brill/Nijhoff, Leiden 2018, pp. 344–77; F. AHMED and A. PERRY, 'The Coherence of the Doctrine of Legitimate Expectations' (2014) 73 *Cambridge Law Journal* 67.

[31] The extensive use of legitimate expectations as a sub-standard of FET is justified by the fact that legitimate expectations are now considered a 'general principle of law', as referred to in the Statute of the International Court of Justice, Article 38(1)(c), being the principle of legitimate expectations common to the legal systems of 'civilized nations' (see M. POTESTÀ, above n. 30, pp. 93–98).

[32] See *Total S.A. v. Argentine Republic* (ICSID Case No. ARB/04/1), Decision on Liability (27 December 2010), §128.

on the host state's regulatory framework (including legislation, treaties, assurances contained in decrees, licences and other executive statements), or on undertakings and representations made – explicitly or implicitly – by the host state.[33]

Further, investment arbitral tribunals have clarified that investors' subjective hopes and perceptions do not qualify as legitimate expectations. Rather, legitimate expectations must be based on objectively verifiable facts; what is 'legitimate' is not what is reasonable for the investor, but what is reasonable from an objective point of view.[34]

For the purposes of this analysis, it is worth noting that, in IIL – differently from the ECHR system, as will be explained below – 'legitimate expectations' are not the direct object of protection (which, as clarified above, must be a 'protected investment'), but are instead used as a substantive standard (more precisely a sub-standard of FET) through which investments are protected.

3.1.2. The Notion of 'Legitimate Expectations' in the ECHR System

In the ECHR system, legitimate expectations are conceptualised as a type of protected property (or, to use the language of Article 1, Protocol 1, a type of 'possession').[35]

Differently from IIL, where legitimate expectations serve as a standard of protection for the underlying investment, in the case law of the ECtHR, legitimate expectations are treated as the direct object of protection against interference by national authorities.[36]

According to the Guide on Article 1, Protocol 1, 'possessions' can either be 'existing possessions', or they can be assets, including claims, in respect of which the applicant can argue that he or she has at least a 'legitimate expectation' of obtaining effective enjoyment of a property right.[37]

---

[33] See R. DOLZER and C. SCHREUER, above n. 3, p. 145.
[34] *Suez, Sociedad General de Aguas de Barcelona, S.A. and Vivendi Universal, S.A. v. Argentine Republic* (ICSID Case No. ARB/03/19), Decision on Liability (20 July 2010), §209. See also R. DOLZER and C. SCHREUER, above n. 3, p. 148.
[35] See M. FANOU and V.P. TZEVELEKOS, above n. 2, p. 125.
[36] Ibid., pp. 111–12; M. RUFFERT, above n. 23, 120.
[37] *Guide on Article 1 of Protocol No. 1*, above n. 24, p. 8.

In an attempt to circumscribe the meaning of 'legitimate expectations' within the concept of 'possessions', the ECtHR affirmed, in *Béláné Nagy v. Hungary*, that:

> Although Article 1 of Protocol No. 1 applies only to a person's existing possessions and does not create a right to acquire property ... in certain circumstances a 'legitimate expectation' of obtaining an asset may also enjoy the protection of Article 1 of Protocol No. 1 ... *A legitimate expectation must be of a nature more concrete than a mere hope and be based on a legal provision or a legal act such as a judicial decision.* The hope that a long-extinguished property right may be revived cannot be regarded as a 'possession'; nor can a conditional claim which has lapsed as a result of a failure to fulfil the condition.[38] (emphasis added)

Despite being treated as a direct object of protection by the ECHR, and as a standard of protection by IIL, 'legitimate expectations' protected under the ECHR are akin to the corresponding notion in IIL, as a matter of definition. Whether the doctrine of 'legitimate expectations' is also applied in the same way by the ECtHR and the investment arbitral tribunals will be verified through consideration of the three questions described in the introduction to this section.

3.2. ARE GENERAL PROVISIONS, INCLUDED IN THE HOST STATE REGULATORY FRAMEWORK, SUFFICIENT TO CREATE A LEGITIMATE EXPECTATION?

3.2.1. Legitimate Expectations and the General Regulatory Framework in IIL

It is undisputed that foreign investors typically derive legitimate expectations from specific commitments addressed to them personally by the host state (for example, in the form of a stabilisation clause).[39]

---

[38] See *Béláné Nagy v. Hungary*, no. 53080/13, §§74–75, ECtHR 13 December 2016.
[39] As clarified in *Total S.A. v. Argentine Republic* (ICSID Case No. ARB/04/1), Decision on Liability (27 December 2010), §101, stabilisation clauses are, 'clauses, which are inserted in state contracts concluded between foreign investors and host states with the intended effect of freezing a specific host State's legal framework at a certain date, such that the adoption of any changes in the legal regulatory framework of the investment concerned (even by law of general application and without any discriminatory intent by the host State) would be illegal'.

On the other hand, it is generally accepted by arbitral tribunals that general provisions of the host state's regulatory framework are not sufficient to create legitimate expectations.

In *Philip Morris v. Uruguay*, the arbitral tribunal stated that:

> It clearly emerges from the analysis of the FET standard by investment tribunals that legitimate expectations depend on *specific* undertakings and representations made by the host State to induce investors to make an investment. *Provisions of* general *legislation applicable to a plurality of persons or of category of persons, do not create legitimate expectations that there will be no change in the law.*[40] (emphasis added)

According to the *Blusun* and *Antaris* arbitral tribunals, respectively:

> As such, it [the thesis of the claimants] faces the second and more fundamental difficulty, which is that *tribunals have so far declined to sanctify laws as promises.*[41] (emphasis added)

And:

> *Provisions of general legislation* applicable to a plurality of persons or a category of persons, *do not create legitimate expectations that there will be no change in the law.*[42] (emphasis added)

Notwithstanding the fact that legitimate expectations cannot normally arise from the host state's general regulatory framework, arbitral tribunals tend to agree that legitimate expectations can instead arise from 'rules that are not specifically addressed to a particular investor but which are put in place with a specific aim to induce foreign investments and on which the foreign investor relied in making his investment'.[43]

---

[40] See *Philip Morris Brands Sàrl, Philip Morris Products S.A. and Abal Hermanos S.A. v. Oriental Republic of Uruguay* (ICSID Case No. ARB/10/7), Award (8 July 2016), §426.
[41] See *Blusun S.A., Jean-Pierre Lecorcier and Michael Stein v. Italian Republic* (ICSID Case No. ARB/14/3), Final Award (27 December 2016), §367.
[42] See *Antaris GMBH and Dr. Michael Göde v. The Czech Republic* (PCA Case No 2014-01), Award (2 May 2018), §360(6).
[43] See UNCTAD, *Fair and Equitable Treatment: A Sequel*, UNCTAD Series on Issues in International Investment Agreements II, 2012, p. 69 <https://unctad.org/system/files/official-document/unctaddiaeia2011d5_en.pdf>. See also *Silver Ridge Power BV v. Italian Republic* (ICSID Case No. ARB/15/37), Award of the Tribunal (26 February 2021), §406.

If the possibility of legitimate expectations being created by general legislation cannot be excluded entirely, it is worth noting, using the words of the *Jürgen Wirtgen* tribunal, that:

> The decisive issue is not whether a state's undertaking is 'specific' or 'general', or statutory or contractual, but whether the statements and actions of the state provide a sufficiently clear commitment to give rise under international law to legitimate expectations or legal rights on the part of the investor.[44]

3.2.2. Legitimate Expectations and the General Regulatory Framework in the ECHR System

As seen in the previous paragraph, one contentious issue in IIL is whether legitimate expectations can be created by general legislation (i.e. by provisions of general character indistinctly directed at any individual), or only by specific commitments towards investors.

The reason why this matter is relevant in IIL is straightforward: IIL is aimed at protecting foreign investors who have made investments based on conduct of the host state that was specifically designed to attract such foreign investments; it is disputable whether this is the case in relation to general legislation (since such legislation is not specifically addressed towards foreign investors).

As seen above, according to most investment arbitral tribunals, general legislation (applicable to any individual meeting certain conditions, irrespective of whether they are a foreign investor) is considered insufficient to create legitimate expectations on the part of foreign investors.

On the other hand, the ECHR system aims to protect fundamental human rights from violation by its Contracting States, irrespective of the nationality or any other circumstance of the victim. Since it puts in place a general and abstract system of guarantees, it is irrelevant whether the source of the violated legal position was directly addressed towards foreign investors.

Not surprisingly, then, in the ECtHR case law on legitimate expectations, the core question is not what the possible sources of legitimate expectations are (general legislation, licences, judicial decisions, etc.), but whether an expectation is sufficiently established to be considered legitimate and worthy of protection.

This issue is examined in the following subsection.

---

[44] *Jürgen Wirtgen and others v. The Czech Republic* (PCA Case No. 2014-03), Dissenting Opinion of Arbitrator Gary Born (11 October 2017), §12.

3.3. IS IT NECESSARY THAT INVESTORS ACQUIRE AN ESTABLISHED LEGAL POSITION, FOR LEGITIMATE EXPECTATIONS TO ARISE?

3.3.1. The Threshold of 'Objective Certainty' under IIL

While investment arbitral tribunals agree that investors' expectations must be 'objectively reasonable' in order to be considered 'legitimate', different arbitral tribunals differ in their criteria for assessing the threshold of 'objective certainty'.[45]

For example, a high degree of inconsistency among arbitral tribunals emerged with regard to claims brought by foreign investors against Italy after a regulatory change, implemented in 2014, which reduced incentive tariffs granted to eligible photovoltaic plants for a period of 20 years.[46]

According to one approach, regulatory changes that intervened before the acquisition of a subjective right (in these cases, the admission to a specific incentive tariff) did not interfere with the legitimate expectations principle, given that, at the time of the investment (normally identified as being the time when the foreign investors acquired the shares in the local companies operating or developing the photovoltaic plants), an investor only had a mere factual aspiration – and not a legal expectation – of obtaining a certain benefit (i.e. the incentive tariff) from the regulatory framework:

> [B]oth the tariff recognitions letter and the GSE Agreement in respect of *Megasol* post-dated Claimant's investment. ... *It enjoyed no guarantee of success at the time of investment*, and nothing in any of Respondent's *Contos* [i.e. the Ministerial Decrees through which Italy had implemented the original incentive scheme] could infer that a party in Claimant's position as of such dates was inevitably going to be awarded the incentives. ... *What is decisive is that as of those dates the protection of Claimant's investment rights had not yet crystallised.*[47] (emphasis added)

---

[45] M.C. MALAGUTI and G. ROJAS ELGUETA, above n. 27, pp. 177–79.
[46] For a more comprehensive analysis of the Italian photovoltaic cases brought before investment arbitral tribunals, see ibid.
[47] See *CEF Energia B.V. v. Italian Republic* (SCC Case No. 2015/158), Award (16 January 2019), §§187–88. See also *Sunreserve Luxco Holdings S.À.R.L. and others v. Italian Republic* (SCC Case No. 2016/32), Final Award (25 March 2020), §§705–10, 839.

Pursuant to a second, contrasting, approach, in order for a legitimate expectation to arise it is not necessary for the investor already to have acquired a subjective right (or, in broader terms, an established legal position), it being sufficient that the general regulatory framework gives an express assurance that, once certain conditions have been met, the investor will acquire a certain benefit (in this case, the incentive tariff):

> From its review of all of the relevant evidence and the Parties' arguments, the majority of the Tribunal has concluded that *the Claimants' expectations arising from the* Conto Energia *regime were legitimate expectations for the purposes of FET under the ECT. Conto Energia* Decrees II, III and IV gave an express assurance or commitment that plants which qualified under the terms of the regime would receive a specified incentive tariff in constant terms for the duration of the incentive period.[48] (emphasis added)

> [T]he adoption of legislative and regulatory acts with the specific aim to induce investment makes the coming into existence of legitimate expectations more likely, and the Italian incentive tariff regime undeniably did just that.[49]

3.3.2. The Threshold of 'Objective Certainty' under the ECHR

In accepting that legitimate expectations can be protected as 'possessions', the ECtHR has tried to clarify in what circumstances the expectation of obtaining an asset or a benefit enjoys the protection granted by Article 1, Protocol 1.

As stated in *Béláné Nagy v. Hungary*:

> In cases concerning Article 1 of Protocol No. 1, the issue that needs to be examined is normally whether the circumstances of the case, considered as a whole, conferred on the applicant *title to a substantive interest protected by that provision*.[50] (emphasis added)

As reported in the Guide on Article 1, Protocol 1:

> By way of example, in a number of cases the Court examined, respectively, whether the applicants had '*a claim which was sufficiently established to be*

---

[48] See *ESPF Beteiligungs GmbH and others v. Italian Republic* (ICSID Case No. ARB/16/5), Award (14 September 2020), §545.
[49] See *Silver Ridge Power BV v. Italian Republic* (ICSID Case No. ARB/15/37), Award of the Tribunal (26 February 2021), §§428–29.
[50] See *Béláné Nagy v. Hungary*, no. 53080/13, §76, ECtHR 13 December 2016.

enforceable' (*Gratzinger and Gratzingerova v. the Czech Republic* (dec.) [GC], §74); whether they demonstrated *the existence of 'an assertable right under domestic law to a welfare benefit*' (*Stec and Others v. the United Kingdom* (dec.) [GC], §51); or whether the persons concerned *satisfied the 'legal conditions laid down in domestic law for the grant of any particular form of benefits*' (*Richardson v. the United Kingdom* (dec.), §17).[51] (emphasis added)

Notwithstanding the diversity of the expressions used in the ECtHR case law, it clearly emerges that, in order to establish the existence of a legitimate expectation, it is necessary for there to be a domestic legal basis generating a proprietary interest, or, to use different words, that the applicant has an 'assertable right'.[52]

Clearly, the threshold set by the ECtHR to establish the existence of a legitimate expectation is much higher than the ones set by investment arbitral tribunals, where, as described above, a foreign investor is not always required to prove that they have already acquired an established legal position or 'assertable right'.

The fact that the threshold set by the ECtHR is certainly higher than the ones identified by investment arbitral tribunals finds further confirmation in a recent judgment of the Court of Justice of the European Union (CJEU). In a preliminary ruling, the CJEU had to decide whether the very same regulatory change implemented by Italy in 2014, which had been the subject of various investment arbitration cases (as analysed in the previous subsection), was consistent with Articles 16 (Freedom to conduct a business) and 17 (Right to property) of the Charter of Fundamental Rights of the European Union.

Interestingly, in ruling that Italy was not precluded from reducing the incentive tariffs, the CJEU relied on the case law of the ECtHR, stating that:

The Court of Justice recalled, in paragraph 61 of the judgment of 3 September 2015, *Inuit Tapiriit Kanatami and Others v Commission* (C–398/13 P, EU:C:2015:535), that *it is apparent from the case-law of the European Court of Human Rights relating to Article 1 of Protocol No 1 to the European Convention for the Protection of Human Rights and Fundamental Freedoms that future income cannot be considered to constitute 'possessions' that may enjoy the protection of Article 17 of the Charter unless it has already been earned, it is definitely*

---

[51] See *Guide on Article 1 of Protocol No. 1*, above n. 24, p. 10.
[52] Ibid. *See also Kopecký v. Slovakia*, no. 44912/98, §§45–52, ECtHR 28 September 2004; C. Schreuer and U. Kriebaum, above n. 2, p. 748.

payable or there are specific circumstances that can cause the person concerned to entertain a legitimate expectation of obtaining an asset.[53] (emphasis added)

If one accepts that the CJEU correctly interpreted the ECtHR case law on 'future income', the different extent of the protection granted under IIL, and under the ECHR, becomes readily apparent.

While investment arbitral tribunals agree that a legitimate expectation certainly arises once a 'future income' (for example, the payment of incentive tariffs for a period of 20 years) has crystallised (for example, through a confirmation letter from the competent authority), the ECtHR seems to require a higher threshold (such as, for example, that the incentive tariff is already payable, and thus the claim is already enforceable).[54]

3.4. DOES THE PROTECTION OF LEGITIMATE EXPECTATIONS IMPLY THAT THE HOST STATE IS ABSOLUTELY PRECLUDED FROM ENACTING REGULATORY CHANGES THAT ARE DETRIMENTAL TO INVESTORS?

3.4.1. Balancing Investment Protection and Regulatory Freedom in IIL

In investment arbitration, it is now well settled that, in the absence of a specific commitment towards the investor, legitimate expectations do not imply a guarantee of immutability of the legal framework, and that the national legislator enjoys a wide discretion in issuing new regulations, especially when these are necessary in light of a public interest.[55]

---

[53] See Joined CJEU Cases C-798/18 and C-799/18, *Federazione nazionale delle imprese elettrotecniche ed elettroniche (Anie) and others and Athesia Energy S.r.l. and others v. Ministero dello Sviluppo Economico and Gestore dei servizi energetici (GSE) S.p.A.*, §39, ECLI:EU:C:2021:280.

[54] As to 'future income' (such as incentive tariffs to be paid in the future), the Guide on Article 1 of Protocol 1 clarifies: 'Article 1 of Protocol No. 1 does not create a right to acquire property (*Denisov v. Ukraine* [GC], §137). Future income constitutes a "possession" only if the income has been earned or where an enforceable claim to it exists.' (emphasis added) (*Guide on Article 1 of Protocol No. 1*, above n. 24, p. 14).

[55] During the 'first phase' of investment arbitration (i.e. from the origins of investment arbitration in the 1930s, when the first 'state contracts' were entered into by sovereign states, granting foreign private companies the concession rights to exploit their natural resources, until the 1960s – see P. BERNARDINI, above n. 10, pp. 675–79),

As a consequence, regulatory changes are not, per se, in breach of the principle of legitimate expectations, which is deemed to have been violated only where the regulatory change is: (i) unpredictable; (ii) irrational or arbitrary; or (iii) unreasonable or disproportionate:

> While the investor is promised protection against unfair changes, *it is well established that the host State is entitled to maintain a reasonable degree of regulatory flexibility to respond to changing circumstances in the public interest.* Consequently, the requirement of fairness must not be understood as the immutability of the legal framework, but as implying *that subsequent changes should be made fairly, consistently and predictably*, taking into account the circumstances of the investment.[56] (emphasis added)

> In the absence of a specific commitment, the state has no obligation to grant subsidies such as feed-in tariffs, or to maintain them unchanged once granted. *But if they are lawfully granted, and if it becomes necessary to modify them, this should be done in a manner which is not disproportionate to the aim of the legislative amendment,* and should have due regard to the reasonable reliance interests of recipients who may have committed substantial resources on the basis of the earlier regime.[57] (emphasis added)

For the purposes of this chapter, it is worth noting that investment arbitral tribunals, when assessing whether a regulatory change has breached investors' legitimate expectations, often resort to the concepts

---

the principle of legitimate expectations, and in general the FET standard, were interpreted as providing foreign investors with a guarantee of strict stability of the legal and business framework. The current trend in investment arbitral awards is one that seeks to find a more cautious balance between foreign investors' protection and host states' regulatory freedom: '[I]f the often repeated formula to the effect that "the stability of the legal and business framework is an essential element of fair and equitable treatment" were true, legislation could never be changed: the mere enunciation of that proposition shows its irrelevance. Such a standard of behaviour, if strictly applied, is not realistic, nor is it the BITs' purpose that States guarantee that the economic and legal conditions in which investments take place will remain unaltered ad infinitum. ... In other words, *the Tribunal cannot follow the line of cases in which fair and equitable treatment was viewed as implying the stability of the legal and business framework. Economic and legal life is by nature evolutionary.*' (emphasis added) (see *El Paso Energy International Company v. The Argentine Republic* (ICSID Case No. ARB/03/15), Award (31 October 2011) §§350, 352).

56   See *Electrabel S.A. v. Republic of Hungary* (ICSID Case No. ARB/07/19), Award (25 November 2015), §7.77.

57   See *Blusun S.A., Jean-Pierre Lecorcier and Michael Stein v. Italian Republic* (ICSID Case No. ARB/14/3), Final Award (27 December 2016), §319(5).

of 'proportionality' and 'margin of appreciation', which are central in the ECHR system.[58]

As to 'proportionality', the *Stadtwerke* and *Antaris* tribunals stated, respectively, that:

> The Tribunal further adopts the analysis of the tribunal in *AES Summit v. Hungary*, which held: 'There are two elements that require to be analyzed to determine whether a state's act was unreasonable: the existence of a rational policy; and the reasonableness of the act of the state in relation to the policy. A rational policy is taken by a state following a logical (good sense) explanation and with the aim of addressing a public interest matter. ... [A] challenged measure must also be reasonable. That is, there needs to be an appropriate correlation between the state's public policy objective and the measure adopted to achieve it. This has to do with the nature of the measure and the way it is implemented.'[59]

And:

> The Tribunal accepts the Respondent's case that for purposes of the reasonableness analysis, it does not matter whether a tribunal believes that a particular course of action is 'good' or 'bad,' that a different solution might have been 'better,' or that a State could have done 'more,' or that other States took different measures. The Tribunal accepts that the Respondent had the rational objective of reducing excessive profits and sheltering consumers from excessive electricity price rises, and that its actions were not arbitrary or irrational. There was an appropriate correlation between the Respondent's objectives and the measures it took.[60]

Investment arbitral tribunals increasingly accord a significant margin of appreciation to states, in relation to the introduction of regulatory changes

---

[58] As highlighted by C. SCHREUER and U. KRIEBAUM, above n. 2, p. 762: 'Notwithstanding evident similarities, there is little interaction and cross citation between decision makers and scholars in the two fields. This in turn is part of a broader phenomenon of fragmentation in international law. Increasing specialization has led to epistemic sub-communities with their own specialized terminologies which barely communicate with each other. Ideas and concepts from one field of international law are virtually unknown in another. Well-tested solutions adopted in one field are absent from another.'

[59] See *Stadtwerke München GmbH and others v. Kingdom of Spain* (ICSID Case No. ARB/15/1), Award (2 December 2019), §318.

[60] See *Antaris GMBH and Dr. Michael Göde v. The Czech Republic* (PCA Case No. 2014-01), Award (2 May 2018), §§443–44.

that are justified by a public interest, and adopt a deferential approach in reviewing domestic regulatory measures.

In *Continental Casualty Company*, and in *S.D. Myers*, the arbitral tribunals remarked, respectively, that:

> An interpretation of a bilateral reciprocal treaty that accommodates the different interests and concerns of the parties in conformity with its terms accords with an effective interpretation of the treaty. Moreover, *in the Tribunal's view, this objective assessment must contain a significant margin of appreciation for the State applying the particular measure.*[61] (emphasis added)

And:

> The Tribunal considers that a breach of Article 1105 occurs only when it is shown that an investor has been treated in such an unjust or arbitrary manner that the treatment rises to the level that is unacceptable from the international perspective. *That determination must be made in the light of the high measure of deference that international law generally extends to the right of domestic authorities to regulate matters within their own borders.* The determination must also take into account any specific rules of international law that are applicable to the case.[62] (emphasis added)

With specific regard to the photovoltaic cases involving Italy, Prof. Giorgio Sacerdoti's dissenting opinion in the *Greentech* case underlined that:

> I recall, finally, the margin of discretion recognized to host countries when acting in the public interest with reasonable measures and taking into account the rights and interests of operators and investors (both domestic and foreigners by equally applicable measures, without discriminations as has been the case here). In this respect the standards applied by the Italian Constitutional Court when it found the tariff reduction of the *Spalma-incentivi* legitimate must be considered. It is not lightly to be presumed or accepted that the Italian legal system, which incorporates the relevant protective principles of the European Convention of Human Rights and of the European Union, would afford a level of protection to

---

[61] See *Continental Casualty Company v. The Argentine Republic* (ICSID Case No. ARB/03/9), Award (5 September 2008), §181; see also *CEF Energia B.V. v. Italian Republic* (SCC Case No. 2015/158), Award (16 January 2019), §185; ibid., §360(9).

[62] See *S.D. Myers, Inc. v. Government of Canada* (UNCITRAL), Partial Award (13 November 2000), §263.

those who enter into long-term relations with the public sector lower than that stemming from the ECT.[63] (emphasis added)

3.4.2. Balancing Investment Protection and Regulatory Freedom in the ECHR System

Similarly to the analysis offered in the previous subsection, in the ECHR system the protection of legitimate expectations does not entail that states are absolutely precluded from introducing regulatory changes that interfere in a detrimental way with those expectations.

In particular, when an interference with the 'peaceful enjoyment of possessions' is declared lawful (having a legal justification in the relevant domestic law), the ECtHR will also resort to the proportionality test (while recognising a high margin of appreciation on the part of national authorities).[64]

As is well known, the proportionality test aims to strike a balance between the general interests of the community and the protection of the

---

[63] See *Greentech Energy Systems A/S, et al. v. Italian Republic* (SCC Case No. 2015/095), Dissenting Opinion of Arbitrator Giorgio Sacerdoti (5 December 2018), §50.

[64] See *Guide on Article 1 of Protocol No. 1*, above n. 24, p. 30: 'In order to be compatible with the general rule set forth in the first sentence of the first paragraph of Article 1 of Protocol No. 1, an interference with the right to the peaceful enjoyment of "possessions", apart from being prescribed by law and in the public interest, must strike a "fair balance" between the demands of the general interest of the community and the requirements of the protection of the individual's fundamental rights.' See also M. FANOU and V.P. TZEVELEKOS, above n. 2, p. 115; M. RUFFERT, above n. 23, 140: 'The Eur. Court H.R. has constantly reiterated that any interference with Article 1 of Protocol No. 1, particularly an interference that fails to be considered under its second paragraph, must strike a "fair balance" between the general interest and the protection of the individual's fundamental right to the enjoyment of one's possessions. Basically this means that *there must be a reasonable relationship of proportionality between the means employed and the aim pursued by the regulatory legislation. … However, the Eur. Court H.R. again recognizes that the state enjoys a wide margin of appreciation with regard both to the choice of means and to the assessment of whether the consequences of enforcement are justified for the purpose of achieving the aim of the relevant law.* The Eur. Court H.R. is not prepared to intervene unless that choice and assessment are made without reasonable foundation.' (emphasis added). See also E. BJORGE, *Domestic Application of the ECHR: Courts as Faithful Trustees*, OUP, Oxford 2015, p. 155: 'The ECHR proportionality test encompasses first legality ("Is the interference prescribed by a clear and accessible law?") and second legitimacy and the giving of reasons.' As underlined by Alec Stone Sweet and Jud Mathews, proportionality analysis has become 'the preferred procedure for managing … an alleged conflict between two rights claims, or between a rights provision and a legitimate state … interest' (see A. STONE SWEET and J. MATHEWS, 'Proportionality Balancing and Global Constitutionalism' (2008) 47 *Columbia Journal of Transnational Law* 72, 73).

individual's fundamental rights (in this analysis, the protection of FDI); or, in other words, to ascertain whether the person concerned had to bear a disproportionate and excessive burden as a consequence of the state's action (or inaction).⁶⁵

In particular, the test is structured in four steps. First, the ECtHR verifies whether the aim was legitimate (i.e. whether the state was legally authorised to take such a measure). Second, the analysis shifts to whether the measure was 'suitable' (i.e. whether the means adopted by the government were rationally related to the stated policy objectives). Third, the ECtHR assesses whether there was proportionality between the interference suffered by the individual and the identified legitimate aim. Fourth, the ECtHR carries out a *stricto sensu* cost–benefit analysis, measuring the benefits brought to society against the costs imposed on the applicant.⁶⁶

While one of the elements of the proportionality test is whether other, less intrusive, measures existed that could reasonably have been resorted to by the public authorities in the pursuance of the public interest, their possible existence does not itself render the contested legislation unjustified, provided that the state remains within the bounds of its margin of appreciation. In other words, it is not for the ECtHR to say whether the contested legislation represented the best solution for dealing with the problem, or whether the legislature's discretion should have been exercised in another way.⁶⁷

In the regulation of property issues, the ECtHR accords a wide margin of appreciation to national authorities, acknowledging 'that national authorities, because of their closer proximity to the social realities of the community that they are entrusted to govern, are better placed to determine what is in the public interest and what is not'.⁶⁸

---

65   See *Guide on Article 1 of Protocol No. 1*, above n. 24, p. 30.
66   See E. BJORGE, above n. 64, p. 155; see also W.W. BURKE-WHITE and A. VON STADEN, 'Private Litigation in a Public Law Sphere: The Standard of Review in Investor-State Arbitrations' (2010) 35 *The Yale Journal of International Law* 283, 334. As clarified in the Guide on Article 1 of Protocol No. 1: 'The purpose of the proportionality test is to establish first how and to what extent the applicant was restricted in the exercise of the right affected by the interference complained of and what were the adverse consequences of the restriction imposed on the exercise of the applicant's right on his/her situation. Subsequently, this impact is balanced against the importance of the public interest served by the interference.' (*Guide on Article 1 of Protocol No. 1*, above n. 24, p. 30).
67   *Guide on Article 1 of Protocol No. 1*, above n. 24, p. 32.
68   W.W. BURKE-WHITE and A. VON STADEN, above n. 66, 309.

As an illustration, in the case of *Broniowski v. Poland*, the ECtHR reaffirmed that:

> Under the system of protection established by the Convention, *it is thus for the national authorities to make the initial assessment as to the existence of a problem of public concern warranting measures to be applied in the sphere of the exercise of the right of property*, including deprivation and restitution of property. Here, as in other fields to which the safeguards of the Convention extend, the national authorities accordingly enjoy a certain margin of appreciation. Furthermore, the notion of 'public interest' is necessarily extensive. In particular, the decision to enact laws expropriating property or affording publicly funded compensation for expropriated property will commonly involve consideration of political, economic and social issues. *The Court has declared that, finding it natural that the margin of appreciation available to the legislature in implementing social and economic policies should be a wide one, it will respect the legislature's judgment as to what is 'in the public interest' unless that judgment is manifestly without reasonable foundation.*[69] (emphasis added)

As a further illustration, in the case of *Jahn and others v. Germany*, the ECtHR reaffirmed that:

> *Because of their direct knowledge of their society and of its needs, the national authorities are in principle better placed than the international judge to appreciate what is 'in the public interest'* ... *the national authorities, accordingly, enjoy a certain margin of appreciation.*[70] (emphasis added)

4. CONCLUSIONS

In light of the analysis carried out in this chapter, it is possible to draw some conclusions in relation to the two objectives set out in the introduction.

As to the first of these (establishing whether the ECHR system can play a role in the protection of FDI), it has been shown that investments can be considered a human right protected by Article 1, Protocol 1. This becomes evident if one compares the notion of 'investment' under IIL with the broad concept of 'possessions' developed by the ECtHR case law.

---

[69] See *Broniowski v. Poland* [GC], no. 31443/96, §149, ECtHR 28 September 2005.
[70] See *Jahn and others v. Germany* [GC], nos. 46720/99, 72203/01 and 72552/01, §91, ECtHR 30 June 2005.

Therefore, it can be concluded that both the ECHR and IIL offer protection to FDI, although on different premises.

As to the second objective (comparing how investment arbitral tribunals and the ECtHR use the principle of 'legitimate expectations' in deciding disputes involving investments), the analysis involved a comparison between the notions of legitimate expectations developed by arbitral tribunals, and by the ECtHR. Although the former treat legitimate expectations as a substantive standard of protection, and the latter treats them as the object of protection, it has been found that the two systems converge towards a similar definition of what constitutes a 'legitimate expectation'.

As to the extent of the protection offered to investments through the use of this doctrine, the following conclusions can be drawn. First, the scope of protection offered by IIL is, by definition, more limited, given that IIL is specifically aimed at protecting foreign investors from changes in the conduct of the host state, on which they had relied when making their investments. This is why most investment arbitral tribunals rule out the possibility that general legislation can give rise to legitimate expectations. On the other hand, the ECHR is a general and abstract system of guarantees, which seems to attribute minor relevance to the source of the legitimate expectation.

Second, the threshold of 'objective certainty', for the investor's legitimate expectations to be considered worthy of protection under the ECHR, is higher than the equivalent threshold in IIL. Pursuant to the ECtHR case law, in order to establish the existence of a legitimate expectation it is necessary for there to be a domestic legal basis under which the applicant has an 'assertable right', whereas investment arbitral tribunals do not always require foreign investors to prove that they have already acquired an established legal position or 'assertable right'.

The foregoing is evident if one considers the same matter in relation to 'future incomes'. While investment arbitral tribunals agree that, once a 'future income' has crystallised, a legitimate expectation certainly arises, the ECtHR seems to require a higher threshold (as has recently been further enlightened by the CJEU).

Third, both systems agree that regulatory changes are not, per se, precluded to states by the doctrine of legitimate expectations. Interestingly, when it comes to the standards of review employed to assess whether a regulatory change was legitimate, there seems to be a convergence of IIL towards the use of two doctrines that are crucial in the ECHR system: 'proportionality' and 'margin of appreciation'.

From the foregoing, it can be concluded that there is space for a fruitful two-way dialogue between the ECHR system and IIL. On one hand, investment arbitral tribunals can draw important lessons from the ECtHR's elaborations of the proportionality test, and of the margin of appreciation doctrine. On the other hand, the ECtHR could take advantage of the more advanced debate on legitimate expectations as a substantive standard of protection, in IIL. Deeper cross-pollination between the two systems is both possible and desirable.

THE EU PRINCIPLE OF MUTUAL RECOGNITION BEFORE THE EUROPEAN COURT OF HUMAN RIGHTS

Denise Wiedemann

1. Introduction 226
2. The Impact of Fundamental Rights on the Implementation of Judgments 227
   2.1. National Dimension 227
   2.2. Recognition and Enforcement of Foreign Judgments 228
      2.2.1. Right of Access to Court (Art. 6(1) ECHR) 228
      2.2.2. Procedural and Institutional Standards (Art. 6(1) ECHR) 229
         2.2.2.1. Fundamental Rights Violation in the State of Recognition or Enforcement 229
         2.2.2.2. Fundamental Rights Violation During the Adjudication of the Dispute in the State of Origin 230
      2.2.3. Substantive Rights 232
3. Recognition and Enforcement of Judgments within the EU 234
4. The Impact of the ECHR on the EU Mechanisms of Recognition and Enforcement 237
   4.1. Matters of Strict International Legal Obligation 238
      4.1.1. Applicability of the ECHR (Art. 1 ECHR) 238
      4.1.2. Presumption of Compliance 240
      4.1.3. Supervisory Mechanism 241
      4.1.4. Substantive Fundamental Rights Protection 242
   4.2. Matters with a Margin of Manoeuvre 247
5. Summary and Outlook 249

1. INTRODUCTION

The European Court of Human Rights (ECtHR) has elaborated obligations both for the enforcement of judgments in situations where adjudication of the dispute and implementation of the judgment occur in the same national legal system, and for the recognition or enforcement of foreign judgments (see section 2 below). As all EU Member States have ratified the European Convention on Human Rights (ECHR or Convention),[1] they are obliged to secure the ECHR's rights and freedoms.[2] Meanwhile, in the European Union (EU), recognition and enforcement of judgments from one Member State in another Member State is, for the most part, no longer a matter of national law. The Treaty of Amsterdam[3] vested judicial cooperation in civil matters within the competence of the EU[4] (today this matter is governed by Art. 81 of the Treaty on the Functioning of the European Union (TFEU)). Since then, the unification and simplification of the recognition and enforcement procedures has developed steadily (see section 3 below). However, it is not obvious whether, and to what extent, the recognition and enforcement of a judgment in accordance with an EU regulation will be measured against rights embodied in the Convention (see section 4 below). First, the EU is not yet a party to the Convention, even though it may ultimately accede to it.[5] The Court of Justice of the European Union (CJEU) gave a negative opinion[6] on the draft Accession Agreement of 5 April 2013, and the renegotiation of the Accession Agreement, which started in October 2019, has not yet come to an end.[7] Thus, the ECHR does not bind the EU directly. Second, the EU Member States are committed in two different ways: as Contracting States to the ECHR, and as EU Member States vis-à-vis the EU.

---

[1] For a chart of signatures and ratifications of the ECHR, see https://www.coe.int/en/web/conventions/full-list?module=signatures-by-treaty&treatynum=005.

[2] See Art. 1 ECHR, which obliges all 'High Contracting Parties' to respect the Convention.

[3] Treaty of Amsterdam amending the Treaty on European Union, the Treaties establishing the European Communities and certain related acts, OJ C 340, 10 November 1997, pp. 1–14.

[4] The European Communities were merged into the EU by the Treaty of Lisbon (Treaty of Lisbon amending the Treaty on European Union and the Treaty establishing the European Community, signed at Lisbon, 13 December 2007, OJ C 306, 17 December 2007, pp. 1–271).

[5] Art. 59(2) ECHR.

[6] CJEU, Opinion 2/13, 18 December 2014, ECLI:EU:C:2014:2454.

[7] On the accession of the EU to the ECHR, see, e.g. F. KORENICA, *The EU Accession to the ECHR*, Springer, Cham 2015.

2. THE IMPACT OF FUNDAMENTAL RIGHTS ON THE IMPLEMENTATION OF JUDGMENTS

2.1. NATIONAL DIMENSION

According to Art. 6(1) ECHR, '[i]n the determination of his civil rights and obligations ... everyone is entitled to a fair and public hearing within a reasonable time by an independent and impartial tribunal established by law.' On the one hand, this provision implicitly guarantees the right of access to a court.[8] On the other hand, Art. 6(1) ECHR sets institutional ('independent and impartial tribunal established by law') as well as procedural ('fair and public hearing within a reasonable time') standards for court proceedings.

For creditors, the right of access to a court first of all secures the right to institute proceedings before a court.[9] But access to court would be illusory if the creditor could obtain a judgment but could not enforce it.[10] Therefore, in a second step, the right of access to court also embodies the creditor's right to enforce a successful judgment against the debtor.[11] In order to comply with Art. 6(1) ECHR, the Contracting States must each establish an adequate and effective procedure for the enforcement of judgments.[12]

---

[8] *Waite and Kennedy v. Germany*, no. 26083/94, ECtHR (GC) 18 February 1999, §50; *Golder v. the United Kingdom*, no. 4451/70, ECtHR 21 February 1975, §§28–36; J. MEYER-LADEWIG, S. HARRENDORF and S. KÖNIG, 'Art. 6 EMRK' in J. MEYER-LADEWIG, M. NETTESHEIM and S. VON RAUMER (eds), *EMRK*, 4th ed., Nomos, Baden-Baden 2017, Art. 6, n. 34; W. PEUKERT, 'Verfahrensgarantien und Zivilprozeß (Art. 6 EMRK)' *Rabels Zeitschrift für ausländisches und internationales Privatrecht* 63 (1998), 600–624, 608.

[9] *Philis v. Greece*, nos. 12750/87, 13780/88, 14003/88, ECtHR 27 August 1991, §59.

[10] *Hornsby v. Greece*, no. 18357/91, ECtHR 19 March 1997, §40: 'However, that right would be illusory if a Contracting State's domestic legal system allowed a final, binding judicial decision to remain inoperative to the detriment of one party.'

[11] Ibid.; *Burdov v. Russia*, no. 59498/00, ECtHR 7 May 2002, §34; *Plotnikovy v. Russia*, no. 43883/02, ECtHR 24 February 2005, §22; *Burdov v. Russia (no. 2)*, no. 33509/04, ECtHR 15 January 2009, §65; B. HESS, 'Comparative Analysis of the National Reports' (2006) *European Business Law Review* 723–43, 727; J. MEYER-LADEWIG, S. HARRENDORF and S. KÖNIG, 'Art. 6 EMRK' in J. MEYER-LADEWIG, M. NETTESHEIM and S. VON RAUMER (eds), *EMRK*, 4th ed., Nomos, Baden-Baden 2017, Art. 6, n. 50; W. PEUKERT, 'Verfahrensgarantien und Zivilprozeß (Art. 6 EMRK)', *Rabels Zeitschrift für ausländisches und internationales Privatrecht* 63 (1998), 600–24, 617 *et seq.*; differently, see the concurring opinion of Judge Spielmann in *Vrbica v. Croatia*, no. 32540/05, ECtHR 1 April 2010: 'The execution of a decision follows on from the trial, unlike the issue of access to a court, which precedes the trial.'

[12] *Fociac v. Romania*, no. 2577/02, ECtHR 3 February 2005, §69.

In addition to the right of access to a court, the institutional and procedural standards set out in Art. 6(1) ECHR apply to enforcement proceedings.[13] States are obliged, vis-à-vis creditors, to carry out enforcement within a reasonable period of time.[14] In addition, the denial of (timely) enforcement may violate other Convention rights. In *Scollo v. Italy*, the ECtHR affirmed a violation of Art. 1 of the Protocol to the ECHR (protection of property) because a flat owner's eviction order against their tenant had not been enforced.[15] Vis-à-vis debtors, states have to secure a fair trial.[16]

2.2. RECOGNITION AND ENFORCEMENT OF FOREIGN JUDGMENTS

2.2.1. Right of Access to Court (Art. 6(1) ECHR)

From the perspective of general international law, judgments produce effects only within the borders of the state in which they have been issued. General international law, thus, does not oblige states to recognise and enforce foreign judgments, except where an international convention requires this.[17] Yet from the perspective of Art. 6(1) ECHR ('right of access to court'), a territorial limitation on the effects of judgments could be questionable.[18] A creditor who has already obtained a judgment in one state would have to incur the costs, time and litigation risk of a second

---

[13] F. MATSCHER, 'Die Einwirkungen der EMRK auf das Internationale Privat- und zivilprozessuale Verfahrensrecht' in F. MATSCHER et al. (eds), *Europa im Aufbruch – Festschrift Fritz Schwind*, Manz, Wien 1993, pp. 71–85, 85.

[14] *Scollo v. Italy*, no. 19133/91, ECtHR 28 September 1995, §44: the inactivity of the competent enforcement authorities engages the responsibility of a Contracting State.

[15] *Scollo v. Italy*, no. 19133/91, ECtHR 28 September 1995, §40.

[16] K.-H. BRUNNER, 'Die europäischen Leitlinien für eine bessere Umsetzung der bestehenden Empfehlung des Europarates über die Zwangsvollstreckung', *Deutsche Gerichtsvollzieher Zeitung*, 2012, 61–69.

[17] P. KINSCH, 'Enforcement as a right', *Nederlands internationaal privaatrecht*, 2014, 540–44, 540 (referring to the case *S.S. Lotus (France v. Turkey)*, no. 9, 7 September 1927, PCIJ (Series A) No. 10, pp. 18–19, which, however, concerned the territorial limitation of jurisdiction); R. MICHAELS, 'Recognition and Enforcement of Foreign Judgments' in R. WOLFRUM (ed), *Max Planck Encyclopedia of Public International Law*, OUP, Oxford 2012, §11.

[18] B. HESS, 'EMRK, Grundrechte-Charta und europäisches Zivilverfahrensrecht' in H.P. MANSEL et al. (eds), *Festschrift für Erik Jayme*, vol. I, Sellier, Munich 2004, pp. 339–59, 340.

trial in another state. Thus, one could argue that the right of access to court encompasses not only the enforcement of a judgment in the same state, but also its recognition and enforcement abroad.[19]

The ECtHR has not, thus far, considered recognition and enforcement of foreign judgments from the angle of the right of access to court, but has distinguished the cross-border 'situation from the one where both adjudication of the dispute and implementation of the judgment occur in the same national legal system'.[20] Instead, the Court has measured recognition and enforcement of foreign judgments from the perspective of procedural standards, in particular the right to a fair trial (see section 2.2.2. below), and from the perspective of substantive rights (see section 2.2.3. below).

2.2.2. Procedural and Institutional Standards (Art. 6(1) ECHR)

2.2.2.1. Fundamental Rights Violation in the State of Recognition or Enforcement

The ECtHR did not accept the argument that the principle of sovereignty allows each Contracting State to decide independently under which conditions it implements a foreign decision in its domestic legal order.[21] Thus, the procedural and institutional standards of Art. 6(1) ECHR are binding for the Contracting States when recognising or enforcing a foreign judgment.[22] First, a refusal to recognise or enforce a foreign judgment

---

[19] Ibid., p. 344; F. MATSCHER, 'Die Einwirkungen der EMRK auf das Internationale Privat- und zivilprozessuale Verfahrensrecht' in F. MATSCHER et al. (eds), *Europa im Aufbruch – Festschrift Fritz Schwind*, Manz, Wien 1993, pp. 71–85, 82 *et seq.*; more cautious is J. ADOLPHSEN, 'Aktuelle Fragen des Verhältnisses von EMRK und Europäischem Zivilprozessrecht' in J. RENZIKOWSKI (ed), *Die EMRK im Privat-, Straf- und Öffentlichen Recht*, Manz, Wien 2004, pp. 39–81, 73.

[20] *Korolev v. Russia*, no. 38112/04, ECtHR 21 October 2010, §50. In the end, the ECtHR did not rule on a violation of Art. 6(1) ECHR, but found the application inadmissible because the applicant had not exhausted the available domestic remedies. By contrast, the refusal of domestic courts to enforce a foreign judgment that has already been declared enforceable may violate the right of access to court: *Vrbica v. Croatia*, no. 32540/05, ECtHR 1 April 2010, §62 – see, however, the concurring opinion of Judge Spielmann: 'The execution of a decision follows on from the trial, unlike the issue of access to a court, which precedes the trial.'

[21] *Sylvester v. Austria*, Decision as to the admissibility of application no. 54640/00, ECtHR 9 October 2003.

[22] *Saccoccia v. Austria*, no. 69917/01, ECtHR 18 December 2008, §62.

might constitute an interference with the judgment creditor's right to a fair trial, if the Contracting State has no relevant justification for such a refusal.[23] And, second, the Contracting States have to observe the parties' rights during the recognition or enforcement proceedings.[24] For example, a creditor might claim a violation of Art. 6(1) ECHR if a foreign judgment has not been recognised or enforced within a reasonable time.[25] Furthermore, both parties, in general, have the right to be heard during the recognition and enforcement proceedings. However, as recognition and enforcement concern rather technical issues, states might be dispensed from holding an oral court hearing.[26]

2.2.2.2. Fundamental Rights Violation During the Adjudication of the Dispute in the State of Origin

In *Pellegrini v. Italy*, the ECtHR acknowledged an obligation on Contracting States to refuse recognition or enforcement of a foreign judgment if the defendant's rights have been violated during the adjudication of the dispute in the state of the judgment's origin.[27] The ECtHR did not examine whether the proceedings before the court of origin complied with Art. 6(1) of the Convention. Instead, the Court scrutinised whether the Italian courts, i.e. courts in the state of enforcement, in reviewing the foreign

---

[23] *McDonald v. France*, no. 18648/04, ECtHR 29 April 2008: 'La Cour reconnaît que le refus d'accorder l'exequatur des jugements du tribunal américain a représenté une ingérence dans le droit au procès équitable du requérant.' – The Court recognises that the refusal to grant the exequatur of the judgments of the American court constituted an interference with the applicant's right to fair trial (author's translation). See also *Negrepontis-Giannisis v. Greece*, no. 56759/08, ECtHR 3 May 2011, §§44, 46; P. KINSCH, 'Enforcement as a right', *Nederlands internationaal privaatrecht*, 2014, 540–44, 542.

[24] F. MATSCHER, 'Die Einwirkungen der EMRK auf das Internationale Privat- und zivilprozessuale Verfahrensrecht' in F. MATSCHER et al. (eds), *Europa im Aufbruch – Festschrift Schwind*, Manz, Wien 1993, pp. 71–85, 84.

[25] *Sylvester v. Austria*, Decision as to the admissibility of application no. 54640/00, ECtHR 9 October 2003, §§25–34.

[26] *Saccoccia v. Austria*, no. 69917/01, ECtHR 18 December 2008, §79.

[27] *Pellegrini v. Italy*, no. 30882/96, ECtHR 20 July 2001, §40; see also *Avotiņš v. Latvia*, no. 17502/07, ECtHR 23 May 2016, §§96, 98; J. ADOLPHSEN, 'Aktuelle Fragen des Verhältnisses von EMRK und Europäischem Zivilprozessrecht' in J. RENZIKOWSKI (ed), *Die EMRK im Privat-, Straf- und Öffentlichen Recht*, Manz, Wien 2004, pp. 39–81, 71; F. MATSCHER, 'Der Begriff des fairen Verfahrens nach Art. 6 EMRK' in H. NAKAMURA et al. (eds), *Festschrift Beys*, Sakkoulas, Athens 2003, pp. 989–1007, 1005; F. MATSCHER, 'Die Einwirkungen der EMRK auf das Internationale Privat- und zivilprozessuale Verfahrensrecht' in F. MATSCHER et al. (eds), *Europa im Aufbruch – Festschrift Schwind*, Manz, Wien 1993, pp. 71–85, 83.

judgment, applied a standard of review which was in conformity with Art. 6(1) ECHR.[28]

As regards the standard of review, the ECtHR required the Italian courts to 'duly satisfy' themselves that the proceedings in the state of the judgement's origin fulfilled the guarantees of Art. 6(1) ECHR.[29] Thus, when recognising or enforcing a civil judgment from a non-Contracting State, Contracting States have to verify that the foreign proceedings complied with Art. 6(1) ECHR.

In other issues, however, the ECtHR has limited the standard of review to the question of a 'flagrant denial of justice': in the criminal law context, the ECtHR held that Contracting States are only obliged to refuse the enforcement of a sentence if 'it emerges that the conviction is the result of flagrant denial of justice'.[30] The same limited review has been applied to extradition cases[31] and to child return cases.[32] It was argued in scholarship that in case of the recognition or enforcement of a foreign civil judgment the review should likewise be limited because the fundamental rights violation in the state of recognition or enforcement would be only of an indirect nature.[33] In opposition to this, the ECtHR confirmed the requirement of an unlimited review of the proceeding in the state of origin in *Dolenc v. Slovenia*.[34] The Court saw 'no reason to depart from the approach set out in *Pellegrini*'.[35] This ruling is convincing with regard to Art. 1 ECHR which obliges the Contracting States to fully secure everyone's rights and

---

[28] *Pellegrini v. Italy*, no. 30882/96, ECtHR 20 July 2001, §40. On the nature of the ecclesiastical court (which was a superior court of the Catholic Church, and not a state court of the Vatican), see P. KINSCH, 'The Impact of Human Rights on the Application of Foreign Law and on the Recognition of Foreign Judgments – A Survey of the Cases Decided by the European Human Rights Institutions' in T. EINHORN and K. SIEHR (eds), *Intercontinental Cooperation Through Private International Law – Essays in Memory of Peter E Nygh*, TMC Asser Press, The Hague 2004, pp. 197–228, 219 *et seq*.
[29] *Pellegrini v. Italy*, no. 30882/96, ECtHR 20 July 2001, §40.
[30] *Drozd and Janousek v. France and Spain*, no. 12747/87, ECtHR 26 June 1992, §110.
[31] *Othman (Abu Qatada) v. the United Kingdom*, no. 8139/09, ECtHR 17 January 2012, §258; P. KINSCH, 'The Impact of Human Rights on the Application of Foreign Law and on the Recognition of Foreign Judgments – A Survey of the Cases Decided by the European Human Rights Institutions' in T. EINHORN and K. SIEHR (eds), *Intercontinental Cooperation Through Private International Law – Essays in Memory of Peter E Nygh*, TMC Asser Press, The Hague 2004, pp. 197–228, 205.
[32] *Eskinazi and Chelouche v. Turkey*, no. 14600/05, ECtHR 6 December 2005.
[33] F. MATSCHER, 'Der Begriff des fairen Verfahrens nach Art. 6 EMRK' in H. NAKAMURA et al. (eds), *Festschrift Beys*, Sakkoulas, Athens 2003, pp. 989–1007, 1005.
[34] *Dolenc v. Slovenia*, no. 20256/20, ECtHR 20 October 2022.
[35] Ibid., §60 (emphasis in the original).

freedoms. A deviation from the requirement set out in Art. 1 ECHR is not justified by the fact that recognition or enforcement of a decision issued in violation of Art. 6(1) ECHR would only be of an indirect nature; rather, such a recognition or enforcement would exacerbate the violation and would, therefore, be in direct breach of the Convention.

Despite of this confirmation in *Dolenc v. Slovenia*, the ECtHR left two loopholes for a more limited review in civil recognition or enforcement cases. First, the *Pellegrini* and the *Dolenc* cases concerned judgments emanating from non-Contracting States.[36] If, in contrast, the recognition or enforcement of a judgment from a Contracting State was at stake, the debtor would be obliged to challenge violations of Art. 6(1) ECHR in the state of the judgment's origin.[37] If the debtor failed to do so, for example if he or she missed a deadline, a further review in the state of enforcement might not be successful. Otherwise, procedural limits for human rights challenges would lose their preclusive effect. Second, the ECtHR qualified *Pellegrini* and *Dolenc* as cases with 'paramount importance to the defendant'.[38] While *Pellegrini* concerned a decision annulling a marriage, i.e. determining the personal status, the foreign judgment in *Dolenc* caused serious financial and reputational damage to the applicant. However, it is questionable whether, for example, judgment for payment of a small amount of money would allow a more limited review as Art. 1 ECHR does not differentiate between important and less important matters.

2.2.3. Substantive Rights

The violated right can also be of a substantive nature. If a domestic court recognises or enforces a foreign judgment, the recognition or enforcement

---

[36] Ibid.; *Pellegrini v. Italy*, no. 30882/96, ECtHR 20 July 2001, §40 '[a] review of that kind is required where a decision in respect of which enforcement is requested emanates from the courts of a country which does not apply the Convention'.

[37] *Sofia Povse and Doris Povse v. Austria*, no. 3890/11, ECtHR 18 June 2013, §86; J. Oster, 'Public Policy and Human Rights' (2015) 11 *Journal of Private International Law* 542–67, 564; see also P. Kinsch, 'The Impact of Human Rights on the Application of Foreign Law and on the Recognition of Foreign Judgments – A Survey of the Cases Decided by the European Human Rights Institutions' in T. Einhorn and K. Siehr (eds), *Intercontinental Cooperation Through Private International Law – Essays in Memory of Peter E Nygh*, TMC Asser Press, The Hague 2004, pp. 197–228, 227 et seq. However, in *Odd F. Lindberg v. Sweden*, no. 48198/99, ECtHR 15 December 2004 the ECtHR refrained from determining the applicable standard in that case (p. 13).

[38] *Dolenc v. Slovenia*, no. 20256/20, ECtHR 20 October 2022, §60; also see *Pellegrini v. Italy*, no. 30882/96, ECtHR 20 July 2001, §40 'capital importance'.

might violate the defendant's rights. The enforcement of a foreign defamation judgment, for instance, could violate the defendant's freedom of expression.[39] In turn, refusal or delay in recognising or enforcing a foreign decision might deprive the creditor of the decision's substantive effects.[40] For example, the ECtHR has found violations of Art. 8 ECHR (right to respect for private and family life) in cases involving such refusals.[41] The Court has drawn the scope of application of Art. 8 ECHR very broadly. First, while the main purpose of Art. 8 ECHR is to protect the individual from arbitrary interferences by the public authorities, the purpose of the provision is not confined to this negative function; the negative obligation is supplemented by positive obligations.[42] These positive obligations may involve the adoption of measures, including the recognition and enforcement of foreign judgments. Second, even if Art. 8 ECHR does not explicitly safeguard procedural requirements, it requires the proceeding leading to interferences with the right to private and family life to be fair.[43] Thus, complaints of a procedural nature may not only be examined from the perspective of Art. 6(1) ECHR but also of Art. 8 ECHR.[44]

---

[39] *Odd F. Lindberg v. Sweden*, no. 48198/99, ECtHR 15 December 2004.
[40] P. KINSCH, 'Enforcement as a right', *Nederlands internationaal privaatrecht*, 2014, 540–44, 540.
[41] *M.A. v. Austria*, no. 4097, ECtHR 15 January 2015, §137 (violation due to the 'failure to act swiftly' during the implementation of an Italian return order); *Labassee v. France*, no. 65941/11, ECtHR 26 June 2014; *Mennesson v. France*, no. 65192/11, ECtHR 26 June 2014 (both finding a violation because France had refused to order the transcription of American judgments recording the births of children conceived by gestational surrogacy); *Negrepontis-Giannisis v. Greece*, no. 56759/08, ECtHR 3 May 2011, §§44, 46 (finding a violation of Art. 8 because Greece had refused to recognise an American adoption judgment); *Leschiutta and Fraccaro v. Belgium*, no. 58081/00, 58411/00, ECtHR 17 July 2008 (finding a violation of Art. 8 ECHR because Belgium did not immediately enforce a foreign judgment on handing over the custody of a child); *Wagner and JMWL v. Luxembourg*, no. 76240/01, ECtHR 28 June 2007 (finding a violation of Art. 8 ECHR because Luxembourg had refused to recognise a judgment concerning the adoption of a child in Peru); *Ignaccolo-Zenide v. Romania*, no. 31679/96, ECtHR 25 January 2000, §113 (finding a violation of Art. 8 ECHR because Romania had refused to enforce an order to return children); B. HESS, 'EMRK, Grundrechte-Charta und europäisches Zivilverfahrensrecht' in H.P. MANSEL et al. (eds), *Festschrift für Erik Jayme*, vol. I, Sellier, Munich 2004, pp. 339–59, 351.
[42] *M.A. v. Austria*, no. 4097, ECtHR 15 January 2015, §104.
[43] *Veres v. Spain*, no. 57906/18, ECtHR 8 November 2022, §53.
[44] The ECtHR recently solely applied Art. 8 ECtHR: *Veres v. Spain*, no. 57906/18, ECtHR 8 November 2022, §54.

3. RECOGNITION AND ENFORCEMENT OF JUDGMENTS WITHIN THE EU

A distinction has traditionally been made between the recognition of the effects of a foreign judgment, especially res judicata, and the enforcement of a foreign judgment, because the two processes follow different mechanisms.

The recognition of a judgment from another Member State usually takes place implicitly, without the need for a special recognition procedure. A proceeding only commences if a party opposes recognition, and this proceeding leads to the refusal of recognition only if the recognition would be manifestly contrary to public policy (*ordre public*), or if any other specific ground for refusal is established.[45] Most EU regulations follow this mechanism of implicit recognition, with the possibility of refusing recognition at the request of a party: for example the Brussels Ibis Regulation for general civil and commercial matters;[46] the Brussels IIter Regulation for matrimonial matters and the matters of parental responsibility;[47] the EU Succession Regulation;[48] the EU Regulations on matrimonial property[49] and on property relationships of registered partnerships;[50] and the EU Insolvency Regulation (for judgments other than the opening

---

[45] See, e.g. Art. 45(1), Brussels Ibis Regulation (Regulation (EU) No. 1215/2012 of the European Parliament and of the Council of 12 December 2012 on jurisdiction and the recognition and enforcement of judgments in civil and commercial matters, OJ L 351, 20.12.2012, pp. 1–32).

[46] Ibid., Art. 36 *et seq.*

[47] Arts. 38 and 39, Brussels IIter Regulation (Council Regulation (EU) 2019/1111 of 25 June 2019 on jurisdiction, the recognition and enforcement of decisions in matrimonial matters and the matters of parental responsibility, and on international child abduction, OJ L 178, 02.07.2019, pp. 1–115).

[48] Art. 39 *et seq.*, EU Succession Regulation (Regulation (EU) No. 650/2012 of the European Parliament and of the Council of 4 July 2012 on jurisdiction, applicable law, recognition and enforcement of decisions and acceptance and enforcement of authentic instruments in matters of succession and on the creation of a European Certificate of Succession, OJ L 201, 27.07.2012, pp. 107–34).

[49] Art. 36 *et seq.*, Council Regulation (EU) 2016/1103 of 24 June 2016 implementing enhanced cooperation in the area of jurisdiction, applicable law and the recognition and enforcement of decisions in matters of matrimonial property regimes, OJ L 183, 08.07.2016, pp. 1–29.

[50] Art. 36 *et seq.*, Council Regulation (EU) 2016/1104 of 24 June 2016 implementing enhanced cooperation in the area of jurisdiction, applicable law and the recognition and enforcement of decisions in matters of the property consequences of registered partnerships, OJ L 183, 08.07.2016, pp. 30–56.

of the insolvency proceeding).[51] Jenard described the mechanism as a 'presumption in favour of recognition, which can be rebutted if one of the grounds for refusal ... is present'.[52] Some EU regulations, however, have abolished the grounds for refusal of recognition, in whole or in part. Those regulations oblige Member States to recognise judgments from other Member States without the possibility of refusing recognition, even if their recognition would violate public policy. Along these lines, the Brussels IIter Regulation exempts from the general regime decisions granting rights of access, and decisions that entail the return of a child; such decisions have to be recognised without the possibility of opposing their recognition.[53] Similar unrestricted recognition mechanisms apply, under the EU Maintenance Regulation, to decisions issued in a EU Member State bound by the 2007 Hague Maintenance Protocol,[54] and to judgments that have been confirmed or established in genuine EU proceedings, such as an EU Enforcement Order,[55] an EU Order for Payment,[56] an EU Small Claims Proceeding,[57] or an EU Account Preservation Order.[58]

---

[51] Arts. 32(1) and 33, EU Insolvency Regulation (Regulation (EU) 2015/848 of the European Parliament and of the Council of 20 May 2015 on insolvency proceedings, OJ L 141, 05.06.2015, pp. 19–72).

[52] P. JENARD, 'Report on the Convention on jurisdiction and the enforcement of judgments in civil and commercial matters', OJ C 59, 5 March 1979, pp. 1–65.

[53] Art. 43, Brussels IIter Regulation (above n. 47). However, the Regulation allows a refusal if, and to the extent that, the decision is found to be irreconcilable with a later decision. Furthermore, Art. 56(4) Brussels IIter Regulation allows the enforcement authority to suspend enforcement in exceptional cases, 'if enforcement would expose the child to a grave risk of physical or psychological harm due to temporary impediments which have arisen after the decision was given, or by virtue of any other significant change of circumstances.'

[54] Art. 17(1), EU Maintenance Regulation (Council Regulation (EC) No. 4/2009 of 18 December 2008 on jurisdiction, applicable law, recognition and enforcement of decisions and cooperation in matters relating to maintenance obligations, OJ L 7, 10.01.2009, pp. 1–79). However, the defendant has the right to apply for a review if their right to be heard has been restricted (ibid., Art. 19).

[55] Art. 5, EU Enforcement Order Regulation (Regulation (EC) No. 805/2004 of the European Parliament and of the Council of 21 April 2004 creating a European Enforcement Order for uncontested claims, OJ L 143, 30.04.2004, pp. 15–39).

[56] Art. 19, EU Order for Payment Regulation (Regulation (EC) No. 1896/2006 of the European Parliament and of the Council of 12 December 2006 creating a European order for payment procedure, OJ L 399, 30.12.2006, pp. 1–32).

[57] Art. 20(1), EU Small Claim Regulation (Regulation (EC) No. 861/2007 of the European Parliament and of the Council of 11 July 2007 establishing a European Small Claims Procedure, OJ L 199, 31.07.2007, pp. 1–22).

[58] Art. 22, EAPO Regulation (Regulation (EU) No. 655/2014 of the European Parliament and of the Council of 15 May 2014 establishing a European Account Preservation Order procedure to facilitate cross-border debt recovery in civil and commercial matters, OJ L 189, 27.06.2014, pp. 59–92).

In relation to the enforcement of judgments from another Member State, three different mechanisms can be distinguished. The first, and oldest, mechanism is the exequatur proceeding. While foreign judgments are implicitly recognised, they are not, traditionally, enforced automatically. With an exequatur decision, the Member State of enforcement formally declares that the foreign judgment is enforceable. On the application of the judgment debtor, the Member State of enforcement can refuse exequatur on the same grounds under which it may refuse recognition; in particular, it may do so if the enforcement would violate its public policy. The Brussels I Regulation[59] (which was replaced by the Brussels Ibis Regulation in 2015) and the Brussels IIbis Regulation[60] (which was replaced by the Brussels IIter Regulation in 2022) both provided for such an exequatur proceeding. The exequatur proceeding still applies in matters of succession,[61] and in matters of matrimonial property, as well as in property relationships stemming from registered partnerships.[62] The second mechanism for enforcement of judgments from other Member States otherwise abolishes the formal exequatur proceeding: judgments from one Member State are automatically enforceable in all other Member States. However, the debtor can still object to enforcement on certain grounds, especially if there would be a violation of the public policy of the Member State of enforcement. Thus, the second mechanism is designed in the same manner as the traditional model for recognition of judgments. The Brussels Ibis Regulation and the Brussels IIter Regulation[63] provide for such an automatic enforceability with the possibility to refuse enforcement on certain grounds. The third and last mechanism not only abolishes the formal exequatur proceeding, but also the grounds for refusal of enforcement. It is followed by those regulations which provide for an unrestricted recognition without the possibility of opposing it (see above in this section).[64] Judgments which

---

[59] Art. 38(1), Brussels I Regulation (Council Regulation (EC) No. 44/2001 of 22 December 2000 on jurisdiction and the recognition and enforcement of judgments in civil and commercial matters, OJ L 12, 16.01.2001, pp. 1–23).

[60] Art. 28(1), Brussels IIbis Regulation (Council Regulation (EC) No. 2201/2003 of 27 November 2003 concerning jurisdiction and the recognition and enforcement of judgments in matrimonial matters and the matters of parental responsibility, repealing Regulation (EC) No. 1347/2000, OJ L 338, 23.12.2003, pp. 1–29).

[61] Art. 43 et seq., EU Succession Regulation (above n. 48).

[62] Art. 42, EU Regulation on matrimonial property regimes (above n. 49); Art. 42, EU Regulation on property consequences of registered partnerships (above n. 50).

[63] Art. 34 et seq., Brussels IIter Regulation (above n. 47).

[64] Ibid., Art. 45 et seq.; Art. 17(2), EU Maintenance Regulation (above n. 54); Art. 5, EU Enforcement Order Regulation (above n. 55); Art. 19, EU Order for Payment

are enforced under regulations that follow the third mechanism are not subject to an *ordre public* review in the Member State of enforcement.

The introduction of common mechanisms for recognition and enforcement was initially understood as a vehicle for achieving a common internal market.[65] The subsequent simplification of the mechanisms follows the principle of mutual trust between the Member States. The principle of mutual trust is a presumption that is based on another presumption; namely that the Member States' legal systems share the common values, and in particular the fundamental rights, on which the EU has been founded.[66] As a result, control mechanisms in the state of recognition or enforcement became a symbol of distrust, the abolition of which was promoted, above all, by the European Commission.[67]

4. THE IMPACT OF THE ECHR ON THE EU MECHANISMS OF RECOGNITION AND ENFORCEMENT

The unification and simplification of cross-border recognition and enforcement within the EU secures a creditor's right to have a judgment recognised and enforced abroad. Yet the integration of Member States into the EU recognition and enforcement scheme raises the question of whether, and to what extent, the Member States are still subject to their obligations flowing from the ECHR.

In matters where Contracting States are bound by other international obligations, particularly to the EU, the ECtHR applies different standards, depending on whether the other international obligation is of a strict nature or whether it leaves a margin of manoeuvre to the Contracting State. The former standard applies to unrestricted recognition and enforcement mechanisms, which do not allow the EU Member States to refuse recognition or enforcement (see section 4.1. below). The latter

---

Regulation (above n. 56); Art. 20(1), EU Small Claim Regulation (above n. 57); Art. 22, EAPO Regulation (above n. 58).

[65] B. Hess, 'EMRK, Grundrechte-Charta und europäisches Zivilverfahrensrecht' in H.P. Mansel et al. (eds), *Festschrift für Erik Jayme*, vol. I, Sellier, Munich 2004, 339–59, 343.

[66] CJEU, Opinion 2/13, 18 December 2014, ECLI:EU:C:2014:2454, §168.

[67] Commission of the European Communities, COM(2008) 465, 18 August 2008, 15 *et seq.*

standard might come into play when considering the application of the public policy reservation (see section 4.2. below).

4.1. MATTERS OF STRICT INTERNATIONAL LEGAL OBLIGATION

4.1.1. Applicability of the ECHR (Art. 1 ECHR)

The ECHR is binding only where a Contracting State exercises its jurisdiction (Art. 1 ECHR). If a Contracting State does not act on its own discretion but, rather, in direct execution of obligations to be complied with under EU law, the question arises whether the Convention is applicable at all. In the case *Bosphorus v. Ireland*, the ECtHR answered this question in the affirmative, provided that the Contracting State implements the law of an international organisation through an act or omission of its own public officials.[68] Thus, a Contracting State exercises jurisdiction, in the sense of Art. 1 ECHR, if it implements the law through its own act or omission, even if it has no discretion in doing so.[69]

Later, the ECtHR seized the chance to confirm its *Bosphorus* jurisprudence for the recognition and enforcement procedures prescribed by EU law. The first case, *Povse v. Austria*,[70] is one of the numerous cases dealing with the human rights aspects of international child abduction.[71] The mother had taken the child from Italy to Austria after leaving the child's father. An Italian court ordered the child's return to Italy, in accordance

---

[68] *Bosphorus Hava Yolları Turizm ve Ticaret Anonim Şirketi v. Ireland*, no. 45036/98, ECtHR 30 June 2005, §153; see also *Boivin v. France, Belgium and 32 other Contracting Parties*, no. 73250/01, ECtHR 9 September 2008: 'intervention directe ou indirecte de l'Etat ou des Etats mis en cause'; *M. & Co. v. Germany*, no. 13258/87, European Commission of Human Rights 9 February 1990: 'Under Article 1 ... of the Convention the Member States are responsible for all acts and omissions of their domestic organs allegedly violating the Convention regardless of whether the act or omission in question is a consequence of domestic law or regulations or of the necessity to comply with international obligations.'
[69] C. JANIK, 'Die EMRK und internationale Organisationen – Ausdehnung und Restriktion der *equivalent protection*-Formel in der neuen Rechtsprechung des EGMR', *Zeitschrift für ausländisches öffentliches Recht und Völkerrecht* 70 (2010), 127–79, 151.
[70] *Sofia Povse and Doris Povse v. Austria*, no. 3890/11, ECtHR 18 June 2013.
[71] E.g. *Kupás v. Hungary*, no. 24720/17, ECtHR 28 October 2021; *Spinelli v. Russia*, no. 57777/17, ECtHR 19 October 2021; *X v. Latvia*, no. 27853/09, ECtHR 26 November 2013; *Neulinger and Shuruk v. Switzerland*, no. 41615/07, ECtHR 6 July 2010; *Maumousseau and Washington v. France*, no. 39388/05, 6 December 2007.

with Art. 11(8) Brussels IIbis Regulation. An Austrian court enforced the order; Art. 42(1) Brussels IIbis Regulation neither required an exequatur decision nor allowed the Austrian courts to refuse enforcement on the basis of public policy (see section 3 above). The CJEU had clarified, in a preliminary ruling, that the requested Austrian court was obliged to enforce the return decision and could not refuse enforcement under any circumstances.[72] The mother and the child filed a complaint against Austria before the ECtHR, alleging that the Austrian courts had violated the ECHR by enforcing the return order.[73]

The second case, *Avotiņš v. Latvia*,[74] concerned the enforcement of a judgment from Cyprus for payment of money. The creditor was enforcing the Cyprian judgment in Latvia in accordance with the exequatur mechanisms of the Brussels I Regulation.[75] During the exequatur proceedings, the debtor tried to secure a refusal of exequatur, based not on *ordre public*, but on Art. 34(2) Brussels I Regulation, which allows for rejection of an exequatur decision where the judgment was given in default of appearance, and the debtor was not served with the lawsuit, and was unable to challenge the judgment.[76] The Latvian courts did not accept the debtor's application, and enforced the Cypriot judgment. The debtor filed a complaint against Latvia before the ECtHR, alleging a violation of his rights under Art. 6(1) ECHR because of this non-refusal.

In both cases, the ECtHR found that the Contracting States had the strict obligation to enforce the judgments, and that there was no margin of manoeuvre. In the *Povse v. Austria* child abduction case, Austria lacked a margin of manoeuvre because the Brussel IIbis Regulation did not allow for a refusal of enforcement.[77] And in *Avotiņš v. Latvia*, there was no margin of manoeuvre because Art. 34(2) Brussels I Regulation did

---

[72] CJEU Case C-211/10 PPU, *Doris Povse v. Mauro Alpago*, 1 July 2010, ECLI:EU:C:2010:400, §82.
[73] The applicants did not base their complaint on Art. 6 of the Convention, but on Art. 8 – the right to respect for family life – because they argued that the child's return to Italy would constitute a serious danger to his well-being.
[74] *Avotiņš v. Latvia*, no. 17502/07, ECtHR 23 May 2016.
[75] The case was decided in accordance with the Brussels I Regulation because the proceedings in the state of origin were commenced before the Brussels Ibis Regulation entered into force (see Art. 66(1) Brussels Ibis Regulation).
[76] On the interpretation of Art. 34(2) Brussels I Regulation, see also Case C-70/15, *Emmanuel Lebek v. Janusz Domino*, ECLI:EU:C:2016:524, §§31–49.
[77] *Sofia Povse and Doris Povse v. Austria*, no. 3890/11, ECtHR 18 June 2013, §§76, 79.

not leave any discretion to Latvia.[78] Yet those strict obligations towards the EU do not free the Contracting States from their obligations under the ECHR. Thus, the Contracting States remain principally responsible, under the Convention, for the recognition and enforcement of judgments prescribed by EU law, even if the applicable EU provision leaves no margin of manoeuvre.

4.1.2. Presumption of Compliance

An unlimited applicability of the ECHR in matters of strict international obligation would lead to a responsibility of the Contracting States to comply with the ECHR whenever there has been a shortcoming in the relevant proceedings. However, the ECtHR has acknowledged that assigning unlimited responsibility to comply with the ECHR's obligations to an EU Member State that implements EU law would not take adequate account of the fact that such a state is bound by EU law, as a Member State of the EU, just as it is bound by the ECHR, as a Contracting State to the ECHR. Furthermore, the ECtHR would have to measure EU law against the standards of the Convention, even though the EU is not a Contracting Party. Thus, in *Povse v. Austria*[79] and *Avotiņš v. Latvia*,[80] the ECtHR avoided conflicting obligations for the Contracting States, and evaded an examination of EU law, by applying the 'presumption of compliance' which it had already established in *Bosphorus v. Ireland*.[81]

---

[78] *Avotiņš v. Latvia*, no. 17502/07, ECtHR 23 May 2016, §§ 106–08; see, however, the joint concurring opinions of Judges Lemmens and Briede (Latvia has not violated Art. 6(1) ECHR) when enforcing the Cyprian judgment (§ 4) and, therefore, there is no need to have recourse to the *Bosphorus* presumption (§ 6) and the dissenting opinion of Judge Sajó. In detail, see P. Gragl, 'An Olive Branch from Strasbourg: Interpreting the European Court of Human Rights' Resurrection of *Bosphorus* and Reaction to Opinion 2/13 in the *Avotins* Case: ECtHR 23 May 2016, Case No. 17502/07, *Avotins v. Latvia*' (2017) 13 *European Constitutional Law Review* 551–67, 563.

[79] *Sofia Povse and Doris Povse v. Austria*, no. 3890/11, ECtHR 18 June 2013, § 76.

[80] *Avotiņš v. Latvia*, no. 17502/07, ECtHR 23 May 2016, § 101; P. Gragl, 'An Olive Branch from Strasbourg: Interpreting the European Court of Human Rights' Resurrection of *Bosphorus* and Reaction to Opinion 2/13 in the *Avotins* Case: ECtHR 23 May 2016, Case No. 17502/07, *Avotins v. Latvia*' (2017) 13 *European Constitutional Law Review* 551–67, 561.

[81] *Bosphorus Hava Yolları Turizm ve Ticaret Anonim Şirketi v. Ireland*, no. 45036/98, ECtHR 30 June 2005, § 156; In *Matthews v. the United Kingdom*, no. 24833/94, ECtHR 18 February 1999, the ECtHR did not approach the UK's application with a presumption of compliance. Rather, the Court focused on the voluntary transfer of sovereign rights. It held the UK responsible, under the Convention, for the absence of elections to the European Parliament in Gibraltar, because the UK had voluntarily ratified the Treaty

The 'presumption of compliance' means that as long as 'equivalent protection' exists within the EU, there is a rebuttable presumption that an EU Member State, that fulfils its obligations towards the EU, does not violate the Convention even if there were shortcomings in the recognition or enforcement proceeding. 'Equivalent protection' exists if 'both the substantive guarantees offered and the mechanisms controlling their observance' are in principle equivalent.[82] Thus, the 'presumption of compliance' will be rebutted if there is a dysfunction in the EU supervisory mechanism (see section 4.1.3. below) or a manifest deficiency in the substantive fundamental rights protection (see section 4.1.4. below).

4.1.3. Supervisory Mechanism

As concerns the EU supervisory mechanism, the ECtHR found that the CJEU offers protection equivalent to the ECtHR, even though private individuals have only limited access to the CJEU. In principle, preliminary reference proceedings initiated by national courts, proceedings initiated by EU institutions, and individual actions for damages provide a sufficient protection.[83] As the preliminary reference proceeding is an essential part of the EU's supervisory mechanism, it will be of importance, first, whether the applicant could avail himself of the possibility of bringing his objections before the domestic courts in the Member State where recognition or enforcement is sought; and, second, the domestic courts have to request a preliminary ruling from the CJEU unless the questions have already been decided, or are clear.[84] Thus, the ECtHR limits the necessity for a

---

of Maastricht as well as the election law that excluded Gibraltar from the elections. However, the *Matthews* case is different from the cases of recognition and enforcement of judgments: in the *Matthews* case, the unlawful act is primary law which the Member States have agreed on directly (C. JANIK, 'Die EMRK und internationale Organisationen – Ausdehnung und Restriktion der *equivalent protection*-Formel in der neuen Rechtsprechung des EGMR', *Zeitschrift für ausländisches öffentliches Recht und Völkerrecht* 70 (2010), 127–79, 142; L. SCHEECK, 'The Relationship between the European Courts and Integration through Human Rights', *Zeitschrift für ausländisches öffentliches Recht und Völkerrecht* 65 (2005), 837–85, 860). The rules on recognition and enforcement, on the other hand, derive from secondary law regulations; these do not come about directly through the agreement of the Member States, but through the agreement of the EU institutions.

[82] *Sofia Povse and Doris Povse v. Austria*, no. 3890/11, ECtHR 18 June 2013, §77.
[83] *Michaud v. France*, no. 12323/11, ECtHR 6 December 2012, §§107–11.
[84] On a possible legal protection gap, because the CJEU decides only on the validity and interpretation of Union law, but not on the application to the specific case, see German Federal Constitutional Court, 6 November 2019 – 1 BvR 276/17 – *Recht auf Vergessen II*.

preliminary ruling in a similar way to that in which the CJEU limits the obligation of last instance courts to request a preliminary ruling (*acte éclairé* and *acte clair*):[85]

> The [ECtHR] considers that the condition of the deployment of the full potential of the supervisory mechanism provided for by European Union law ... should be applied without excessive formalism and taking into account the specific features of the supervisory mechanism in question. It considers that it would serve no useful purpose to ... request a ruling from the CJEU in all cases without exception, including those cases where no genuine and serious issue arises with regard to the protection of fundamental rights by EU law, or those in which the CJEU has already stated precisely how the applicable provisions of EU law should be interpreted in a manner compatible with fundamental rights.[86]

Furthermore, in *Povse v. Austria*, the ECtHR did not demand that the CJEU assesses the fundamental rights comparability of the enforcement mechanism. Rather, the Member State of origin has the responsibility to observe fundamental rights during the adjudication of the dispute. If the Member State of origin does not respect fundamental rights, the applicant would be in a position to file an application with the ECtHR against that state.[87]

4.1.4. Substantive Fundamental Rights Protection

As for the substantive guarantees, the EU is, in principle, respectful of fundamental rights in a manner equivalent to the ECHR, since, first, the CJEU has started to refer specifically to the ECHR,[88] and, second, Art. 6 TEU has conferred primary law status to the human rights guaranteed by

---

[85] On the exception to the obligation to refer a question to the CJEU, see, e.g. P. GRAGL, 'An Olive Branch from Strasbourg: Interpreting the European Court of Human Rights' Resurrection of *Bosphorus* and Reaction to Opinion 2/13 in the *Avotins* Case: ECtHR 23 May 2016, Case No. 17502/07, *Avotins v. Latvia*' (2017) 13 *European Constitutional Law Review* 13 551–67, 562; W. WEGENER in C. CALLIESS and M. RUFFERT (eds), *EUV/AEUV*, 6th ed., C.H. Beck, Munich 2022, Art. 267 AEUV n. 33. Last instance courts, however, have the obligation to justify any decision not to refer a preliminary question: see *Avotiņš v. Latvia*, no. 17502/07, ECtHR 23 May 2016, §110.

[86] *Avotiņš v. Latvia*, no. 17502/07, ECtHR 23 May 2016, §109.

[87] *Sofia Povse and Doris Povse v. Austria*, no. 3890/11, ECtHR 18 June 2013, §86.

[88] CJEU Case C-7/98, *Dieter Krombach v. André Bamberski*, ECLI:EU:C:2000:164, §39; see also section 4.2. below.

the EU Charter on Fundamental Rights,[89] the ECHR and the Member States' common constitutional traditions (the latter two as general principles).[90] Art. 47(2) of the EU Charter contains guarantees similar to those in Art. 6(1) ECHR. The EU Charter is binding for the Member States when they recognise or enforce a foreign judgment in accordance with EU law,[91] and it is to be interpreted in accordance with the case law of the ECtHR.[92]

Povse v. Austria seemed to indicate that the ECtHR had accepted that a fundamental rights review should take place only in the Member State of origin. This would pave the way for an unrestricted recognition and enforcement of foreign judgments, without the possibility of a refusal on the ground of public policy, as it is foreseen in the Brussels IIbis/ter Regulation (access and return orders), the Maintenance Regulation, the EU Enforcement Order Regulation, the EU Order for Payment Regulation, the EU Small Claims Proceeding Regulation, and the EU Account Preservation Order Regulation (see section 3 above).[93]

The ECtHR discarded this reading of the *Povse* case, in *Avotiņš v. Latvia*.[94] The presumption of compliance will be rebutted not only where the supervisory mechanism was in state of dysfunction; as already stated in *Bosphorus*,[95] a rebuttal will also be possible if it can be shown, in

---

[89] Charter of Fundamental Rights of the European Union, OJ 18.12.2000 C 364/1.
[90] *Avotiņš v. Latvia*, no. 17502/07, ECtHR 23 May 2016, §102; *Michaud v. France*, no. 12323/11, ECtHR 6 December 2012, §106.
[91] The recognition and enforcement of judgments in accordance with EU law is an implementation of EU law within the meaning of Art. 51(1) of the Charter: CJEU Case C-156/12, *GREP GmbH v. Freistaat Bayern*, ECLI:EU:C:2012:342, §31.
[92] Art. 52, EU Charter. For doubts on the binding nature of ECtHR jurisprudence, however, see J. ADOLPHSEN, 'Aktuelle Fragen des Verhältnisses von EMRK und Europäischem Zivilprozessrecht' in J. RENZIKOWSKI (ed), *Die EMRK im Privat-, Straf- und Öffentlichen Recht*, Manz, Wien 2004, pp. 39–81, 47.
[93] These unrestricted recognition and enforcement mechanisms have previously been viewed with scepticism ('hyper-efficient' recognition and enforcement): see J. OSTER, 'Public Policy and Human Rights' (2015) 11 *Journal of Private International Law* 542–67, 548, with further references.
[94] This was predicted by P. KINSCH, 'The Impact of Human Rights on the Application of Foreign Law and on the Recognition of Foreign Judgments – A Survey of the Cases Decided by the European Human Rights Institutions' in T. EINHORN and K. SIEHR (eds), *Intercontinental Cooperation Through Private International Law – Essays in Memory of Peter E Nygh*, TMC Asser Press, The Hague 2004, pp. 197–228, 208: 'There is little doubt that, should an irremediable conflict occur in the future, the ECtHR would consider that the convention obligation of the Contracting States must prevail over any contrary treaty obligations.'
[95] *Bosphorus Hava Yolları Turizm ve Ticaret Anonim Şirketi v. Ireland*, no. 45036/98, ECtHR 30 June 2005, §156.

the 'individual case', that the protection of Convention rights has been 'manifestly deficient'.[96] With regard to the focus on the individual case, the ECtHR case law differs from the German Federal Constitutional Court's *Solange* case law:[97] the Federal Constitutional Court does not examine the individual case, asking instead whether the standard of fundamental rights in the EU has, in general, fallen below the level of German fundamental rights. With regard to the necessary standard of fundamental rights, the ECtHR emphasised that this standard has to be comparable with, and not identical to, the ECHR's standard, as the necessity for an identical standard would run counter to the interest of international cooperation.[98]

The ECtHR's focus on the 'individual case', has been a reaction to the CJEU's ban on the accession of the EU to the ECHR. The CJEU has stated that EU mechanisms might require the Member States 'to presume that fundamental rights have been observed by the other Member States, so that ... save in exceptional cases, they may not check whether that other Member State has actually, in a specific case, observed the fundamental rights guaranteed by the EU'.[99] The Accession Agreement's failure to respect those mechanisms was one reason why the CJEU found the Agreement to be incompatible with primary EU law.

The ECtHR has adamantly refused to accept the CJEU's position:

> Limiting to exceptional cases the power of the State in which recognition is sought to review the observance of fundamental rights by the State of origin of the judgment could, in practice, run counter to the requirement imposed by the Convention according to which the court in the State addressed must at least be empowered to conduct a review commensurate with the gravity of any serious allegation of a violation of fundamental rights in the State of origin, in order to ensure that the protection of those rights is not manifestly deficient.[100]

---

[96] *Avotiņš v. Latvia*, no. 17502/07, ECtHR 23 May 2016, §112; *Bosphorus Hava Yolları Turizm ve Ticaret Anonim Şirketi v. Ireland*, no. 45036/98, ECtHR 30 June 2005, §156.
[97] German Federal Constitutional Court, 29 May 1974, BVerfGE 37, 271 ('*Solange I*') and 22 October 1986, BVerfGE 73, 339 ('*Solange II*').
[98] *Bosphorus Hava Yolları Turizm ve Ticaret Anonim Şirketi v. Ireland*, no. 45036/98, ECtHR 30 June 2005, §155.
[99] CJEU, Opinion 2/13, 18 December 2014, ECLI:EU:C:2014:2454, §192.
[100] *Avotiņš v. Latvia*, no. 17502/07, ECtHR 23 May 2016, §114.

The ECtHR came close to rebutting the presumption of compliance in *Avotiņš v. Latvia*. But even though there were shortcomings in the Latvian proceedings the Court did not, ultimately, find a manifestly deficient process.[101] But the Court made clear that an EU mechanism for cross-border recognition and enforcement would be manifestly deficient if it obliged a Member State to enforce a judgment despite a serious violation of fundamental rights in the Member State of origin. The *Avotiņš* judgment indicates that the applicant's possibility of filing an application with the ECtHR against the Member State of origin does not free the Member State of recognition or enforcement from its obligations under the Convention.

In recent cases on the European arrest warrant, the ECtHR has also clarified that the Member State addressed will be liable if it strictly follows a manifestly deficient EU proceeding,[102] and does not make an exception for serious violations of fundamental rights. It is for Member States to interpret and apply the rules of EU law in conformity with the Convention:

> En revanche, s'il leur est soumis un grief sérieux et étayé dans le cadre duquel il est allégué que l'on se trouve en présence d'une insuffisance manifeste de protection d'un droit garanti par la Convention et que le droit de l'UE ne permet pas de remédier à cette insuffisance, elles ne peuvent renoncer à examiner ce grief au seul motif qu'elles appliquent le droit de l'UE … Il leur appartient dans ce cas de lire et d'appliquer les règles du droit de l'UE en conformité avec la Convention.[103]

For the recognition and enforcement of civil judgments, it follows that the Member State where recognition or enforcement takes place has to review the proceeding in the state of origin, in order to prevent a manifestly deficient protection of fundamental rights, even if the wording of an EU

---

[101] Ibid., §125.
[102] Similarly, see P. GRAGL, 'An Olive Branch from Strasbourg: Interpreting the European Court of Human Rights' Resurrection of *Bosphorus* and Reaction to Opinion 2/13 in the *Avotins* Case: ECtHR 23 May 2016, Case No. 17502/07, *Avotins v. Latvia*' (2017) 13 *European Constitutional Law Review* 551–67, 565.
[103] However, if they receive a serious and substantiated complaint alleging that there is a manifest inadequacy in the protection of a right guaranteed by the Convention and that EU law does not remedy that inadequacy, they cannot waive consideration of that complaint merely because they are applying EU law … It is for them to read and apply the rules of EU law in conformity with the Convention (author's translation). *Sousa v. Portugal*, no. 28/17, ECtHR 7 December 2021, §76; see also *Romeo Castano/Belgium*, no. 8351/17, ECtHR 9 July 2019, §84; *Pirozzi v. Belgium*, no. 21055/11, ECtHR, 17 April 2018, §§105 *et seq*.

regulation demands recognition and enforcement without the possibility of refusal.[104] Nevertheless, as the debtor's right is confronted with the creditor's right to a fair trial, the finding that such a violation exists must have a 'sufficient factual basis'.[105]

Ultimately, the disparity between the CJEU's *Opinion 2/13* and the fundamental rights test called for by the ECtHR is likely to be less serious than the ECtHR presented it to be in *Avotiņš*. Indeed, the CJEU has sometimes been reluctant to place limits on the concept of mutual trust.[106] Thus, it seemed unclear whether the CJEU would accept a derogation from the obligation to implement a measure from another EU Member State. However, *Opinion 2/13* left a loophole for 'exceptional cases'. In *Aranyosi* and *Căldăraru*, the CJEU used this exception,[107] thus bringing its case law into harmony with the ECtHR's requirements.[108] Accordingly, the principles of mutual recognition and mutual trust between Member States could be subject to limitation.[109] Even if the wording of the EU law does not allow refusal of the implementation of a European arrest warrant, a Member State may postpone or refuse to execute a European arrest warrant if the surrender exposes the applicant to a 'real risk' of being detained in conditions contrary to Art. 4 of the EU Charter, due to 'systemic' or concrete deficiencies in certain places of detention.[110]

---

[104] The ECtHR recently confirmed its decision for return orders under the Brussels IIbis/ter Regulation in an *obiter dictum*: see *Royer v. Hungary*, no. 9114/16, ECtHR 6 March 2018, § 50: 'As the Court has previously held, it must verify that the principle of mutual recognition is not applied automatically and mechanically.'; see also H. Schack, 'Die Entwicklung des europäischen Internationalen Zivilverfahrensrechts – aktuelle Bestandsaufnahme und Kritik' in R. Stürner et al. (eds), *Festschrift Leipold*, Mohr Siebeck, Tübingen 2009, 317–34, 333.

[105] *Romeo Castano v. Belgium*, no. 8351/17, ECtHR 9 July 2019, §85.

[106] See, for instance, CJEU Case C-116/02, *Erich Gasser GmbH v. MISAT Srl.*, ECLI:EU:C:2003:657 (Italian torpedo); B. Hess, 'EMRK, Grundrechte-Charta und europäisches Zivilverfahrensrecht' in H.P. Mansel et al. (eds), *Festschrift für Erik Jayme*, vol. I, Sellier, Munich 2004, 339–59, 357.

[107] CJEU Case C-404/15, C-659/15 PPU, *Aranyosi* and *Căldăraru*, 5 April 2016, §82.

[108] More sceptical because subsequent cases seem to ignore *Aranyosi* and *Căldăraru*: P. Gragl, 'An Olive Branch from Strasbourg: Interpreting the European Court of Human Rights' Resurrection of *Bosphorus* and Reaction to Opinion 2/13 in the Avotins Case: ECtHR 23 May 2016, Case No. 17502/07, *Avotins v. Latvia*' (2017) 13 *European Constitutional Law Review* 551–67, 566.

[109] CJEU Case C-404/15, C-659/15 PPU, *Aranyosi* and *Căldăraru*, §82.

[110] CJEU Case C-404/15, C-659/15 PPU, *Aranyosi* and *Căldăraru*, §104; see also the ECtHR's reaction in *Bivolaru and Moldovan v. France*, nos. 40324/16, 12623/17, ECtHR 25 March 2021. For limitations similar to those applicable to the recognition or enforcement of a civil judgment, see C. Kohler, 'Grenzen des gegenseitigen Vertrauens im Europäischen Justizraum', *Praxis des internationalen Privat- und*

The limits on the execution of a European arrest warrant cannot be transferred directly to the recognition and enforcement of foreign civil judgments. While the European arrest warrant requires a prognosis of whether there is a 'real risk' in the future, recognition and enforcement require an assessment of the past adjudication proceedings. Therefore, systemic deficiencies in the judicial system of the state of origin can lead to a refusal of recognition or enforcement only if they have had an effect on the concrete adjudication proceeding.

4.2. MATTERS WITH A MARGIN OF MANOEUVRE

The ECtHR has announced that a Contracting State will be 'fully responsible under the Convention for all acts falling outside its strict international legal obligations, notably where it has exercised State discretion'.[111] Beyond the EU recognition and enforcement mechanism, the ECtHR requires the Contracting States to 'duly satisfy' themselves that the adjudication process in the state of origin complied with Art. 6(1) ECHR; the Court, however, limited this standard of review to the recognition or enforcement of judgments from non-Contracting States where the defendant's interests at stake are of 'paramount importance' (see section 2.2.2. above). If the judgment originates from an EU Member State, the influence of the Convention might be reduced by the facts, first, that all EU Member States are Contracting States, and so the applicant might thus challenge fundamental rights violations in the state of origin; and, second, that the ECtHR shares competence with the CJEU to supervise the application of EU law. Parties may challenge an interference with fundamental rights not only in Strasbourg, but also in Luxembourg.

An EU Member State has a margin of manoeuvre when it recognises or enforces a judgment from another Member State and considers the application of the public policy reservation.[112] In *Royer v. Hungary*, a

---

Verfahrensrechts, 2017, 333–38, 337 et seq.; C. KOHLER and W. PINTENS, 'Entwicklungen im europäischen Personen- und Familienrecht' 2015–2016 *Zeitschrift für das gesamte Familienrecht*, 1509–29, 1522.

[111] *Michaud v. France*, no. 12323/11, ECtHR 6 December 2012, §103; *Bosphorus Hava Yolları Turizm ve Ticaret Anonim Şirketi v. Ireland*, no. 45036/98, ECtHR 30 June 2005, §§156–57.

[112] *Royer v. Hungary*, no. 9114/16, ECtHR 6 March 2018; see also J. OSTER, 'Public Policy and Human Rights' (2015) 11 *Journal of Private International Law* 542–67, 559. A further type of decision which also does not fall under matters of strict international responsibility, but leaves discretion to the EU Member States, has been introduced by Art. 56(4) of the Brussels IIter Regulation.

Hungarian court refused to enforce French judgments on custody, on the basis of Art. 23(a) Brussels IIbis Regulation (*ordre public*). It found that the judgments ran counter to Hungarian public policy because they had considered the child's best interests in only a purely formalistic manner, and thus did not respect fundamental rights.[113] With this decision, the Hungarian court was in line with the CJEU's guidelines for the interpretation of *ordre public* clauses. As a first step, the CJEU accepts that the *ordre public* encompasses those rules that are regarded as essential in the addressed state's national system. But, in a second step, the *ordre public* is subject to boundaries; namely, recourse to the public policy clause is allowed only where the judgment is 'at variance to an unacceptable degree with the legal order of the State in which enforcement is sought inasmuch as it infringes a fundamental principle'.[114] Those fundamental principles include, amongst others, the fundamental rights embodied in the ECHR.[115]

The ECtHR found that the Hungarian court's assessment of the case did not amount to a violation of Art. 8 ECHR. Even though the ECtHR does not apply a presumption of compliance, it nevertheless limits its review in such a way that does not 'question the assessment of [Article 23(a) of the Brussels II bis Regulation by] the domestic authorities, unless there is clear evidence of arbitrariness.'[116] Thus, in assessing whether a legal provision such as a public policy clause has been applied correctly, the ECtHR takes an observatory position:

> In particular, it is not [the ECtHR's] function to deal with errors of fact or law allegedly committed by a national court or to substitute its own assessment for

---

[113] *Royer v. Hungary*, no. 9114/16, ECtHR 6 March 2018, §34.
[114] CJEU Case C-7/98, *Dieter Krombach v. André Bamberski*, ECLI:EU:C:2000:164, §37.
[115] Ibid., §39; see also *Krombach v. France*, no. 29731, ECtHR 13 February 2001; and J. Adolphsen, 'Aktuelle Fragen des Verhältnisses von EMRK und Europäischem Zivilprozessrecht' in J. Renzikowski (ed), *Die EMRK im Privat-, Straf- und Öffentlichen Recht*, Manz, Wien 2004, 39–81, 71; B. Hess, 'EMRK, Grundrechte-Charta und europäisches Zivilverfahrensrecht' in H.P. Mansel et al. (eds), *Festschrift für Erik Jayme*, vol. I, Sellier, Munich 2004, 339–59, 345.
[116] *Royer v. Hungary*, no. 9114/16, ECtHR 6 March 2018, §60; differently, see J. Oster, 'Public Policy and Human Rights' (2015) 11 *Journal of Private International Law* 542–67, 564 *et seq.*, arguing for a strict standard of scrutiny regarding the refusal of recognition or enforcement based on a public policy clause. By contrast, Oster argues for a reduced standard of scrutiny where the addressed state recognises or enforces a judgment from another Contracting State, and the applicant argues that the court should have refused recognition or enforcement because, due to fundamental rights violations in the state of origin, the recognition or enforcement is in breach of public policy.

that of the national courts or other national authorities unless and in so far as they may have infringed rights and freedoms protected by the Convention.[117]

As the Hungarian court gave particular consideration to the best interests of the child and, in this respect, stayed within the ECtHR's guidelines, the ECtHR found no such clear evidence of arbitrariness.[118] It thus seems to be essential that the Member States interpret the public policy clause on the basis of fundamental rights, as required by the CJEU, and also take into account the case law of the ECtHR.

5. SUMMARY AND OUTLOOK

This chapter has attempted to describe the relationships of the various EU recognition and enforcement mechanisms with the ECHR. In the case of recognition and enforcement under strict EU procedures (without the possibility of refusal), Member States benefit from the 'presumption of compliance'. With this presumption, the ECtHR seeks to establish a balance between its own review powers vis-à-vis states, and its respect for the activities of the EU. If the Member States have a margin of manoeuvre, in particular through the public policy clause, the ECtHR will not require the Member State of recognition or enforcement to 'duly satisfy' itself that the adjudication proceeding in the Member State of origin complied with Art. 6(1) ECHR. Rather, the ECtHR will assess whether the application of the public policy clause has been 'clearly arbitrary'.

The picture is certainly not yet complete, and will develop further nuances. In October 2019, the EU and the Steering Committee for Human Rights (CDDH) resumed negotiations on the EU's accession to the ECHR.[119] The revised Art. 5b of the Draft Accession Agreement attempts to outline the balance between the principles of mutual trust and fundamental rights protection:

> Accession of the European Union to the Convention shall not affect the application of the principle of mutual trust within the European Union. In this

---

[117] *Sisojeva and Others v. Latvia*, no. 60654/00, ECtHR 15 January 2007, §89.
[118] *Royer v. Hungary*, no. 9114/16, ECtHR 6 March 2018, §61.
[119] For the status of the negotiations, see https://www.coe.int/en/web/human-rights-intergovernmental-cooperation/accession-of-the-european-union-to-the-european-convention-on-human-rights.

context, the protection of human rights guaranteed by the Convention shall be ensured.[120]

The first sentence gives priority to the principle of mutual trust. The ECtHR has accepted that this principle has gradually led to an abolition of the control proceedings in the Member State of recognition or enforcement.[121] The second sentence is intended to refer to the guidelines given in the cases *Aranyosi* and *Căldăraru*.[122] In those cases, the Court placed a limit on the principle of mutual trust; a Member State is allowed to postpone or refuse to execute a European arrest warrant if the surrender exposes the applicant to a 'real risk' of being detained in conditions contrary to Art. 4 of the EU Charter.

As for civil judgments, the Draft Accession Agreement, so far, does not specify under which conditions EU Member States would be allowed to refuse recognition or enforcement even if an EU regulation contains no provision for such a refusal. In line with the ECtHR's case law, a refusal of recognition or enforcement should be allowed if recognition or enforcement of a judgment would lead to a manifestly deficient protection of fundamental rights in the individual case. Systemic deficiencies in the judicial system of the state of origin would allow for a refusal of recognition or enforcement only if they have had an effect on the individual adjudication proceeding in the state of origin.

---

[120] 12th negotiation meeting of the CDDH ad hoc negotiation group ('47+1 Group') on the accession of the European Union (EU) to the European Convention on Human Rights (ECHR) (7–10 December 2021), meeting report, https://perma.cc/HF2C-F7RK, p. 21.

[121] *Avotiņš v. Latvia*, no. 17502/07, ECtHR 23 May 2016, §113; *Royer v. Hungary*, no. 9114/16, ECtHR 6 March 2018, §50.

[122] 12th negotiation meeting of the CDDH ad hoc negotiation group ('47+1 Group') on the accession of the European Union (EU) to the European Convention on Human Rights (ECHR) (7–10 December 2021), meeting report, https://perma.cc/HF2C-F7RK, p. 21.

PART V
LABOUR LAW

FREEDOM OF ASSOCIATION FOR THE ARMED FORCES

A Fruitful Dialogue between the European Court of Human Rights and the Italian Constitutional Court

Edoardo ALES

1. The Collective Dimension in the Armed Forces and the Decisions of the Italian Constitutional Court. 254
2. Freedom of Association and the State as Employer in the ECHR, as Interpreted by the ECtHR. 260
3. The Case Law of the Italian Constitutional Court on the Impact of ECHR Provisions on National Legislation 264
4. The Case Law of the ECHR on the Armed Forces. 266
5. The Case Law of the Italian Constitutional Court in Light of Article 117, Para. 1 of the Constitution. 268
6. Conclusion. 271

This chapter aims to investigate the influence of the European Convention on Human Rights (ECHR) on Italian labour law. From the examples that could have been taken into consideration, the chapter focuses on the long-standing issue of the prohibition on military personnel establishing and joining unions, which has characterised the Italian legal order for decades.[1]

In order to shed light on this issue, this chapter adopts a chronological approach; first, it analyses some decisions of the Italian Constitutional

---

[1] For a view in context, see M. FALSONE, 'Union Freedoms in the Armed Forces: Still a Taboo?' (2022) 51(2) *Industrial Law Journal* 375, https://doi.org/10.1093/indlaw/dwab003.

Court of the 1980s and 1990s regarding provisions, adopted during the fascist period, that criminalise the collective exercise of freedom of expression, assembly and association, which has otherwise been recognised, since 1948, by the Italian Constitution. Second, the chapter examines the case law of the European Court of Human Rights (ECtHR) on Article 11(2) ECHR, with reference to the state as an employer, between the 1970s and the first decade of this century. Third, it comes back to the decisions of the Italian Constitutional Court, adopted after the 2001 constitutional reform, which recognise the sub-constitutional status of international provisions, including the ECHR as interpreted by the ECtHR, in testing the constitutionality of national legislation. Fourth, the chapter returns to the case law of the ECtHR, with specific reference to the recognition of freedom of association with regard to the armed forces. Fifth, and last, it shows how the sub-constitutional status of the ECHR, as interpreted by the ECtHR, played a decisive role in the 2018 decision of the Constitutional Court recognising the freedom of military personnel to establish and join a union, which had been denied by the same Court in the 1990s, when international provisions did not enjoy such status. The chapter elaborates on such analysis in order to draw some conclusions about the influence of the ECHR on Italian labour law, and on the merit of the issue at stake.

1. THE COLLECTIVE DIMENSION IN THE ARMED FORCES AND THE DECISIONS OF THE ITALIAN CONSTITUTIONAL COURT

According to the Italian Constitution, 'homeland defence is a sacred duty of the citizen' (Article 52, para. 1). At the same time, 'the military order shall conform to the democratic spirit of the Republic' (Article 52, para. 3). The principle of homeland defence as a sacred duty of the citizen, which specifies the more general duty of loyalty to the Republic, and obedience to the Constitution, and to the laws (Article 54), includes the military duties organised within the armed forces as a stronghold of the independence and freedom of the nation.[2]

During the 1980s, these principles had already been confronted with the exercise, by military personnel, of some basic constitutional rights such as freedoms of assembly and opinion, affirmed, respectively by Articles 17

---

[2] Constitutional Court, decision n. 16 of 1973.

and 21 of the Italian Constitution. Indeed, these freedoms had been denied by the fascist regime that had enacted, in 1941 – some months after Italy had declared war on France and United Kingdom – the Military Penal Codes in Time of War and Peace.[3]

After the fall of the fascist regime and the end of World War II, the Republican legislator adopted an abstentionist stance towards the above-mentioned codifications, leaving to the Constitutional Court the task of checking the compatibility of civil and penal provisions with the new fundamental rights framework provided by the Constitution.

As for the military, such a compatibility test had to be run mainly against the already-mentioned statements that, even if, on the one hand, 'homeland defence is a sacred duty of the citizen', on the other hand, 'the military order shall conform to the democratic spirit of the Republic' (Article 52, paras. 1 and 3 const.), i.e by adopting statutory provisions respectful of fundamental rights and freedoms of any human beings, militaries included.

A paramount example of how the Constitutional Court applied that test can be found in decision n. 31 of 1982, by which Article 184, para. 2 of the Military Penal Code in Time of Peace (MPCTP) was scrutinised, as it looked at any unauthorised assemblies of militaries as a crime. By doing so, it raised an issue of compatibility with Article 21 of the Italian Constitution, on freedom of expression, contradicting the statement that 'the military order shall conform to the democratic spirit of the Republic' (Article 52, para. 3). In particular, Article 184, para. 2 MPCTP provided that a six-month prison sentence would apply to any military personnel who, in order to deal with issues related to service or discipline, promoted, without authorisation, a meeting of militaries, or took part in such a meeting.

According to the Constitutional Court, even though the freedoms of peaceful assembly, and to express an opinion, are fundamental rights recognised, respectively, by Articles 17 and 21 of the Constitution, limits and conditions are implied, as with any other freedom right, with a view to avoiding other constitutional goods being sacrificed through the exercise of these freedoms. Furthermore, these constitutional goods included those protected by Article 52 of the Constitution.

In the view of the Court, within this framework, the statement that 'the military order shall conform to the democratic spirit of the Republic' (Article 52, para. 3) does not exclude, at all, that the exercise of freedom

---

[3] Royal Decree n. 303 of 1941.

rights by military personnel should harmonise with the institutional goals of the armed forces, as realised by their organisation. Therefore, it was not a constitutional requirement to recognise a right for the military to take part, without authorisation, in a meeting on issues related to military service, if that meeting is going to take place in a military area, instead of in a public space, as provided by Article 17 of the Constitution. Authorisation aims to guarantee the regular performance of military duties, which would be compromised if unauthorised meetings were allowed. Authorisation also aims to allow a previous assessment, by the superior authority, of the topic and the modalities of the meeting, in order to avoid any possible prejudices towards military duties.

From such a perspective, the Constitutional Court highlighted that Act n. 382 of 1978 on 'Regulatory principles on military discipline', after stating that military personnel enjoy the same rights, recognised by the Constitution, as every other citizen, provides that, in order to guarantee the fulfilment of constitutional armed forces duties, limits to the exercise of those rights, and the observance of specific duties, are imposed by the law.[4]

Four years later, the Constitutional Court was again called upon to assess the compatibility of Article 184, para. 2 MPCTP with Article 17 of the Constitution (freedom of assembly), in the absence of any hostile and seditious characteristics of the meeting.

According to the Court, there can be no doubt that the criminalisation of unauthorised military meetings should be based on their hostile and seditious character, which represents a violation of discipline, and at the same time jeopardises the effective exercise of armed forces' constitutional duties. Consequently, withdrawing Article 184, para. 2 MPCTP would mean leaving such hostile and seditious collective actions unpunished, a situation that cannot be acceptable from a constitutional point of view.

However, as phrased by the legislator, Article 184, para. 2 MPCTP is likely also to punish meetings that, being peaceful in their modalities and unharmful or even helpful in their contents, do not jeopardise any constitutional goods. In such cases, courts should exclude the application of penal sanctions in the absence of any hostile and seditious characteristics, and in the presence of a legitimate goal for the meeting, such as discussing how to obtain better living conditions, but without prejudice to any disciplinary sanctions in the case of an unauthorised meeting.

---

[4] Constitutional Court, decision n. 24 of 1989.

Such decision is consistent with the stance the Constitutional Court took in 1985, on Article 180 MPCTP, according to which, when ten or more military personnel, collectively or individually, although by previous agreement, ask the same question of, or lodge the same claim with, their superiors, each of them can be punished with imprisonment of up to one year.[5]

According to the Court, it is clear that Article 180 MPCTP, which renders any moral pressure exercised by a group on the military authorities liable to prosecution, in order to preserve those authorities' freedom of decision, actually punishes any collective claims against those authorities. By doing so, it violates the fundamental right of the military personnel to express their opinions, which, according to Article 21 of the Constitution, also includes peaceful collective expressions of discontentedness.

As already highlighted above, even if the Court does admit that the modalities of freedom of expression may be regulated and, consequently, that freedom of expression may be limited accordingly, it makes such limitations conditional upon the dual requirement that they do not make the exercise of such a freedom difficult or even impossible, and that they are justified by the protection of other constitutional values.

In the Court's view, there were no conditions justifying the limitations imposed by Article 180 MPCTP. Indeed, according to the Court, neither the harshest criticism against the institutions, nor intentions of changing them, nor even an ideological challenge against the political set-up, could justify such limitations and sanctions, which could be admitted only in cases of violence against the established legal order.

The limitation provided by Article 180 MPCTP affects collective freedom of expression as such, criminalising it to the extent that an essential part of its exercise is made difficult or even impossible. As a matter of fact, according to the Court, the collective aspect of the freedom of expression is crucial from the viewpoint of realising the democratic principle that characterises the Italian legal and political order. Moreover, the general significance of Article 52, para. 3 of the Constitution, according to which 'the military order shall conform to the democratic spirit of the Republic', has to be taken into consideration. A combined consideration of both aspects leads to the exclusion of the possibility that the fundamental freedom of expression can be subject to a limitation of such extent and seriousness due to the exigencies of the military order.

---

[5] Constitutional Court, decision n. 126 of 1985.

On the contrary, according to the Court, the peaceful exercise of dissent by military personnel against the authorities – also, and above all, in a collective form, and on collective needs relating to discipline or service issues – not only contributes to supporting grounded requests, but is even likely to stimulate a democratisation of the armed forces with a view to realising the relevant constitutional goal.

This does not mean to obliterate the specific needs of cohesion that characterise military corps, as expressed by the values of discipline and hierarchy; it means to disagree that such values could profit from excessive protection, which could prejudice fundamental freedoms and the same democratic nature of the armed forces.

Such excessive protection is not justified by the need to guarantee the freedom of decisions of the military authority as though it were jeopardised by the collective exercise of freedom of expression, taking into consideration the fact that such a jeopardy can be detected only when sedition is at stake.

Such excessive protection is not downscaled by the provisions of Act n. 382 of 1978, which established representative bodies within the armed forces, elected by the military personnel. As a matter of fact, the competence of these bodies is limited to some areas, and does not cover the whole spectrum of potential collective issues. In any case, according to the Court, the criminalisation of claims relating to areas excluded from the scope of such representative bodies is not justified at all.

The same issues raised in relation to freedom of expression and assembly have been dealt with by the Constitutional Court with reference to the relationship between the military order and freedom of association, as affirmed by Article 18 of the Constitution, for citizens, and by Article 39, for employees and employers.

In this case, the Court confronted the prohibition from forming and joining trade unions within the military, as confirmed by Article 8, para. 1 of Act n. 382 of 1978, on the grounds of a potential incompatibility of unions with the internal cohesion and neutrality of the military order.[6] More specifically, Article 8 does not allow military personnel to exercise the right to strike, to establish professional organisations with union characteristics, or to join already-established unions.

Raising a constitutionality question, the Council of State not only suspected a violation of Article 39 on freedom of association, but also of the equality principle, in comparison with the police. In fact, police

---

[6] Constitutional Court, decision n. 449 of 1999.

officers although deprived of the right to strike, enjoy the freedom and the right to negotiate on working conditions, which includes the possibility of refusing the government's proposals, which is not the case for armed forces personnel. A violation of Article 52, para. 3 ('the military order shall conform to the democratic spirit of the Republic') of the Constitution could be at stake as well.

The Council of State insisted that the lack of recognition of freedom of association within the military could not be compensated, as such, by the establishment of military representation bodies, as provided by the law, with a limited and predefined scope of action. The Council of State also alleged a violation of freedom of organisation and union pluralism in the fact that representation was channelled into a predetermined body, albeit one freely elected by the military personnel.

Had it been found to be grounded, the question raised by the Council of State would have resulted in the withdrawal of the prohibition provided by Act n. 382 of 1978, and in the extension of freedom of association and organisation to its full extent, understood both as a prerogative for military personnel to establish unions of their own, and as a right to join already-established unions, without prejudice to the prohibition on strikes.

According to the Constitutional Court, the fact that the armed forces are not a separate legal order, instead representing a part of the democratic state in which the military personnel are embedded, does not make that prohibition unconstitutional. The recognition of fundamental rights to military personnel as individual citizens and employees is not under discussion. What is at stake is the prevailing character of the service they provide in a sensitive area, as the sacred duty of homeland defence. In the view of the Court, the withdrawal of the prohibition from exercising freedom of association and union organisation would produce a result incompatible with the internal cohesion and neutrality that should characterise the military order.

On the other hand, according to the Court, and as recognised by the Council of State, Act n. 382, even if it denies freedom of association to military personnel, recognises some prerogatives aimed at safeguarding their collective claims. Although the legal order should guarantee forms of protection for the fundamental collective rights of military personnel as citizens and employees, this should not necessarily happen through the recognition of union rights.

With reference to discrimination against military personnel as alleged by the Council of State, the Court observed that the legislator had not only deprived them of the right to strike, but had also prohibited any collective actions that might jeopardise public security and investigations (articles 82, 83, 84, Act n. 121 of 1981). In any case, in the view of the Court, a decisive point was represented by the demilitarisation of police that had accompanied the recognition of freedom of association and union organisation. Enjoying a different status, a different treatment cannot result in a discrimination.

2. FREEDOM OF ASSOCIATION AND THE STATE AS EMPLOYER IN THE ECHR, AS INTERPRETED BY THE ECtHR

As is well known, a person's 'right to freedom of peaceful assembly and to freedom of association with others, including the right to form and to join trade unions for the protection of his interests' is also recognised by Article 11(1) ECHR. According to Article 11(2),

> [n]o restrictions shall be placed on the exercise of these rights other than such as are prescribed by law and are necessary in a democratic society in the interests of national security or public safety, for the prevention of disorder or crime, for the protection of health or morals or for the protection of the rights and freedoms of others.

However, the application of Article 11 'shall not prevent the imposition of lawful restrictions on the exercise of these rights by members of the armed forces, of the police or of the administration of the State'.[7]

The ECtHR has been called on to clarify the meaning of such provisions, first of all with reference to the alleged distinction between 'the functions of a Contracting State as holder of public power and its responsibilities as employer'. The Court has concluded that the ECHR 'nowhere express such a distinction'.[8] According to the Court, the fact that 'the State is bound to

---

[7] On Article 11 ECHR, see A. SAGAN, 'Article 11 ECHR Freedom of assembly and association' in E. ALES, M. BELL, O. DEINERT and S. ROBIN-OLIVER, *International and European Labour Law*, Nomos, Baden-Baden 2018, p. 1513 *et seq.*; I. VAN HIEL, 'The Right to Form and Join a Trade Union Protected by Article 11 ECHR' in F. DORSSEMONT, K. LÖRCHER and I. SCHÖMANN (eds), *The European Convention on Human Rights and the Employment Relation*, Hart Publishing, Oxford 2013, p. 287 *et seq.*

[8] *Swedish Engine Drivers' Union v. Sweden*, no. 5614/72, ECtHR 6 February 1976, para. 36.

respect the freedom of assembly and association of its employees, subject to the possible imposition of "lawful restrictions" in the case of members of its armed forces, police or administration' confirms that Article 11 'is accordingly binding upon the "State as employer", whether the latter's relations with its employees are governed by public or private law'.[9]

Among the limitations that the state, as an employer, may impose on its employees, the Court allows the selective recognition of collective bargaining prerogatives only to the most representative unions, since employees retain the personal freedom to join or remain a member of a union to which such prerogatives are denied, even if it might be that the stagnation or fall in the membership of such a union 'is to be explained at least in part … by the disadvantage the applicant is placed at compared with trade unions enjoying a more favourable position', as it might be 'that this state of affairs is capable of diminishing the usefulness and practical value of belonging to the applicant union'. However, according to the Court, this policy is 'not on its own incompatible with trade union freedom'.[10]

An important, although controversial, contribution to the interpretation of Article 11(2) ECHR was offered by the European Commission of Human Rights, with reference to the decision by the British prime minister, as minister for the civil service, that the conditions of service applicable to civil servants in Government Communications Headquarters (GCHQ) should be revised so as to exclude membership of any trade union other than a departmental staff association approved by the director of GCHQ.[11]

Elaborating a position on that decision, the Commission deemed such restrictions justified, under Article 11(2) ECHR, as being 'necessary in a democratic society in the interests of national security', and their purpose to be consistent with the legitimate goal set out in Article 11(2) of protecting the interests of national security, of which GCHQ formed a vital part.

The Commission highlighted that 'steps were taken to secure, so far as possible, a fair balance between the interests of national security and the individual rights and freedoms'. In particular, 'those serving at GCHQ were given the choice between continuing to remain there under the revised conditions (including receiving payment of £1,000) and requesting a transfer to a similar alternative post elsewhere in the Civil Service with a continuing right of membership of a national trade union'. Moreover,

---

[9] Ibid., para. 37.
[10] Ibid., para. 42.
[11] Commission decision of 20 January 1987, *Council of Civil Service Unions et al v. the United Kingdom*, no. 11603/85.

'a staff association ... has now been formed by members of the staff at GCHQ. It has been statutorily listed as a trade union and has been granted recognition by GCHQ and by the Treasury to represent the staff and negotiate on their behalf'.

According to the Commission, the second sentence of Article 11(2) ECHR does more than just highlight the fact that members of the armed forces, of the police, or of the administration of the state, have special duties and responsibilities which must be considered under the first sentence. As the Commission emphasised, 'in a number of European countries persons in the three categories are made subject to special restrictions in relation to union membership and union activities. Indeed, the word "restrictions" is sufficiently wide to introduce a prohibition on membership of a trade union.'

In the Commission's view, even if the second sentence did not exclude all supervision by the Convention organs, the signatory parties enjoyed wider powers to impose restrictions in relation to the three specified categories than they did in relation to other employees, and the supervisory role of the Convention institutions was correspondingly reduced. Moreover, even the substance of the right to join a trade union had not been sacrificed entirely, since GCHQ staff were free to join the departmental staff association, which served to protect the interests of all GCHQ staff.

Finally, according to the Commission, the word 'lawful', in the second sentence, was equivalent to the expression 'prescribed by law' in the first sentence, thus requiring that any restrictions should be both prescribed by law and necessary in a democratic society.

When called on, some years later, to decide on the compatibility with Article 11(2) ECHR of the dissolution – by the Turkish government, as approved by the Court of Cassation – of Tüm Haber Sen, a trade union of public sector contractual staff working in the communications field, the ECtHR took the opposite stance with regard to the interpretation of 'restrictions' as a sufficiently wide notion to introduce a prohibition on unionisation.[12]

As to whether an interference was 'necessary in a democratic society', the Court reiterated that

> it must be borne in mind that the exceptions set out in Article 11 are to be construed strictly; only convincing and compelling reasons can justify restrictions on such parties' freedom of association. In determining whether a

---

[12] *Tüm Haber Sen et Çınar v. Turkey*, no. 28602/95, ECtHR 21 February 2006.

necessity within the meaning of Article 11 §2 exists, the Contracting States have only a limited margin of appreciation, which goes hand in hand with rigorous European supervision embracing both the law and the decisions applying it, including those given by independent courts.[13]

The mere fact that national legislation did not provide the possibility of establishing unions in the public sector was not sufficient to warrant a measure as radical as the dissolution of an already-established union.[14]

In the absence of 'any concrete evidence to show that the founding or the activities of Tüm Haber Sen represented a threat to Turkish society or the Turkish State', the Court could not accept that an argument based solely on an absolute statutory provision was sufficient to ensure that the union's dissolution complied with the conditions on which freedom of association may be restricted.[15]

The Court specified its position in an individual follow-up to the *Tüm Haber Sen* decision, in joint cases *Demir and Baykara*.[16] In the Court's view, the restrictions imposed on the three groups (public sector employees, police and armed forces) were to be construed strictly, and should therefore be confined to the 'exercise' of the freedom in question; these restrictions must not impair the very essence of the freedom to organise. Indeed, the Court did not share the Commission's view[17] that the term 'lawful', in the second sentence of Article 11(2), required no more than that the restriction in question should have a basis in national law and should not be arbitrary, and that it did not entail any requirement of proportionality. On the contrary, the Court held that it was incumbent on the state concerned to show the legitimacy of any restrictions on the right to organise.[18]

From such a perspective, the Court also recalled that Article 5 of the Revised European Social Charter (RESC) guaranteed the freedom of

---

[13] Ibid., para. 35.
[14] Ibid., para. 36.
[15] Ibid., para. 40.
[16] *Demir and Baykara v. Turkey*, no 34503/97, ECtHR 12 December 2008. See, on this, K. LÖRCHER, 'The New Social Dimension in the Jurisprudence of the European Court of Human Rights (ECHR): The *Demir and Baykara* Judgment, its Methodology and Follow-up' in F. DORSSEMONT, K. LÖRCHER and I. SCHÖMANN (eds), *The European Convention on Human Rights and the Employment Relation*, Hart Publishing, Oxford 2013, p. 3 *et seq.*
[17] *Council of Civil Service Unions et al v. the United Kingdom*, no. 11603/85, ECtHR Decisions and Reports 50, p. 228.
[18] *Demir and Baykara v. Turkey*, above n. 16, para. 97.

workers and employers to form local, national or international organisations for the protection of their economic and social interests, and to join those organisations.[19] Nevertheless, the Court had to admit that, according to Article 5 RESC, national legislation may impose partial restrictions on police officers, and total or partial restrictions on members of the armed forces.[20] In the same vein, the Court highlighted, as to European practice, that 'in the majority of member States, the few restrictions that can be found are limited to judicial offices, the police and the fire services, with the most stringent restrictions, culminating in the prohibition of union membership, being reserved for members of the armed forces'.[21]

3. THE CASE LAW OF THE ITALIAN CONSTITUTIONAL COURT ON THE IMPACT OF ECHR PROVISIONS ON NATIONAL LEGISLATION

Coming back to the Italian perspective, it must be stressed that the value and effect of ECHR provisions, as interpreted by the ECtHR, have been issues for a long time. Only in 2007 did the Constitutional Court clarify the situation in two landmark decisions, issued on the same day, and on the same topic: expropriation.[22]

First, the Constitutional Court has confirmed that ECHR provisions do not enjoy the same status as EU Law. In fact, the latter has full mandatory effect and direct application within the EU Member States, without the need for adaptation.[23] Such effect derives from Article 11 of the Italian Constitution, which allows limitations to national sovereignty in order to promote and favour the establishment of international organisations aimed at ensuring peace and justice among nations. On the other hand, according to the Court, Article 11 of the Constitution does not apply to

---

[19] On Article 5 RESC, see T. JASPERS, 'Article 5 RESC The right to organize' in E. ALES, M. BELL, O. DEINERT and S. ROBIN-OLIVIER, *International and European Labour Law*, Nomos, Baden-Baden 2018, p. 277 *et seq.*; A. JACOBS, 'Article 5 The Right to Organise' in N. BRUUN, K. LÖRCHER, I. SCHÖMANN and S. CLAUWAERT (eds), *The European Social Charter and the Employment Relation*, Hart, Oxford 2017, p. 220 *et seq.*
[20] *Demir and Baykara v. Turkey*, above n. 16, para. 103.
[21] Ibid., para. 106.
[22] Constitutional Court, decisions n. 348 and n. 349 of 2007.
[23] Constitutional Court, decisions n. 183 of 1973 and n. 170 of 1984.

ECHR provisions, since they stem from a specific agreement which does not entail any limitations on national sovereignty.[24] Therefore, despite their great value in protecting the fundamental rights and freedoms of the human being, ECHR provisions do not produce such a direct effect on the national legal order, so as to allow national judges to disapply national provisions deemed to violate the ECHR.

The Court has highlighted that Article 117, para. 1 of the Constitution, as modified by the 2001 constitutional reform, confirmed the correctness of such an interpretation by substantially distinguishing obligations deriving from EU Law from those stemming from international conventions. Through the signature of the EEC, EC and EU treaties, Italy became part of a wider legal order of a supranational nature, handing over, to this legal order, a part of its legislative prerogatives, within the competences recognised as applying to the EU institutions, the only limits being the inalienability of constitutional principles and rights. On the contrary, the ECHR does not establish a supranational legal order, and its provisions are not directly applicable to the signatory parties. The ECHR thus has to be regarded as a multilateral international treaty, which produces obligations for the parties without incorporating their national legal orders in a supranational legal order.

On the other hand, Article 117, para. 1 of the Constitution makes the exercise of legislative prerogatives at a national level conditional upon international obligations being respected, and ECHR provisions undoubtedly fall within the scope of such obligations. Therefore, even if a constitutional value is not attributed to ECHR provisions, Article 117 para. 1 acknowledges them as parameters to be considered when deciding on the constitutionality of a national provision. Therefore, if a national court believes that a national provision violates any international obligations, it should raise a question of constitutionality, and the Constitutional Court should verify this, with reference both to the national and the international provisions.

Indeed, not being of constitutional rank, international provisions such as the ECHR enjoy a sub-constitutional status, concretising the benchmark of international obligations, as referred to by Article 117, para. 1 of the Constitution, against national legislative provisions. Moreover, since, unlike other international treaties, the ECHR is characterised by the establishment of a court that is in charge, among other things, of

---

[24] Constitutional Court, decision n. 188 of 1980.

interpreting its provisions (Article 32 ECHR), the case law of the ECtHR, which specifies the obligations deriving from the ECHR, also falls within the scope of the constitutionality test.

The constitutionality of sub-constitutional provisions is unavoidable and absolute. As a consequence, in cases of alleged inconsistency between a national provision and an international one, the Constitutional Court is called on to apply the constitutionality test to both provisions: for the former, with reference to the relevant sub-constitutional provision; and for the latter, in relation to the relevant constitutional provisions.

If a sub-constitutional provision in the case at stake, as interpreted by the ECtHR, does not pass the test, the Constitutional Court must deny its effect within the national legal order. Such a denial affects, at the same time, the relevant case law of the ECtHR.

4. THE CASE LAW OF THE ECHR ON THE ARMED FORCES

In light of the aforementioned matters, it is apparent that, since 2007, ECHR provisions, as interpreted by the European Court of Human Rights, play a relevant role within the case law of the Italian Constitutional Court.

As far as Article 11(2) ECHR and its application to the armed forces is concerned, that role has been checked against two decisions of the ECtHR further limiting the lawfulness of restrictions on the freedom of association.

In *Matelly v. France*,[25] the claimant, a French gendarme, alleged that an order he had received to withdraw from an organisation aimed at protecting the professional interests of military personnel constituted a violation of Article 11 ECHR. This view was not shared by the French Council of State, according to whom such an order was in line with Article 11 ECHR, since it did not prohibit the gendarme from joining organisations of a different kind.[26]

The national provision under scrutiny was Article L. 4121-4, para. 2 of the Code de la défence, according to which the existence of military professional organisations of a union nature, as well as military staff's membership of any professional organisations, is incompatible with military discipline.

---

[25] *Matelly v. France*, no. 10609/10, ECtHR 2 January 2015.
[26] Ibid., para. 26. See also the 'twin' case *ADefDroMil v. France*, para. 36.

In the Council of State's view, such a provision, interpreted in the sense that it does not exclude belonging to professional organisations not aimed at defending professional interests, constituted a lawful restriction within the meaning of Article 11(2) ECHR.[27] According to the French government, such a restriction was lawful, necessary within a democratic society and proportionate, being imposed with the legitimate aim of defending national order and security, as well as of guaranteeing the operational effectiveness of the armed forces, and the discipline required by this kind of organisation.[28]

Furthermore, the French government claimed that dedicated social dialogue systems had been established within the armed forces, in order to protect the collective interests of military personnel; these included the Conseil Supérieur de la Fonction Militaire (CSFM), to which seven *conseils de la fonction militaire* (CFM) had to be added, one for each branch of the armed forces, including the *conseils de la fonction militaire de la gendarmerie national* (CFMG).[29]

The Court reacted by recalling that Article 11(1) ECHR reflects an understanding of the freedom to organise a union as a specific feature of freedom of association. Indeed, the expression 'for the defence of their interests' refers to unions' freedom to support their members' claims collectively, as authorised or made possible by the national legislators.[30]

In the view of the Court, Article 11(2) ECHR did not exclude any group of workers from the scope of application of the freedom to organise a union, since it explicitly named armed forces among those to whom 'lawful restrictions' could be imposed without, consequently, putting their right to organise under discussion.[31]

The Court also recalled its view that any restrictions have to be limited to the exercise of the freedoms at stake, without jeopardising their very essence, such as the freedom to organise a union, and to join it.[32] Moreover, the Court stressed that, although the word 'order' can also be understood

---

[27] *Matelly vs. France*, above n. 25, para. 30.
[28] Ibid., para. 50.
[29] Ibid., para. 53. The French government also claimed that the Haut Comité de l'évaluation de la condition militaire had been established in order to monitor living and working conditions within the armed forces: see *ADefDroMil v. France*, above n. 26, para. 39.
[30] *Matelly v. France*, above n. 25, para. 55. See also *National Union of Belgian Police v. Belgium*, no. 4464/70, ECtHR 27 October 1975, paras. 38–40.
[31] *Matelly v. France*, above n. 25, para. 56.
[32] Ibid., paras. 57–58, referring to *Demir and Baykara*, above n. 16, para. 97, 119, 144–45.

as the internal discipline of a specific group, such as the armed forces, since disorder within such a group may affect society as a whole, the denial of the freedom to organise a union and to join it can never represent a measure 'necessary within a democratic society', within the meaning of Article 11(2) ECHR.[33]

Even where the armed forces take care of military personnel's living and working conditions through dedicated social dialogue systems provided by law, these could not, in the Court's view, be a substitute for the freedom to organise a union, and to join one.[34]

5. THE CASE LAW OF THE ITALIAN CONSTITUTIONAL COURT IN LIGHT OF ARTICLE 117, PARA. 1 OF THE CONSTITUTION

In 2017, the Italian Constitutional Court was once again called on by the Council of State to test the constitutionality of the prohibition on military personnel forming or joining trade unions, as then provided by Article 1475(2) of Legislative Decree n. 66 of 2010 (Code of the Armed Forces). Well aware of the stance taken by the Court in relation to Article 39 of the Constitution, the Council of State raised its question by focusing on the alleged violation, by the aforementioned prohibition, of Article 117, para. 1 of the Constitution, and Article 11 ECHR as a sub-constitutional provision, as interpreted by the ECtHR in *Matelly v. France* and *ADefDroMil v. France*.

The Council of State also alleged a violation of Article 5 RESC, which, as mentioned above, commits the signatory parties to undertake that national law shall not be such as to impair, nor shall it be so applied as to impair, the freedom of workers and employers to form local, national or international organisations for the protection of their economic and social interests, and to join those organisations. Article 5 RESC also states that 'the principle governing the application to the members of the armed forces of these guarantees and the extent to which they shall apply to persons in this category shall equally be determined by national laws or regulations', a statement whose complexity seems not to have taken into due consideration by either the Constitutional Court or the Council of State, as will be highlighted below.

---

[33] *Matelly v. France*, above n. 25, para. 62.
[34] Ibid., paras. 69–70. See also *ADefDroMil v. France*, above n. 26, paras. 43–44.

The Constitutional Court, in light of the case law of the ECtHR, recognised that a prohibition such as the one provided in Article 1475(2) of Legislative Decree n. 66 of 2010 violated Article 11(2) ECHR.[35] In doing so, the Court also stressed that the French legislator, in compliance with *Matelly* and *ADefDroMil*, had modified Article L 4121-4 Code de la défence, recognising the right of military personnel to establish professional organisations within the framework of specific legislation.[36]

The Constitutional Court, moreover, also recognised the provisions of the RESC as having sub-constitutional status, as a natural complement to the social field of the ECHR. On top of this, the Court highlighted that Article 5 RESC had a precise content, similar to that of Article 11(2) ECHR. Therefore, the denial of the freedom to organise a union, and to join it, was also in violation of Article 5 RESC.

However, as envisaged in the above, it is submitted here that there is no coincidence between the contents of Article 11(2) ECHR and the third sentence of Article 5 RESC. As a matter of fact, the latter provision clearly recognises that signatory parties have the right to determine 'the principle governing the application to the members of the armed forces of [the] guarantees and the extent to which they shall apply to persons in this category'. By exercising this right, the signatory parties may also decide to deny such members the freedom to organise a union, and to join it.[37] If applied in its true significance, as a social complement to the ECHR, Article 5 RESC could also be used as an interpretative tool in relation to Article 11(2) ECHR, in order to make such denial compatible with the latter.

Such a reflection cannot be found in the reasoning of the Constitutional Court, which concluded by considering both Article 11(2) ECHR and

---

[35] Constitutional Court, decision n. 120 of 2018.
[36] Article L 4121-4, as modified by Article 10 Act n. 2015-917 of 2015, provides that 'L'existence de groupements professionnels militaires à caractère syndical ainsi que, sauf dans les conditions prévues au troisième alinéa, l'adhésion des militaires en activité à des groupements professionnels sont incompatibles avec les règles de la discipline militaire. *Les militaires peuvent librement créer une association professionnelle nationale de militaires régie par le chapitre VI du présent titre, y adhérer et y exercer des responsabilités.* Il appartient au chef, à tous les échelons, de veiller aux intérêts de ses subordonnés et de rendre compte, par la voie hiérarchique, de tout problème de caractère général qui parviendrait à sa connaissance.'
[37] In the same vein, see T. Jaspers, 'Article 5 RESC The right to organize' in E. Ales, M. Bell, O. Deinert and S. Robin-Olivier, *International and European Labour Law*, Nomos, Baden-Baden 2018, p. 281; A. Jacobs, 'Article 5 The Right to Organise', in N. Bruun, K. Lörcher, I. Schömann and S. Clauwaert (eds), *The European Social Charter and the Employment Relation*, Hart, Oxford 2017, p. 241.

Article 5 RESC as sub-constitutional provisions the constitutionality test had to be carried out against, according to Article 117, para. 1 of the Constitution, in order to recognise the right to organise a union and to join it to militaries.

However, the Court recalled that both provisions allowed some legislative restrictions, and decided to verify if, and to what extent, such prerogatives could or should be exercised in light of the constitutional principles relating to the military order.

From this perspective, the constitutionality of the prohibition on military personnel joining 'other unions', i.e. those already established outside the military force as provided by Article 1475 of Legislative Decree n. 66 of 2010 had to be tested, since this issue did not fall within the scope of the case law of the ECtHR.

In the Constitutional Court's view, such a prohibition did not seem to be incompatible with Article 11(2) ECHR, since it did not jeopardise an essential element of freedom of association. On the other hand, as illustrated above (section 1), the Court has been consistent in admitting the possibility, and the need, for the military to set some limits on the exercise of that freedom, in order to make it compatible with the institutional goals attributed to the armed forces by the Constitution.[38]

Consequently, according to the Court, the constitutionality of the prohibition on military personnel joining other unions, as provided by Article 1475 Legislative Decree n. 66 of 2010, was affirmed. Therefore, military personnel should be allowed to join unions whose membership is reserved only to them, and those unions cannot federate with other unions under the meaning of Article 1475.

However, in the Court's view, a proper implementation of the constitutional framework requires a further check to be carried out, since its underpinnings make a non-specifically regulated recognition of the freedom of association incompatible with that framework. As a matter of fact, if, according to international parameters, the provision of such conditions and restrictions is optional it is mandatory from the national perspective, in view of excluding the possibility of a legislative vacuum which would impede the same recognition of military personnel's freedom to organise unions and to join them.

According to the Court, is up to the legislator to set such restrictions. However, in order not to postpone the recognition of freedom of association,

---

[38] See the Constitutional Court decisions n. 126 of 1985, n. 278 of 1987 and n. 449 of 1999.

and the adjustments required by the case law of the ECtHR, the Court has presumed that, pending a legislative intervention, the legislative vacuum can be filled by those provisions of Legislative Decree n. 66 of 2010 that exclude from the competences of the military representation bodies any subjects relating to the structure and the organisation of the armed forces, thus safeguarding their cohesion and neutrality.

On the other hand, Article 1475, para. 2 of Legislative Decree n. 66 of 2010 should be declared unconstitutional, insofar as it states that 'military personnel may not establish professional trade union associations or join other trade union associations' rather than stating that 'military personnel may establish professional trade union associations in accordance with the conditions and subject to the limits laid down by the law'.[39]

6. CONCLUSION

Elaborating on the aforementioned analysis, it is possible to draw some conclusions both on the impact of the ECHR on Italian (labour) law, and on the merit of the issues relating to the recognition of the freedom right for military personnel to establish and join unions of their own.

As for the first of these matters, it is apparent that the amendment to Article 117, para. 1 of the Italian Constitution has stimulated the Constitutional Court to recognise the sub-constitutional status of international provisions, thus affirming their crucial role within the constitutionality test that national provisions have to pass in order to keep producing effects within the legal order. As for the more specific issue at stake, that amendment has allowed the Court to change its position on the prohibition of unionisation within the military without abandoning the negative stance taken in the late 1990s with reference to Article 39, para. 1 of the Constitution.

As for the second of these matters, what is worth underlining is the refusal, common to both the ECtHR and the Italian Constitutional Court, to look at representative bodies established by the law, with participatory competences on living and working conditions, as suitable alternatives

---

[39] The Italian Legislator has regulated the exercise of freedom of association for armed forces by Act 28 April 2022, n. 46, which, among the others, modifies Article 1475 para. 2 MPCTP according to the wording of the Constitutional Court's decision.

to the recognition of freedom of association, in guaranteeing a collective voice to military personnel. Taking into consideration the fact that in no case will such recognition be followed by an entitlement to collective bargaining and collective action rights, it is difficult to see how a 'works council' approach could be of any detriment to the representation of these personnel's collective interests.

THE IMPACT OF THE EUROPEAN CONVENTION ON HUMAN RIGHTS ON GERMAN LABOUR LAW

A Special Focus on Collective Labour Law

Gabriele BUCHHOLTZ

1. Introduction 273
2. Case Law History 275
   2.1. Case Law History of the ECtHR. 275
      2.1.1. *Demir and Baykara* 276
      2.1.2. *Enerji Yapi-Yol Sen* 276
   2.2. Reactions of the German Courts 277
3. Binding Effect of the ECHR 278
4. Assessing the Impact of the ECHR on the German Right to Strike 279
5. Conclusion and Outlook 281

1. INTRODUCTION

For some time now, an increasing influence of European law on the legal orders of European countries has been observable. This is also the case in the area of labour law, which, with its social dimension,[1] is said to have socially 'integrative' potential for Europe.[2] The European Court of

---

[1] V. MANTOUVALOU, 'Labour Rights in the European Convention on Human Rights: An Intellectual Justification for an Integrated Approach to Interpretation' (2013) 13 *HRL Rev.* 529, 530 *et seq.*; T. NOVITZ, 'A Human Rights Analysis of the *Viking* and *Laval* Judgments' (2008) 16 *CYELS* 540 *et seq.*

[2] T. KINGREEN, 'Grundrechtsverbund oder Grundrechtsunion?' (2010) 3 *EuR* 338, 361.

Human Rights (ECtHR) in Strasbourg, in particular, has distinguished itself as a central player in this field, by declaring the European Convention on Human Rights (ECHR) to be a 'living instrument'. In the course of this development, national labour law, in particular the right to strike, has increasingly received an impetus from Strasbourg. The most prominent legal cases have been *Demir and Baykara*[3] and *Enerji Yapi-Yol Sen*.[4] In these decisions, the ECtHR has deduced a very far-reaching right to strike from Article 11 ECHR (freedom of assembly).

These decisions have attracted considerable attention, including in Germany. Not only numerous lower courts, but also the Federal Constitutional Court (Bundesverfassungsgericht or BVerfG) have recently had to deal with the right to strike. The BVerfG had to rule on the constitutionality of the ban on strike action for civil servants, and in so doing, the judges had to take into account the provisions of Article 11 ECHR, as well as related decisions by the ECtHR. However, in its decision, on 12 June 2018, the BVerfG showed an unwillingness to abandon the German civil service strike ban to the provisions of Article 11 ECHR. This, however, is not surprising, given that the German right to strike and the civil service strike ban are strongly influenced by tradition, and have so far been regarded as an inviolable sphere of domestic law. This is reason enough to take a closer look at the right to strike provided for in Article 11 ECHR, and its influence on German national law.

First, a closer look will be taken at the case law history, in particular the *Demir and Baykara* and *Enerji Yapi-Yol Sen* decisions and the German courts' reactions to these (section 2). Thereafter, the binding effect of the Charter provisions will be examined, from both the ECHR perspective and a national constitutional perspective (section 3): it is especially important to adopt a constitutional perspective, as the impact of the ECHR on the German legal system is largely determined by constitutional law. Following this, it will be determined where the possibilities and boundaries of the ECHR implementation lie, by critically examining the BVerfG decision of 12 June 2018 (section 4).

---

[3] *Demir and Baykara v. Turkey*, no. 34503/97, ECtHR 12 November 2008.
[4] *Enerji Yapi-Yol Sen v. Turkey*, no. 68959/01, ECtHR 21 April 2009.

2. CASE LAW HISTORY

2.1. CASE LAW HISTORY OF THE ECtHR

Since the right to strike is not expressly stipulated in Article 11 ECHR, the ECtHR has traditionally been reluctant when it comes to its recognition:[5] the original position of the ECHR was that the 'grant of a right to strike represents without any doubt one of the most important of these means [of exercising freedom of association], but there are others.'[6]

In other words, the right to strike is not an indispensable part of the guarantee in Article 11 ECHR.[7] However, a 'paradigm shift'[8] followed in *Demir and Baykara* and *Enerji Yapi-Yol Sen*. Both of these decisions have been recognised in the literature as landmark decisions.

---

[5] A. JACOBS, 'Article 11 ECHR: The Right to Bargain Collectively under Article 11 ECHR' in F. DORSSEMONT, K. LÖRCHER and I. SCHÖMANN (eds), *The European Convention on Human Rights and the Employment Relation*, Hart, Oxford 2013, pp. 309–32, §12, p. 310 *et seq.*; J.F. LINDNER, 'Dürfen Beamte doch streiken?' (2011) *DöV* 305, 307; A. SEIFERT, 'Recht auf Kollektivverhandlungen und Streikrecht für Beamte – Anmerkungen zur neuen Rechtsprechung des EGMR zur Vereinigungsfreiheit' (2009) *KritV* 357; V. MANTOUVALOU, 'Labour Rights in the European Convention on Human Rights: An Intellectual Justification for an Integrated Approach to Interpretation' (2013) 13 *HRL Rev.* 529, 532 *et seq.*; Critical of the ECtHR's reluctance, T. NOVITZ, *International and European Protection of the Right to Strike: A Comparative Study of Standards Set by the International Labour Organization, the Council of Europe and the European Union*, OUP, Oxford 2003, p. 238; B. WEDDERBURN, *Employment Rights in Britain and Europe*, Lawrence & Wishart, London 1991, p. 144.

[6] *Schmidt and Dahlström v. Sweden*, no. 5589/72, §36, ECtHR 6 February 1976.

[7] *National Union of Belgian Police v. Belgium*, no. 4464/70, §39, ECtHR 27 October 1975; *Unison v. the United Kingdom*, no. 53574/99, ECtHR 10 January 2002; P. FÜTTERER, 'Das Koalitions- und Streikrecht im EU-Recht nach dem Wandel der Rechtsprechung des EGMR zur Koalitionsfreiheit gemäß Art. 11 EMRK (*Demir und Baykara* und andere)' (2011) *EuZA* 505, 511.

[8] P. FÜTTERER, 'Das Koalitions- und Streikrecht im EU-Recht nach dem Wandel der Rechtsprechung des EGMR zur Koalitionsfreiheit gemäß Art. 11 EMRK (*Demir und Baykara* und andere)' (2011) *EuZA* 505, 511; similarly, see also K. LÖRCHER, 'Das Menschenrecht auf Kollektivverhandlung und Streik – auch für Beamte – Zu den EGMR-Urteilen v. 12.11.2008, *Demir und Baykara*, und 21.4.2009, *Enerji Yapi-Yol Sen*' (2009) *ArbuR* 229; K. LÖRCHER, 'Meilenstein der Menschenrechtsentwicklung' in W. DÄUBLER (ed), *Arbeitskampfrecht*, vol. 4, Baden-Baden 2018, §10 Rn. 41; K. LÖRCHER, 'The New Social Dimension in the Jurisprudence of the European Court of Human Rights (ECtHR): The *Demir and Baykara* Judgment, its Methodology and Follow-up' in F. DORSSEMONT, K. LÖRCHER and I. SCHÖMANN (eds), *The European Convention on Human Rights and the Employment Relation*, Hart, Oxford 2013, pp. 3–46, §1, p. 3. In the international context, see the discussion in K.D. EWING and J. HENDY, 'The Dramatic Implications of *Demir and Baykara*' (2010) 39 *ILJ* 2, 47.

2.1.1. Demir and Baykara

This decision was based on the following facts: the two Turkish applicants were public servants, and were members of a union. This union signed a collective agreement with the city council. Because the city council did not comply with its obligations under this collective agreement, the union brought a successful action at the District Court. However, the Court of Cassation subsequently quashed the decision, because – according to their reasoning – public servants may set up a trade union, under Turkish law, but are not allowed to conclude collective agreements. Finally, the two complainants brought an action before the ECtHR alleging a violation of Article 11 ECHR. The Grand Chamber of the ECtHR unanimously found such a violation.

The Court elaborated on the 'living instrument doctrine', and pointed out that the Convention must be interpreted in the light of present-day conditions, and in accordance with developments in international law, so as to reflect the increasingly high standards being required in the area of the protection of human rights. With regard to international standards, the court recognised, for the first time, that the right to collective bargaining was an essential element of the right to freedom of association in Article 11 ECHR.[9] Furthermore, the Court stated that public servants cannot, per se, be denied the right to collective bargaining, under Article 11 ECHR.

2.1.2. Enerji Yapi-Yol Sen

This decision was based on facts similar to those in *Demir and Baykara*. A circular was published by the Turkish prime minister, banning public sector employees from a strike being organised by a trade union. Despite the ban, members of the union went on strike and were disciplined. In its application to the ECtHR, the trade union alleged a breach of Article 11 ECHR by the Turkish authorities.

On 21 April 2009, the ECtHR held that there had been a violation of Article 11 ECHR. The Court stated that not only the right to collective bargaining, but also the right to strike, was an essential part of the provisions in Article 11 ECHR.[10] The Court acknowledged that the right to strike was not totally guaranteed, and could be subject to certain conditions and restrictions. However, the circular in this particular case, which had

---

[9] *Demir and Baykara v. Turkey*, no. 34503/97, §154, ECtHR 12 November 2008.
[10] *Enerji Yapi-Yol Sen v. Turkey*, no. 68959/01, §24, ECtHR 21 April 2009.

been drafted in general terms, completely deprived all public servants from the right to take strike action, and thus constituted a violation of Article 11 ECHR. In other words, a general strike ban is inconsistent with the provisions of Article 11 ECHR. Civil servants cannot be denied the right to strike simply because of their formal status. Restrictions are only conceivable for members of the 'administration of the state' (Art. 11 (2)), for example those who exercise sovereign powers.[11]

2.2. REACTIONS OF THE GERMAN COURTS

Encouraged by the decisions from Strasbourg, several teachers with civil servant status all over Germany dared to strike, and took legal action against disciplinary measures imposed against them, before the German administrative courts.[12] At first instance, the courts took quite different positions. The administrative court of Düsseldorf (31 K 3904/10.O) waived the plaintiffs' fines by paying attention to the judgments of the ECtHR, especially *Demir and Baykara* and *Enerji Yapi-Yol Sen*. The administrative court of Kassel (28 K 1208/10.KS.D) even found the two plaintiffs to be right, in light of the decisions from Strasbourg. In contrast, the Osnabrück administrative Court (9 A 1/11) and the Bremen administrative Court (D K 20/11) adhered to the traditional ban on civil servants' strikes.

However, the decisions of second instance were more uniform. The Higher Administrative Court of Münster (3d A 317/11.O) regarded the judgments of the ECtHR just like the Higher Administrative Court of Lüneburg (20 BD 7/11) did – as no real threat to the German civil service strike ban. In 2014, the Federal Administrative Court in Leipzig confirmed the ban on strike action for civil servants (2 C 1/13). Nevertheless, the Court admitted that the ban was contrary to the provisions of Article 11 ECHR.

And, finally, in 2018, the BVerfG confirmed the constitutionality of the ban on strike action for civil servants.[13]

---

[11] Ibid., §32.
[12] In Schleswig-Holstein, more than 1,800 civil servant teachers are said to have gone on strike in 2010; in Hesse, several thousand are said to have gone on strike since 1979. For these figures, see U. BATTIS, *Streikverbot für Beamte*, Arbeitsgemeinschaft der Verbände des höheren Dienstes, Bonn 2013, p. 5 (with further details).
[13] BVerfG, Urt. v. 12.06.2018 – 2 BvR 1738/12 (u.a.), ECLI:DE:BVerfG:2018:rs20180612. 2bvr173812.

3. BINDING EFFECT OF THE ECHR

The starting point for determining the binding effect of the ECHR is Article 46 of the ECHR, which provides that 'The High Contracting Parties undertake to abide by the final judgment of the Court in any case to which they are parties'. In other words, the binding effect of a certain ECtHR decision is limited to the parties to the individual case. From the perspective of Convention law, ECtHR decisions therefore only have an effect *inter partes*. Only in exceptional cases, may decisions have an effect that extends beyond the individual case (*erga omnes*). In order to determine the scope of this effect, it is necessary to take a closer look at the relevant provisions of national law, especially the Federal Constitution. This is because the ECHR leaves it up to the Member States to determine what rank they assign to the ECHR, in their national law, and how they comply with the judgments of the ECHR.

First of all, reference shall be made to the BVerfG decision *Görgülü* (2004).[14] Here, the judges in Karlsruhe made some remarkable comments on the bindingness of the ECHR and decisions by the ECtHR:

> In the German legal system, the European Convention on Human Rights has the status of a federal statute, and it must be taken into account in the interpretation of domestic law, including fundamental rights and constitutional guarantees … Courts are at all events under a duty to take into account a judgment that relates to a case already decided by them if they … are able to take the judgment into account without a violation of substantive law.

Thus, in short, even if a certain ECtHR decision is only binding *inter partes*, there exists a *constitutional duty of consideration*, which takes as its normative starting point the 'principle of the Constitution's openness to international law, in particular, the guarantees of the ECHR' (Article 1, paragraph 2; Article 25; and Article 59, paragraph 2, sentence 1 of the Basic Law). Decisions from Strasbourg thus have a normative guiding function beyond the specific legal dispute to which they relate. According to the BVerfG, national courts are obliged to 'take into account' the ECHR, as interpreted by the ECtHR, but that is as far as it goes.

---

[14] BVerfG, Urt. v. 14.10.2004 – 2 BvR 1481/04, ECLI:DE:BVerfG:2004:rs20041014.2b vrl48104.

4. ASSESSING THE IMPACT OF THE ECHR ON THE GERMAN RIGHT TO STRIKE

The 'duty of consideration' might cause difficulties in individual cases where Convention law and national law cannot be easily harmonised. This is demonstrated by the recent example of the ban on strike action for civil servants. With its decision of 12 June 2018, Karlsruhe rejected the idea of a civil servants' right to strike, and thus destroyed any further hope for changes in this area of law.[15]

The BVerfG pointed out that, under constitutional law, the ban on strike action for civil servants is a traditional principle with constitutional status laid down in Art. 33(5) of the Basic Law.[16] It is 'fundamental':[17]

> A right to strike, even for some groups of civil servants only, would fundamentally reshape the understanding and regulations of the civil service. … it would require fundamental changes to these principles, which are essential to the functioning of the civil service.[18]

The BVerfG also elaborated on the bindingness of the ECHR by stating that:

> The ban on strike action for civil servants in Germany is in accordance with the principle of the Constitution's openness to international law; in particular, it is compatible with the guarantees of the European Convention on Human Rights.

Furthermore, the Court briefly summarised that:

> [A] conflict between German law and the European Convention on Human Rights can presently not be established.[19]

And even if there was a conflict between national law and Article 11 ECHR, the BVerfG continued, it could be overcome. Here, the Court introduced a new line of argumentation and stated that:

> special importance must be attached to the specific context of the decision by the European Court of Human Rights when interpreting the Basic Law. Where

---

[15] BVerfG, Urt. v. 12.06.2018 – 2 BvR 1738/12 (u.a.), ECLI:DE:BVerfG:2018:rs20180612. 2bvr173812.
[16] BVerfG, Urt. v. 12.06.2018 – 2 BvR 1738/12, Rn. 143 et seq.
[17] BVerfG, Urt. v. 12.06.2018 – 2 BvR 1738/12, Rn. 152.
[18] BVerfG, Urt. v. 12.06.2018 – 2 BvR 1738/12, Rn. 153.
[19] BVerfG, Urt. v. 12.06.2018 – 2 BvR 1738/12, Rn. 163.

it is methodologically untenable or incompatible with the Basic Law to include values of the European Convention on Human Rights, the Constitution's openness to international law is limited.[20]

The judges added that:

> [T]he case-law of the European Court of Human Rights must be integrated as carefully as possible into the existing, dogmatically differentiated national legal system ... Therefore, international law concepts must not be adopted indiscriminately.[21]

These statements are remarkable because the BVerfG thereby specified the boundaries of the principle of the Constitution's 'openness to international law', and even drew these boundaries more restrictively. However, this line of argumentation must be criticised. Human rights standards apply regardless of the context, and guarantee an inviolable minimum standard.[22] The context does not allow for relativisations of the minimum standard.

What other options would have been available to the judges in Karlsruhe? One might easily argue that the wording of Article 33(5) is open to a new interpretation in accordance with Article 11 ECHR. This new interpretation would not change or touch the identity or core of the constitution. The consequence would have been a right to strike for some groups of civil servants who do not exercise sovereign powers, for example teachers. Incidentally, teachers in Germany can be employed as civil servants or as non-civil servants, so why should we differentiate between these two groups when it comes to the right to strike? It is difficult to justify why some teachers would be allowed to strike, while others working in the same classroom would not.

Moreover, a function-related ban on civil servants' strikes would correspond much more closely to the German doctrine of fundamental rights than the status-related ban. It is well known that encroachments on a fundamental right – in this case, Article 9(3) of the Basic Law – require a legitimate purpose and objective justification. Against this background, an encroachment on the right to strike, under Article 9(3) of the Basic Law,

---

[20] BVerfG, Urt. v. 12.06.2018 – 2 BvR 1738/12, Rn. 126.
[21] BVerfG, Urt. v. 12.06.2018 – 2 BvR 1738/12, Rn. 133 *et seq.*
[22] J. HEUSCHMID, 'Aktuelle Rechtsprechung des EGMR im Bereich des Arbeitsrechts' (2018) 3 *NZA Beilage* 68, 69.

can be justified much better in relation to function-related bans than in relation to status-related bans. Incidentally, this is how most neighbouring European countries understand the right to strike.

5. CONCLUSION AND OUTLOOK

Whether we like it or not, the BVerfG has decided against a civil service right to strike, and has denied any influence of the ECHR in this field of law. However, one thing has become clear: decisions from Strasbourg will no longer be ignored, especially in the field of labour law. It should be welcomed that Karlsruhe has dealt, in detail, with the decisions from Strasbourg. Although it may not have happened yet, greater coherence in the European system of fundamental rights should be expected soon, including in relation to labour law.

PART VI
CONCLUSIONS

COMPARATIVE LAW AT THE EUROPEAN COURT OF HUMAN RIGHTS

Does Context Still Matter?

Filippo VIGLIONE

1. Introduction 285
2. The Use of Comparative Remarks 287
3. European Consensus and its Contradictions 292
4. Comparative Law in the Advisory Opinions of the ECtHR: Conclusions 297

1. INTRODUCTION

According to Günter Frankenberg, comparative legal scholars must decide 'how to compare, what to compare and, especially, what to look out for'.[1] It would appear that this definitive statement sets a sort of preliminary task for all comparative studies to achieve. However, the outcome may depend on several variables, with context and scope of comparison playing a pivotal role. Nevertheless, no matter the subject of comparison, comparative discussions tend to share a fundamental characteristic: the capacity to debunk myths and superficial narratives.

Whether from a functional, structural or critical comparative perspective, it is generally agreed that the study of legal phenomena across jurisdictions is a complex undertaking. A broad awareness of 'cognitive limitations' and the need for 'cultural immersion' have become the methodological bases for conducting an adequate comparison.

---

[1] G. FRANKENBERG, *Comparative Law as Critique*, Edward Elgar, Cheltenham 2016, p. viii.

When comparison is performed by judges, the method and scope of comparison is certainly relevant. On the other hand, in cases where comparison is merely a factor considered when reaching a judicial decision, cultural awareness and cognition of unspoken rules are both required, in order to avoid decisions founded on biased and erroneous premises.

Based on the above, the recourse to comparative analysis by the European Court of Human Rights (ECtHR) raises several problems, which derive both from the very nature and scope of the Strasbourg Court, and on its oversimplified use of comparison. Although this issue has already been extensively addressed by the literature, it seems appropriate to analyse the problem once again, both in light of some important recent decisions, and under the new consultative mechanism provided by Protocol no. 16 to the European Convention of Human Rights (ECHR).[2]

In general, the Court's area of competence puts it in the position to reconcile two apparently conflicting requirements: on the one hand, the uniformity of the protection of fundamental rights in the Member States of the Council of Europe, and, on the other, the necessity of respecting the legal, social and cultural differences between the said Member States. In this context, comparison may constitute a useful balancing tool, but only if applied with a mindful approach that goes beyond the idea of a mere 'comparison by columns', i.e. a mere comparison of legislation currently in force in different legal systems.

In particular, the advisory opinion mechanism raises the question of whether a more abstract approach, less linked to the specific case, can modify the dynamics of legal comparison, and whether it might help to overcome the numerous criticisms that have emerged in this respect.

Taking this as a basis and opportunity for reflection, this chapter is divided into three main parts. The first part concerns a topic which has been analysed repeatedly in the literature: the ECtHR's recourse to the comparative law method, and its connection with the doctrines of European consensus and the margin of appreciation. In the second part of

---

[2] A persistent broad interest in the doctrine of consensus and the use of comparative law by the ECtHR is testified by the large number of scholarly writings published in the last few years. Among many, see K. DZEHTSIAROU, *European Consensus and the Legitimacy of the European Court of Human Rights*, CUP, Cambridge, 2015; E. POLGARI, 'European Consensus: A Conservative and a Dynamic Force in European Human Rights Jurisprudence' (2017) 12 *ICL Journal* 59–84; P. KAPOTAS and V. TZEVELEKOS, *Building Consensus on European Consensus: Judicial Interpretation of Human Rights in Europe and Beyond*, CUP, Cambridge, 2019; D. PEAT, *Comparative Reasoning in International Courts and Tribunals*, CUP, Cambridge, 2019, pp. 140–77.

the chapter, some potential contradictions in the use of these two doctrines are addressed, with particular reference to the area of family relationships. The third part discusses the use of legal comparison in the context of the advisory opinions of the ECtHR, according to Protocol no. 16 ECHR, exploring the problematic aspects of the application of the comparative law method, in terms of consistency and transparency.

2. THE USE OF COMPARATIVE REMARKS

The debate over comparative law as a tool available to national and supranational courts has been much discussed. Several studies have attempted to analyse the influence of foreign legal data on case law, particularly in cases that encompass international elements, such that the focus on the use of comparative law in the courts has become a classical locus of comparative legal studies.[3]

The subject matter acquires a somewhat different practical connotation when it comes to the analysis of the ECtHR's case law. Even the idea of universality, which comes with the protection of fundamental rights, may appear in contrast with the cultural relativism of any comparative approach.[4] We may then wonder whether different human rights

---

[3] Among others, see T. KOOPMANS, 'Comparative Law and the Courts' (1996) 45 *Int'l & Comp. L. Quarterly* 545-56; U. DROBNIG and S. VAN ERP, *The Use of Comparative Law by Courts*, XIVth International Congress of Comparative Law, Kluwer Law International, The Hague 1999; B. MARKESINIS and J. FEDTKE, 'The Judge as Comparatist' (2005) 80 *Tul. L. Rev.* 11-167; C.L. ROZAKIS, 'The European Judge as Comparatist' (2005) 80 *Tul. L. Rev.* 257-79; G.F. FERRARI and A. GAMBARO, *Corti nazionali e comparazione giuridica*, Esi, Napoli 2006; T.H. BINGHAM, *Widening Horizons: The Influence of Comparative Law and International Law on Domestic Law*, CUP, Cambridge 2010; M. BOBEK, *Comparative Reasoning in European Supreme Courts*, OUP, Oxford 2013; M. GELTER and M. SIEMS, 'Citations to Foreign Courts. Illegitimate and Superfluous, or Unavoidable? Evidence from Europe' (2014) 62 *Am. J. Comp. Law* 35-85; M. ANDENAS and D. FAIRGRIEVE (eds), *Courts and Comparative Law*, OUP, Oxford 2015; N. VOGIATZIS, 'The Relationship Between European Consensus, the Margin of Appreciation and the Legitimacy of the Strasbourg Court' (2019) 25 *EPL* 445-80.

[4] See M.-T. MEULDERS-KLEIN, 'Internationalisation des droits de l'Homme et évolution du droit de la famille: un voyage sans destination?' in *Internationalisation des droits de l'Homme et évolution du droit de la famille*, Actes du Colloque du Laboratoire d'études et de recherches appliquées au droit privé, Université Lille II, LGDJ, Paris 1996, pp. 180-213, at p. 211 (explaining that the use of a comparative approach by the ECtHR may introduce relativism and social self-reference as a mode of transforming norms into universal and transcendent sources).

perceptions, founded on national peculiarities, should be permitted to prevent the implementation of analogous rights throughout the Member States of the Council of Europe.

The balance between the universality of fundamental rights and the peculiarities of national diversities has been pursued through some degree of 'flexibility' in the implementation of the provisions of the ECHR, and in particular through the doctrine of the so-called European consensus.

In other words, the decisions of the Strasbourg Court are often influenced by the existence of a common sentiment among national legal systems in relation to each specific problem: the higher the level of consensus identified, the smaller the 'room for manoeuvre' granted by the Court to the national authorities.[5]

In the first two advisory opinions issued by the Court (as in many recent judgments of the ECtHR), specific paragraphs of comparison, entitled 'Comparative Law', 'Comparative Law materials' or 'Comparative survey', were included; in all these parts of the decisions, the Court briefly described the relevant practices of the Member States, but only to paint a picture of the legal state of the art, while the reasoning that led the Court's decision was not be necessarily affected by this information.[6]

The use of comparative argumentative techniques – which inevitably require strong comparative sensitivity and the ability to recognise the 'operational rules'[7] in each Member State's legal system – has not been completely accepted by a considerable portion of the scholarship. Especially among human rights scholars, the relativism that the doctrine

---

[5] On the relationship between the doctrine of the margin of appreciation and European consensus, see E. KASTANAS, *Unité et Diversité: Notions Autonomes et Marge d'Appréciation des Etats dans la Jurisprudence de la Cour Européenne des Droits de L'Homme*, Bruylant, Brussels 1996; E. BREMS, *Human Rights: Universality and Diversity*, Martinus Nijhoff Publishers, The Hague/Boston/London 2001; G. LETSAS, 'Two Concepts of the Margin of Appreciation' (2006) 26 *OJLS* 705–32; J. GERARDS, 'Pluralism, Deference and the Margin of Appreciation Doctrine' (2011) 17 *ELJ* 80–120; G. REPETTO, *Argomenti comparativi e diritti fondamentali in Europa. Teorie dell'interpretazione e giurisprudenza sovranazionale*, Jovene, Napoli 2011; K. DZEHTSIAROU, above n. 2, pp. 132 *et seq.*

[6] In an often-cited dissenting opinion, Judge Matscher criticised the superficial character of the Court's comparative approach and argued that 'autonomous interpretation would call for comparative studies of a far more detailed nature than those carried out so far by the Convention institutions'. See *Öztürk v. Federal Republic of Germany*, no. 8544/79, ECtHR 21 February 1984, Dissenting Opinion of Judge Matscher.

[7] The idea of 'operational rules' was introduced into the comparative debate by R. SACCO, 'Legal Formants: A Dynamic Approach to Comparative Law (Installment I of II)' (1991) 39 *Am. J. Comp. Law* 1–34.

of consensus encompasses is often remarked on, due to its potential to 'soften' the protection of human rights.[8]

According to this perspective, this issue poses some questions in relation to the idea of the ECtHR as a vehicle for the integration of the national legal orders in the area of human rights, but also – and above all – as to the functions of comparative law, and in particular to its harmonising dimension.[9]

In any case, it may be useful to distinguish between academic comparative research and comparative surveys drafted on behalf of the ECtHR. While the latter are not expected to be as accurate or scientific as the former (which have a more theoretical, historical, and 'cultural' dimension), it is clear that an oversimplified process of comparison undermines the objectiveness of the findings in the ECtHR's decisions. Even the recurrence of a European consensus may be wrongly detected by the Court if the process of comparison omits important data other than the mere legislation.[10]

A prime example is provided by the analysis of the 'margin of appreciation' with reference to the rules concerning the right to respect for private and family life (Article 8 ECHR) and the non-discrimination principle (Article 14 ECHR). Regarding such provisions of the Convention, the ECtHR often recognises a broad discretion of member states to establish the limits of said principles.[11] Accordingly, preliminary comparative investigations allow the Court to avoid addressing the issue of whether

---

[8] E. BENVENISTI, 'Margin of Appreciation, Consensus, and Universal Standards' (1999) 31 Int'l Law and Politics 843–54, at 844: 'Margin of appreciation, with its principled recognition of moral relativism, is at odds with the concept of the universality of human rights.'

[9] For a comprehensive analysis, see M. GRAZIADEI, 'The Functionalist Heritage' in P. LEGRAND and R. MUNDAY (eds), Comparative Legal Studies: Traditions and Transitions, CUP, Cambridge 2003, pp. 100–28; E. BANAKAS, 'The Contribution of Comparative Law to the Harmonisation of European Private Law' in A. HARDING and E. ORUCU (eds), Comparative Law in the Twenty First Century, Kluwer Law Intl., The Hague 2002, pp. 179–91.

[10] The risk of superficial analysis was particularly high until the end of the last century, when the Court started a process of 'professionalisation' in its approach to the common standard inquiry. See K. DZEHTSIAROU, above n. 2, p. 86.

[11] A few cases on Articles 8 and 14 where states have been allowed a wide margin of appreciation on the ground of lack of consensus include: Mata Estevez v. Spain, no. 56501/00, ECtHR 10 May 2001; Fretté v. France, no. 36515/97, ECtHR 26 February 2002; Evans v. United Kingdom, no. 6339/05, ECtHR 10 April 2007; Schalck and Kopf v. Austria, no. 30141/04, ECtHR 24 June 2010; A, B and C v. Ireland, no. 25579/05, ECtHR 16 December 2010.

'commonly accepted standards'[12] indeed exist, or may be established. A more audacious position suggests that, when a fundamental right is at stake and there is no substantial argument to deny its recognition, the absence of common standards within states should not play a specific and decisive role in granting protection of the fundamental right.

The problem seems to have been augmented by the recent tendency of the ECtHR to combine a 'procedural' approach to the margin of appreciation with the doctrine of European consensus. The former means that, when the ECtHR is confronted with conflicting fundamental rights, scrutiny of the availability of procedural safeguards in the respondent state will take place. In many cases, where the ECtHR has associated the level of the margin of appreciation to the quality of the parliamentary process, European consensus has also played a pivotal role in the Court's reasoning. In a significant number of these cases, both the analysis of European consensus and the procedural approach to the margin of appreciation led the Court to widen the overall margin of appreciation, thus restricting the effectiveness of protection of the human right at stake.[13]

The technique of using comparative surveys to identify the level of consensus may also lead to a potential underestimation of the importance of comparative law, which is then identified as the tool of 'moral relativism' inherent in the doctrine of consensus. From the perspective of the view that this may lead to the underestimation described above, it has been argued that 'the adjudicating organ must either adopt a moral standard or defer to a relativistic approach based on a comparative analysis',[14] thus suggesting that comparative law, applied to the field of human rights, can only lead to a paralysing outcome for the evolution of the protection of fundamental rights. In contrast, other authors have highlighted the tendency to create a '*ius commune* of human rights', which has its roots in comparative law,

---

[12] *Tyrer v. United Kingdom*, no. 5856/72, ECtHR 28 April 1978 (usually considered the first occurrence of the European consensus).

[13] Clear examples of this connection are provided in *Shindler v. United Kingdom*, no. 19840/09, ECtHR 7 May 2013; *Animal Defenders International v. United Kingdom*, no. 48876/08, ECtHR 22 April 2013; *S.A.S. v. France*, no. 43835/11, ECtHR 1 July 2014; *Parrillo v. Italy*, no. 46470/11, ECtHR 27 August 2015. On the distinction between the structural and procedural margins of appreciation, see G. LETSAS, above n. 5. The 'procedural approach' is also illustrated by the former President of the ECtHR, David Spielmann, in D. SPIELMANN, 'Whither the Margin of Appreciation?' (2014) 67 CLP 49–65, at 64.

[14] E. BENVENISTI, above n. 8, 851.

as an instrument to convey the contents of a growing expansion of global humanitarian protections.[15]

Similar viewpoints may, however, confuse some of the features of comparative law with the purpose of comparison. The latter is inherently impartial and, in its consolidated dimension, is neutral towards the choices of the best model possible. Comparison, in other words, is strictly linked to the knowledge of the law in general, and when applied by the courts, offers the chance to test the various solutions adopted in different legal systems with regard to a particular problem.[16]

As opposed to application of the 'neutral' comparative approach, some authors have suggested that the Court use the consensus doctrine as a means for reaching the optimal legal regulation of the issue under review. Consequently, 'if all the states in Europe have the same propensity to adopt good laws and if the ECHR is able to survey all of their national laws, the best results under the Jury Theorem will be achieved by following the majority of states'.[17]

Whichever premise we assume about the functions of comparison (and even if such comparison is limited to short comparative surveys), the collection of legal data from multiple Member States requires a coherent method of acquisition. This means that comparison cannot be used mechanically and without an adequate method of investigation. Otherwise, the identification of a sort of 'majority solution' among the Member States, identified through an analysis conducted in an abstract manner,[18] may be grounded in a dangerous interpretative bias. Moreover, an instrumental

---

[15] See A. HARDING and P. LEYLAND, 'Comparative Law in Constitutional Context' in E. ORUCU and D. NELKEN (eds), *Comparative Law: A Handbook*, OUP, Oxford 2007, pp. 313–38, at p. 328.

[16] The gathering of knowledge is widely considered the main function of a correct comparative law analysis. Moreover, legal comparison has been asserted as a rebellion against formalism and dogmatism. In this respect, a mere reproduction of legal data without a proper analysis of the context of law might produce the same enemies that comparative law fought against. On the aims and functions of comparative law, still fundamental is R. SACCO, above n. 7.

[17] S. DOTHAN, 'The Optimal Use of Comparative Law' (2014) 43 *Denver J. Int'l L. & Policy* 21–44, at 27, with a particular reference to Condorcet's jury theorem that justifies the use of majority rule and assesses the optimal size of deliberative bodies.

[18] Commendable exceptions, where the case law of a Member State was considered, are *Cooper v. United Kingdom*, no. 48843/99, ECtHR 16 December 2003; and *Eriksen v. Norway*, no. 17391/90, ECtHR 27 May 1997. See M. ANDENAS and D. FAIRGRIEVE, '"There is a World Elsewhere" – Lord Bingham and Comparative Law' in M. ANDENAS and D. FAIRGRIEVE (eds), *Tom Bingham and the Transformation of the Law*, OUP, Oxford 2009, p. 855.

use of comparison may also emerge from a methodologically suspect 'cherry-picking', which tends to use comparative data with the exclusive purpose of justifying a decision taken on different grounds.[19]

3. EUROPEAN CONSENSUS AND ITS CONTRADICTIONS

The European consensus is one of the most frequently used interpretative tools of the ECtHR. If comparison shows that the 'domestic law and practice of the Contracting States reveal a fairly substantial measure of common ground', then 'a more extensive European supervision corresponds to a less discretionary power of appreciation'.[20] The Court often conducts a comparative study on different legal systems and then identifies the dominant position in its decisions. As such, an interpretation that is dependent on national law becomes the basis of the ECtHR's decisions, as the guardian of fundamental rights. On the other hand, without uniform solutions, as the states' margin of appreciation expands, the Court's discretion becomes more limited and, in turn, the discrepancies between different states' legislation are left intact. In this sense, the dynamic circulation of the judicial rules linked with fundamental rights shows two sides of the same coin: the case law of the ECtHR influences the evolution of domestic legislation but, at the same time, appears affected by existing models.

The way in which the ECtHR has applied the doctrine of consensus in the areas of family law and bio-law indicates almost invariably that comparative analysis is performed to measure the extent to which specific policy problems impact on national law, and whether a trend exists between different countries.[21] The choices of lawmakers in individual countries,

---

[19] This risk seems particularly evident when the Court draws data from jurisdictions outside the Council of Europe, in a clear demonstration of the technique of 'cherry-picking', which is also one of the main objections that has arisen in the American debate against the judicial use of comparative law. See the case of *Sukhovetskyy v. Ukraine*, no. 13716/02, ECtHR 28 March 2006, where the Court found no violation of Conventional norms in the refusal to register a candidate for parliamentary elections because he had failed to pay an electoral deposit. In the list of 'relevant comparative international practice', the Court went into detail about the solutions offered in Ireland, Canada, the United Kingdom and Mauritius, showing a sketchy selection of comparators.

[20] *Sunday Times v. United Kingdom*, no. 6538/74, ECtHR 26 April 1979, §59.

[21] I. GIESEN, 'The Use and Influence of Comparative Law in "Wrongful Life" Cases' (2012) 8 *Utrecht Law Rev.* 35–54.

therefore, appear to guide the interpretation of the provisions of the ECHR, which are often subject to evolutionary and flexible interpretation.[22]

Moreover, analysis of the ECtHR's decisions in the realm of private law clearly illustrates the significant role played by comparative analysis in the justification of certain of the Court's interpretations. For instance, in the field of family law, decisions confirming a violation of the Convention often reflect new trends in the delineation of boundaries of new family models amongst Member States,[23] while judgments that do not find any violation often invoke the lack of a widespread consensus justifying a limitation of the margin of appreciation afforded to the individual states.

In family law, it is sufficient to consider the seminal decisions in matters of filiation in which the ECtHR influenced national legislation through a path of gradual assimilation between children born in and out of wedlock. Thus, the Court's first judgments in the area of filiation – confirming what took more than 35 years for some Member States to put into law, such as Italy with the 2015 filiation reform – were progressive. The landmark case dates to 1979, when the ECtHR, in *Marckx v. Belgium*, upheld the appeal of Ms Marckx with regard to the inheritance rights of children born out of wedlock. Indeed, at the time, children born out of wedlock in Belgium were only entitled to inherit property from their mother or their mother's family estate. Instead, as early as 1979, the ECtHR found not only that Article 8 ECHR (right to respect for private and family life) had been violated, but also Article 14 ECHR (prohibition of discrimination), and ruled that the Marckx's daughter – despite being born to unwed parents and notwithstanding no apparent consensus amongst Member States on the matter – was entitled to inherit from both biological parents (and, therefore, also from Mr Marckx).

Following the *Marckx* decision, it became necessary to safeguard the right to private and family life without distinguishing between children

---

[22] Since the ECHR can be regarded as a system of rules that expresses a common cultural heritage, the role of comparative law becomes a fundamental tool of interpretation in the search for this common ground. Within a traditional voluntarist conception of international law, see E. BREMS, 'The Margin of Appreciation Doctrine in the Case-Law of the European Court of Human Rights' (1996) 56 *Zeitschrift für ausländisches öffentliches Recht* 230–314, at 276: 'it is because the European System is supposed to be derived from the national systems of the member states that the comparative argument takes so much weight'.

[23] The reshaping of the family can be traced in some of the most important ECtHR cases. A complete list can be found in C. DRAGHICI, *The Legitimacy of Family Rights in Strasbourg Case Law: 'Living Instrument' or Extinguished Sovereignty?*, Hart, Oxford 2017, pp. 26 *et seq.*

born in or out of wedlock. Hence, *Marckx v. Belgium* can be identified as the inspiration for subsequent cases where inheritance rights, family life and the principle of non-discrimination merged. Additionally, it has prompted national legislators to comply with the necessity of ensuring full equality in children's rights of succession.

This case is considered to be the first one in which the reasoning of the Strasbourg Court manifestly shaped the evolutionary patterns of domestic legislation in family and succession law.

Belgium has, albeit following a cumbersome legislative path, and with a great deal of influence from its Constitutional Court's case law, recognised all biological children as part of the family and, as such, entitled to inheritance. Both France and Germany have modified their national law on succession as a direct consequence of the ECtHR's judgments and decisions. More specifically, following the judgment in *Mazurek v. France*,[24] France enacted Law no. 2001/1135, and equalised the position of biological and legitimate children in matters of inheritance, removing any discriminatory differences.[25] The Italian legislative reform on filiation, which recognised all biological children as part of the family, had some significant consequences for inheritance rights too – full equality of all children – following a long and tedious process of recognition that had found its spark in the decisions of the ECtHR.[26]

All the cases where the ECtHR has dealt with family law by searching for commonly accepted standards show, in some way, a declining attitude of the Court towards judicial activism, inversely proportional to the growing relevance of the doctrine of European consensus. In this respect, in a significant number of recent decisions where the Court has excluded the presence of a violation of Convention norms, the issue of consensus has played a decisive role, although it is not clear whether it is being used as a shield in highly sensitive areas. The most significant cases concern,

---

[24] *Mazurek v. France*, no. 34406/97, ECtHR 1 February 2000.
[25] Notwithstanding this legislative intervention, the transitional arrangements still showed some flaws. Hence, the ECtHR, in a more recent case, *Fabris v. France*, no. 16574/08, ECtHR 21 July 2011, recognised that excluding a child born from an adulterous relationship from a *donation-partage* (to which legitimate children were admitted), in 1970, constituted a breach of the principle of non-discrimination, following Additional Protocol no. 1, Article 1.
[26] F. Giardini, 'Unification of Child Status and Parental Responsibility: The Reform of Filiation Remodels the Family in the Legal Sense in the Italian Legal System' (2017) 22 *IJFS* 2–16.

once again, the right of family relations and, in particular, marriage between persons of the same sex.²⁷ In *Schalk and Kopf v. Austria*,²⁸ the alleged violations related to Articles 12, 8 and 14 ECHR, in connection with Austrian national legislation that recognised the right to marry only for persons of a different sex (Article 44, ABGB).²⁹ In this case, the Court rejected the complaint of the Austrian citizens, stating that the Convention did not oblige Member States to legislate for, or legally recognise, same-sex marriages.

Although accepting same-sex relationships as a form of 'family life', the reasoning of the Court insisted on three kinds of considerations, ranging from the wording of Article 12 to the original intent of the framers of the Convention, and also the final, and perhaps decisive, observation that there was 'little common ground' between Contracting States in this area. In fact, in recent years the ECtHR has repeatedly been called upon to hear cases on issues concerning the right of homosexual couples to adopt. The dominant position thus far has proved to be ambivalent. On the one hand, the Court has linked the relationship between same-sex persons with the scope of 'family life' under Article 8 ECHR, resulting in an enhancement of the principle of non-discrimination.³⁰ On the other hand, however, the judges in Strasbourg do not believe that Contracting States have an obligation to provide for the institution of same-sex marriage. This position has recently been confirmed in *Chapin and Charpentier v. France*,

---

27   See also the chapter by M.G. STANZIONE, 'Shaping New Families: Same-Sex Couples' Rights in the Dialogue between the Courts', in this volume.
28   *Schalck and Kopf v. Austria*, no. 30141/04, ECtHR 24 June 2010.
29   Note, however, that when the application was submitted to the Strasbourg Court, the Austrian law on registered partnerships (Eingetragene Partnerschaft-Gesetz) had not yet entered into force. This law, starting from 1 January 2010, gives same-sex couples the right to access a form of legal recognition (and to a series of protections that go with it), even if this is not comparable to the institution of marriage.
30   The consequences of this have been of great importance. Consider, to mention just some of the most significant applications: the affirmation of the right to have sex with a consenting person of the same sex (*Dudgeon v. United Kingdom*, no. 7525/76, ECtHR 22 October 1981); the right of a lesbian woman to seek an adoption (*EB v. France*, no. 43546/02, ECtHR 22 January 2008); the finding of a violation of the ECHR in relation to denial of custody of a child to their biological father, motivated only by his sexual orientation (*Salgueiro da Silva Mouta v. Portugal*, no. 33290/96, ECtHR 21 December 1999); as well as the violation that resulted from the exclusion of gay couples from civil partnerships reserved for heterosexual couples in Greek legislation (*Vallianatos and others v. Greece*, nos. 29381/09 and 32684/09, ECtHR 11 July 2013).

where the Court showed no hesitation in again declaring that there was no European consensus on same-sex marriage.[31]

From this perspective, the doctrine of European consensus seems to serve as a brake on the protection of rights granted by the ECtHR, since the examination of solutions adopted in other Member States plays a major role in the Court's judgments on the existence of a violation of the Convention.[32] If there is no doubt that the Court tends to balance the needs of protection of fundamental rights with the need to ensure a degree of legitimacy in its decisions,[33] then a non-systematic implementation of the 'consensus argument' seems to diminish the level of protection, when the 'politically' sensible choice would call for a more radical position, in order to strengthen the quality of life of minority groups.[34]

In a significant number of cases, then, the ECtHR seems to have given up adopting a proactive role and contributing to the formation of a generally accepted approach among Contracting States. This leads to a paradox: the ECtHR adopts this statistical criterion even where the protection of

---

[31] *Chapin and Charpentier*, no. 40183/07, ECtHR 9 June 2016. After the application had been made in *Chapin and Charpentier*, France changed its laws, in May 2013, introducing the so called '*mariage pour tous*'. This circumstance led the ECtHR to consider that there was no violation of Article 12 in combination with Article 14: the applicants were, indeed, free to marry if they desired to, at the time of the decision.

[32] See *Hämäläinen v. Finland*, no. 37359/09, ECtHR 16 July 2014, where the Court confirmed the approach taken with regard to Article 12 in *Schalk and Kopf*. The question related to the case of a transsexual woman who had married another woman before her gender transition. The rejection of the applicant's claim – a full legal recognition of her gender without putting an end to her marriage – was grounded, among other reasons, on the lack of a European consensus in this regard.

[33] P. MAHONEY and R. KONDAK, 'Common Ground: A Starting Point or Destination for Comparative-Law Analysis by the European Court of Human Rights?' in M. ANDENAS and D. FAIRGRIEVE (eds), *Courts and Comparative Law*, above n. 3, p. 120 ('Convincing and reliable interpretative techniques, such as the search for common European ground, brings as much objectivity to the exercise as possible and serve to justify any law-making accomplished by the Court when filling interpretative gaps left in the Convention law. The comparative-law process thereby adds legitimacy to the judgments of the Court.').

[34] See E. BRIBOSIA, I. RORIVE and L. VAN DEN EYNDE, 'Same-Sex Marriage – Building an Argument before the European Court of Human Rights in Light of the US Experience' (2014) 32 *Berkeley J. Int'l L.* 1–43, at 19 (stating that 'the use of the consensus argument is often fraught with methodological imprecision and is often a means to conceal or justify a moral positioning of ECtHR judges'). Similar criticisms can be found in L. HODSON, 'A Marriage by Any Other Name? *Schalk and Kopf v Austria*' (2011) 11 *Human Rights L. Rev.* 170–79, at 177, which criticised the use of the instrument of consensus, reputed as 'clearly an unsatisfactory approach that leaves minorities vulnerable to majoritarian domination'.

minorities is at stake, thus using the European consensus as a tool to justify its hesitancy to intervene.[35]

Moreover, even where commonly accepted standards exist, the ECtHR sometimes abdicates its role as the guardian of fundamental rights, as emerged clearly in a case relating to abortion. In *A, B and C v. Ireland*,[36] the Court recognised a consensus amongst a substantial majority of the Contracting States of the Council of Europe towards allowing abortion on broader grounds than those accorded under Irish law. At that time, Ireland was the only Contracting State that allowed abortion solely where there was a risk to the life of the expectant mother. Nonetheless, the Court did not consider that this common approach decisively narrowed the broad margin of appreciation of the state, confirming the idea that an unsystematic and flexible use of comparison, and of the doctrine of European consensus, inevitably diminishes their value and epistemological strength.

4. COMPARATIVE LAW IN THE ADVISORY OPINIONS OF THE ECtHR: CONCLUSIONS

The special importance given to comparative law in the argumentative paths of the ECtHR has caused a mixed reaction among legal scholars. European consensus has been regarded as an interesting laboratory for the circulation of different legal models, but it has also given rise to scepticism, based on the relativisation of human rights' implementation.[37]

It is likely that, if the Court uses comparative analysis in the same way as it has done so far, this outcome will also be repeated within the advisory opinion system.[38] As illustrated in the Explanatory Report to Protocol no. 16

---

[35] A different approach was adopted by the Inter-American Court of Human Rights, in the decision *Atala Riffo and Daughters v. Chile*, Inter-Am. CtHR 24 February 2012, case no. 12.502: 'the alleged lack of consensus in some countries regarding full respect for the rights of sexual minorities cannot be considered a valid argument to deny or restrict their human rights or to perpetuate and reproduce the historical and structural discrimination that these minorities have suffered'.

[36] *A, B and C v. Ireland*, no. 25579/05, ECtHR 16 December 2010.

[37] See V. GREMENTIERI, 'Comparative Law and Human Rights in Europe' in A.M. RABELLO (ed), *European Legal Traditions and Israel*, The Hebrew University of Jerusalem, Jerusalem 1994, p. 375.

[38] European consensus and the advisory opinion mechanism are jointly considered as instruments of dialogue between judges, by P. BUREŠ, 'The dialogue between judges leading to a consensus? On a mute and a silent dialogue before ECtHR' (2017) 1 *Eur. J. Public Matters* 63–73.

to the ECHR,[39] all advisory opinions form part of the case law of the Court, alongside its judgments and decisions. From this perspective, 'the interpretation of the Convention and the Protocols thereto contained in such advisory opinions would be analogous in its effect to the interpretative elements set out by the Court in judgments and decisions'.

Indeed, in its recent implementation of the advisory opinion mechanism, the ECtHR has confirmed the usual practice of attributing a fundamental role to comparative remarks. Protocol no. 16 allows the 'highest domestic courts' to request the ECtHR to give an advisory opinion on 'questions of principle relating to the interpretation or application of the rights and freedoms defined in the Convention or the protocols thereto'. The objective of the Protocol is to 'further enhance the interaction between the Court and national authorities and thereby reinforce implementation of the Convention, in accordance with the principle of subsidiarity'. Both of the opinions so far issued under Protocol no. 16 demonstrate a vast recourse to comparison.

In the Court's first advisory opinion,[40] comparative law materials were widely examined, even if they were not, ultimately, considered crucial in determining the outcome of the opinion. Indeed, the Court recalled that there was no European consensus among the 47 Member States on whether intended parenthood resulting from surrogacy should be recognised. The absence of European consensus would lead, in line with the Court's practice, to a wide margin of appreciation. However, in this specific case, the Court's opinion was that such margin should be abridged, because the concern at stake encompassed particularly important features of an individual's identity as well as 'essential aspects of the (children's) private life'.[41]

---

[39] Available at https://www.echr.coe.int/Documents/Protocol_16_explanatory_report_ENG.pdf.

[40] ECtHR, *Advisory Opinion concerning the recognition in domestic law of a legal parent-child relationship between a child born through a gestational surrogacy arrangement abroad and the intended mother Requested by the French Court of Cassation*, 10 April 2019, Request no. P16-2018-001.

[41] The lack of consensus, on the contrary, is considered crucial in relation to the choice of means by which to permit recognition of the legal relationship between the child and the intended parents. As a consequence of the first advisory opinion, the French Cour de Cassation ordered the transcription of the foreign birth certificate to be proceeded with, thus recognising the maternity *ex lege* of the intended mother (Cour de Cassation, Ass. plén., 4 October 2019, n. 648). See J. HOUSSIER, 'L'affaire Mennesson ou la victoire du fait sur le droit' (2019) *AJ Famille*, 11, 592–94; L. MARGUET, 'GPA: Quand la Cour de cassation facilite la reconnaissance du lien de filiation du second parent … au-delà même des exigences européennes?' (2020) *La Revue des droits de l'homme. Actualités Droits-Libertés* 1–11.

In the second advisory opinion,[42] the ECtHR undertook a comparative survey addressing two issues: the first issue concerned the use of the 'blanket reference' or 'legislation by reference' technique for setting out the constituent elements of criminal offences in general, and offences against the constitutional order of a country in particular. The second issue concerned the principle of non-retroactivity of (less favourable) criminal law and the principle of retrospective application of more favourable criminal law.[43]

Comparative law material may become even more important if one considers the structure of the first advisory opinions; that is, while the Court usually only narrowly adapts its legal reasoning to the concrete facts of each case, under the mechanism of Protocol no. 16 the ECtHR disregards its engagement with the background facts altogether, and applies a more abstract reasoning.[44] Indeed, proceedings will still be pending at the domestic level when the European Court is asked to give its opinion and, as clarified in the Explanatory Report to Protocol no. 16, §11, the aim of an application for an advisory opinion 'is not to transfer the dispute concerned to the Court', given that the Court has 'no jurisdiction either to assess the facts of a case … or to rule on the outcome of the proceedings'.[45] Such a more abstract way of considering the question submitted by a national high court may increase the relevance of comparative surveys, which could become more effective when questions are posed in more general terms.[46]

---

[42] ECtHR, *Advisory Opinion concerning the use of the 'blanket reference' or 'legislation by reference' technique in the definition of an offence and the standards of comparison between the criminal law in force at the time of the commission of the offence and the amended criminal law*, 29 May 2020, Request no. P16-2019-001.

[43] Unanimous consensus among Member States has been detected on the principle of non-retroactivity of (less favourable) criminal law, and on the principle of retrospective application of more favourable criminal law (§36 of the opinion cited in n. 42). On the other hand, in relation to the use of the 'blanket reference', the ECtHR found no consensus among Member States on whether the referenced norms must be, or may be, of a certain nature or hierarchical level (§35).

[44] N. Posenato, 'New opinions ex Protocol no. 16 to the ECHR and the Inter-American advisory practice: some comparative remarks' (2020) *Eurojus*, 353–70, at 361 (explaining that 'the issues admitted to the European consultative procedure, although defined in the context of the dispute in which they arose, may have a more abstract character not strictly limited to the factual framework of the case under analysis').

[45] ECtHR, Advisory Opinion 10 April 2019, §25.

[46] An appropriate use of comparative method in the Court's advisory opinions would help promote a better understanding that a ratification of Protocol no. 16 does not cause any risk for national 'sovereignty', as wrongly claimed by the Italian Parliament (on this basis, the Chamber of Deputies of the Italian Parliament recently decided to postpone *sine die* the ratification of the Protocol). The request for an advisory opinion

The interpretative technique of European consensus – reached through a comparative analysis – and the requests of advisory opinions formulated by national supreme or superior courts enhance a kind of dialogue between national and European judges. Nevertheless, the concrete way in which the advisory opinion mechanism is to be used will influence the dialogue between national and European judges.

At present, following the release of only two advisory opinions, it is not possible to verify whether the use of legal comparison in this context is going to operate in a different way than it does with respect to the generality of the Court's case law. However, some positive aspects can already be expected. First, the advisory function will be nourished by the elements of knowledge that legal comparison can provide. This seems particularly true in the case of judicial protection of new rights, such as those rooted in the field of bio-law. Second, in the advisory opinions, the ECtHR's legal reasoning can be developed, to a more consistent extent, through general principles, and in a manner that is less linked to specific cases. This makes it possible to avoid the distortions of a purely functional comparison,[47] which is very much at risk of bias linked to the different regulatory contexts of reference. The legal reasoning '*per principia*',[48] enriched by the information derived from an adequate comparison, would then open the way, at the domestic level, to judicial specifications more respectful of the local context, but at the same time consistent with the Court's guidelines.

The first advisory opinion, however, shows some uncertainties and inconsistencies regarding the role of comparative materials. This circumstance clearly emerges from the division of the opinion into two parts. In the first, the Court considered that Article 8 ECHR should be read as requiring domestic law to recognise the relationship between the intended parent and the child born through gestational surrogacy abroad. Even though there is no consensus among Member States in this regard, the Court gave priority to the doctrine of the best interest of the child.

---

does not have, as its object, the conformity of national law with the ECHR, but relates instead to the interpretation of the Convention – an interpretation which, to be complete and adequate, requires the consistent and transparent use of comparison.

[47] J. Husa, 'Methodology of Comparative Law Today: From Paradoxes to Flexibility?' (2006) *Rev. int. droit comp.* 1095–117, at 1104 (summarising the defects of functionalism and explaining that, in its theory, functionalism recognises the importance and relevance of the context of laws but, 'in its practice it fails to live to the high standards it sets for itself').

[48] A. Ruggeri, 'Ancora sul prot. 16: verrà dai giudici la sollecitazione al legislatore per il suo recepimento in ambito interno?' (2020) *diritticomparati.it*, 81–97, at 84.

In the second part, however, the Court affirmed that each Member State can achieve the recognition of filiation by transcription, or by adoption, or even by other means, thus allowing for wide margins of appreciation. Although the lack of consensus emerging from the comparative survey was referred to in both of the different questions, only in one case was the doctrine of consensus considered conclusive.[49]

Notwithstanding the cautious approach of the ECtHR in its first advisory opinion,[50] the importance of the consultative mechanism can be attested to by a recent Italian case on surrogacy. Despite an interpretation offered by the Italian Court of Cassation, *en banc*, only one year previously,[51] the Italian Constitutional Court has been called upon to decide whether the prohibition on registering the name of the second father of a child born abroad through a surrogate mother violates the same-sex couple's constitutional rights. In particular, this question, raised by the Supreme Court,[52] asks whether Italian laws limiting the recognition of foreign documents and judgments, on grounds of public policy, conflict with the Constitution and the international rules on the protection of minors, insofar as they do not allow the registration of children of homosexual couples born through 'surrogate motherhood' practices, which are prohibited (and punishable under criminal law) in Italy. The potential

---

[49] On the first part, see §43 of the advisory opinion, where the Court clarifies that 'despite a certain trend towards the possibility of legal recognition of the relationship between children conceived through surrogacy abroad and the intended parents, there is no consensus in Europe'; on the second part, see §51: 'The Court notes that there is no consensus in Europe on this issue: where the establishment or recognition of a legal relationship between the child and the intended parent is possible, the procedure varies from one State to another.' Moreover, the comparative survey shows a certain superficiality. It is sufficient to think about the Italian situation, which is not mentioned in any way, even though there are various judicial decisions that tend to admit the filiation relationship through adoption of minors within families (*adozioni in casi particolari*), or through transcription, both for same-sex and opposite-sex parents. The evolution of the case law and the complex legal framework have recently been illustrated by S. Izzo, '"From status to contract": la trascrizione dei provvedimenti stranieri dichiarativi dello status del figlio d'intenzione' (2019) 6 *GenIUS* 48–60; see also M. Winkler and K.T. Schappo, 'A tale of two fathers' (2019) 5 *Ital. Law J.* 359–87.

[50] L. Lavrysen, 'The Mountain Gave Birth to a Mouse: The First Advisory Opinion under Protocol No. 16' in *strasbourgobservers.com*, 14 April 2019, https://strasbourgobservers.com/2019/04/24/the-mountain-gave-birth-to-a-mouse-the-first-advisory-opinion-under-protocol-no-16/.

[51] Italian 'Corte di Cassazione', sez. un., 8 May 2019, n. 12193, in *Fam. e dir.*, 2019, p. 653 (with comments by M. Dogliotti and G. Ferrando).

[52] Italian 'Corte di Cassazione', ord. 29 April 2020, n. 8325, in *Fam. e dir.*, 2020, p. 675 (with comments by G. Recinto).

conflict emerged following the first advisory opinion of the ECtHR, which was, at least in part, based on comparative law analysis.

Although the Italian Constitutional Court subsequently rejected the arguments of the Court of Cassation (invoking an objective to discourage the use of surrogacy),[53] it is undeniable that the advisory opinion procedure, created with the aim of strengthening the dialogue between national courts and the ECtHR (but also to alleviate the Court's burden and reduce its backlog), may constitute another effective instrument with a general harmonising effect. Nonetheless, the first two decisions of the Court seem to replicate the reasons for criticism that have been articulated over the past two decades,[54] especially with regard to the opacity of the methodology used to detect the European consensus, and to define the margin of appreciation.

The primary shortcomings that have emerged, so far, in applying the doctrine of consensus appear to be its inconsistent use, the absence of a real method of comparative investigation, the focus solely on the legislative formant, and the total lack of consideration for the context in which a specific rule is regarded by the courts.[55]

The outcome of these observations reveals a role for comparison more linked to justification than to interpretation,[56] as confirmed by the first advisory opinion on parenthood and cross-border surrogacy. In other words, the exercise of the comparative analysis is carried out in an inevitably superficial manner in the ECtHR's decisions, without the implementation of a clear method differing from the mere listing of Member States that (apparently) adhere to a given solution, or (at other times) simply quoting

---

[53] Italian Constitutional Court, 9 March 2021, n. 33, in Nuova *giur. civ. comm.*, 2021, II, p. 930.

[54] Among others, see J.A. BRAUCH, 'The Dangerous Search for an Elusive Consensus: What the Supreme Court Should Learn from the European Court of Human Rights' (2009) 52 *Howard L.J.* 277–318, at 278 (arguing that '[d]espite hundreds of cases and over thirty years of experience, the ECHR has still not made clear what a European consensus is, or even how one would identify the consensus if it existed').

[55] From the ECtHR's case law, it is possible to consider that, on certain occasions, the recognition of a broad consensus is not crucial, while in other decisions a mere 'trend' may be useful for justifying an innovative outcome. See, in this regard, the case of *Goodwin v. United Kingdom*, no. 28957/95, ECtHR 11 July 2002, where the Court found no justification for barring a transgender individual from enjoying the right to marry under any circumstances, despite there not being any European consensus on the matter.

[56] P.G. CAROZZA, 'Uses and Misuses of Comparative Law in International Human Rights: Some Reflections on the Jurisprudence of the European Court of Human Rights' (1999) 73 *Notre Dame L. Rev.* 1217–37, at 1225.

a majority trend among the Member States.[57] This circumstance means that, once the Court has taken into account certain considerations, it can make use of comparative surveys to strengthen its arguments.[58]

This is demonstrated by the total lack of awareness regarding the importance of 'operational rules' beyond definitions and general provisions;[59] this is an essential prerequisite for any comparative study, since comparison must look for the outcome of a complex numbers of factors, and cannot limit itself to the mere consistency of the statements made in different jurisdictions.

Furthermore, this approach demeans the potential of comparative law in human rights practice, which has been accurately expressed by Christopher McCrudden: 'the role of comparison is that of persuasion to an essentially moral position. Lawyers in the human rights context often use comparison to legitimate their argument that a particular interpretation of an existing human rights norm should be adopted, or as part of the process of generating further norms. The use of comparison as part of the process of persuasion not infrequently gives rise to highly selective, often rather simplistic comparative arguments.'[60]

Reducing the impact of comparative law to the search for a European consensus, enlarging or reducing the states' margin of appreciation, might ultimately contrast with the very spirit of the Convention, and does not explain why the shared perspective of the majority of member States should determine the content and purpose of the provisions of the ECHR,[61] or,

---

[57] For mere references to the majority guidelines, see *Opuz v. Turkey*, no. 33401/02, ECtHR 9 June 2009, §87, on domestic violence; and *Konstantin Markin v. Russia*, no. 30078/06, ECtHR 22 March 2012, paras. 71–75, on 'parental leave'.

[58] According to part of the legal doctrine, the Court of Justice of the European Union shares with the ECtHR the same absence of a clear comparative methodology. In this sense, see S. DOUGLAS-SCOTT, 'A Tale of Two Courts: Luxembourg, Strasbourg and the Growing European Human Rights Acquis' (2006) 43 *Common Market L.R.* 629–65, at 657 ('Although the European Court of Human Rights and the ECJ are transnational courts par excellence, and much of their case law is built out of general principles of law from Member States, there is very little clear comparative law methodology in their jurisprudence.').

[59] Every jurist trained in comparative law knows that general provisions and theoretical formulations might be incoherent with the operational rules. On the other hand, it might be that some operational rules are not contained in official sources (e.g. civil codes), but are nevertheless applicable. See R. SACCO, above n. 7.

[60] C. MCCRUDDEN, 'Judicial Comparativism and Human Rights' in E. ÖRÜCÜ and D. NELKEN (eds), *Comparative Law – A Handbook*, Hart, Oxford/Portland 2007, pp. 371–97, at p. 376.

[61] P.G. CAROZZA, above n. 56, 1228.

conversely, why the absence of such consensus necessarily implies the exercise of self-restraint by the Court.

During its 60 years of existence, the ECtHR has developed from a small institution into the world's most influential regional human rights court, with more than 800 million people entitled to submit a complaint about the violation of rights protected under the ECHR. Given the complexity of the entire system of protection of human rights, a superficial use of comparative law may have detrimental consequences for the fairness of its decisions.

HARMONISATION THROUGH THE BACK DOOR?

The Impact of the European Convention on Human Rights on National Private Law

Matteo FORNASIER

1. Introduction 306
2. The Channels of Harmonisation 308
   2.1. Direct Harmonisation 308
   2.2. Indirect Harmonisation 309
   2.3. Soft Harmonisation 310
3. Direct Harmonising Effects 314
   3.1. Harmonisation in Procedure 314
   3.2. Harmonisation in Substantive Law 318
      3.2.1. Harmonising Effects Resulting from Autonomous Interpretation of the Convention 318
      3.2.2. The Inductive Approach: Harmonising Effects Resulting from the Notion of 'European Consensus' 320
      3.2.3. Inconsistencies in the Court's Case Law: The Deductive Approach 324
4. Indirect Harmonising Effects 327
   4.1. Embedding the Guarantees of the Convention into the System of EU Law 327
   4.2. An Example of Indirect Harmonising Effects: Judicial Review of the Duty of Loyalty in Church Employment 328
5. Conclusion 332
   5.1. Factors Weakening the Convention's Harmonising Effects 333
   5.2. How Activist is the European Court of Human Rights? 336

1. INTRODUCTION

When we talk about harmonisation of private law in Europe, we are usually referring to the framework of European Union (EU) law and its impact on the Member States' domestic legal systems. In other words, we focus on what is known as 'EU private law',[1] i.e. the creation of directly applicable uniform law through regulations under Article 288(2) of the Treaty on the Functioning of the European Union (TFEU),[2] and the approximation of national private law through directives under Article 288(3) TFEU. Undoubtedly, EU law has an enormous impact on the Member States' national laws, and plays a key role in shaping a common European legal order. This chapter, however, deals with a different topic: it seeks to explore to what extent the European Convention on Human Rights (ECHR) and the case law of the European Court of Human Rights (ECtHR) also contribute to the 'Europeanisation' of private law. It will argue that, if the institutional framework of the EU represents the 'main door' for the harmonisation of private law in Europe, the ECHR may be described, in some circumstances, as the often overlooked 'back door'.[3]

In hindsight, it may appear surprising that the main promoter of legal harmonisation in Europe has been the EU rather than the Council of Europe, the organisation that gave birth to the ECHR. The European Economic Community, the predecessor of the EU, started off as a market-oriented organisation with the primary aim of furthering economic integration among European states. By contrast, the Council of Europe, established in 1949 in the immediate aftermath of World War II, had a broader focus from the outset. It sought to 'achieve a greater unity between its members', placing a great emphasis on the protection of human rights

---

[1] See, on this concept, J. BASEDOW, 'EU Private Law' in J. BASEDOW, K. HOPT and R. ZIMMERMANN (eds), *The Max Planck Encyclopedia of European Private Law*, OUP, Oxford 2012, pp. 537–41.

[2] OJ C 202, 7 June 2016, p. 47.

[3] The same metaphorical phrase is sometimes used in a different, yet similar, context, namely to describe the case law of the Court of Justice of the European Union relating to the Charter of Fundamental Rights of the European Union and its impact on the EU Member States' domestic private law: see O. MÖRSDORF, 'Europäisierung des Privatrechts durch die Hintertür?', *Juristenzeitung* 2019, 1066. The common feature is that, in both instances, harmonisation of private law results not from legislation, but from the jurisprudence of quasi-constitutional international courts – the ECtHR and the CJEU respectively – on the basis of human rights law.

and fundamental freedoms, as well as the rule of law and democracy.[4] The divergent approaches underlying the two organisations are also reflected by the fact that it was only one year after the foundation of the Council of Europe that the ECHR was adopted. Thus, the Convention was – and still is – at the very heart of that organisation. By contrast, it took the EU more than 40 years to elaborate a similar human rights instrument, namely the Charter of Fundamental Rights of the EU,[5] which became legally binding only after the entry into force of the Treaty of Lisbon in 2009. Nonetheless, the impact of the EU on domestic law has been significantly more substantial than that of the Council of Europe. A common market, one may argue, is a much more effective catalyst for legal convergence than common values.

As the number of cases brought before the ECtHR grows, so too does the impact of the Convention on national law – including national private law. Against this backdrop, it is worthwhile exploring the potential harmonising effects of the ECHR on national law, for two reasons in particular. First, if the Convention is indeed found to harmonise domestic private law, such harmonising effects would extend well beyond the boundaries of the EU, affecting all 46 Members States[6] of the Council of Europe, with an overall population of more than 600 million. Second, the ECHR could also impact fields of private law such as family law[7] or collective labour law, which have not, so far, been harmonised by the EU due to its lack of legislative power on these matters. Thus, with respect to some countries and certain areas of the law, the ECHR could represent not just the back door, but even the main door for European harmonisation.

This chapter is structured as follows: section 2 provides a brief overview of the main channels through which the Convention and the case law of the Strasbourg Court can contribute to the harmonisation of national private

---

[4] See Article 1 of the Statute of the Council of Europe of 5 May 1949, ETS No. 1, which sets out the aims of the Council of Europe. For a closer look at the goals pursued with the establishment of the Council of Europe, see E. BATES, *The Evolution of the European Convention on Human Rights*, OUP, Oxford 2010, pp. 49 *et seq.*

[5] OJ C 202, 7 June 2016, p. 391.

[6] Up until 2022, the Council of Europe had 47 Member States. However, following its aggression against Ukraine, the Russian Federation has been expelled from the Council of Europe, as of 16 March 2022. As a result, the Russian Federation is no longer a party to the ECHR.

[7] See G. RIXE, 'Der EGMR als Motor einer Harmonisierung des Familienrechts in Europa', *FPR* 2008, 222, who characterises the ECtHR as an 'engine of harmonisation of family law in Europe'.

law; sections 3 and 4 deal in more depth with the 'direct harmonising effects' and 'indirect harmonising effects' of the ECHR, respectively; finally, section 5 summarises the main findings of the chapter, and concludes with some general considerations on the topic.

2. THE CHANNELS OF HARMONISATION

Generally speaking, one can discern different channels through which the ECHR can produce harmonising effects on the States Parties' national private law.

2.1. DIRECT HARMONISATION

First, there is what will be referred to in this chapter as *direct harmonising effect*. This kind of harmonisation results from the fact that the private law of the Contracting States, as well as its application by national courts and other authorities, is subject to judicial scrutiny by the ECtHR.[8] Since the standard of judicial review adopted by the Strasbourg Court is a uniform minimum standard, applicable to all Contracting States – namely the rights and freedoms guaranteed by the Convention – it follows that the domestic legal systems of the various Contracting States must all satisfy, in principle, the same minimum requirements, to be assessed as being in conformity with the Convention. The result is clearly some sort of approximation between the Contracting States' domestic laws. The 'harmonising role' of the Convention's case law has been also highlighted by several judges of the Strasbourg Court, in their joint dissenting opinion in the case *A, B and C v. Ireland*:

> Indeed, one of the paramount functions of the case-law [of the ECtHR] is to gradually create a harmonious application of human rights protection, cutting across the national boundaries of the Contracting States and allowing the individuals within their jurisdiction to enjoy, without discrimination, equal protection regardless of their place of residence.[9]

---

[8] See, for a more detailed description of the judicial supervision exercised by the ECtHR in the realm of private law, M. FORNASIER and M.G. STANZIONE, 'The European Convention on Human Rights and its Impact on National Private Law: An Introduction', in this volume.

[9] Joint Dissenting Opinion of Judges Rozakis, Tulkens, Fura, Hirvelä, Malinverni and Poalelungi, *A, B and C v. Ireland*, no. 25579/05, § 5, ECtHR (GC) 16 December 2010.

It is important to note that, according to the settled case law of the ECtHR, the duty to respect the rights and freedoms under the Convention does not apply solely to national courts and other public authorities when they are handling individual cases. Rather, contrary to what the drafters envisaged at the time they elaborated the Convention, the ECHR is also binding on national legislatures.[10] This is especially true of the positive obligations arising from the Convention, which require the Contracting States to protect individuals in the enjoyment of the rights guaranteed under the Convention, not only against acts committed by public authorities, but also against interferences from private actors.[11] Thus, the ECtHR assumes the role of a 'quasi-constitutional court', also exercising supervision over the domestic legislation passed by the Contracting States.[12] As will be shown below, this aspect is crucial for the direct harmonising effects of the Convention on national private law.

2.2. INDIRECT HARMONISATION

The second channel through which the ECHR can produce harmonising effects is the law of the EU. Though, to date, the EU has not become a party to the ECHR, the Convention is formally embedded into the framework of EU law. Article 6(3) of the Treaty on European Union (TEU)[13] states that fundamental rights guaranteed by the Convention shall constitute general principles of EU law. Moreover, the 'equivalence clause' enshrined in Article 52(3) of the EU Charter of Fundamental Rights provides that, where the rights contained in the Charter correspond to rights and freedoms guaranteed by the ECHR, the meaning and scope of those rights shall be, as a minimum, the same as those laid down by the Convention. In other words, the Charter can be said to incorporate the human right guarantees of the Convention.[14] Thus, when called upon to interpret the

---

[10] This principle was acknowledged by the European Commission of Human Rights as early as 1958, in the case of *de Becker v. Belgium*, no. 214/56, ECommHR 9 June 1958, *International Law Reports* 25 (1958–I), 172, 180: '[T]he Convention is binding on all the authorities of the Contracting Parties, including the legislative authority.'
[11] See, on the concept of 'positive obligations', the groundbreaking decision *Marckx v. Belgium*, no. 6833/74, § 31, ECtHR 13 June 1979.
[12] See, on this particular aspect, E. BATES, above n. 4, pp. 157 *et seq.*
[13] OJ C 202, 7 June 2017, p. 15.
[14] This is the language used by the German Federal Constitutional Court to describe the relationship between the Convention and the Charter: see BVerfGE 152, 152, para. 57 = *NJW 2020*, 300.

content of the EU Charter of Fundamental Rights, the European Court of Justice (CJEU), as well as the national courts of the Member States, have to consider the corresponding rights and freedoms under the Convention, and take into account the apposite case law of the ECtHR. As legislative acts adopted by the EU are to be interpreted and applied in a manner consistent with EU primary law, including the EU Charter of Fundamental Rights,[15] it follows from what has been said above that the ECHR has a bearing on the interpretation and application of EU law, and the Member States' national laws transposing EU law. This may be referred to as the *indirect harmonising effect*, as the ECHR affects domestic law not directly, but only through the framework of EU law. Obviously, this channel of harmonisation does not encompass all States Parties to the Convention, but is limited to the Member States of the EU.

2.3. SOFT HARMONISATION

Finally, one can discern a third way in which the ECHR contributes to legal convergence across Europe. The Convention serves not only as a yardstick for scrutinising the Contracting States' domestic laws, and for concretising, in accordance with Article 6(3) TEU and Article 52(3) of the EU Charter of Fundamental Rights, the fundamental rights guaranteed under EU law. The Convention also has an impact on the evolution of the law in Europe, as it embodies constitutional values and principles of justice that are fundamental for liberal and democratic societies. Thus, it has been argued that the normative framework established by the Convention can constitute a key element for the creation of a common European legal culture, and thus fill a gap left by EU law, which is often considered to be a 'technocratic' legal order, dealing primarily with specific market-related issues.[16]

The values and principles embodied in the Convention constitute important guidelines for domestic courts, especially where they face the task of interpreting the law in light of international legal trends or changing moral views on issues such as family law, protection of personality rights, or workers' rights. The case law of the German Federal Constitutional Court (FCC)

---

[15] See, e.g. CJEU Case C-131/12, *Google Spain SL and Google Inc. v. Agencia Española de Protección de Datos (AEPD) and Mario Costeja González*, ECLI:EU:C:2014:317, para. 68; see also CJEU Case C-684/16, *Max-Planck-Gesellschaft zur Förderung der Wissenschaften eV v. Tetsuji Shimizu*, paras. 57 *et seq.*

[16] J. BASEDOW, 'Europäische Menschenrechtskonvention und Europäisches Privatrecht', *RabelsZ* 63 (1999), 409, 412.

provides an illustration of how the Convention may be relied upon to further develop national law. According to the Constitutional Court, the provisions of the German Constitution are to be interpreted in a manner that is 'open to international law'.[17] In particular, the Constitutional Court emphasises that the ECHR and the jurisprudence of the ECtHR serve as 'guidelines' for the interpretation of the fundamental rights and freedoms enshrined in domestic constitutional law.[18] The German doctrine of the legal order's 'openness' to international law makes it possible for national courts to incorporate the values and principles underlying the ECHR into domestic law, and to keep pace with international trends and developments in the protection of human rights, thus aligning national and international protection standards. An illustrative example is the decision of the German Federal Court of Justice on the recognition of a foreign judgment establishing legal parenthood of the intended parents of a child born abroad through gestational surrogacy.[19] Although the law in Germany bans surrogacy agreements, and hence does not confer parenthood on the intended parents, the Federal Court of Justice held that the judgment, delivered by a court in California, was not contrary to German public policy and, therefore, also had to be recognised in Germany. When assessing whether the establishment of the legal parent–child relationship between the twins and the intended parents was in line with public policy, the Federal Court of Justice, drawing upon the notion of German law's 'openness' to international law, relied heavily on the right to private and family life under Article 8 of the Convention, and the interpretation given to that provision by the ECtHR in *Mennesson v. France*.[20]

Moreover, it should be noted that using the ECHR as a guideline for the interpretation of fundamental rights under domestic law has the additional side effect of bringing domestic law and EU law into line with one another, given that the rights flowing from the EU Charter of Fundamental Rights are to be construed in conformity with corresponding rights enshrined in the Convention.[21]

---

[17] BVerfGE 148, 296 para. 126 = *NJW* 2018, 2695.
[18] Ibid.
[19] BGHZ 203, 350 = *NJW* 2015, 479.
[20] *Mennesson v. France*, no. 65192/11, ECtHR 26 June 2014.
[21] This aspect has been emphasised recently by the German Constitutional Court: see BVerfGE 152, 152, para. 58 = *NJW 2020*, 300: 'Just as the Convention serves as a guiding principle for the Charter, the fundamental rights of the Basic Law, too, are interpreted in light of the Convention. ... However, this shows that the fundamental rights of the Basic Law, just like the fundamental rights of the Charter, are interpreted and applied in light of the European Convention on Human Rights and generally incorporate its guarantees.'

In addition to stimulating judicial dialogue between domestic and European courts, the jurisprudence of the Strasbourg Court may also have an impact on domestic legislation. Some landmark cases brought before the ECtHR may trigger public debates on certain human rights issues and eventually give rise to legislative initiatives aimed at improving the protection of human rights. Thus, the adoption of EU Directive 2019/1937 on the protection of persons who report breaches of Union law[22] may be viewed as a response to recent rulings of the ECtHR strengthening the position of whistle-blowers.[23]

It is important to bear in mind that the kind of harmonising effect discussed here differs from the models of direct and indirect harmonisation described above. The difference lies in the fact that, when courts draw upon the values enshrined in the ECHR to interpret their national laws, or when legislatures refer to the Convention when amending existing laws, or passing new laws, they often go beyond what the Convention requires them to do. Often, such state practice merely relies on *obiter dicta* by the Strasbourg Court. Moreover, as will be shown below, the ECtHR generally grants to the Contracting States a wide margin of appreciation as to how to protect the rights guaranteed by the Convention. Nonetheless, the Contracting States may sometimes choose not to make use of the latitude in judgment conceded to them. In the case on gestational surrogacy mentioned above, protection of the child's rights under Article 8 ECHR did not necessarily require recognition of the Californian judgment establishing legal parenthood of the intended parents. As the ECtHR has pointed out in other cases, the legal family ties between the child and the intended parents may be also established through adoption[24] or foster parenting.[25] However, the German Federal Court of Justice took a narrower view,[26] arguing that, to protect the child's best interests under Article 8 ECHR, the legal parenthood of the intended parents established through the foreign court decision had to be recognised.

---

[22] Directive (EU) 2019/1937 of the European Parliament and of the Council of 23 October 2019 on the protection of persons who report breaches of Union law.

[23] *Heinisch v. Germany*, no. 28274/08, ECtHR 21 July 2011; *Guja v. Moldova*, no. 14277/04, ECtHR (GC), 12 February 2008. See also the reference to the case law of the ECtHR in Recital 31 of Directive (EU) 2019/1937.

[24] Advisory Opinion, P16-2018-001, §§ 48 *et seq.*, ECtHR (GC) 10 April 2019; *D v. France*, no. 11288/18, §§ 63 *et seq.*, ECtHR 16 July 2020.

[25] *Valdís Fjölnisdóttir and Others v. Iceland*, no. 71552/17, §§ 71 *et seq.*, ECtHR 18 May 2021.

[26] T. HELMS, 'Elternteil in einem Staat – Elternteil in jedem Staat (der EU)?' *ZEuP* 2022, 747, 749.

A similar example is provided by a recent ruling of the Austrian Constitutional Court. The case concerned the rules on filiation in the Austrian Civil Code. According to Article 144 of the Code, the man married to the mother of the child at the time of birth is recognised *ex lege* as the legal father of the child. In case the biological mother of the child lives in a registered same-sex partnership, the partner is recognised as parent *ex lege* only where the mother can prove that the pregnancy resulted from assisted reproductive treatment. Thus, access to legal parenthood for the spouse of the child's mother is easier in an opposite-sex partnership than in a same-sex partnership. Against this background, the Austrian Constitutional Court declared Article 144 of the Civil Code void, arguing that the provision was discriminatory against same-sex couples and thus violated the prohibition of discrimination under Article 14 ECHR as well as the right to respect of private and family life under Article 8 ECHR.[27] Again, it seems doubtful whether the ECtHR would have arrived at the same conclusion, especially if one bears in mind that the Court usually affords a broad margin of discretion to Contracting States where delicate moral and ethical issues are at stake, such as reproductive rights and parental rights of same-sex couples.[28] While it is safe to assume that the Strasbourg Court would require Contracting States to offer, within their domestic law, the possibility to establish some kind of legal relationship between the child and the same-sex partner of the child's mother where the two have developed *de facto* family ties, it is rather unlikely that the Court would prescribe the particular legal mechanism through which such legal relationship should be achieved, e.g. through an *ex lege* recognition of the parenthood of the mother's partner, through the voluntary acknowledgement of parenthood, or through adoption.[29]

What the aforementioned examples show is that national courts and other authorities, when assuming human rights friendly positions, sometimes rely on the ECHR, not because they are legally obliged to do so in the given circumstances, but instead because they regard the Convention and the Strasbourg Court as an authoritative institution in the

---

[27] VfGH 30 June 2022 – G 230/2021-20.
[28] *S.H. and Others v. Austria*, no. 57813/00, § 97, ECtHR (GC) 3 November 2011.
[29] See also *Boeckel and Gessner-Boeckel v. Germany*, no. 8017/11, ECtHR 7 May 2013, where the Court, in a case similar to that decided by the Austrian Constitutional Court, denied there had been a violation of the Convention, highlighting the fact that the partner of the biological mother of the child had been given the possibility to adopt the child.

field of human rights law, compliance with which is deemed desirable from a political point of view. Thus, the harmonising effect described here may be referred to as *soft harmonisation*. While the distinction between *hard* and *soft harmonisation* appears quite clear in theory, it is admittedly more difficult to distinguish between the two concepts in practice: in the cases outlined above, the national authorities may have *felt* under an obligation to follow the case law of the ECtHR, even though, objectively, such an obligation does not exist.

The following sections 3 and 4 will deal in more depth with the channels of 'hard harmonisation', namely the direct and the indirect harmonising effects.

3. DIRECT HARMONISING EFFECTS

The 'direct' harmonising effects on domestic law, resulting from the case law of the ECtHR, can relate either to procedural issues or to substantive law.

3.1. HARMONISATION IN PROCEDURE

Viewed through the lens of human rights law, private law is about striking a fair balance between competing fundamental individual rights and interests. This is true for the legislature, which seeks to regulate private relations, and it is equally true for courts, who are called on to settle disputes between private parties. Thus, in private law disputes, the task of the Strasbourg Court is usually to assess whether the authorities of the respondent state – generally the legislature or the judiciary – have struck a fair balance between the competing human rights of the parties involved.

In this context, the Court usually reiterates that, in accordance with the principle of subsidiarity, the States Parties enjoy a 'margin of appreciation'[30] when it comes to striking a balance between competing rights and interests.[31] Nonetheless, the ECtHR reserves the right to exercise what it refers to as 'European supervision' over how the respondent state has

---

[30] The 'margin of appreciation' doctrine, which is closely intertwined with the principle of subsidiarity, has recently been inserted into the preamble of the Convention through Protocol No. 15, which entered into force on 1 August 2021.

[31] See, in the context of the right to respect of private life under Article 8 of the Convention, *X and Y v. Netherlands*, no. 8978/80, § 24, ECtHR 26 March 1985: 'The Court ... observes that the choice of the means calculated to secure compliance with

weighed up the interests at stake.³² The supervision is primarily concerned with procedural issues:³³ the Court examines whether the domestic authorities have identified the interests at stake, whether they have attached sufficient weight to those interests, and whether they have made efforts to achieve a proper balance between those interests.³⁴ Thus, the ECtHR is not concerned with the outcome of the balancing test *in casu* – whether the national authorities were right to value the rights and interests of individual A over the competing rights and interests of individual B;³⁵ rather, the Court inquires whether the domestic authorities have provided a plausible explanation as to why they gave priority to the interests of party A over those of party B.

Especially in the context of the right to respect for family life under Article 8 of the Convention, the ECtHR has often emphasised that the Convention gives rise to 'procedural obligations'.³⁶ This is particularly true

---

Article 8 (art. 8) in the sphere of the relations of individuals between themselves is in principle a matter that falls within the Contracting States' margin of appreciation.'; *Evans v. United Kingdom*, no. 6449/05, §§ 77 et seq., ECtHR (GC) 10 April 2007; similarly, in the context of Articles 9 and 11 of the Convention, *Sindicatul 'Păstorul Cel Bun' v. Romania*, no. 2330/09, § 160, ECtHR (GC) 9 July 2013: '[T]he State generally enjoys a wide margin of appreciation ... where a balance has to be struck between competing private interests or different Convention rights.'

32 *López Ribalda and others v. Spain*, nos. 1874/13, 8567/13, § 111, ECtHR (GC) 17 October 2019; *Eweida and Others v. United Kingdom*, nos. 48420/10, 36516/10, 51671/10 and 36516/10, § 84, ECtHR 15 January 2013; *Von Hannover v. Germany (no. 2)*, nos. 40660/08 and 60641/08, § 105, ECtHR (GC) 7 February 2012.

33 See, for a more general analysis of the 'procedural approach' in the more recent case law of the ECtHR, T. KLEINLEIN, 'The Procedural Approach of the European Court of Human Rights: Between Subsidiarity and Dynamic Evolution' (2019) 68 *Int'l & Comp. L.Q.* 90; A. NUSSBERGER, *The European Court of Human Rights*, OUP, Oxford 2020, pp. 94 and 98–101; see also the contributions by E. BREMS, 'The "Logics" of Procedural-Type Review by the European Court of Human Rights'; J. GERRARDS, 'Procedural Review by the ECtHR: A Typology'; and A. NUSSBERGER, 'Procedural Review by the ECHR: View from the Court' in J. GERRARDS and E. BREMS (eds), *Procedural Review in European Fundamental Rights Cases*, CUP, Cambridge 2017.

34 See, e.g. *Sahin v. Germany*, no. 30943/96, § 66, ECtHR (GC) 8 July 2003 ('Article 8 requires that the domestic authorities should strike a fair balance between the interests of the child and those of the parents and that, in the balancing process, particular importance should be attached to the best interests of the child, which, depending on their nature and seriousness, may override those of the parents.').

35 A. NUSSBERGER, 'Die Europäische Menschenrechtskonvention und das Privatrecht', *RabelsZ* 80 (2016), 817, 824.

36 See, e.g. *Wetjen and Others v. Germany*, nos. 68125/14 and 72204/14, § 70, ECtHR 22 March 2018 ('The Court further notes that while Article 8 contains no explicit procedural requirements, the decision-making process involved in measures of interference must be fair and such as to afford due respect to the interests safeguarded by Article 8.').

for cases concerning the withdrawal of child custody or parental access rights.[37] Here, the Court generally states that its task is not to take the place of national authorities but, rather, to review the decision-making process of the national authorities in the case at issue. In *Petrov and X v. Russia*, a case involving a residence order for a child, by a Russian court in favour of the child's mother, the ECtHR held that its role was limited to:

> determin[ing] whether the reasons adduced by the domestic courts in child residence proceedings were relevant and sufficient. In particular, the Court has competence to ascertain whether the domestic courts, when taking such a decision, conducted an in-depth examination of the entire family situation and a whole series of relevant factors and made a balanced and reasonable assessment of the respective interests of each person, with a constant concern for determining what the best solution would be for the child. A failure to make a sufficiently thorough examination will amount to a violation of Article 8.[38]

On a similar note, the Court often stresses that, in order to effectively protect the rights and freedoms under the Convention in private relations, the Contracting States must set up 'a legislative framework taking into consideration the various interests to be protected in a particular context'.[39] Here, again, the Court does not specify the substantive content of such a legislative instrument: it does not specify the mutual rights of the parties involved, and, in particular, the degree of protection to be afforded to a certain right. Rather, the requirement to pass legislation regulating the conflicting private interests is a mere procedural requirement designed to safeguard the rights protected under the Convention against arbitrary interference from private parties, and also to promote clarity and predictability in private relations.[40] Similarly, the ECtHR has, on some occasions, held that certain rights guaranteed by the Convention need to be protected against infringements by private individuals, through

---

[37] See on this aspect K. DUDEN, 'Parental Autonomy and Child Protection Measures: Procedural and Substantive Standards', in this volume.

[38] *Petrov and X v. Russia*, no. 23608/16, § 106, ECtHR 23 October 2018.

[39] *Bărbulescu v. Romania*, no. 61496/08, § 115, ECtHR (GC) 5 September 2017; see also *Codarcea v. Romania*, no. 31675/04, § 102, ECtHR 2 June 2009; *López Ribalda and others v. Spain*, nos. 1874/13, 8567/13, § 113, ECtHR (GC) 17 October 2019.

[40] See also, on this issue, *Evans v. United Kingdom*, no. 6449/05, § 89, ECtHR (GC) 10 April 2007.

criminal law provisions.⁴¹ Here, again, the Court is primarily concerned with the form, and not the substance, of the regulatory measures Contracting States must adopt in order to fulfil the positive obligations arising from the Convention. Another example of this type of case law is the Court's ruling in *Schüth v. Germany*, a case involving an organist employed by the Catholic Church who had been dismissed for having an extramarital relationship.⁴² When assessing whether the dismissal violated the organist's right to respect for his private life under Article 8 of the Convention, the Court noted that:

> by putting in place both a system of employment tribunals and a constitutional court having jurisdiction to review their decisions, Germany has in theory complied with its positive obligations towards citizens in the area of labour law, an area in which disputes generally affect the rights of the persons concerned under Article 8 of the Convention. In the present case the applicant was thus able to bring his case before an employment tribunal, which had to determine whether the dismissal was lawful under ordinary domestic labour law, while having regard to ecclesiastical labour law, and to balance the competing interests of the applicant and the employing Church.⁴³

That said, the Court found a violation of the applicant's rights under the Convention, on the grounds that the domestic courts in Germany had failed to explain why the rights of the employing Church outweighed the rights of the applicant.⁴⁴

This line of case law reflects a deferential approach by the Strasbourg Court. By applying a standard of judicial review which is procedural rather than substantive in nature, the Court grants to domestic authorities a significant degree of leeway when it comes to delineating the scope of the various Convention rights, and striking a fair balance between them where they clash. Accordingly, the Court stresses that its 'task is not to substitute itself for the competent national authorities in determining the most appropriate policy for regulating' conflicting individual rights and interests.⁴⁵

---

41   *X and Y v. Netherlands*, no. 8978/80, § 27, ECtHR 26 March 1985; *Nicolae Virgiliu Tănase v. Romania*, no. 41720/13, § 115, ECtHR (GC) 25 June 2019.
42   For a more detailed analysis of this case, see section 4.2. below.
43   *Schüth v. Germany*, no. 1620/03, § 59, ECtHR 23 September 2010.
44   Ibid., § 74.
45   *Valdís Fjölnisdóttir and others v. Iceland*, no. 71552/17, § 67, ECtHR 18 May 2021.

3.2. HARMONISATION IN SUBSTANTIVE LAW

In some cases, the ECtHR assumes a less restrained role and sets up substantive requirements for the protection of human rights, thus contributing to the harmonisation of substantive private law in Europe. From a methodological point of view, these harmonising effects rest on two important principles embraced by the Court, namely the principles of autonomous interpretation and evolutive interpretation of the Convention.

3.2.1. Harmonising Effects Resulting from Autonomous Interpretation of the Convention

In the case law of the Court, the method of *autonomous interpretation* is crucial to determining the scope of the entitlements granted by the Convention. The Court's ruling in *Sindicatul Păstorul Cel Bun v. Romania* illustrates this approach. In this case, the Court had to decide whether a trade union founded by priests and other members of the clergy of the Romanian Orthodox Church fell within the scope of Article 11 of the Convention, which guarantees freedom of association and, in particular, the right to form and join trade unions. The Court took the view that this depended on whether the members of the clergy could be said to be in an employment relationship with their Church.[46] At the level of national law, views differ quite considerably among European jurisdictions as to whether priests and other members of the clergy are to be classified as 'employees', and thus whether they fall within the ambit of (domestic) labour law.[47] For the ECtHR, however, the classification of employment status under national law was of no relevance. In order to assess whether the priests had the status of employees, the Court did not refer to the applicable national law – *in casu* to Romanian law; instead, it opted for an autonomous interpretation of the concept of an employment relationship, relying on criteria set out in international instruments such as the Recommendations and Conventions of the International Labour Organization. Based on

---

[46] *Sindicatul 'Păstorul Cel Bun' v. Romania*, no. 2330/09, §§ 141 et seq., ECtHR (GC) 9 July 2013.

[47] In Germany, for instance, members of the clergy are generally not regarded as being employees: see the ruling by the Federal Labour Court BAG, *NJW* 1990, 2082, 2083. The courts in Romania, on the other hand, seem to take the opposite view: see the references in *Sindicatul 'Păstorul Cel Bun' v. Romania*, no. 2330/09, §§ 27 et seq., ECtHR (GC) 9 July 2013.

these criteria, the Court arrived at the conclusion that priests were indeed employees and, therefore, could invoke the right to form a trade union under the Convention. The result of this case law is that collective labour rights under Article 11 of the Convention are also applicable to individuals who belong to occupational groups whose members do not qualify as employees under the relevant national law, and so fall outside the sphere of domestic employment law. As the above example shows, the method of autonomous interpretation bridges differences between national legal systems, by ensuring that individuals enjoy the rights and freedoms under the Convention regardless of whether these individuals are entitled to the corresponding rights guaranteed by domestic law.

Similar observations can be made with regard to the concept of 'family life' in Article 8 of the Convention. The Court interprets this term in an autonomous manner, in such a way as to also cover de facto relationships which the applicable national law does not formally acknowledge as family relationships.[48] This is true, for example, for same-sex couples in jurisdictions which restrict access to marriage to opposite-sex couples, and which lack other forms of legal recognition for same-sex relationships, such as civil unions or registered partnerships.[49] Likewise, the Court has held that the concept of 'family life' encompasses the relationship between a child born out of wedlock, on the one hand, and his or her natural parents,[50] as well as the natural parents' relatives, on the other hand, even where the relevant national law does not establish a legal relationship between such persons.[51] In such cases, the positive obligations arising from Article 8 ECHR may require the national legislature to accord certain family rights[52] to de facto relationships or, alternatively, to enable the parties involved

---

[48] *Marckx v. Belgium*, no. 6833/74, § 31, ECtHR 13 June 1979; *Kroon and Others v. The Netherlands*, no. 18535/91, § 30, ECtHR 27 October 1994.

[49] *Schalk and Kopf v. Austria*, no. 30141, § 94, ECtHR 24 June 2010; *Vallianatos and Others v. Greece*, nos. 29381/09 and 32684/09, § 73, ECtHR (GC) 7 November 2013; *Oliari and Others v. Italy*, nos. 18766/11 and 36030/11, § 103, ECtHR 21 July 2015. For more details, see M.G. STANZIONE, 'Shaping New Families: Same-Sex Couples' Rights in the Dialogue between the Courts', in this volume.

[50] See on the ECtHR's case law on parental rights of biological, but non-legal, fathers A. DUTTA, 'The Status of Biological Fathers: An Example for the Impact of the European Convention on Human Rights on National Family Law', in this volume.

[51] *Keegan v. Ireland*, no. 16969/90, § 44, ECtHR 26 May 1994; *Chavdarov v. Bulgaria*, no. 3465/03, § 40, ECtHR 21 December 2010.

[52] See *Marckx v. Belgium*, no. 6833/74, § 31, ECtHR 13 June 1979, regarding statutory inheritance rights.

to create legal family ties between them, for example through registered partnerships,[53] the recognition of parenthood, etc.[54] Thus, the method of autonomous interpretation has the effect of providing a European minimum standard of family law protection to people who, despite having biological or social family ties, lack a legally recognised family status in the relevant national jurisdiction. In this respect, the case law of the ECtHR results in harmonisation of the rights of, and protections for, individuals, not only from a procedural point of view, but also in substance.

3.2.2. The Inductive Approach: Harmonising Effects Resulting from the Notion of 'European Consensus'

A second element in the case law of the ECtHR, favouring the harmonisation of private law in the Contracting States, is the doctrine of evolutive interpretation of the Convention. As the Court famously spelt out in *Tyrer v. United Kingdom*, and has reiterated on many occasions ever since, the Convention 'is a living instrument which … must be interpreted in the light of present-day conditions'.[55] When interpreting the provisions of the Convention, the Court looks at the overall legal picture, also taking into account legal sources other than the Convention itself, and assessing how the law in the area at issue has evolved both at the international and national levels. Thus, current legal trends and developments affect the way the Court interprets the Convention. In particular, the Court often looks for a 'European consensus' among Contracting States on certain values, principles or rules. Where such consensus is found already to exist or – more likely – to be in the process of emerging, the Court tends to be less deferential to national courts and authorities when concretising the rights and freedoms guaranteed by the Convention: the broader the consensus among Contracting States, the narrower the margin of appreciation granted to them. Thus, if a state engages in practices that deviate from the European consensus, such practices are likely to be judged in breach of the Convention by the Court. By contrast, where there is no common ground among Contracting States on a given issue, and the approaches taken by the domestic legal systems differ significantly from each other, the Court will usually grant a wider margin of appreciation to the respondent state,

---

[53] *Oliari and Others v. Italy*, nos. 18766/11 and 36030/11, § 174, ECtHR 21 July 2015.
[54] *Kroon and Others v. The Netherlands*, no. 18535/91, § 36, ECtHR 27 October 1994, regarding the right of a natural father to have his fatherhood recognised.
[55] *Tyrer v. United Kingdom*, no. 5856/72, § 31, ECtHR 25 April 1978.

and refrain from setting up substantive requirements for the protection of the rights and interests at issue.

Two examples, both from labour law, may be illustrative. In the case *Sørensen and Rasmussen v. Denmark*, the Court was confronted with a Danish law which permitted the conclusion of closed-shop agreements between trade unions and employers. Under such an agreement, the employer would promise to solely hire and employ workers who were members of the trade union that was party to the agreement. The ECtHR had to examine whether the Danish law permitting such agreements violated freedom of association under Article 11 of the Convention. In most European countries, closed-shop agreements are deemed contrary to negative freedom of association, i.e. the right of individual workers not to be compelled to join a trade union, which is generally also protected under Article 11 of the Convention.[56] The Strasbourg Court found that Denmark, by allowing closed-shop agreements, had violated Article 11 of the Convention. One major argument the Court relied upon was the fact that the Danish position on the legality of closed-shop agreements ran contrary to the law and practice in the majority of Contracting States. The Court noted that closed-shop agreements were inconsistent with other instruments of international and European law, such as the European Social Charter,[57] the Community Charter of the Fundamental Social Rights of Workers,[58] and the Charter of Fundamental Rights of the EU. Against this backdrop, the Court concluded that, 'it appears that there is little support in the Contracting States for the maintenance of closed-shop agreements'.[59]

In the case of *National Union of Rail, Maritime and Transport Workers (RMT) v. United Kingdom*,[60] on the other hand, the Court had to deal with a statutory ban on secondary strike action under UK law. Secondary strike action, sometimes also referred to as 'sympathy action' or 'solidarity action', is a form of industrial action aimed at supporting workers employed by a different employer, in their quest for better working conditions. Unlike in a primary strike, in which the workers involved refuse to work, in order

---

[56] *Sigurður A. Sigurjónsson v. Iceland*, no. 16130/90, § 35, ECtHR 30 June 1993.
[57] European Social Charter of 18 October 1961, ETS No. 35, and European Social Charter (Revised) of 3 May 1996, ETS No. 163.
[58] COM(89) 254 final.
[59] *Sørensen and Rasmussen v. Denmark*, nos. 52562/99 and 52620/99, § 75, ECtHR (GC) 11 January 2006.
[60] *National Union of Rail, Maritime and Transport Workers (RMT) v. United Kingdom*, no. 31045/10, ECtHR 8 April 2014.

to obtain better terms of employment for themselves, the workers taking secondary action seek to strengthen the bargaining position of the workers involved in the primary dispute vis-à-vis their own employer. Secondary action often occurs in the context of maritime employment: if the crew of a cargo ship goes on strike to obtain, say, better pay from the shipowner, the dock workers employed in the port where the ship is moored may decide to join in the collective action and refuse to load or unload the ship, thus increasing the economic pressure on the shipowner. The side effect of such form of action is that the employer of the workers taking secondary action – in the aforementioned example, the company running the port – is equally affected by the strike, even though they are not a party to the industrial dispute. This is why, in the UK and many other jurisdictions, secondary strike actions are either banned altogether, or are subject to legal restrictions. In the *RMT* case, the applicant trade union took the view that the UK rules prohibiting secondary action violated the right to freedom of association under Article 11 of the ECHR. The union relied heavily on the case of *Enerji Yapı-Yol Sen v. Turkey*, in which the Court, only five years earlier, had famously acknowledged that freedom of association under Article 11 of the Convention also comprised the right to strike.[61] That ruling, however, had been concerned with primary strike action. In *RMT*, the Court clarified that secondary industrial action also falls within the ambit of trade union activities protected by Article 11 ECHR. The key question was whether the statutory ban on secondary strike action was a legitimate measure adopted by the national legislature to safeguard third party interests, in particular the economic interests of the employers who, without being connected to the industrial dispute, were nonetheless affected by the strike action. The Court reiterated its well-settled case law, according to which national authorities enjoy a margin of appreciation when they are faced with the task of striking a balance between competing rights and interests: in the case at issue, trade unions' right to strike and the economic interests of employers. The breadth of the margin depended on a variety of factors, one being the 'degree of common ground between the Member States of the Council of Europe'.[62] With regard to secondary strike action, the Court observed that there was a 'high degree of divergence ... between the domestic systems in this field'.[63] In the absence of a European consensus on the lawfulness

---

[61] *Enerji Yapı-Yol Sen v. Turkey*, no. 68959/01, § 24, ECtHR 21 April 2009.
[62] *National Union of Rail, Maritime and Transport Workers (RMT) v. United Kingdom*, no. 31045/10, § 86, ECtHR 8 April 2014.
[63] Ibid.

of secondary industrial action, the Court was satisfied that the statutory ban on this form of collective action, under UK law, was a legitimate interference with freedom of association, as the UK legislature had struck a fair balance between the competing rights and interests at stake. In sum, the Court found no violation of Article 11 of the Convention.[64]

Though the doctrine of 'European consensus' is highly controversial, and raises a number of methodological questions which cannot be addressed here,[65] it shows quite clearly that the Court is well aware of the impact its case law has on the Contracting States' domestic legal systems. Where approaches to a certain private law issue are inconsistent among the Contracting States, the Court is reluctant to set rigid substantive standards and, therefore, gives considerable leeway to national authorities as to how to balance the competing rights and interests at issue. The focus of judicial review is on procedural aspects, rather than on the outcome of the balancing test. However, the situation is different where legal convergence exists among the Contracting States: here, the Court tends to show significantly less judicial restraint, and to be more specific about which rights and interests should take precedence in the balancing test. The effect of this approach is to force Contracting States whose practices deviate from the European consensus on the protection of human rights to adhere to the common standards. Thus, the degree to which the case law of the ECtHR contributes to the harmonisation of substantive private law in Europe varies; where national laws and values are in the process of converging, the jurisprudence of the Strasbourg Court has the effect of further intensifying such developments. Conversely, substantive harmonisation is all but absent where the national legal orders differ from each other in the ways that they regulate private law relationships, and in such cases no trend towards approximation is in sight.

---

[64] The Court has also taken a similar approach in other recent cases concerning collective labour law: see *Trade Unions (LO) and Norwegian Transport Workers' Union (NTF) v. Norway*, no. 45487/17, § 97, ECtHR 10 June 2021 (on the lawfulness of a boycott by a trade union); *Association of Civil Servants and Union for Collective Bargaining and Others v. Germany*, nos. 815/18, 3278/18, 12380/18, 12693/18, 14883/18, § 55, ECtHR 5 July 2022 (on a German statute giving precedence to collective agreements concluded by the largest trade union in the relevant business unit).

[65] See G. LETSAS, *A Theory of Interpretation of the European Convention on Human Rights*, OUP, Oxford 2007, pp. 120 et seq.; A. NUSSBERGER, *The European Court of Human Rights* (above n. 33), p. 86; L. WILDHABER, A. HJARTARSON and S. DONNELLY, 'No Consensus on Consensus – The Practice of the European Court of Human Rights' (2012) 33 *HRLJ* 248; see also F. VIGLIONE, 'Comparative Law at the European Court of Human Rights: Does Context Still Matter?', in this volume.

3.2.3. Inconsistencies in the Court's Case Law: The Deductive Approach

The Court's case law, however, is not always consistent. In some decisions, the Court has set out quite rigid substantive criteria on how conflicting interests should be balanced, without bothering whether its approach reflects an existing or emerging European consensus. A prominent example is the case of *Von Hannover v. Germany*,[66] based on an application by Princess Caroline of Monaco, where the Court found that German courts, including the FCC, had violated the right to respect for private and family life, under Article 8 of the Convention, by allowing the press to publish certain pictures of the applicant's private life. The Court held that, when balancing freedom of the press, protected under Article 10 of the Convention, against the applicant's right to privacy, German courts had failed to attach sufficient weight to the latter. As the photographs at issue pictured the princess in a purely private context, and were totally unrelated to her official role as a representative of the State of Monaco, the publication of the photos was not justified by a public interest. Thus, in the Court's view, the right to respect for private life should have trumped the freedom of the press.[67] What is remarkable about this decision is that the ECtHR, unlike in other cases concerning private law relationships, did not confine itself to setting out open-ended procedural requirements for the balancing test, but, rather, gave clear instructions as to which of the competing rights had to prevail. Furthermore, the Court, also in contrast to its other rulings, refrained from conducting a comparative analysis examining whether the solution it prescribed was in line with the law in the bulk of Contracting States. In fact, the approach taken by the Court in the *Von Hannover* case, in particular the strong weight attached to the protection of private life, in the absence of a 'general interest' in publication of the photographs, does not appear to reflect common ground among European states. As commentators have pointed out,[68] the reasoning of the ECtHR seems primarily to reflect the legal position adopted by the French courts on the issue.

---

[66] *Von Hannover v. Germany*, no. 59320/00, ECtHR 24 June 2004.

[67] For more details on the ECtHR's case law on the protection of the right to privacy K. DE LA DURANTAYE, 'Shaping the Right to Privacy: The Interplay between Karlsruhe, Strasbourg, and Luxembourg', in this volume; see also C. SCHMITT-MÜCKE, *Persönlichkeitsschutz und Presseberichterstattung im deutschen und italienischen Recht*, Nomos, Baden-Baden 2023, pp. 155 et seq.; 200 et seq.

[68] S. ENGELS and U. JÜRGENS, 'Auswirkungen der EGMR-Rechtsprechung zum Privatsphärenschutz – Möglichkeiten und Grenzen der Umsetzung des „Caroline"-Urteils im deutschen Recht', *NJW* 2007, 2517.

It is true that the Strasbourg Court does not always refer to the doctrine of European consensus when called on to assess whether the laws or practices of a Contracting State violate the Convention. Especially where 'core rights', such as the right to life or the prohibition of torture and slavery, are concerned, the ECtHR generally adopts an 'autonomous' standard of review, based on criteria formulated by the Court itself; whether or not the values embraced by the Court are broadly shared among European States is of little or no relevance.[69] The *Von Hannover* case, however, did not centre on such core fundamental rights. Rather, it involved the conflict between two rights which do not fall under the category of 'core rights', namely the right to protection of private and family life under Article 8, and freedom of expression under Article 10 of the Convention. It is important to recall that the Court generally grants a margin of appreciation to national authorities where such a clash of competing rights and interests arises.[70] Against this backdrop, it comes as a surprise that, although the German courts had conducted a thorough balancing test, the Strasbourg Court found a violation of the Convention on the grounds that the protection of private life outweighed the freedom of the press. By second-guessing the outcome of the balancing test conducted by the German courts, the ECtHR essentially substituted itself for the domestic judiciary, and thus performed a role it is generally reluctant to assume.[71] Thus, unlike in the *Sørensen* and *RMT* cases mentioned above,[72] where the Court took an inductive

---

[69] See, on the distinction between 'core' or 'absolute' rights, on the one hand, and 'qualified rights' (such as Articles 8, 9 and 10 ECHR), on the other, and the different degrees of discretion accorded to national authorities with regard to the protection of these distinct categories of rights, R. SPANO, 'The Future of the European Court of Human Rights – Subsidiarity, Process-Based Review and the Rule of Law' (2018) 18 HRL Rev. 473, 483.

[70] See above n. 31.

[71] See section 3.2.2. above. In a similar case, involving the same applicant and decided a few years later, the Court appeared to adopt a more deferential approach, and to grant more discretion to domestic courts: see *Von Hannover v. Germany (No. 2)*, nos. 40660/08 and 60641/08, ECtHR (GC) 7 February 2012. However, one important reason for the Court's restraint in this case seems to be that the German courts, whose case law on the protection of private life against media reports was, again, at the centre of the dispute, had indeed changed their approach to comply with the judgment of the Strasbourg Court in the earlier *Von Hannover* case. The Court stressed that, '[w]here the balancing exercise has been undertaken by the national authorities in conformity with the criteria laid down in the Court's case-law, the Court would require strong reasons to substitute its view for that of the domestic courts' (see para. 107 of the judgment). Thus, the Court did not abandon the rigid substantive standard of review adopted in the earlier case.

[72] See section 3.2.2.

(bottom-up) approach, inferring the scope of the rights guaranteed by the Convention from legal developments both in international law, and in the Contracting States' domestic law, the reasoning in the *Von Hannover* case worked in the opposite direction, and can be described as deductive (top-down) in nature: the Court determined the substantive content of the Convention rights at issue on the basis of its own views and ideas.

A similar deductive, and thus more activist, approach can be found in other rulings. The case of *Barbulescu v. Romania* dealt with an employer monitoring an employee's online communications in the workplace. The ECtHR had to decide whether the Romanian courts, by regarding the surveillance measures taken by the employer to be lawful, had violated the employee's right to protection of their private life, under Article 8 of the Convention. At the outset of its reasoning, the Court observed that there appeared to be no European consensus on the level of protection to be afforded to employees against the monitoring of their private communications, by their employers, in the workplace. Therefore, a 'wide margin of appreciation' needed to be granted to Contracting States in regulating the issue. Yet, the Court set out a very detailed list of no less than six criteria that must be met for the surveillance of the worker to be lawful.[73] Remarkably, the judgment is silent on the legal sources from which the Court derives those criteria. Here, the Strasbourg Court set uniform substantive standards for the protection of privacy rights in the field of employment, thus filling a regulatory vacuum left by the legislature, both at the national and supranational levels. In *Heinisch v. Germany*, a case concerning the protection of whistle-blowing employees, the Court adopted a similar approach. Here, the Strasbourg Court meticulously spelt out the factors domestic authorities have to take into account when assessing whether the signalling of an employer's illegal action by an employee constitutes a breach of the duty of loyalty owed to the employer, or whether it is legitimate behaviour, protected by freedom of expression under Article 10 ECHR.[74] Again, the ruling makes no reference to European consensus, and contains no indication as to whether the criteria set out by the Court represent common ground among European states.

---

[73] *Bărbulescu v. Romania*, no. 61496/08, § 121, ECtHR (GC) 5 September 2017; confirmed in *López Ribalda and Others v. Spain*, nos. 1874/13, 8567/13, §§ 115 *et seq.*, ECtHR (GC) 17 October 2019. For more details on the *Bărbulescu* case as well as on the impact of the ECHR on data protection C. Heinze and D. Ebel, 'Data Protection in Private Relations and the European Convention on Human Rights', in this volume.

[74] *Heinisch v. Germany*, no. 28274, §§ 65 *et seq.*, ECtHR 21 July 2011.

4. INDIRECT HARMONISING EFFECTS

4.1. EMBEDDING THE GUARANTEES OF THE CONVENTION INTO THE SYSTEM OF EU LAW

Thus far, we have seen how the ECtHR, by scrutinising the Contracting States' legislation, as well as its application by national authorities, has a direct impact on domestic legal orders, contributing to the harmonisation of the protection of human rights in Europe, both from a procedural and a substantive point of view. In this section, the focus is on how the Convention and the Strasbourg Court's case law influence the jurisprudence of the CJEU, and thus affect the Member States' legal systems *indirectly*, namely through the framework of EU law.

Paradoxically, the indirect harmonising effect may be stronger than the direct effect. The reason for this is that the Contracting States hold divergent views on how the content of the ECHR is to be implemented into their domestic legal systems, and how the Convention and domestic law interact.[75] Only in a few jurisdictions is the ECHR, being an international treaty, accorded the status of constitutional law. In some states, the Convention ranks below the constitution, but still above ordinary statutory law, whereas in other legal systems it has the same status as ordinary statutory law. Thus, to the extent that the Convention and domestic law contain conflicting rules, there is no consistent approach among the Contracting States as to which source of law is to prevail. These inconsistencies among European states clearly hamper the harmonising effect of the Convention. The situation is quite different with regard to EU law. Over the years, the CJEU has established the principle of primacy of EU law: EU law, be it primary or secondary law, takes precedence over any conflicting rule in the Member States' internal law, including constitutional law.[76] This principle is, by and large, accepted by all Member States. Thus,

---

[75] For an overview, see E. BATES, above n. 4, pp. 158 *et seq.* See, in particular, on the contrasting approaches taken by the German and Italian legal orders, the contributions, respectively, by A. ENGEL, 'The European Convention on Human Rights in the German Legal System: A Qualitative and Quantitative Introduction' and L. VAGNI, 'The Role of the Italian Courts in the Effective Implementation of the European Convention on Human Rights: Introductory Remarks', both contained in this volume.

[76] See, in particular, the landmark rulings CJEU Case 6/64, *Flaminio Costa v. E.N.E.L*, ECLI:EU:C:1964:66; CJEU Case 11/70, *Internationale Handelsgesellschaft mbH v. Einfuhr- und Vorratsstelle für Getreide und Futtermittel*, ECLI:EU:C:1970:114, para. 3; CJEU Case 106/77, *Amministrazione delle Finanze dello Stato v. Simmenthal SpA*, paras. 17 *et seq*.

by being embedded into the framework of EU law, the ECHR and the case law of the Strasbourg Court can achieve a higher hierarchical status within the EU Member States' legal systems: they can, in principle, also override domestic constitutional law. Moreover, as it falls under the ambit of the doctrine of primacy of EU law, the ECHR produces uniform legal effects in all Member States of the EU.

4.2. AN EXAMPLE OF INDIRECT HARMONISING EFFECTS: JUDICIAL REVIEW OF THE DUTY OF LOYALTY IN CHURCH EMPLOYMENT

The case law on the protection of Church employees against dismissal for allegedly breaching the duty of loyalty towards their employers provides an illustrative example of the indirect harmonising effects of the Convention on the EU Member States' private law. In particular, this case law shows how the CJEU can actually enhance the effectiveness of the rights and freedoms guaranteed by the Convention, at the level of domestic law.

In 2011, the ECtHR handed down its landmark decision in the case of *Schüth v. Germany*.[77] The applicant, Mr Schüth, had been employed as an organist and choirmaster at a Roman Catholic parish church in Germany, and had also served as a head musician in the deanery. After more than ten years of service to the church, Mr Schüth, who was himself of the Roman Catholic faith, broke up with his wife and started a relationship with a new partner, with whom he later had a child. In the Catholic Church's view, the applicant's conduct amounted to adultery and bigamy, and thus constituted a violation of the duty of loyalty that church employees owe towards their employer. Therefore, the parish church dismissed Mr Schüth. The applicant challenged the termination of his employment contract, in vain, before the labour courts and the FCC. The applicant then took his case to the ECtHR, which found that the German courts, in upholding the dismissal, had failed to strike a fair balance between the applicant's right to respect for his private life, under Article 8 ECHR, on the one hand, and the church's right to self-regulation, protected by Articles 9 and 11 of the

---

[77] *Schüth v. Germany*, no. 1620/03, ECtHR 23 September 2010. The Court also had to deal with similar disputes in the cases of *Obst v. Germany*, no. 425/03, ECtHR 23 September 2010; *Siebenhaar v. Germany*, no. 18136/02, ECtHR 3 February 2011; and *Fernández Martínez v. Spain*, no. 56030/07, ECtHR (GC) 12 June 2014; however, unlike in *Schüth*, the Court found no violations of the Convention in these cases.

Convention, on the other. In particular, the Court held that the German employment tribunals had attached too much weight to the Church's right of autonomy, as they had subjected the decision to dismiss the applicant 'only to a limited judicial scrutiny … without having regard to the nature of the post in question and without properly balancing the interests involved in accordance with the principle of proportionality'.[78] In fact, the approach adopted by the labour courts reflected the position of the FCC. According to the case law of the FCC,[79] Churches enjoy a wide margin of discretion when determining the content and scope of the duties of loyalty they impose on their employees. More specifically, the right of autonomy accorded to Churches, by the German Constitution, requires state courts to respect the Church's own perception as to whether the conduct of an employee may be at odds with the Church's proclamatory mission, and thus affect its credibility. Consequently, employment tribunals may scrutinise the employing Church's decision to dismiss an employee for breach of the duty of loyalty, only subject to very strict limits. In the ECtHR's view, the reduced standard of review applied by German courts violated the right to respect for private life and family life of Church employees. In *Fernández Martínez v. Spain*, the Grand Chamber of the ECtHR confirmed the position taken by the Court in *Schüth*, holding that national courts must conduct an 'in-depth examination' when balancing the Church's right of autonomy against the employee's right to respect for private or family life.[80]

A few years later, the labour courts in Germany were confronted with a similar dispute. The plaintiff, a doctor and member of the Roman Catholic Church, had served as a head of department in a hospital run by a private company owned by the Catholic Church. After divorcing his first wife and getting married to his new partner, the plaintiff was dismissed on the grounds that the remarriage was contrary to the precepts of the Catholic Church, and thus amounted to a violation of the duty of loyalty. The doctor initiated legal proceedings against the termination of his employment relationship, claiming that the dismissal was discriminatory since, under the regulations of the Catholic Church, the remarriage of a head of department of the Protestant faith, or of no faith, would not have been regarded as a breach of the duty of loyalty, and thus would not have resulted in the dismissal of the employee. The labour courts, including the Federal Labour Court, ruled in favour of the plaintiff, and held that

---

[78] *Schüth v. Germany*, no. 1620/03, § 69, ECtHR 23 September 2010.
[79] See the leading judgment BVerfGE 70, 138 = *Juristenzeitung* 1986, 131.
[80] *Fernández Martínez v. Spain*, no. 56030/07, § 132, ECtHR (GC) 12 June 2014.

the dismissal was wrongful, one of the arguments being that remarriage could be not regarded as behaviour harming the Church's credibility, given that the Church tolerated the same behaviour on the part of non-Catholic employees in similar positions. Therefore, the employer was not entitled to dismiss the plaintiff.[81] The employer, however, brought the case before the FCC, which set aside the judgment of the Federal Labour Court. The FCC reiterated its case law, according to which the contractual duties of loyalty a Church imposes on its employees are subject only to limited judicial scrutiny. The FCC found that the labour courts, by examining whether remarriage of employees performing managerial roles could negatively affect the Church's proclamatory mission, had unduly interfered with the discretion accorded to the Church. In its ruling, the FCC also addressed the question whether its own approach was in line with the case law of the ECtHR, especially in light of the Strasbourg Court's decision in *Schüth v. Germany*.[82] The FCC answered the question in the affirmative. This was rather a disputable interpretation of the ECtHR's case law,[83] given that, in *Schüth*, the Strasbourg Court had made it quite clear that the reduced standard of judicial review advocated by the FCC violated the employee's rights under Article 8 of the Convention. Having found that the labour courts had erred in upholding the doctor's application, the FCC referred the case back to the Federal Labour Court.

At this point, the proceedings took an unexpected turn. Instead of establishing that the dismissal of the doctor had been lawful, the Federal Labour Court referred the case to the CJEU,[84] seeking to ascertain whether the decision of the employer to dismiss the doctor was contrary to Directive 2000/78/EC on equal treatment in employment and occupation.[85] Undoubtedly, the termination of the doctor's contract of employment represented unequal treatment on the grounds of religion, within the meaning of Article 1 of the Directive, since a non-Catholic employee holding a similar position would not have been dismissed for the same conduct. The employing Church, however, asserted that the differentiation was justified on the basis of Article 4(2) of the Directive. Under this provision, employees of Churches or other religious organisations may

---

[81] BAG *NZA* 2012, 443.
[82] BVerfGE 137, 273 paras. 127 *et seq.* = *NZA* 2014, 1387.
[83] See, especially, BVerfGE 137, 273, para. 143 = *NZA* 2014, 1387.
[84] BAG *NZA* 2017, 388.
[85] Council Directive 2000/78/EC of 27 November 2000 establishing a general framework for equal treatment in employment and occupation, OJ 2000 L 303/16.

be subject to unequal treatment because of their religion, provided that the employee's religion constitutes a 'genuine, legitimate and justified occupational requirement, having regard to the [employing] organisation's ethos'. The key question here is the leeway to be granted to the employing Church when assessing whether the test under Article 4(2) of the Directive has been met. Again, in order to determine the proper standard of judicial review, the rights of the employee are to be balanced against the Church's right of autonomy.

Although, unlike in the cases decided by the ECtHR, the right invoked by the employee was not the right to respect for private or family life, but instead the principle of equal treatment, the reasoning of the Grand Chamber of the CJEU was very much in line with the case law of the Strasbourg Court: the CJEU stressed that the criteria set out in Article 4(2) of the Directive must be subject to 'effective judicial review'.[86] Thus, when evaluating whether the difference in treatment on the grounds of religion is justified, the national courts may not simply defer to the employing Church's own view. Instead, they have to conduct an objective test, examining thoroughly whether the reasons brought forward by the employer in justification of the differentiation are plausible. The Court made it clear that it was not satisfied that the employer had presented plausible arguments for imposing stricter duties of loyalty on Catholic employees than on non-Catholic employees, though it was ultimately for the referring court to establish whether the criteria in Article 4(2) of the Directive had been met. The CJEU's decision contains no direct reference to the case law of the ECtHR. However, the influence of the ECtHR on the approach taken by the CJEU is evident. The judgment relies heavily on the decision in *Vera Egenberger v. Evangelisches Werk für Diakonie und Entwicklung E.V.*, delivered by the Grand Chamber of the CJEU earlier in the same year, which also concerned unequal treatment on the grounds of religion, in the context of Church employment.[87] Here, the Grand Chamber followed the opinion of the Advocate General, who had drawn upon the ECtHR's rulings in *Schüth v. Germany* and *Fernández Martínez v. Spain* to argue that the assertions made by the Church to justify differences in treatment on the basis of religion should be subject to unrestricted judicial review.[88]

---

[86] CJEU Case C-68/17, *IR v. JQ*, ECLI:EU:C:2018:696, paras. 43 *et seq.*
[87] CJEU Case C-414/16, *Vera Egenberger v. Evangelisches Werk für Diakonie und Entwicklung E.V.*, ECLI:EU:C:2018:257.
[88] Ibid., Opinion of Advocate General Tanchev, ECLI:EU:C:2017:851, paras. 68 *et seq.*

Following the preliminary ruling delivered by the CJEU, the case of the dismissed Catholic doctor returned, for the third time, to the Federal Labour Court, which now conducted an in-depth examination of the duty of loyalty imposed by the Church on the employee. Again, just as in its initial ruling, the Federal Labour Court held that the dismissal of the doctor was discriminatory, and hence unlawful.[89] Thus, the CJEU's ruling had the effect of setting aside the decision of the FCC, which had sought to restrict the scope of judicial review in order not to interfere with the employing Church's right of autonomy – an approach that seems at odds with the rulings of the ECtHR in both *Schüth* and *Fernández Martínez*. This case shows how the CJEU can accentuate the impact of the ECHR and the case law of the Strasbourg Court on domestic law, by embedding the guarantees of the Convention into EU law. If it had not been for the decision of the CJEU, which relied heavily on the jurisprudence of the ECtHR, the position of the FCC would probably have prevailed.

5. CONCLUSION

The brief survey of the case law of the ECtHR, in the sections above, has shown that the Convention and the Strasbourg Court do indeed contribute to the harmonisation of private law in Europe. In some cases, the Court has developed uniform procedural requirements for the protection of human rights in private law relationships. In other rulings, the Court has set up substantive standards for the protection of the rights and freedoms guaranteed by the Convention, thus directly affecting the substantive content of the Contracting States' private law. In this respect, the approaches taken by the Court vary to some extent: in some decisions, the Court has chosen an inductive approach, setting the standard of protection on the basis of a comparative analysis of international legal trends and the Contracting States' domestic law (doctrine of 'European consensus'). In other cases, the reasoning of the ECtHR has followed a deductive approach, with the Court defining the content and scope of the Convention rights in an autonomous manner, i.e. in accordance with its own views and ideas. Moreover, we have

---

[89] BAG *NZA* 2019, 901. The employing Church eventually refrained from challenging the decision of the Federal Labour Court before the Federal Constitutional Court: see the press release issued by the Archdiocese of Cologne on 2 July 2019, available at <https://www.erzbistum-koeln.de/news/Keine-Verfassungsbeschwerde-im-Chefarzt-Fall/>.

seen that the case law of the Strasbourg Court sometimes has an influence on the interpretation of EU law by the CJEU, and thus affects national private law indirectly, through the framework of EU law.

The harmonising effects of the Convention on national private law raise numerous questions: is the ECtHR a well-suited institution to adjudicate disputes between private parties?[90] Is the Court sufficiently legitimate to harmonise private law? Does the case law of the Court leave enough leeway for legislatures, both at national and supranational level, to regulate private law relationships? Based on which considerations does the Court opt for setting solely procedural standards in some cases, while in other cases it chooses to develop substantive standards for the protection of human rights? It would go beyond the scope of this chapter to deal with all of these questions. Therefore, I will limit myself to addressing two aspects which seem particularly important to me. First, I shall briefly discuss why the harmonisation effects on domestic private law resulting from the ECHR are generally significantly weaker than those produced by EU law. Finally, I will explore whether, by setting uniform European standards for the protection of human rights in private law relationships, the Strasbourg Court is assuming too activist a judicial role.

5.1. FACTORS WEAKENING THE CONVENTION'S HARMONISING EFFECTS

The Convention's potential for harmonising private law in Europe is diminished by the lack of a consistent doctrine among European states as to how the rights and freedoms guaranteed by the ECHR interact with domestic law. As has already been pointed out,[91] the Contracting States take different views on the hierarchical status to be accorded to the ECHR within their respective legal systems. The legal effects of the case law of the ECtHR also give rise to uncertainty. The Convention is clear only on the binding force of the Court's decisions vis-à-vis the Contracting States which are parties to the proceedings. In accordance with Article 46 ECHR, those states are under an obligation to abide by the final judgment delivered by the Court, the execution of which is supervised by the

---

[90] See, on this issue, P. WINDEL, 'Die Bedeutung der Europäischen Menschenrechtskonvention für das Privatrecht', *Juristische Rundschau* 2011, 323, 327.
[91] See section 4.1. above.

Committee of Ministers of the Council of Europe. There is, however, no common ground among Contracting States as to the binding effect of the Court's case law on states that are not involved in the dispute. In Germany, for example, the FCC takes the view that the decisions of the ECtHR provide a guideline for the interpretation of domestic fundamental rights, no matter whether those decisions were directed against Germany or another State Party.[92] However, the FCC emphasises the need for 'contextualisation' where national courts take into account the case law of the ECtHR beyond the scope of application of Article 46 ECHR.[93] In other words, German courts are required to read the decisions of the Strasbourg Court in light of, inter alia, the peculiarities of the national law applicable to the individual case, before using those decisions as guidelines for the interpretation of German constitutional law. Such an approach renders it more difficult to infer, from the jurisprudence of the ECtHR, uniform rules and standards that are binding on all Contracting States.[94]

Italy, on the other hand, seems to follow a different approach, as far as the impact of judgments by the ECtHR on domestic law is concerned, though the case law of the Italian Constitutional Court is not yet settled on the issue.[95] In its judgment no. 49 of 2015, the Italian Constitutional Court held that, besides pilot judgments pursuant to Rule 61 of the Rules of Court, only decisions of the ECtHR reflecting a 'consolidated case-law' of the Strasbourg Court may serve as guidelines for the interpretation of domestic law, and are to be taken into account by national courts.[96] Similarly to the doctrine of 'contextualisation' developed by the FCC in Germany, the approach adopted by the Italian Constitutional Court also has the effect of reducing the impact of the ECtHR's case law on domestic

---

[92] BVerfGE 148, 296, para. 129 = *NJW* 2018, 2695.
[93] Ibid., para. 132: 'Beyond the scope of application of Art. 46 ECHR, however, the specific circumstances of the case must particularly be considered to provide for contextualisation when using the case-law of the European Court of Human Rights as guidelines.'
[94] Another factor limiting the impact of the Convention on the domestic legal system, especially in the context of private law relationships, is the FCC's interpretation of Article 53 ECHR: see, for details, A. ENGEL, above n. 75, in this volume.
[95] For more details, see the contribution by L. VAGNI, above n. 75, in this volume.
[96] Corte Costituzionale, 14 January 2015, no. 49, GU 01.04.2015, no.13, § 7: 'It is thus only "consolidated law" resulting from the case law of the European Court on which the national courts are required to base their interpretation, whilst there is no obligation to do so in cases involving rulings that do not express a position that has not become final.'

law. This, in turn, also diminishes the Convention's potential for the harmonisation of private law in Europe.

Another difficulty arises from the fact that the judgments of the ECtHR focus on individual cases. The Court often stresses that 'its task is not to review the relevant domestic law and practice *in abstracto*, but to determine whether the manner in which they were applied has infringed [Convention Rights]'.[97] This is an important difference compared to the role of the CJEU, in preliminary ruling proceedings, whose task is confined to the interpretation of EU law in the abstract, leaving it to the referring national courts to apply the law in the concrete dispute. Thus, the case law of the CJEU lends itself significantly better to generalisation than the judgments of the ECtHR do.[98]

However, it has been rightly pointed out that the judicial review conducted by the Strasbourg Court tends to be more abstract where the alleged violation of Convention rights is caused by national legislation or, likewise, by the lack of national legislation protecting the Convention rights at issue.[99] In such cases, it is easier to infer general rules and standards from the jurisprudence of the Court. Moreover, where the object of judicial scrutiny is an individual decision such as a court ruling or an administrative practice, the Court usually makes an effort to formulate general rules of law, in order to provide guidance to national courts that may be called upon to adjudicate similar cases in the future.[100] This approach is reflected by the structure of the Court's reasoning: in most cases, when assessing whether a Convention right has been violated, the Court generally starts off by reiterating the 'general principles' of the relevant right, and then goes on to apply these principles to the case at hand. This way of reasoning facilitates the emergence of a coherent body of general rules and principles. The same is true for the publication of comprehensive case law guides on the Court's website.[101]

---

[97] *Von Hannover v. Germany (no. 2)*, nos. 40660/08 and 60641/08, § 116, ECtHR (GC) 7 February 2012.

[98] P. KINSCH, 'European Court of Human Rights (ECtHR)' in J. BASEDOW, K. HOPT and R. ZIMMERMANN, above n. 1, pp. 579, 580: '[Compared with the approach of the CJEU] there is [in the case law of the ECtHR] a greater emphasis on the protection of individual rights in the concrete case at hand and a correspondingly less far-reaching trend towards the express formulation of judge-made rules of law.'

[99] J. GERARDS, 'Abstract and Concrete Reasonableness Review by the European Court of Human Rights' (2020) 1 *ECHR L. Rev.* 218, 233 *et seq.*

[100] R. SPANO, above n. 69, 487.

[101] Available at <https://www.echr.coe.int/Pages/home.aspx?p=caselaw/analysis/guides&c=#>.

5.2. HOW ACTIVIST IS THE EUROPEAN COURT OF HUMAN RIGHTS?

Undoubtedly, the rights and freedoms guaranteed by the Convention need to be protected against interference, not only from public authorities, but likewise from private individuals. Consequently, the ECtHR should also give effect to human rights in private law relationships, and scrutinise private law legislation, as well as court decisions in disputes between private parties. However, the 'constitutionalisation' of private law, i.e. the process of deriving specific rights and duties in the relationships between private individuals, from constitutional or quasi-constitutional law such as human rights law, reduces the margin of discretion for the legislature to regulate private law relationships.[102] As the rules and principles of private law, developed by the courts on the basis of constitutional provisions, have the same status as constitutional law, they may not be modified by the ordinary legislature. Being immune from legislative amendments, 'constitutionalised' private law risks becoming 'petrified' law. Against this backdrop, the ECtHR faces the difficult task of also ensuring effective protection of human rights in private law relationships, without, at the same time, unduly interfering with the regulatory discretion of the legislature.

Another difficulty for the ECtHR arises from the principle of subsidiarity. As an international court, the ECtHR is charged with setting standards for the protection of human rights that cut across national boundaries. However, due to the great variety of legal traditions, sociocultural conditions and moral views among the Member States of the Council of Europe, it is often difficult to develop standards that are acceptable to all Member States. This is especially true in the context of private law, which involves – as demonstrated above – the balancing of competing individual rights and interests. While often the rights and interests at stake are, in principle, recognised and protected in all legal orders, the Contracting States may take different views as to the outcome of the balancing test – that is, which of the clashing rights and interests are to prevail. Imposing rigid uniform rules and standards on the States Parties without accommodating national needs and conditions is likely to undermine the Court's authority, and is also at odds with the purpose of the Convention, which embraces

---

[102] R. REBHAHN, 'Zivilrecht und Europäische Menschenrechtskonvention', AcP 210 (2010) 489, 538 *et seq.*

the notion of subsidiarity.[103] Here, again, the Court has to strike a balance between European supervision of the rights and freedoms guaranteed by the Convention, on the one hand, and deference to the Contracting States, on the other.

How well does the ECtHR succeed in reconciling effective protection of Convention Rights and respect for the legislature's regulatory discretion as well as national idiosyncrasies? The answer seems mixed. Where the Court confines itself to defining procedural requirements for the protection of human rights,[104] it leaves leeway for the legislature, both at national and European levels, to regulate private law relationships, and allows for legal variety among Contracting States. Conversely, the scope of the legislature's regulatory discretion is narrow where the Court sets substantive standards. Here, the ECtHR assumes a more activist role. This approach appears more acceptable to the extent that the Court opts for the 'inductive method', defining the content and scope of the rights guaranteed by the Convention on the basis of the 'European consensus', thus showing awareness of the differences between national legal systems.[105] The opposite is true where the ECtHR adopts the 'deductive approach', and develops substantive criteria without taking into account the law and practices of the Contracting States. While this approach might be appropriate with regard to the protection of 'core' Convention rights against state interference, it should be reconsidered in the context of private law, where a balance needs to be struck between competing rights and interests; here, in the absence of a European consensus on the issue, the Court should allow for more discretion for national legislatures and courts. Harmonisation of private law on the basis of human rights law is not an end in itself.

---

[103] See the reference to the principle of subsidiarity introduced into the preamble of the Convention by Protocol No. 15.
[104] See section 3.1. above.
[105] See section 3.2.2. above.

BIBLIOGRAPHY

J. ADOLPHSEN, 'Aktuelle Fragen des Verhältnisses von EMRK und Europäischem Zivilprozessrecht' in J. RENZIKOWSKI (ed), *Die EMRK im Privat-, Straf- und Öffentlichen Recht*, Manz, Wien 2004

F. AHMED and A. PERRY, 'The Coherence of the Doctrine of Legitimate Expectations' (2014) 73 *Cambridge Law Journal* 67

J.P. ALBRECHT and F. JOTZO, *Das neue Datenschutzrecht der EU*, Nomos, Baden-Baden 2017

M. ANDENAS and D. FAIRGRIEVE (eds), *Courts and Comparative Law*, OUP, Oxford 2015

M. ANDENAS and D. FAIRGRIEVE, '"There is a World Elsewhere" – Lord Bingham and Comparative Law' in M. ANDENAS and D. FAIRGRIEVE (eds), *Tom Bingham and the Transformation of the Law*, OUP, Oxford 2009

C. ANGELOPOULOS and J.P. QUINTAIS, 'Fixing Copyright Reform. A Better Solution to Online Infringement' (2019) 10 *Journal of Intellectual Property, Information Technology and E-Commerce Law* 147

H. AUERNHAMMER, *DSGVO/BDSG*, 7th ed., Carl Heymanns, Cologne 2020

L. BACCAGLINI, G. DI PAOLO and F. CORTESE, 'The value of Judicial precedent in the Italian Legal System' (2016) 7(1) *Civil Procedure Review* 3

J.M. BALKIN, 'Obergefell v. Hodges: A Critical Introduction' in J.M. BALKIN (ed.), *What Obergefell v. Hodges Should Have Said: The Nation's Top Legal Experts Rewrite America's Same-Sex Marriage Decision*, Yale University Press, New Haven 2020

E. BANAKAS, 'The Contribution of Comparative Law to the Harmonisation of European Private Law' in A. HARDING and E. ORUCU (eds), *Comparative Law in the Twenty First Century*, Kluwer Law Intl., The Hague 2002

V. BARSOTTI, P. CAROZZA, M. CARTABIA and S. SIMONCINI, *Italian Constitutional Justice in Global Context*, OUP, Oxford 2016

J. BASEDOW, 'EU Private Law' in J. BASEDOW, K. HOPT and R. ZIMMERMANN (eds), *The Max Planck Encyclopedia of European Private Law*, OUP, Oxford 2012

J. BASEDOW, 'Europäische Menschenrechtskonvention und Europäisches Privatrecht', *RabelsZ* 63 (1999), 409

E. BATES, *The Evolution of the European Convention on Human Rights*, OUP, Oxford 2010

U. BATTIS, *Streikverbot für Beamte*, Arbeitsgemeinschaft der Verbände des höheren Dienstes, Bonn 2013

M. BENEDETTELLI, 'Human rights as a litigation tool in international arbitration: reflecting on the ECHR experience' (2015) 31 *Arbitration International* 631

E. BENVENISTI, 'Margin of Appreciation, Consensus, and Universal Standards' (1999) 31 *Journal of International Law and Politics* 843

P. BERNARDINI, 'Investimento straniero e arbitrato' [2017] *Rivista dell'arbitrato* 673

G. BERNINI, 'Cultural Neutrality: A Prerequisite to Arbitral Justice' (1989) 10(1) *Michigan Journal of International Law* 39

R. BIFULCO and D. PARIS, 'The Italian Constitutional Court' in A.V. BOGDANDY, P.M. HUBER and C. GRABENWARTER (eds), *Constitutional Adjudication: Institutions*, vol. III, 3rd ed., OUP, Oxford 2020

T.H. BINGHAM, *Widening Horizons: The Influence of Comparative Law and International Law on Domestic Law*, CUP, Cambridge 2010

F. BIONDI DAL MONTE and F. FONTANELLI, 'The Decisions No. 348 and 349/2007 of the Italian Constitutional Court: The Efficacy of the European Convention in the Italian Legal System' (2008) 7 *German Law Journal* 889

D. BISHOP and L. REED, 'Practical Guidelines for Interviewing, Selecting and Challenging Party-Appointed Arbitrators in International Commercial Arbitration' (1998) 14(4) *Arbitration International* 395

E. BJORGE, *Domestic Application of the ECHR: Courts as Faithful Trustees*, OUP, Oxford 2015

M. BOBEK, *Comparative Reasoning in European Supreme Courts*, OUP, Oxford 2013

N. BOBBIO, *L'età dei diritti*, Einaudi, Torino 1990

K. BOELE-WOELKI and A. FUCHS (eds), *Legal Recognition of Same-Sex Relationships in Europe: National, Cross-border and European Perspectives*, 3rd ed., Intersentia, Cambridge 2017

I. BOONE, 'Co-parenting before conception – The Low Countries' approach to intentional multi-parent families', *Family & Law*, February 2018

J.A. BRAUCH, 'The Dangerous Search for an Elusive Consensus: What the Supreme Court Should Learn from the European Court of Human Rights' (2009) 52 *Howard Law Journal* 277

E. BREMS, 'The Margin of Appreciation Doctrine in the Case-Law of the European Court of Human Rights' (1996) 56 *Zeitschrift für ausländisches öffentliches Recht* 230

E. BREMS, *Human Rights: Universality and Diversity*, Martinus Nijhoff Publishers, The Hague/Boston/London 2001

S. BRETTHAUER 'Verfassungsrechtliche Grundlagen, Europäisches und nationales Recht', in L. SPECHT and R. MANTZ (eds), *Handbuch Europäisches und deutsches Datenschutzrecht*, C.H. Beck, Munich 2019

E. BRIBOSIA, I. RORIVE and L. VAN DEN EYNDE, 'Same-Sex Marriage: Building an Argument before the European Court of Human Rights in Light of the US Experience' (2014) 32 *Berkeley Journal of International Law* 1

G. BRITZ, 'Kindesgrundrechte und Elterngrundrecht: Fremdunterbringung von Kindern in der verfassungsgerichtlichen Kontrolle', *FamRZ* 2015, 793

A. BROWN, *A Theory of Legitimate Expectations for Public Administration*, OUP, Oxford 2017

K.-H. BRUNNER, 'Die europäischen Leitlinien für eine bessere Umsetzung der bestehenden Empfehlung des Europarates über die Zwangsvollstreckung', *Deutsche Gerichtsvollzieher Zeitung*, 2012

M. BUNGERBERG, J. GRIEBEL, S. HOBE and A. REINISCH (eds), *International Investment Law: A Handbook*, Bloomsbury Publishing, London 2015

F.M. BUONAIUTI, 'The Effects of Judgments of The European Court of Human Rights on the Final Decisions of Domestic Courts: Recent Developments in the Italian Case Law' (2019) 28(1) *The Italian Yearbook of International Law Online* 159

P. BUREŠ, 'The dialogue between judges leading to a consensus? On a mute and a silent dialogue before ECtHR' (2017) 1 *European Journal of Public Matters* 63

C. CALLIESS and M. RUFFERT (eds), *EUV/AEUV*, 6th ed., C.H.Beck, Munich 2022

E. CALZOLAIO, 'National Judges and Strasbourg Case Law: Comparative Reflections about the Italian Experience' in M. ANDENAS and D. FAIRGRIEVE (eds), *Courts and Comparative Law*, OUP, Oxford 2015

M. CAREDDA, 'Quando "reinterpretare" dovrebbe equivalere ad "accogliere"' (2015) 1 *Giurisprudenza Costituzionale* 30

P.G. CAROZZA, 'Subsidiarity as a Structural Principle of International Human Rights Law' (2003) 97 *American Journal of International Law* 38

P.G. CAROZZA, 'Uses and Misuses of Comparative Law in International Human Rights: Some Reflections on the Jurisprudence of the European Court of Human Rights' (1999) 73 *Notre Dame Law Review* 1217

S. CASSESE, 'Ruling Indirectly Judicial Subsidiarity in the ECtHR' in *Subsidiarity: a two-sided coin? Dialogue between Judges 2015*, seminar organised by the ECtHR, Strasbourg, 30 January 2015, https://images.irpa.eu/wp-content/uploads/2011/10/Subsidiarity-a-two-sided-coin_1.pdf

J. CHRISTOFFERSEN, *Fair Balance: Proportionality, Subsidiarity and Primarity in the European Convention on Human Rights*, Martinus Nijhoff, Laiden/Boston 2009

M. COESTER, 'Reformen im Kindschaftsrecht', *Brühler Schriften zum Familienrecht* 18 (2014), 43

D. COESTER-WALTJEN, 'Statusrechtliche Folgen der Stärkung der Rechte der nichtehelichen Väter', *FamRZ* 2013, 1693

L.J. CONSTANTINESCO, *Traité de droit comparé, t. II, La méthode comparative*, Librairie générale de droit et de jurisprudence, Paris 1974

C. COUPETTE and A. FLECKNER, 'Quantitative Rechtswissenschaft' [2018] *Juristenzeitung* 379

C. COUPETTE, *Juristische Netzwerkforschung*, Mohr Siebeck, Tübingen 2019

E. CRIVELLI, 'La Corte costituzionale garantisce i rapporti di parentela a tutti i minori adottati: nota alla sentenza n. 79 del 2022' (2022) 5 *Osservatorio Costituzionale* 1

E. CRIVELLI, 'The Italian Debate about the Ratification of Protocol 16' (2020) 4 *Eurojus* 371

I. CURRY-SUMNER, 'Same-Sex Relationships in a European Perspective' in J.M. SCHERPE (ed), *European Family Law*, vol. III, Edward Elgar Publishing, Cheltenham 2016

K. DE LA DURANTAYE and CÉLINE M. LALÉ, 'Hurbain v. Belgien: Eine Entscheidung zum Vergessen?' (2022) *Zeitschrift für Europäisches Privatrecht* 660

D.P. DE MARTINO and K. PLAVEC, 'Has COVID-19 Unlocked Digital Justice? Answers from the World of International Arbitration' (2021) 6(1) *Cambridge Law Review* 45

V. DI GRAVIO, 'L'indipendenza dell'arbitro' (2018) *Rivista dell'arbitrato* 195

M. DICOSOLA, C. FASONE and I. SPIGNO, 'The Prospective Role of Constitutional Courts in the Advisory Opinion Mechanism before the European Court of Human Rights: A First Comparative Assessment with the European Union and the Inter-American System' (2015) 16(6) *German Law Journal* 1387

R. DOLZER and C. SCHREUER, *Principles of International Investment Law*, 2nd ed., OUP, Oxford 2012

S. DOTHAN, 'The Optimal Use of Comparative Law' (2014) 43 *Denver Journal of International Law & Policy* 21

S. DOUGLAS-SCOTT, 'A Tale of Two Courts: Luxembourg, Strasbourg and the Growing European Human Rights Acquis' (2006) 43 *Common Market Law Review* 629

S. DRACKERT, *Die Risiken der Verarbeitung personenbezogener Daten*, Duncker & Humblot, Berlin 2014

C. DRAGHICI, *The Legitimacy of Family Rights in Strasbourg Case Law: 'Living Instrument' or Extinguished Sovereignty?*, Hart, Oxford 2017

J. DREXL, 'Constitutional Protection of Authors' Moral Rights in the European Union – Between Privacy, Property and the Regulation of the Economy' in K.S. ZIEGLER (ed), *Human Rights and Private Law: Privacy as Autonomy*, Hart Publishing, Oxford 2007

U. DROBNIG and S. VAN ERP, *The Use of Comparative Law by Courts*, XIVth International Congress of Comparative Law, Kluwer Law International, The Hague, 1999

A. DRZEMCZEWSKI and J. MEYER-LADEWIG, 'Grundzüge des neuen EMRK-Kontrollmechanismus nach dem am 11.5.1994 unterzeichneten Reform-Protokoll (Nr. 11)' (1994) *Europäische Grundrechtezeitschrift* 317

K.A.N. DUGALL and N.J. DIAMOND, 'Regime Interaction in Investment Arbitration: Crowded Streets; Are Human Rights Law and International Investment Law Good Neighbors?' [2021] *Kluwer Arbitration Blog*

K. DZEHTSIAROU, *European Consensus and the Legitimacy of the European Court of Human Rights*, CUP, Cambridge, 2015

A. ENGEL, 'Staatenimmunität in der Rechtsprechung des Bundesverfassungsgerichts' in D. MÜLLER and L. DITTRICH (eds), *Linien der Rechtsprechung des Bundesverfassungsgerichts*, vol. 6, De Gruyter, Berlin 2022

S. ENGELS and U. JÜRGENS, 'Auswirkungen der EGMR-Rechtsprechung zum Privatsphärenschutz – Möglichkeiten und Grenzen der Umsetzung des „Caroline"-Urteils im deutschen Recht', *NJW* 2007, 2517

K.D. EWING and J. HENDY, 'The Dramatic Implications of *Demir and Baykara*' (2010) 39 *Industrial Law Journal* 2

M. Falsone, 'Union Freedoms in the Armed Forces: Still a Taboo?' (2022) 51(2) *Industrial Law Journal* 375

M. Fanou and V.P. Tzevelekos, 'The Shared Territory of the ECHR and International Investment Law' in Y. Radi (ed), *Research Handbook on Human Rights and Investment*, Edward Elgar, Cheltenham 2018

A Federico, 'La "maternità surrogata" ritorna alle Sezioni Unite' (2022) 5 *Nuova Giurisprudenza Civile Commentata* 1047

R. Feehily, 'Neutrality, Independence and Impartiality in International Commercial Arbitration, A Fine Balance in the Quest For Arbitral Justice' (2019) 7(1) *Penn State Journal of Law & International Affairs* 88

G.F. Ferrari and A. Gambaro, *Corti nazionali e comparazione giuridica*, Esi, Napoli 2006

A. Fleckner, 'Anlegermitverschulden vor dem Bankensenat – Eine quantitative juristische Studie' in S. Grundmann, H. Merkt and P.O. Mülbert (eds), *Festschrift für Klaus J. Hopt zum 80. Geburtstag am 24. August 2020*, De Gruyter, Berlin 2020

A. Fleckner, 'Anlegermitverschulden vor dem Bankensenat – Eine quantitative juristische Studie' in S. Grundmann, H. Merkt and P.O. Mülbert (eds), *Festschrift für Klaus J. Hopt zum 80. Geburtstag am 24. August 2020*, De Gruyter, Berlin 2020

M. Fornasier, 'Europäische Menschenrechtskonvention' in U. Preis and A. Sagan (eds), *Europäisches Arbeitsrecht*, 2nd ed., Otto Schmidt, Köln 2019

R. Frank, 'Art. 8 EMRK und die Anfechtung wahrheitswidriger Vaterschaftsanerkennungen durch den biologischen Vater (§1600 Abs. 2 BGB)', *FamRZ* 2021, 1081

G. Frankenberg, *Comparative Law as Critique*, Edward Elgar, Cheltenham 2016

P. Fütterer, 'Das Koalitions- und Streikrecht im EU-Recht nach dem Wandel der Rechtsprechung des EGMR zur Koalitionsfreiheit gemäß Art. 11 EMRK (*Demir und Baykara* und andere)' (2011) *EuZA* 505

C. Geiger, 'Intellectual Property Shall be Protected!? – Article 17(2) of the Charter of Fundamental Rights of the European Union: a Mysterious Provision with an Unclear Scope' (2009) *European Intellectual Property Review* 115

C. Geiger, 'The Role of the Court of Justice of the European Union: Harmonizing, Creating and Sometimes Disrupting Copyright Law in the European Union' in I. Stamatoudi (ed), *New Developments in EU and International Copyright Law*, Kluwer Law International, Alphen aan den Rijn 2016

C. Geiger and E. Izyumenko, *Shaping Intellectual Property Rights Through Human Rights Adjudication: The Example of the European Court of Human Rights*, Center for International Intellectual Property Studies Research Paper No. 2020-02 (2020)

R. Geiger, Staatsrecht III, 7th ed., C.H. Beck, München 2018

M. Gelter and M. Siems, 'Citations to Foreign Courts. Illegitimate and Superfluous, or Unavoidable? Evidence from Europe' (2014) 62 *American Journal of Comparative Law* 35

J. Gerards, 'Abstract and Concrete Reasonableness Review by the European Court of Human Rights' (2020) 1 *European Convention on Human Rights Law Review* 218

J. Gerards, 'Advisory Opinions, Preliminary Rulings, and the new Protocol no. 16 to the European Convention of Human Rights. A Comparative and Critical Appraisal' (2014) 21 *Maastricht Journal* 648

J. Gerards, *General Principles of the European Convention of Human Rights*, CUP, Cambridge 2019

J. Gerards, 'Pluralism, Deference and the Margin of Appreciation Doctrine' (2011) 17 *European Law Journal* 80

J. Gerrards, 'Procedural Review by the ECtHR: A Typology'; and A. Nussberger, 'Procedural Review by the ECHR: View from the Court' in J. Gerrards and E. Brems (eds), *Procedural Review in European Fundamental Rights Cases*, CUP, Cambridge 2017

J. Gerards, 'The European Court of Human Rights and the National Courts: Giving Shape to the Notion of "Shared Responsibility"' in J. Gerards and J. Fleuren, *Implementation of the European Convention of Human Rights and of the judgments of the ECtHR in national case-law: A comparative Analysis*, Intersentia, Cambridge 2014

F. Giardini, 'Unification of Child Status and Parental Responsibility: The Reform of Filiation Remodels the Family in the Legal Sense in the Italian Legal System' (2017) 22 *Interdisciplinary Journal of Family Studies* 2

T. Giegerich, 'Wirkung und Rang der EMRK in den Rechtsordnungen der Mitgliedstaaten' in O. Dörr, R. Grote and T. Marauhn (eds), *EMRK/GG*, 2nd ed., Mohr Siebeck, Tübingen 2013

I. Giesen, 'The Use and Influence of Comparative Law in "Wrongful Life" Cases' (2012) 8 *Utrecht Law Review* 35

L.R. Glas, *The Theory, Potential and Practice of Procedural Dialogue in the European Convention on Human Rights System*, Intersentia, Cambridge 2016

I. Götz, in J. Ellenberg et al., *Grüneberg – Bürgerliches Gesetzbuch mit Nebengesetzen*, 81st ed, C.H. Beck, Munich 2022

C. Grabenwarter, '*Schutz der Privatsphäre versus Pressefreiheit*: Europäische Korrektur des deutschen Sonderweges?' (2004) *Zeitschrift für das gesamte Medienrecht: Archiv für Presserecht* 309

C. Grabenwarter and K. Pabel, *EMRK*, 7th ed., C.H. Beck, München 2021

P. Gragl, 'An Olive Branch from Strasbourg: Interpreting the European Court of Human Rights' Resurrection of *Bosphorus* and Reaction to Opinion 2/13 in the *Avotins* Case: ECtHR 23 May 2016, Case No. 17502/07, *Avotins v. Latvia*' (2017) 13 *European Constitutional Law Review* 551

M. Graziadei, 'The Functionalist Heritage' in P. Legrand and R. Munday (eds), *Comparative Legal Studies: Traditions and Transitions*, CUP, Cambridge 2003

V. Grementieri, 'Comparative Law and Human Rights in Europe' in A.M. Rabello (ed), *European Legal Traditions and Israel*, The Hebrew University of Jerusalem, Jerusalem 1994

J. GRIEBEL 'Europäische Grundrechte als Prüfungsmaßstab der Verfassungsbeschwerde' [2014] *Deutsches Verwaltungsblatt* 204

J. GRIFFITHS and L. MCDONAGH, 'Fundamental Rights and European IP Law: The Case of Art 17(2) of the EU Charter' in C. GEIGER (ed), *Constructing European Intellectual Property: Achievements and New Perspectives*, Edward Elgar Publishing, Cheltenham, UK/Northampton, MA, US 2013

D. GRIMM et al., 'European Constitutionalism and the German Basic Law' in A. ALBI and S. BARDUTZKY (eds), *National Constitutions in European and Global Governance: Democracy, Rights, the Rule of Law*

S. GROSSI and M.C. PAGNI (eds), *Commentary on the Italian Code of Civil Procedure*, OUP, Oxford 2010

H. HAMANN, 'Der blinde Fleck der deutschen Rechtswissenschaft – Zur digitalen Verfügbarkeit instanzgerichtlicher Rechtsprechung' [2021] *Juristenzeitung* 656

H. HAMANN, *Evidenzbasierte Jurisprudenz*, Mohr Siebeck, Tübingen 2014

S. HAMMER, in H. PRÜTTING and T. HELMS (eds), *FamFG*, 5th ed., Otto Schmidt, Cologne 2020

A. HARDING and P. LEYLAND, 'Comparative Law in Constitutional Context' in E. ORUCU and D. NELKEN (eds), *Comparative Law: A Handbook*, OUP, Oxford 2007

M. HEESE, 'Veröffentlichung gerichtlicher Entscheidungen im Zeitalter der Digitalisierung' in C. ALTHAMMER and C. SCHÄRTL (eds), *Dogmatik als Fundament für Forschung und Lehre, Festschrift für Herbert Roth*, Mohr Siebeck, Tübingen 2021

B. HEIDERHOFF, 'Herausforderungen durch neue Familienformen – Zeit für ein Umdenken', *NJW* 2016, 2629

B. HEIDERHOFF, 'Kann ein Kind mehrere Väter haben?', *FamRZ* 2008, 1901

L.R. HELFER, 'Toward a Human Rights Framework for Intellectual Property' (2007) 40 *U.C. Davis Law Review* 971

T. HELMS, 'Elternteil in einem Staat – Elternteil in jedem Staat (der EU)?' *ZEuP* 2022, 747

T. HELMS, *Rechtliche, biologische und soziale Elternschaft – Herausforderungen durch neue Familienformen, Gutachten F zum 71. Deutschen Juristentag*, CH Beck, Munich 2016

M. HERTIG RANDALL, 'Der grundrechtliche Dialog der Gerichte in Europa' (2014) *Europäische Grundrechte-Zeitschrift* 5

B. HESS, 'Comparative Analysis of the National Reports' (2006) *European Business Law Review* 723

B. HESS, 'EMRK, Grundrechte-Charta und europäisches Zivilverfahrensrecht' in H.P MANSEL et al. (eds), *Festschrift für Erik Jayme*, vol. I, Sellier, Munich 2004

J. HEUSCHMID, 'Aktuelle Rechtsprechung des EGMR im Bereich des Arbeitsrechts' (2018) 3 *NZA Beilage* 68

L. HODSON, 'A Marriage by Any Other Name? Schalk and Kopf v Austria' (2011) 11 *Human Rights Law Review* 170

F. HOFFMEISTER, 'Germany: Status of European Convention on Human Rights in domestic law' (2006) 4 *International Journal of Constitutional Law* 723

G. Horsmann, 'La fusione della giustizia pubblica e della giustizia privata. L'arbitrato privato/pubblico' (2017) *Contratto e impresa* 1238

J. Houssier, 'L'affaire Mennesson ou la victoire du fait sur le droit' (2019) *AJ Famille*, 11

P.M. Huber, 'Die Einwirkungen des Unionsrechts und der EMRK auf das Grundgesetz' in H.-J. Blanke, S. Magiera, J.C. Pielow and A. Weber (eds), *Verfassungsentwicklungen im Vergleich – Italien 1947 – Deutschland 1949 – Spanien 1978*, Duncker & Humblot, Berlin 2021

M. Hunter, 'Ethics of the International Arbitrator' (1987) 53(4) *Arbitration* 219

H. Hurpy, 'La judiciarisation par défaut du lien de filiation des enfants nés d'une GPA transfrontière avec le mère d'intention' (2019) 631 *Revue de l'Union Européenne* 486

J. Husa, 'Methodology of Comparative Law Today: From Paradoxes to Flexibility?' (2006) *Rev. int. droit comp.* 1095

M. Husovec, 'The Essence of Intellectual Property Rights Under Article 17(2) of the EU Charter' (2019) 20 *German Law Journal* 840

S. Izzo, '"From status to contract": la trascrizione dei provvedimenti stranieri dichiarativi dello status del figlio d'intenzione' (2019) 6 *GenIUS* 48

A. Jacobs, 'Article 5 The Right to Organise', in N. Bruun, K. Lörcher, I. Schömann and S. Clauwaert (eds), *The European Social Charter and the Employment Relation*, Hart, Oxford 2017

A. Jacobs, 'Article 11 ECHR: The Right to Bargain Collectively under Article 11 ECHR' in F. Dorssemont, K. Lörcher and I. Schömann (eds), *The European Convention on Human Rights and the Employment Relation*, Hart, Oxford 2013

A. Jaksic, 'Procedural Guarantees of Human Rights in Arbitration Proceedings – A Still Unsettled Problem?' (2007) 24(2) *Journal of International Arbitration* 159

C. Janik, 'Die EMRK und internationale Organisationen – Ausdehnung und Restriktion der *equivalent protection*-Formel in der neuen Rechtsprechung des EGMR', *Zeitschrift für ausländisches öffentliches Recht und Völkerrecht* 70 (2010), 127

C. Jarrosson, 'L'arbitrage et la Convention européenne des droits de l'homme' (1989) *Revue de l'arbitage* 573

T. Jaspers, 'Article 5 RESC The right to organize' in E. Ales, M. Bell, O. Deinert and S. Robin-Olivier, *International and European Labour Law*, Nomos, Baden-Baden 2018

G.G.T. Jun, 'An Arbitral Tribunal's Dilemma: The Plea of Financially Impecunious Parties' (2020) 37(4) *Journal of International Arbitration* 479

P. Kapotas and V. Tzevelekos, *Building Consensus on European Consensus: Judicial Interpretation of Human Rights in Europe and Beyond*, CUP, Cambridge 2019

A. Karila-Danziger and F.G. Joly, 'Transcription à l'état civil français des actes de naissance étrangers dresses dans le cadre d'une GPA, «Fin de partie»' (2021) 11 *AJ Famille* 582

U. Karpenstein and F.C. Mayer, *Konvention zum Schutz der Menschenrechte und Grundfreiheiten*, 3rd ed., C.H. Beck, München 2022

E. KASTANAS, *Unité et Diversité: Notions Autonomes et Marge d'Appréciation des Etats dans la Jurisprudence de la Cour Européenne des Droits de L'Homme*, Bruylant, Brussels 1996

G. KAUFMANN-KOHLER, 'Soft Law in International Arbitration Codification and Normativity' [2010] *Journal of International Dispute Settlement* 1

T. KINGREEN, 'Grundrechtsverbund oder Grundrechtsunion?' (2010) 3 *EuR* 338

P. KINSCH, 'Enforcement as a right', *Nederlands internationaal privaatrecht*, 2014, 540

P. KINSCH, 'The Impact of Human Rights on the Application of Foreign Law and on the Recognition of Foreign Judgments – A Survey of the Cases Decided by the European Human Rights Institutions' in T. EINHORN and K. SIEHR (eds), *Intercontinental Cooperation Through Private International Law – Essays in Memory of Peter E Nygh*, TMC Asser Press, The Hague 2004

N. KLEIN, 'Human Rights and International Investment Law: Investment Protection as Human Right?' (2012) 4 *Goettingen Journal of International Law* 199

T. KLEINLEIN, 'The Procedural Approach of the European Court of Human Rights: Between Subsidiarity and Dynamic Evolution' (2019) 68 *International & Comparative Law Quarterly* 90

M. KNIGGE and P. RIBBERS, 'Waiver of the Right to Set-Aside Proceedings in Light of Article 6 ECHR: Party-Autonomy on Top?' (2017) 34(5) *Journal of International Arbitration* 775

C. KOHLER, 'Grenzen des gegenseitigen Vertrauens im Europäischen Justizraum', *Praxis des internationalen Privat- und Verfahrensrechts*, 2017

C. KOHLER and W. PINTENS, 'Entwicklungen im europäischen Personen- und Familienrecht' 2015–2016 *Zeitschrift für das gesamte Familienrecht*, 1509

M. KONEN, 'A New (Deepwater) Horizon For Arbitrator Bias' (2021) *Arbitration Law Review* 11

T. KOOPMANS, 'Comparative Law and the Courts' (1996) 45 *International & Comparative Law Quarterly* 545

F. KORENICA, *The EU Accession to the ECHR*, Springer, Cham 2015

D. KOSAŘ and L. LIXINSKI, 'Domestic Judicial Design by International Human Rights Courts' (2015) 109(4) *American Journal of International Law* 713

S. KRALJIĆ, 'Same-Sex Partnerships in Eastern Europe: Marriage, Registration or No Regulation?' in K. BOELE-WOELKI and A. FUCHS (eds.), *Legal Recognition of Same-Sex Relationships in Europe: National, Cross-border and European Perspectives*, 3rd ed., Intersentia, Cambridge 2017

R. KRÄMER and J. MÄRTEN, 'Der Dialog der Gerichte – Die Fortentwicklung des Persönlichkeitsschutzes im europäischen Mehrebenenrechtsverbund' (2015) *Europarecht* 169

I. KRIARIM and A VALONGO, 'International Issues Regarding Surrogacy' (2016) 2 *The Italian Law Journal* 331

U. KRIEBAUM, 'Is the European Court of Human Rights an Alternative to Investor-State Arbitration?' in P.M. DUPUY, E.U. PETERSMANN and F. FRANCIONI (eds), *Human Rights in International Investment Law and Arbitration*, OUP, Oxford 2009

T. KRUMINS, *Arbitration and Human Rights*, Springer, Cham 2020

J. Kudrna, 'Arbitration and Right of Access to Justice: Tips for a Successful Marriage', *New York University Journal of International Law and Politics (JILP) Online Forum*, February 2013, https://www.nyujilp.org/arbitration-and-right-of-access-to-justice-tips-for-a-successful-marriage/

J. Kühling, M. Klar and F. Sackmann (eds), *Datenschutzrecht*, 5th ed., C.F. Müller, Heidelberg 2021

M. L. Christensen, H. P. Olsen and F. Tarissan, 'Identification of Case Content with Quantitative Network Analysis: An Example from the ECtHR' in F. Bex and S. Villata (eds), *Legal Knowledge and Information Systems*, IOS Press, Amsterdam 2016

J. Lafranque, 'Dialogue between judges. Implementation of the judgments of the European Court of Human Rights: a shared judicial responsibility?', Strasbourg, 31 January 2014

H. Lal, B. Casey and L. Defranchi, 'Rethinking Issue Conflicts in International Commercial Arbitration' (2020) 14(1) *Dispute Resolution International* 3

P. Lalive, 'On the Neutrality of the Arbitrator and of the Place of Arbitration' (1970) *Revue de l'arbitrage* 59

E. Lamarque, 'The Failure by Italy to Ratify Protocol no. 16 to the ECHR' (2021) 1(1) *The Italian Review of International and Comparative Law* 159

L. Lavrysen, 'The Mountain Gave Birth to a Mouse: The First Advisory Opinion under Protocol No. 16' in *strasbourgobservers.com*, 14 April 2019, https://strasbourgobservers.com/2019/04/24/the-mountain-gave-birth-to-a-mouse-the-first-advisory-opinion-under-protocol-no-16/

G. Letsas, 'Two Concepts of the Margin of Appreciation' (2006) 26 *Oxford Journal of Legal Studies* 705

G. Letsas, *A Theory of Interpretation of the European Convention on Human Rights*, OUP, Oxford 2007

K. V. Lewinski, 'Rechtsgeschichte des Datenschutzes', in G. Rüpke, K. V. Lewinski and J. Eckardt (eds), *Datenschutzrecht*, C.H. Beck, Munich 2018

C.L. Lim, J. Ho and M. Paparinskis, *International Investment Law and Arbitration: Commentary, Awards and Other Materials*, CUP, Cambridge 2018

J.F. Lindner, 'Dürfen Beamte doch streiken?' (2011) *DöV* 305

M. Löhnig, 'Die leibliche, nicht rechtliche Mutter', *FamRZ* 2015, 806

M Löhnig, *Früher hatten Eltern viele Kinder – heute haben Kinder viele Eltern – Zum Wandel des Familienbildes unserer Rechtsordnung*, Nomos, Baden-Baden 2015

K. Lörcher, 'Das Menschenrecht auf Kollektivverhandlung und Streik – auch für Beamte – Zu den EGMR-Urteilen v. 12.11.2008, *Demir und Baykara*, und 21.4.2009, *Enerji Yapi-Yol Sen*' (2009) *ArbuR* 229

K. Lörcher, 'Meilenstein der Menschenrechtsentwicklung' in W. Däubler (ed), *Arbeitskampfrecht*, vol. 4, Baden-Baden 2018

K. Lörcher, 'The New Social Dimension in the Jurisprudence of the European Court of Human Rights (ECHR): The *Demir and Baykara* Judgment, its Methodology and Follow-up' in F. Dorssemont, K. Lörcher and I. Schömann (eds), *The European Convention on Human Rights and the Employment Relation*, Hart Publishing, Oxford 2013

G. Lübbe-Wolff, 'Der Grundrechtsschutz nach der Europäischen Menschenrechtskonvention bei konfligierenden Individualrechten – Plädoyer für eine Korridor-Lösung' in M. Hochhuth (ed), *Nachdenken über Staat und Recht. Kolloquium zum 60. Geburtstag von Dietrich Murswiek*, Duncker & Humblot, Berlin 2010

A. Lucas-Schloetter, 'Is there a concept of European Copyright Law? History, Evolution, Policies and Politics and the Acquis Communautaire' in I. Stamatoudi and P. Torremans (eds), *EU Copyright Law: A Commentary*, Edward Elgar Publishing, Northampton 2014

Y. Lupu, 'Precedent in International Courts: A Network Analysis of Case Citations by the European Court of Human Rights' (2012) 42 *British Journal of Political Science* 413

F. Macmillan, '"Speaking Truth to Power": Copyright and the Control of Speech' in O. Pollicino, G.M. Riccio and M. Bassini (eds), *Copyright and Fundamental Rights in the Digital Age. A Comparative Analysis in Search of a Common Constitutional Ground*, Edward Elgar Publishing, Cheltenham, UK/Northampton, MA, US 2020

M.C. Malaguti and G. Rojas Elgueta, 'Alcance y fuentes de las expectativas legítimas de los inversores en las sagas de energía renovable españolas e italianas' (2021) 13 *Arbitraje: Revista de arbitraje comercial y de inversiones* 151

V. Mantouvalou, 'Labour Rights in the European Convention on Human Rights: An Intellectual Justification for an Integrated Approach to Interpretation' (2013) 13 *Human Rights Law Review* 529

R. Mantz and J. Marosi 'Vorgaben der Datenschutz-Grundverordnung', in L. Specht and R. Mantz (eds), *Handbuch Europäisches und deutsches Datenschutzrecht*, C.H. Beck, Munich 2019

L. Marguet, 'GPA: Quand la Cour de cassation facilite la reconnaissance du lien de filiation du second parent … au-delà même des exigences européennes?' (2020) *La Revue des droits de l'homme. Actualités Droits-Libertés* 1

B. Markesinis and J. Fedtke, 'The Judge as Comparatist' (2005) 80 *Tulane Law Review* 11

F. Marongiu Buoinaiuti, 'Recognition in Italy of Filiation Established Abroad by Surrogate Motherhood, between Transnational Continuity of Personal Status and Public Policy' (2019) 11(2) *Cuadernos de Derecho Transnacional* 294

N. Marsch, *Das europäische Datenschutzgrundrecht*, Mohr Siebeck, Tübingen 2018

F. Matscher, 'Der Begriff des fairen Verfahrens nach Art. 6 EMRK' in H. Nakamura et al. (eds), *Festschrift Beys*, Sakkoulas, Athens 2003

F. Matscher, 'Die Einwirkungen der EMRK auf das Internationale Privat- und zivilprozessuale Verfahrensrecht' in F. Matscher et al. (eds), *Europa im Aufbruch – Festschrift Fritz Schwind*, Manz, Wien 1993

F.C. Mayer, 'Einleitung' in U. Karpenstein and F.C. Mayer, *Konvention zum Schutz der Menschenrechte und Grundfreiheiten*, 3rd ed., C.H. Beck, München 2022

C. McCrudden, 'Judicial Comparativism and Human Rights' in E. Örücü and D. Nelken (eds), *Comparative Law – A Handbook*, Hart, Oxford/Portland 2007

M.-T. MEULDERS-KLEIN, 'Internationalisation des droits de l'Homme et évolution du droit de la famille: un voyage sans destination?' in F. DEKEUWER-DÉFOSSEZ (ed.), *Internationalisation des droits de l'Homme et évolution du droit de la famille, Actes du Colloque du Laboratoire d'études et de recherches appliquées au droit privé*, Université Lille II, L.G.D.J., 1996

J. MEYER-LADEWIG, S. HARRENDORF and S. KÖNIG, 'Art. 6 EMRK' in J. MEYER-LADEWIG, M. NETTESHEIM and S. VON RAUMER (eds), *EMRK*, 4th ed., Nomos, Baden-Baden 2017

J. MEYER-LADEWIG and M. NETTESHEIM, 'Einleitung' in J. MEYER-LADEWIG, M. NETTESHEIM and S. VON RAUMER (eds), *EMRK*, 4th ed., Nomos, Baden-Baden 2017

R. MICHAELS, 'Recognition and Enforcement of Foreign Judgments' in R. WOLFRUM (ed), *Max Planck Encyclopedia of Public International Law*, OUP, Oxford 2012

I. MOTOC and M. VOLIKAS, 'The dialogue between the ECHR and the Italian Constitutional Court' in R. CHENAL et al. (eds), *Intersecting Views on National and International Human Rights Protection*, Liber Amicorum *Guido Raimondi*, Wolf Legal Publishers, Chicago 2019

A. MOWBRAY, 'Subsidiarity and the European Convention on Human Rights' (2015) 15(2) *Human Rights Law Review* 313

S. MÜLLER-RIEMENSCHNEIDER, *Pressefreiheit und Persönlichkeitsschutz*, Kovac, Hamburg 2013

N.W. NETANEL, *Copyright's Paradox*, OUP, Oxford 2008

T. NOVITZ, 'A Human Rights Analysis of the *Viking* and *Laval* Judgments' (2008) 16 *Cambridge Yearbook of European Legal Studies* 540

T. NOVITZ, *International and European Protection of the Right to Strike: A Comparative Study of Standards Set by the International Labour Organization, the Council of Europe and the European Union*, OUP, Oxford 2003

A. NUSSBERGER, 'Die Europäische Menschenrechtskonvention und das Privatrecht', *RabelsZ* 80 (2016), 817

A. NUSSBERGER, 'The European Court of Human Rights and the German Federal Constitutional Court', https://www.cak.cz/assets/pro-advokaty/mezinarodni-vztahy/the-echr-and-the-german-constitutional-court_angelika-nussberger.pdf

A. NUSSBERGER, *The European Court of Human Rights*, OUP, Oxford 2020

S. O'LEARY and T. EICKE, 'Some Reflections on Protocol 16' (2018) 3 *European Human Right Law Review* 220

A. OHLY, 'Harmonisierung des Persönlichkeitsrechts durch den Europäischen Gerichtshof für Menschenrechte? Rechtsvergleichende Anmerkungen zum Urteil in der Sache von Hannover/Deutschland' (2004) *GRUR International* 902

J. OSTER, 'Public Policy and Human Rights' (2015) 11 *Journal of Private International Law* 542

J. OSTŘANSKÝ, 'An Exercise in Equivocation: A Critique of Legitimate Expectations as a General Principle of Law under the Fair and Equitable Treatment Standard' in A. GATTINI, A. TANZI and F. FONTANELLI (eds), *General Principles of Law and International Investment Arbitration*, Brill/Nijhoff, Leiden 2018

J. P. ALBRECHT and F. JOTZO, *Das neue Datenschutzrecht der EU*, Nomos, Baden-Baden 2017

K.P. PAPANIKOLAOU, 'Arbitration Under the Fair Trial Safeguards of Art. 6 §1 ECHR' in *Essays in Honour of Prof. C. Calavros* (forthcoming), https://papers.ssrn.com/sol3/papers.cfm?abstract_id=3567706

D. PEAT, *Comparative Reasoning in International Courts and Tribunals*, CUP, Cambridge 2019

L.M. PESCHEL-GUTZEIT, 'Der doppelte Vater – Kritische Überlegungen zum Gesetz zur Stärkung der Rechte des leiblichen, nicht rechtlichen Vaters', *NJW* 2013, 2465

C. PETTA, 'Res Iudicata in breach of the ECHR: The Italian Constitutional Court Point of View' (2018) *The Italian Law Journal* 225

H. PETZOLD, 'The Convention and the Principle of Subsidiarity' in R. MACDONALD, F. MATSCHER and H. PETZOLD (eds), *The European System for the Protection of Human Rights*, Martinus Nijhoff, Dordrecht 1993

W. PEUKERT, 'Verfahrensgarantien und Zivilprozeß (Art. 6 EMRK)' *Rabels Zeitschrift für ausländisches und internationales Privatrecht* 63 (1998), 600

M. PICCHI, 'Surrogate Motherhood: Protecting the Best Interests of the Child in Light of Recent Case Law' (2019) 3(3) *Peace Human Rights Governance* 307

S. PICHARD, 'La Transcription totale des actes étrangers des enfants nés d'une GPA: un schisme antre loi and jurisprudence' (2020) 7 *Requeil Dalloz* 426

J. PILA, 'Copyright and Its Categories of Original Works' (2010) 30 *Oxford Journal of Legal Studies* 229

A.M. PINELLI, 'Le persistenti ragioni del divieto di maternità surrogata e il problema della tutela di colui che nasce dalla pratica illecita. In attesa della pronuncia delle Sezioni Unite' (2022) 12 *Famiglia e diritto* 1175

W. PINTENS, 'Familienrecht und Rechtsvergleichung in der Rechtsprechung des Europäischen Gerichtshofes für Menschenrechte', *FamRZ* 2016, 341

I. PLETTENBERG, *Vater, Vater, Mutter, Kind – Ein Plädoyer für die rechtliche Mehrelternschaft*, Mohr Siebeck, Tübingen 2016

E. POLGARI, 'European Consensus: A Conservative and a Dynamic Force in European Human Rights Jurisprudence' (2017) 12 *ICL Journal* 59

O. POLLICINO, 'Italy: Constitutional Court at the Crossroads between Constitutional Parochialism and Co-Operative Constitutionalism. Judgments No. 348 and 349 of 22 and 24 October 2007' (2008) 4 *European Constitutional Law Review* 363

N. POSENATO, 'New opinions ex Protocol no. 16 to the ECHR and the Inter-American advisory practice: some comparative remarks' (2020) *Eurojus*, 353

M. POTESTÀ, 'Legitimate Expectations in Investment Treaty Law: Understanding the Roots and the Limits of a Controversial Concept' (2013) 28 *ICSID Review – Foreign Investment Law Journal* 88

Y. RADI, 'The "Human Nature" of International Investment Law' [2013] *Transnational Dispute Management*, https://www.transnational-dispute-management.com/article.asp?key=1928

R. REBHAHN, 'Zivilrecht und Europäische Menschenrechtskonvention', *AcP* 210 (2010) 489

L. REED, J. PAULSSON and N. BLACKABY, *Guide to ICSID Arbitration*, 2nd ed., Wolters Kluwer, Alphen aan den Rijn 2011

Reflection Paper on the proposal to extend the Court's advisory jurisdiction, https://www.echr.coe.int/Documents/2013_Courts_advisory_jurisdiction_ENG.pdf

A. REINER, 'Impecuniosity of Parties and Its Effects on Arbitration – From the Perspectives of Austrian Law' in German Institution of Arbitration (ed.), *Financial Capacity of the Parties: A Condition for the Validity of Arbitration Agreements? (Schriftenreihe Der August-Maria- Berges-Stiftung Für Arbitrales Recht, vol. 16)*, Peter Lang, Frankfurt am Main 2004

G. REPETTO, *Argomenti comparativi e diritti fondamentali in Europa. Teorie dell'interpretazione e giurisprudenza sovranazionale*, Jovene, Napoli 2011

P. RESCIGNO, 'Rapporti associativi, indipendenza e ricusazione dell'arbitro (il caso dell'Opus Dei)' *Rivista dell'arbitrato*, 2012, 263

G. RIXE, 'Der EGMR als Motor einer Harmonisierung des Familienrechts in Europa', *FPR* 2008, 222

E. ROSATI, 'Linking and Copyright in the Shade of VG Bild-Kunst', (2021) 58 *Common Market Law Review* 1875

C.L. ROZAKIS, 'The European Judge as Comparatist' (2005) 80 *Tulane Law Review* 257

M. RUFFERT, 'The Protection of Foreign Direct Investment by the European Convention on Human Rights' (2000) 43 *German Yearbook of International Law* 116

A. RUGGERI, 'Ancora sul prot. 16: verrà dai giudici la sollecitazione al legislatore per il suo recepimento in ambito interno?' (2020) *diritticomparati.it*, 81

H.G. RUSE-KHAN, 'Overlaps and conflict norms in human rights law: Approaches of European Courts to Address Intersections with Intellectual Property Rights' in C. GEIGER (ed), *Research Handbook on Human Rights and Intellectual Property*, Edward Elgar Publishing, Cheltenham 2015

R. SABATO, 'The Experience of Italy' in A. MÜLLER (ed), *Judicial Dialogue and Human Rights*, CUP, Cambridge 2017

R. SACCO, 'Legal Formants: A Dynamic Approach to Comparative Law (Installment I of II)' (1991) 39 *American Journal of Comparative Law* 1

U. ŠADL and H.P. OLSEN, 'Can Quantitative Methods Complement Doctrinal Legal Studies? Using Citation Network and Corpus Linguistic Analysis to Understand International Courts' (2017) 30 *Leiden Journal of International Law* 327

A. SAGAN, 'Article 11 ECHR Freedom of assembly and association' in E. ALES, M. BELL, O. DEINERT and S. ROBIN-OLIVER, *International and European Labour Law*, Nomos, Baden-Baden 2018

A. SAMUEL, 'Arbitration, Alternative Dispute Resolution Generally and the European Convention on Human Rights' (2004) 21(5) *Journal of International Arbitration* 413

A. SANDERS, *Mehrelternschaft*, Mohr Siebeck, Tübingen 2018

W. SANDHOLTZ, 'Human Rights Courts and Global Constitutionalism: Coordination Through Judicial Dialogue' (2020) 10(3) *Global Constitutionalism* 439

N.F. ŞANLI, 'Party Impecuniosity and International Arbitration: The Interplay between Failure to Pay the Advance Costs and Validity of Arbitration Agreement in International Arbitration' (2020) 40 *Public and Private International Law Bulletin* 573

F. SAUERWEIN, 'Beyond anecdotal Reference: A Quantitative Assessment of ICTY References to the jurisprudence of the ECtHR' in P. LOBBA and T. MARINIELLO (eds), *Judicial Dialogue on Human Rights*, Brill, Leiden 2017

H. SCHACK, 'Die Entwicklung des europäischen Internationalen Zivilverfahrensrechts – aktuelle Bestandsaufnahme und Kritik' in R. STÜRNER et al. (eds), *Festschrift Leipold*, Mohr Siebeck, Tübingen 2009

L. SCHEECK, 'The Relationship between the European Courts and Integration through Human Rights', *Zeitschrift für ausländisches öffentliches Recht und Völkerrecht* 65 (2005), 837

M. SCHERER, 'Remote Hearings in International Arbitration: An Analytical Framework' (2020) 37(4) *Journal of International Arbitration* 407

J. SCHERPE, 'Breaking the existing paradigms of parent-child relationships' in G. DOUGLAS, M. MURCH and V. STEPHENS (eds.), *International and National Perspectives on Child and Family Law: Essays in Honour of Nigel Lowe*, Intersentia, Cambridge 2018

J. SCHERPE, 'Legal Recognition of Same-Sex Couples in Europe and the Role of the European Court of Human Rights' (2013) 10 *The Equal Rights Review* 83

V. SCHLETTE, 'Das neue Rechtsschutzsystem der Europäischen Menschenrechtskonvention. Zur Reform des Kontrollmechanismus durch das 11. Protokoll' (1996) *Zeitschrift für ausländisches öffentliches Recht und Völkerrecht* 905

C. SCHMITT-MÜCKE, *Persönlichkeitsschutz und Presseberichterstattung im deutschen und italienischen Recht*, Nomos, Baden-Baden 2023

C. SCHREUER and U. KRIEBAUM, 'The Concept of Property in Human Rights Law and International Investment Law' in S. BREITENMOSER (ed), *Human Rights, Democracy and the Rule of Law: Liber Amicorum Luzius Wildhaber*, Dike, Zurich 2007

E. SCHUMANN, in T. RAUSCHER (ed), *Münchener Kommentar zum FamFG*, 3rd ed, C.H. Beck, Munich 2018

R.J. SCHWEIZER, 'Die Rechtsprechung des Europäischen Gerichtshofes für Menschenrechte zum Persönlichkeits- und Datenschutz', *DuD* 2009, 462

V. SCIARABBA, *Il Giudicato e la CEDU*, Cedam, Padova 2012

A. SEIFERT, 'Recht auf Kollektivverhandlungen und Streikrecht für Beamte – Anmerkungen zur neuen Rechtsprechung des EGMR zur Vereinigungsfreiheit' (2009) *KritV* 357

C. SGANGA, *Propertizing European Copyright: History, Challenges and Opportunities*, Edward Elgar Publishing, Northampton 2018

L.A. SICILIANOS, 'L'élargissement de la compétence consultative de la Cour européenne des droits de l'homme. A' propos du Protocole n. 16 à la Convention européenne des droits de l'homme?' (2014) 1 *Revue Trimestrielle des Droit de l'Homme* 9

M. SIEMS, 'Citation Patterns of the German Federal Supreme Court and the Court of Appeal of England and Wales?' (2010) 21 *King's Law Journal* 152

M. SIEMS, 'Numerical Comparative Law: Do We Need Statistical Evidence in Order to Reduce Complexity?' (2005) 13 *Cardozo Journal of International and Comparative Law* 521

S. SIMITIS, 'Die informationelle Selbstbestimmung – Grundbedingung einer verfassungskonformen Informationsordnung', *NJW* 1984, 389

S. SIMITIS, G. HORNUNG and I. SPIECKER (eds), *Datenschutzrecht*, Nomos, Baden-Baden 2019

M. SIMONATO, 'Confiscation and fundamental rights across criminal and non-criminal domains' (2017) 18 *ERA Forum* 365

S. SÖPPER, 'Note on BVerfG, 13.07.2017', *NZFam* 2017, 795

C. SPACCAPELO, 'Imparzialità, terzietà, neutralità e indipendenza degli arbitri' in D. MANTUCCI (ed), *Trattato di diritto dell'arbitrato*, vol. III, Edizioni Scientifiche Italiane, Napoli 2021

R. SPANO, 'The Future of the European Court of Human Rights – Subsidiarity, Process-Based Review and the Rule of Law' (2018) 18 *Human Rights Law Review* 473

L. SPECHT and R. MANTZ (eds), *Handbuch Europäisches und deutsches Datenschutzrecht*, C.H. Beck, Munich 2019

A. SPERTI, 'La sentenza *Obergefell v. Hodges* e lo storico riconoscimento del diritto al matrimonio per le coppie same-sex negli Stati Uniti. Introduzione al focus' (2015) 2 *Genius* 6

D. SPIELMANN, 'Whither the Margin of Appreciation?' (2014) 67 *Current Legal Problems* 49

M.G. STANZIONE, *Filiazione e genitorialità. Il problema del terzo genitore*, Giappichelli, Torino 2010

M.G. STANZIONE, 'Ordine pubblico costituzionale e status filiationis in Italia e negli ordinamenti europei: la normativa e l'esperienza giurisprudenziale', in *Comparazione e diritto civile*, www.comparazionedirittocivile, 2016

A. STONE SWEET and J. MATHEWS, 'Proportionality Balancing and Global Constitutionalism' (2008) 47 *Columbia Journal of Transnational Law* 72

R. STREINZ, 'Art. 24 GG' in M. SACHS (ed), *Grundgesetz*, 9th ed., C.H. Beck, München 2021

R. STREINZ, 'Art. 25 GG' in M. SACHS (ed), *Grundgesetz*, 9th ed., C.H. Beck, München 2021

A. STROWEL, 'Copyright strengthened by the Court of Justice interpretation of Article 17(2) of the EU Charter of Fundamental Rights' in O. POLLICINO, G.M. RICCIO and M. BASSINI (eds), *Copyright and Fundamental Rights in the Digital Age. A comparative Analysis in Search of a Common Constitutional Ground*, Edward Elgar Publishing, Cheltenham, UK/Northampton, MA, US 2020

D. TEGA, 'The Constitutional Background of 2007 Revolution. The Jurisprudence of the Constitutional Court' in G. REPETTO (ed), *The Constitutional Relevance of the ECHR in Domestic and European Law: An Italian Perspective*, Intersentia, Cambridge 2013

F. THOUVENIN, 'Informational Self-Determination: A Convincing Rationale for Data Protection Law?' 12 (2021) *JIPITEC* 246

C. TOMUSCHAT, 'The Effects of Judgments of the European Court of Human Rights According to the German Constitutional Court' (2010) 11 *German Law Journal* 513

C. TOMUSCHAT, 'The European Court of Human Rights and Investment Protection' in C. BINDER, U. KRIEBAUM, A. REINISCH and S. WITTICH (eds), *International Investment Law for the 21st Century: Essays in Honour of Christoph Schreuer*, OUP, Oxford 2009

R. UERPMANN-WITTZACK, 'Rechtsprechung des Europäischen Gerichtshofs für Menschenrechte zum Familienrecht seit 2014', *FamRZ* 2016, 1897

R. UERPMANN-WITTZACK and A. PRECHTL, 'Rechtsprechung des Europäischen Gerichtshofs für Menschenrechte zum Familienrecht seit Ende 2016', *FamRZ* 2020, 469

UNCTAD, *Fair and Equitable Treatment: A Sequel*, UNCTAD Series on Issues in International Investment Agreements II, 2012

L. VAGNI, 'The relationship between Human Rights and Property and the need for comparison in International Law' (2019) 54 *Questions of International Law* 51

J. VAN HAERSOLTE and J. VAN HOF, 'Impartiality and independence: fundamental and fluid' (2021) 37(3) *Arbitration International* 599

I. VAN HIEL, 'The Right to Form and Join a Trade Union Protected by Article 11 ECHR' in F. DORSSEMONT, K. LÖRCHER and I. SCHÖMANN (eds), *The European Convention on Human Rights and the Employment Relation*, Hart Publishing, Oxford 2013

N. VOGIATZIS, 'The Relationship Between European Consensus, the Margin of Appreciation and the Legitimacy of the Strasbourg Court' (2019) 25 *European Public Law* 445

S. WALPER, 'Wieviele Eltern verträgt ein Kind? Mehrelternfamilien aus sozialwissenschaftlicher Sicht', all in K. LUGANI and P.M. HUBER (eds.), *Moderne Familienformen – Symposium zum 75. Geburtstag von Michael Coester*, De Gruyter, Berlin 2018

B. WEDDERBURN, *Employment Rights in Britain and Europe*, Lawrence & Wishart, London 1991

L. WILDHABER, A. HJARTARSON, and S. DONNELLY, 'No Consensus on Consensus – The Practice of the European Court of Human Rights' (2012) 33 *Human Rights Law Journal* 248

P. WINDEL, 'Die Bedeutung der Europäischen Menschenrechtskonvention für das Privatrecht', *Juristische Rundschau* 2011, 323

M. WINKLER and K.T. SCHAPPO, 'A tale of two fathers' (2019) 5 *Italian Law Journal* 359

H.-L. YU and L. SHORE, 'Independence, impartiality, and immunity of arbitrators – US and English Perspectives' (2003) 52(4) *International and Comparative Law Quarterly* 935

P.K. Yu, 'Reconceptualizing Intellectual Property Interests in a Human Rights Framework' (2007) 40 *U.C. Davis Law Review* 1039

G. Zagouras, 'Bildnisschutz und Privatsphäre im europäischen und nationalen Kontext – Das Springreiter-Urteil des BGH vor dem Hintergrund der Caroline-Entscheidung des EGMR' (2004) *Archiv für Presserecht* 509

D.L. Zimmerman, 'Authorship Without Ownership: Reconsidering Incentives in a Digital Age' (2003) 52 *DePaul Law Review* 1121

INDEX

A
access rights   235, 316
adoption   3, 313
advanced costs   181
advisory opinion   52, 58
arbitration   195
  annulment of award   181, 192
  impartiality of the tribunal   184
  independence of the tribunal   184
  neutrality of the tribunal   183
  voluntary   177
armed forces   253, 266
assisted reproductive technology   88, 313
autonomous interpretation   318

B
balancing test   3, 7, 93, 121, 124, 132–133, 154, 161, 168–169, 171, 216, 232, 314, 323–325, 329, 336
best interests of the child   72, 77–78, 83, 94, 96, 248, 312
Brussels Ibis Regulation   234
Brussels IIter Regulation   234, 243

C
Charter of Fundamental Rights of the European Union, *see* EU Charter of Fundamental Rights
child custody   66, 73, 248, 316
child protection measures   78, 81
child return cases   231, 235, 238
church employee   5, 317–318, 328
civil service   274
civil unions   320
closed shop agreement   321
collective agreement   276, 321
collective bargaining   5, 261, 276
Committee of Ministers of the Council of Europe   334
Community Charter of the Fundamental Social Rights of Workers   321
co-motherhood   89, 313; *see also* parenthood
comparative analysis   286, 302, 320, 324
comparative argumentative techniques   288
comparative survey   288, 290
constitutionalisation of private law   336

constitutionally oriented interpretation   46
contact rights   74, 95–96, 235, 316; *see also* parental rights
Convention for the Protection of Individuals with regard to Automatic Processing of Personal Data   139, 144, 148, 154
copyright   157, 160, 162, 169–170
corporal punishment   80
Council of Europe   307
cross-fertilisation   113

D
data protection   138, 169; *see also* General Data Protection Regulation
Data Protection Directive   139, 142
deductive approach   324–326, 332, 337
de facto family relationships   5, 100, 319; *see also* social family
dialogue between national and European judges   44, 112, 300; *see also* judicial dialogue
dialogue between national and international courts   49
divorce settlement   152
doctrine of consolidated case law   47–48
doctrine of European consensus   93, 104, 288, 292, 297, 320, 325, 337
doctrine of openness to international law   19, 22, 123, 279, 311
domestic courts   44–45
  role of   44–45
duty of disclosure   191–192
duty of homeland defence   259
duty of loyalty   328

E
employment law   5, 41, 151, 253, 273, 317–318, 321, 326, 328
enforcement of judgments   226, 228, 236
EU Account Preservation Order   235
EU Account Preservation Order Regulation   243
EU Charter of Fundamental Rights   24, 39, 100–101, 136, 140, 162–163, 243, 307, 309, 321
  Article 4 (prohibition of torture)   246, 250

Article 9 (right to marry and right to found a family)   101
Article 11 (freedom of expression and information)   169
Article 17(2) (right to intellectual property)   162–163
Article 21 (non-discrimination)   100; *see also* non-discrimination
Article 47(2) (right to a fair trial)   243
Article 52(3) (equivalence clause)   24, 309
EU Enforcement Order   235
EU Enforcement Order Regulation   243
EU Insolvency Regulation   234
EU Maintenance Regulation   235, 243
EU Order for Payment   235
EU Order for Payment Regulation   243
EU private law   306
EU Regulations on matrimonial property   234
EU Small Claims Proceeding   235
EU Small Claims Proceeding Regulation   243
EU Succession Regulation   234
European arrest warrant   245
European consensus, *see* doctrine of European consensus
European Convention on Human Rights (ECHR)
   Article 1 (obligation to respect human rights)   162, 169, 214
   Article 6, *see* right to a fair trial
   Article 8, *see* family life, right to respect for; private life, right to respect of
   Article 9, *see* freedom of religion
   Article 10, *see* freedom of expression
   Article 11, *see* freedom of association
   Article 12, *see* right to marry
   Article 14, *see* non-discrimination
   effectiveness of   45
   implementation of   43, 59, 62
   interpretation of national law in conformity with   46
   Protocol 1   162, 169, 214
   Protocol 16   50, 52, 60, 298
European Social Charter   263, 268, 321
European Union law   13, 24, 309
evolutive interpretation   100, 320; *see also* living instrument doctrine
exequatur proceeding   236, 239

F
family life   3, 65, 70, 75–77, 92–94, 96, 100, 109–110, 295, 311, 313, 315, 319, 324, 329
   right to respect for   3, 65, 70, 75–77, 92–94, 96, 100, 109–110, 311, 313, 315, 319, 324, 329
family separation   66–67, 71, 73, 82
fatherhood   5, 88–89, 92, 313

foster family   73, 312
foreign direct investment *see* protected investment
freedom of assembly   254–255, 261
freedom of association   5, 254, 260, 266, 270, 274–275, 318, 321
freedom of decisions of the military authority   258
freedom of expression   121, 132, 169, 172, 233, 254, 325–326; *see also* freedom of the press
freedom of religion   76, 81, 329
freedom of the press   4, 121, 126, 135, 325

G
General Data Protection Regulation   136, 140, 153; *see also* data protection
Grundgesetz (German Constitution)   13, 39, 90, 122, 139, 279

H
Hague Maintenance Protocol   235
harmonisation of national law   84, 306
harmonisation of private law   306
horizontal relations between private parties   2
human and fundamental rights   2

I
impartiality   190, 194
inductive approach   320–323, 332, 337
influence of international and domestic case law on human rights   49
informational self-determination   141–142, 146, 154
inheritance rights of children born out of wedlock   3, 293
intellectual property   157, 164
interaction between the ECtHR and the national courts, *see* judicial dialogue
International Bar Association (IBA) Guidelines   188
international child abduction   238
International Covenant on Economic, Social and Cultural Rights of 1966 (ICESCR)   164
   Article 15(1)(c)   164
International Labour Organization   319
international obligations   265
international public policy   59, 114
   notion of   114
investment   206, 222
   arbitral tribunals   217, 224
   arbitration   216
   protection   199
Italian Constitution   254, 264–265
   Article 11   264
   Article 117 para. 1   265

Index

J
judicial activism   326, 336–337
judicial dialogue   55, 124, 135, 248, 278, 310, 312, 327, 331

L
labour law, *see* employment law
legal person   147
legitimate expectations   209
living instrument doctrine   43, 274, 276, 320; *see also* evolutive interpretation

M
margin of appreciation   54, 70, 78, 81, 84, 94, 104, 122–123, 131, 150, 152, 155, 221, 289, 312, 314, 320, 322, 326
maritime employment   322
military personnel   253, 266
   collective interests of   267
   discrimination against   259
   freedom of association to   259
   peaceful exercise of dissent by   258
   professional interests of   266
   prohibition on military personnel forming or joining trade unions   268, 270
   right of military personnel to express their opinions   257
military professional organisations   266
multiparentality   89, 97; *see also* parenthood
mutual trust principle   237

N
negative obligations   149, 233
non-discrimination   3, 100, 289, 330–331; *see also* EU Charter of Fundamental Rights, Article 21
notion of legitimate expectations   207
nullification of marriage   232

O
online press archives   125, 128–129, 132, 135

P
parental rights   21, 65, 82, 91, 95, 316; *see also* contact rights
parenthood   5, 53, 88–89, 97, 311–313, 320
patrimonialisation of the copyright rules   159
positive obligations   2, 66, 142, 149–150, 233, 309, 317
preliminary reference proceeding   25, 241
presumption of compliance doctrine   241
primacy of application   13, 15, 327–328
principle of homeland defence   254
principle of 'legitimate expectations'   207, 223
principle of mutual trust   246
principle of non-discrimination   100

principle of proportionality   76, 83, 154, 218; *see also* proportionality test
principle of sovereignty   229
principle of subsidiarity   44–45, 50, 298, 336; *see also* margin of appreciation
private life   4, 121, 127, 136, 139, 141, 144–145, 152–153, 317, 324–326, 328–329
   right to respect for   4, 121, 127, 136, 139, 141, 144–145, 152–153, 317, 324–325, 328–329
procedural requirements   70, 79, 93, 227, 229, 233, 315, 323, 332, 337
procedural standards   70, 79, 93, 227, 229, 233, 315, 323, 332, 337
professional nature of arbitrators   186
prohibition of discrimination, *see* non-discrimination
property rights   228; *see also* European Convention on Human Rights, Protocol 1
proportionality test   220–221; *see also* principle of proportionality
protected investment   198, 201, 223
protection of personal data, *see* data protection
protection of 'possessions'   204
public policy   59, 234, 236, 248, 311
public servants, *see* civil service

R
recognition of foreign judgments   226, 228–234, 311
registered partnerships   320
regulatory changes   217, 223
religious freedom, *see* freedom of religion
res judicata   234
Revised European Social Charter (RESC)
   Article 5   268
right of access to court   227–229
right of defence   181
right of military personnel to express their opinions, *see* military personnel, right of military personnel to express their opinions
right to a fair trial   181, 230
right to an effective remedy   74
right to a speedy trial   73
right to be forgotten   120, 125, 135, 143
right to be heard   71, 79, 230
right to expedited proceedings   73
right to found a family   101
right to marry   101, 105, 109; *see also* EU Charter of Fundamental Rights, Article 9
right to privacy   4, 27, 41, 100, 119, 143, 145, 233, 324, 326; *see also* private life, right to respect for
right to strike   259, 274, 276
role of national judges   44

S

same-sex couples   3, 99, 103–105, 108
   legal recognition of   103–105, 108
same-sex marriage   106, 295
same-sex partners   88, 313, 319
same-sex relationships   103
same-sex unions   107, 108
search engines   125, 128, 132, 135
social family   92–93, 95; *see also* de facto family relationships
sperm donation   88, 91, 97
Steering Committee for Human Rights   249
strike action   18, 27, 258, 276, 321
subsidiarity, *see* principle of subsidiarity
substantive requirements   76, 232, 318, 332
substantive standards   76, 232, 318, 332
succession law   3
surrogacy   5, 53, 55–56, 59, 97, 311

T

trade union   5, 254, 258, 261, 267, 276, 318, 322
Treaty on European Union (TEU)   242, 265, 309
Treaty on the Functioning of the European Union (TFEU)   161, 226, 306

U

unauthorised assemblies of militaries   255
uniform standard of adjudication   189
Universal Declaration of Human Rights (UDHR)   164

V

voluntary arbitration, *see* arbitration, voluntary

W

waiver's validity   179, 180
whistle-blower   5, 312, 326

ABOUT THE EDITORS

MATTEO FORNASIER holds a Chair of Civil Law, Labour Law, Private International Law and Comparative Law at Ruhr University Bochum. Previously, he was a Research Fellow at the Max Planck Institute for Comparative and International Private Law in Hamburg (2008–2018) and was Professor at the University of Greifswald (2019–2020). Matteo Fornasier is a member of the New York Bar, and his main area of research is the Europeanisation of private law, in particular in the ambit of labour and contract law.

MARIA GABRIELLA STANZIONE is Associate Professor of Comparative Law at the University of Salerno, where she holds a Chair of Comparative Legal Systems, Anglo-American Law and Comparative Media Law. She is a member of the academic board of the PhD 'Scienze e culture dell'umano Società, Educazione, Politica e Comunicazione', University of Salerno. She is also a member of the Editorial Board of the Italian A-ranked law review *Comparazione e diritto civile*. Her research interests range from fundamental rights and family law to the general theory of comparative law, from personal data protection law to civil liability. She is an author of numerous monographs, articles and scientific essays.